World Literature
An Anthology
700 BC – AD 1922

World Literature

An Anthology
700 BC – AD 1922

Compiled for use in
English 221: Survey of World Literature
at the Baptist College of Florida

Edited by
Elisabeth G. Wolfe

Printed by CreateSpace
Charleston, SC

World Literature: An Anthology, 700 BC – AD 1922
Edited by Elisabeth G. Wolfe
Copyright © 2017 Elisabeth G. Wolfe
All rights reserved.

ISBN-10: 1977506704
ISBN-13: 978-1977506702

This book is set in Palatino Linotype, 12 point typeface.

Cover art and interior illustrations by Elisabeth G. Wolfe.

Contents

Foreword

This anthology is a very idiosyncratic collection, created to fit a very particular need. I have yet to find a world literature anthology from which I actually want to teach, but I also know that students prefer to have a hard-copy collection of their readings rather than hunting them down all over the Internet. However, because I intend this anthology only for use in my own classes (at least for now), I need to avoid duplicating information presented in my lectures.

Thus, students will not find lengthy introductory notes or anything of that sort in these pages. Nor are there selections included here that will not be covered in my class. Rather, this book is a collection of only the public-domain readings assigned on the syllabus; readings that remain under copyright will be made available in another format. The primary additional information included in this volume is the section of study helps on the Greek and Roman pantheon in the Mythology section. I have also added explanatory footnotes on some of the more difficult texts, especially Malory.

Future editions may begin to look more like a conventional anthology that admits of broader use. For the present, however, I hope it will serve my students well.

Many, many thanks to Dr. Geoffrey Reiter for his encouragement and to my dad, Bill Wolfe, for his help in rounding up texts for me so that I could meet my very tight deadline.

Elisabeth G. Wolfe
September 2017
Llano, Texas

Mythology and the Myth Made Fact

Greek and Roman Mythology
Study Helps

The Greco-Roman pantheon can be hard to keep straight, and Hesiod packs a lot of information into a comparatively short poem. In the hope of making matters easier for you, I present this "Who's Who" chart and a set of family trees based on the *Theogony*. (Some of the details differ in later sources; for example, as you will see in the *Aeneid*, later myths have Aphrodite marrying Hephaestus instead of Ares and present Eros as Aphrodite's son. Since you will be reading the *Theogony* first, however, I have kept to Hesiod as much as possible.)

Class	Greek Name	Roman Name	Attribute or Patronage
Eldest Gods	Chaos	Chaos	First thing to exist
	Gaea	Terra Mater	Mother Earth
	Tartarus	Tartarus	Underworld
	Eros	Cupid	Romantic love
Descendants of Chaos	Erebus	Erebus	Darkness
	Nyx	Nox	Night
	Aether	Aether	The bright upper atmosphere
	Hemera	Dies	Day
	Moros	Fatum	Doom
	Thanatos	Mors	Death
	Hypnos	Somnus	Sleep
	Nemesis	Nemesis/Invidia	Retribution
	Apate	Fraus	Deceit
	Eris	Discordia	Strife
Descendants of Gaea[1]	Ouranos	Caelus	Heaven, Father Sky
	Ourea	Mons (Montes)	Mountains
	Pontus	—	Deep sea
	Nereus	—	Old Man of the Sea
	Thaumas	—	Wonder of the sea
	Iris	Iris/Arcus	Rainbow
	Phorcys	—	Hidden dangers of the sea
	Ceto	—	Goddess of sea monsters
	Eurybia	—	Mastery of the sea
Titans	Cronos	Saturn	Harvest[2]
	Rhea	Ops/Magna Mater	Great Mother
	Iapetus	—	Mortality

---

[1] Most of the primordial gods and Titans either were ignored in Roman mythology or were incorporated wholesale as literary figures; almost none still had active cults by the time Rome began expanding.

[2] Despite the similar English spellings, Cronos (Κρονος) was not originally the same as Chronos (Χρονος), Father Time; but they became conflated over the centuries.

Class	Greek Name	Roman Name	Attribute or Patronage
Titans (cont.)	Themis	—	Divine law
	Oceanus	—	Ocean
	Tethys	—	Fresh water
	Hyperion	—	Light
	Theia	—	Sight, aetheric light
	Crius	—	Mastery, leadership
	Mnemosyne	Moneta	Memory
	Coeus	Polus	Rational intelligence, curiosity
	Phoebe	—	"Shining" intellect and poetry
	Helios	Sol	Sun
	Selene	Luna	Moon
	Eos	Aurora	Dawn
	Eosphoros	Lucifer	Morning star
	Astraeus	—	Dusk, stars, planets, astronomy
	Pallas[1]	—	War
	Perses	—	Destruction
	Atlas	—	Upheld heaven
	Menoetius	—	Doomed might
	Prometheus	—	Forethought
	Epimetheus	—	Afterthought
	Pandora	—	"All-gifted," wife of Epimetheus
	Zelus	Invidia[2]	Emulation, rivalry
	Nike	Victoria	Victory
	Cratos	Potestas	Strength
	Bia	Vis	Force
	Leto	Latona	Motherhood, modesty
	Asteria	Asteria	Nighttime oracles, falling stars
	Hecate	Hecate (Trivia?)[3]	Magic
	Metis	Metis	Prudence
Cyclopes	Brontes	(A different group, sons of Neptune, appears in Roman mythology following Homer)	One orbed eye
	Steropes		
	Arges		

[1] A later individual named Pallas, daughter of Triton, was Athena's best friend and was killed in a javelin training accident, whereupon Athena took on the name (i.e. Pallas Athena) in memory of her friend.

[2] Invidia was the female personification of envy, and as such she was connected with the (male) Greek daimon Zelus; but she was more commonly associated with justified outrage over another person's undeserved good fortune, and as such she was equated with Nemesis.

[3] Sources differ as to whether Trivia, goddess of the three-way crossroads, was indeed the Roman version of Hecate.

Class	Greek Name		Roman Name	Attribute or Patronage
Hecatonchires	Cottus		—	100 arms, 50 heads
	Briareos			
	Gyes			
Rivers			Styx	River surrounding Tartarus
Olympians	Aphrodite		Venus	Love
	Hestia		Vesta	Hearth
	Demeter		Ceres	Fertility
	Hera		Juno	Queen of the gods
	Hades		Pluto	God of the underworld
	Poseidon		Neptune	God of the sea
	Zeus		Jupiter/Jove	King of the gods
	Ares		Mars	God of war
	Hebe		Juventas	Youth
	Eileithyia		Lucina/Natio	Childbirth
	Athena		Minerva	Wisdom
	Horae[1]	Eunomia	Eunomia	Order
		Dike	Iustitia	Justice
		Eirene	Pax	Peace
	Persephone		Proserpine	Spring
	Apollo		Apollo	Music and prophecy
	Artemis		Diana	Goddess of the hunt
	Hephaestus		Vulcan	God of the forge
	Hermes		Mercury	Messenger of the gods
	Dionysius		Bacchus	Wine and revelry
	Triton		Triton	Messenger of Poseidon
Nymphs[2]	Hesperides		—	Daughters of the evening
	Meliae		—	Ash-tree nymphs
	Nereids (50)		—	Ocean nymphs, daughters of Nereus and Doris
	Oceanids (3,000)		—	Ocean nymphs, daughters of Oceanus and Tethys
Moirae/Fates	Clotho		Nona	Spins the thread of life
	Lachesis		Decima	Measures the thread
	Atropos		Morta	Cuts the thread
Winds[3]	Zephyrus		Favonius	West wind
	Notus		Auster	South wind
	Boreas		Aquilo/Septentrio	North wind

[1] Other sources list a different triad of Horae, and the name is also applied to twelve goddesses who personify the hours of the day.

[2] Roman mythology tends to lump all nymphs together and includes in their number a great many local deities that do not appear in Greek mythology. The Hesperides, in particular, were treated as only a poetic convention in Roman literature. The Romans tended to prefer to honor the *genius loci*, the spirit of the place.

[3] Eurus (Vulturnus), the East Wind, is not named in the *Theogony*, but other sources include him with the other three as a son of Astraeus and Eos.

Class	Greek Name	Roman Name	Attribute or Patronage
Muses		Clio	History
		Euterpe	Music
		Thalia	Comedy
		Melpomene	Tragedy
		Terpsichore	Dance
		Erato	Lyric poetry
		Polyhymnia	Sacred music
		Urania	Astronomy
		Calliope	Epic poetry
Offspring of Ouranos	Erinyes	Dirae/Furiae	Furies: goddesses of retribution
	Gigantes	Gigantes	Giants
Monsters		Harpies[1]	Monstrous bird-women (whirlwinds)
		Graiae (Pemphredo, Enyo, Deino)	Old women with only one eye and one tooth between them
		Gorgons (Medusa, Sthenno, Euryale)	Snake-haired hags who could turn men to stone
		Geryones	Three-headed herdsman killed by Heracles
		Echidna	Mother of monsters
	Typhoeus/Typhaon[2]	Typhon	Father of dangerous winds
		Orthus	Two-headed hound of Geryones
		Cerberus	Three-headed hound of Hades
		Hydra	Killed by Heracles
		Chimaera	Killed by Bellerophon
		Sphinx	Killed by Oedipus
		Nemean Lion	Killed by Heracles

The giant Chrysaor and his twin brother Pegasus, the winged horse, are not usually numbered among the monsters. Chrysaor has a relatively minor role in the mythology, but Pegasus becomes the faithful steed of the gods and carries Bellerophon on his heroic journeys.

Heracles is better known in the present day by his Roman name, Hercules.

---

[1] Hesiod does not describe the Harpies as monsters, but Aeschylus describes them as ugly, and later writers go further still.

[2] Hesiod uses both of these names for Typhon at separate points in the *Theogony*, which makes it seem (to a modern audience) as if he is talking about two separate monsters.

Family Trees from the *Theogony*

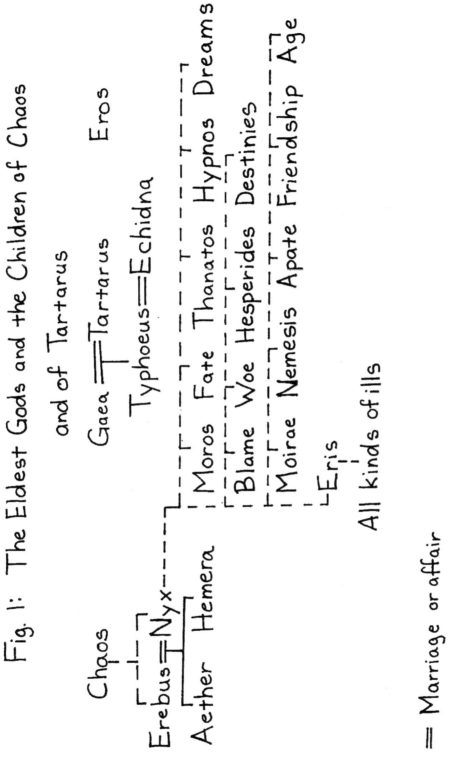

Fig. 1: The Eldest Gods and the Children of Chaos and of Tartarus

Chaos

Erebus=Nyx

Aether Hemera

Moros Fate Thanatos Hypnos Dreams

Blame Woe Hesperides Destinies

Moirae Nemesis Apate Friendship Age

Eris

All kinds of ills

Gaea=Tartarus

Typhoeus=Echidna

Eros

= Marriage or affair

— Child

-- Child conceived asexually

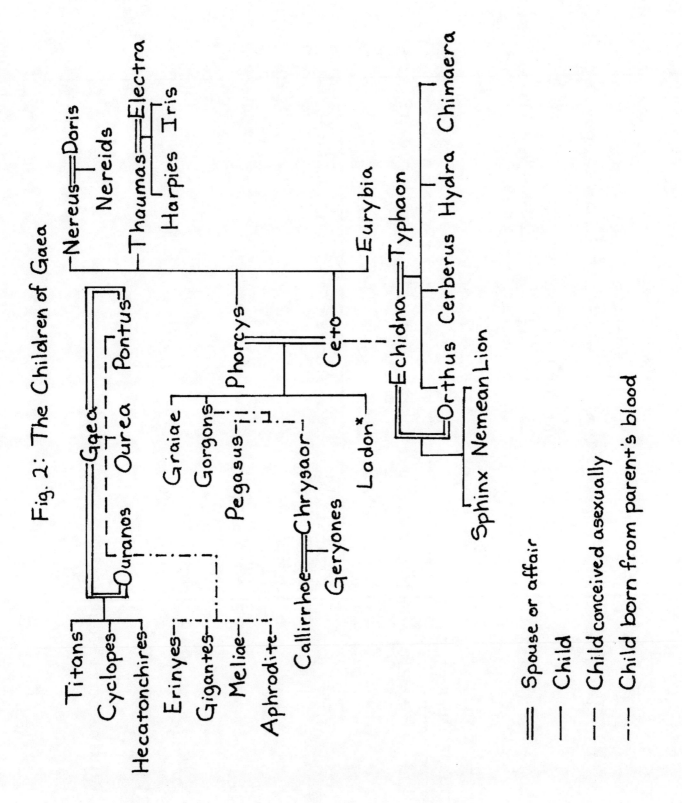

Fig. 2: The Children of Gaea

* Dragon that guards the Golden Apples of the Hesperides—Hesiod does not give his name

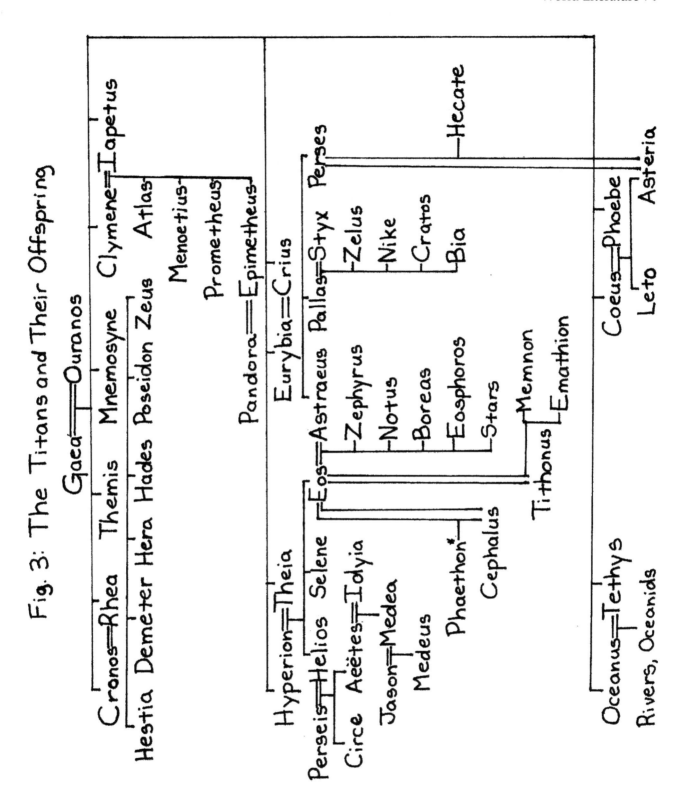

Fig. 3: The Titans and Their Offspring

* This Phaethon is not to be confused with the son of Apollo who nearly crashed the Sun. The son of Eos was stolen by Aphrodite as a child to become the guard of her most sacred shrines.

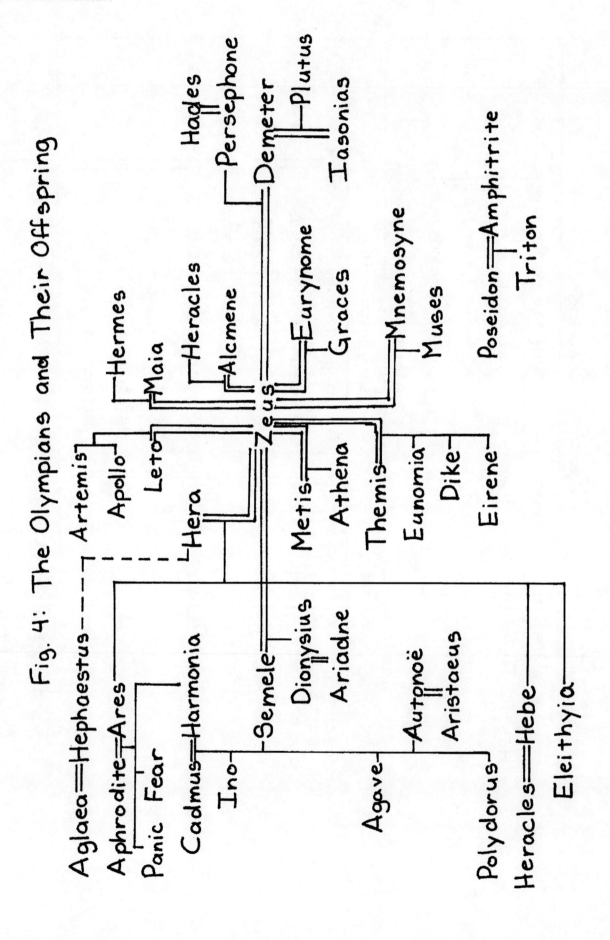

Fig. 4: The Olympians and Their Offspring

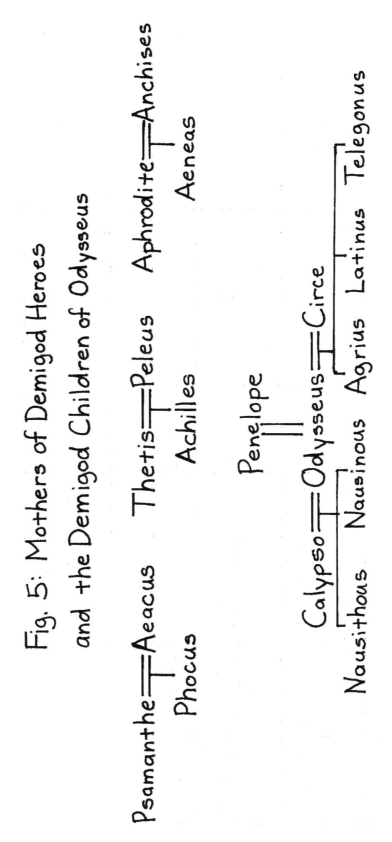

Fig. 5: Mothers of Demigod Heroes and the Demigod Children of Odysseus

Note: Hesiod never names Odysseus' faithful wife Penelope (or their son, Telemachus) in the *Theogony*, but he may have expected his audience to be familiar enough with the *Odyssey* not to need the reminder.

Hesiod
The Theogony
Translated by Hugh G. Evelyn-White[1]

From the Heliconian Muses let us begin to sing, who hold the great and holy mount of Helicon, and dance on soft feet about the deep-blue spring and the altar of the almighty son of Cronos, and, when they have washed their tender bodies in Permessus or in the Horse's Spring or Olmeius, make their fair, lovely dances upon highest Helicon and move with vigorous feet. Thence they arise and go abroad by night, veiled in thick mist, and utter their song with lovely voice, praising Zeus the aegis-holder and queenly Hera of Argos who walks on golden sandals and the daughter of Zeus the aegis-holder bright-eyed Athene, and Phoebus Apollo, and Artemis who delights in arrows, and Poseidon the earth-holder who shakes the earth, and reverend Themis and quick-glancing[2] Aphrodite, and Hebe with the crown of gold, and fair Dione, Leto, Iapetus, and Cronos the crafty counsellor, Eos and great Helius and bright Selene, Earth too, and great Oceanus, and dark Night, and the holy race of all the other deathless ones that are for ever. And one day they taught Hesiod glorious song while he was shepherding his lambs under holy Helicon, and this word first the goddesses said to me—the Muses of Olympus, daughters of Zeus who holds the aegis:

'Shepherds of the wilderness, wretched things of shame, mere bellies, we know how to speak many false things as though they were true; but we know, when we will, to utter true things.'

So said the ready-voiced daughters of great Zeus, and they plucked and gave me a rod, a shoot of sturdy laurel, a marvellous thing, and breathed into me a divine voice to celebrate things that shall be and things there were aforetime; and they bade me sing of the race of the blessed gods that are eternally, but ever to sing of themselves both first and last. But why all this about oak or stone?[3]

Come thou, let us begin with the Muses who gladden the great spirit of their father Zeus in Olympus with their songs, telling of things that are and that shall be and that were aforetime with consenting voice. Unwearying flows the sweet sound from their lips, and the house of their father Zeus the loud-thunderer is glad at the lily-like voice of the goddesses as it spread abroad, and the peaks of snowy Olympus resound, and the homes of the immortals. And they uttering their immortal voice, celebrate in song first of all the reverend race of the gods from the beginning, those whom Earth and wide Heaven begot, and the gods sprung of these, givers of good things. Then, next, the goddesses sing of Zeus, the father of gods and men, as they begin and end their strain, how much he is the most excellent

---

[1] Unless otherwise marked, notes on this text are taken from Evelyn-White's 1848 translation.
[2] The epithet probably indicates coquettishness.
[3] A proverbial saying meaning, 'why enlarge on irrelevant topics?'

among the gods and supreme in power. And again, they chant the race of men and strong giants, and gladden the heart of Zeus within Olympus,—the Olympian Muses, daughters of Zeus the aegis-holder.

Them in Pieria did Mnemosyne (Memory), who reigns over the hills of Eleuther, bear of union with the father, the son of Cronos, a forgetting of ills and a rest from sorrow. For nine nights did wise Zeus lie with her, entering her holy bed remote from the immortals. And when a year was passed and the seasons came round as the months waned, and many days were accomplished, she bare nine daughters, all of one mind, whose hearts are set upon song and their spirit free from care, a little way from the topmost peak of snowy Olympus. There are their bright dancing-places and beautiful homes, and beside them the Graces and Himerus (Desire) live in delight. And they, uttering through their lips a lovely voice, sing the laws of all and the goodly ways of the immortals, uttering their lovely voice. Then went they to Olympus, delighting in their sweet voice, with heavenly song, and the dark earth resounded about them as they chanted, and a lovely sound rose up beneath their feet as they went to their father. And he was reigning in heaven, himself holding the lightning and glowing thunderbolt, when he had overcome by might his father Cronos; and he distributed fairly to the immortals their portions and declared their privileges.

These things, then, the Muses sang who dwell on Olympus, nine daughters begotten by great Zeus, Cleio and Euterpe, Thaleia, Melpomene and Terpsichore, and Erato and Polyhymnia and Urania and Calliope,[1] who is the chiefest of them all, for she attends on worshipful princes: whomsoever of heaven-nourished princes the daughters of great Zeus honour, and behold him at his birth, they pour sweet dew upon his tongue, and from his lips flow gracious words. All the people look towards him while he settles causes with true judgements: and he, speaking surely, would soon make wise end even of a great quarrel; for therefore are there princes wise in heart, because when the people are being misguided in their assembly, they set right the matter again with ease, persuading them with gentle words. And when he passes through a gathering, they greet him as a god with gentle reverence, and he is conspicuous amongst the assembled: such is the holy gift of the Muses to men. For it is through the Muses and far-shooting Apollo that there are singers and harpers upon the earth; but princes are of Zeus, and happy is he whom the Muses love: sweet flows speech from his mouth. For though a man have sorrow and grief in his newly-troubled soul and live in dread because his heart is distressed, yet, when a singer, the servant of the Muses, chants the glorious deeds of men of old and the blessed gods who inhabit Olympus, at once he forgets his heaviness and remembers not his sorrows at all; but the gifts of the goddesses soon turn him away from these.

Hail, children of Zeus! Grant lovely song and celebrate the holy race of the deathless gods who are for ever, those that were born of Earth and starry Heaven and gloomy Night and them that briny Sea did rear. Tell how at the first gods and earth came to be, and rivers,

---

[1] 'She of the noble voice': Calliope is queen of Epic poetry.

and the boundless sea with its raging swell, and the gleaming stars, and the wide heaven above, and the gods who were born of them, givers of good things, and how they divided their wealth, and how they shared their honours amongst them, and also how at the first they took many-folded Olympus. These things declare to me from the beginning, ye Muses who dwell in the house of Olympus, and tell me which of them first came to be.

Verily at the first Chaos came to be, but next wide-bosomed Earth, the ever-sure foundations of all[1] the deathless ones who hold the peaks of snowy Olympus, and dim Tartarus in the depth of the wide-pathed Earth, and Eros (Love), fairest among the deathless gods, who unnerves the limbs and overcomes the mind and wise counsels of all gods and all men within them. From Chaos came forth Erebus and black Night; but of Night were born Aether[2] and Day, whom she conceived and bare from union in love with Erebus. And Earth first bare starry Heaven, equal to herself, to cover her on every side, and to be an ever-sure abiding-place for the blessed gods. And she brought forth long Hills, graceful haunts of the goddess-Nymphs who dwell amongst the glens of the hills. She bare also the fruitless deep with his raging swell, Pontus, without sweet union of love. But afterwards she lay with Heaven and bare deep-swirling Oceanus, Coeus and Crius and Hyperion and Iapetus, Theia and Rhea, Themis and Mnemosyne and gold-crowned Phoebe and lovely Tethys. After them was born Cronos the wily, youngest and most terrible of her children, and he hated his lusty sire.

And again, she bare the Cyclopes, overbearing in spirit, Brontes, and Steropes and stubborn-hearted Arges,[3] who gave Zeus the thunder and made the thunderbolt: in all else they were like the gods, but one eye only was set in the midst of their fore-heads. And they were surnamed Cyclopes (Orb-eyed) because one orbed eye was set in their foreheads. Strength and might and craft were in their works.

And again, three other sons were born of Earth and Heaven, great and doughty beyond telling, Cottus and Briareos and Gyes, presumptuous children. From their shoulders sprang an hundred arms, not to be approached, and each had fifty heads upon his shoulders on their strong limbs, and irresistible was the stubborn strength that was in their great forms. For of all the children that were born of Earth and Heaven, these were the most terrible, and they were hated by their own father from the first.

And he used to hide them all away in a secret place of Earth so soon as each was born, and would not suffer them to come up into the light: and Heaven rejoiced in his evil doing. But vast Earth groaned within, being straitened, and she made the element of grey flint and

[1] Earth, in the cosmology of Hesiod, is a disk surrounded by the river Oceanus and floating upon a waste of waters. It is called the foundation of all (the qualification 'the deathless ones...' etc. is an interpolation), because not only trees, men, and animals, but even the hills and seas (ll. 129, 131) are supported by it.
[2] Aether is the bright, untainted upper atmosphere, as distinguished from Aer, the lower atmosphere of the earth.
[3] Brontes is the Thunderer; Steropes, the Lightener; and Arges, the Vivid One.

shaped a great sickle, and told her plan to her dear sons. And she spoke, cheering them, while she was vexed in her dear heart:

'My children, gotten of a sinful father, if you will obey me, we should punish the vile outrage of your father; for he first thought of doing shameful things.'

So she said; but fear seized them all, and none of them uttered a word. But great Cronos the wily took courage and answered his dear mother:

'Mother, I will undertake to do this deed, for I reverence not our father of evil name, for he first thought of doing shameful things.'

So he said: and vast Earth rejoiced greatly in spirit, and set and hid him in an ambush, and put in his hands a jagged sickle, and revealed to him the whole plot.

And Heaven came, bringing on night and longing for love, and he lay about Earth spreading himself full upon her.[1]

Then the son from his ambush stretched forth his left hand and in his right took the great long sickle with jagged teeth, and swiftly lopped off his own father's members and cast them away to fall behind him. And not vainly did they fall from his hand; for all the bloody drops that gushed forth Earth received, and as the seasons moved round she bare the strong Erinyes and the great Giants with gleaming armour, holding long spears in their hands and the Nymphs whom they call Meliae[2] all over the boundless earth. And so soon as he had cut off the members with flint and cast them from the land into the surging sea, they were swept away over the main a long time: and a white foam spread around them from the immortal flesh, and in it there grew a maiden. First she drew near holy Cythera, and from there, afterwards, she came to sea-girt Cyprus, and came forth an awful and lovely goddess, and grass grew up about her beneath her shapely feet. Her gods and men call Aphrodite, and the foam-born goddess and rich-crowned Cytherea, because she grew amid the foam, and Cytherea because she reached Cythera, and Cyprogenes because she was born in billowy Cyprus, and Philommedes[3] because sprang from the members. And with her went Eros, and comely Desire followed her at her birth at the first and as she went into the assembly of the gods. This honour she has from the beginning, and this is the portion allotted to her amongst men and undying gods,—the whisperings of maidens and smiles and deceits with sweet delight and love and graciousness.

But these sons whom he begot himself great Heaven used to call Titans (Strainers) in reproach, for he said that they strained and did presumptuously a fearful deed, and that vengeance for it would come afterwards.

And Night bare hateful Doom and black Fate and Death, and she bare Sleep and the tribe of Dreams. And again the goddess murky Night, though she lay with none, bare Blame

---

[1] The myth accounts for the separation of Heaven and Earth. In Egyptian cosmology Nut (the Sky) is thrust and held apart from her brother Geb (the Earth) by their father Shu, who corresponds to the Greek Atlas.

[2] Nymphs of the ash-trees, as Dryads are nymphs of the oak-trees.

[3] 'Member-loving': the title is perhaps only a perversion of the regular φιλομειδής (laughter-loving).

and painful Woe, and the Hesperides who guard the rich, golden apples and the trees bearing fruit beyond glorious Ocean. Also she bare the Destinies and ruthless avenging Fates, Clotho and Lachesis and Atropos,[1] who give men at their birth both evil and good to have, and they pursue the transgressions of men and of gods: and these goddesses never cease from their dread anger until they punish the sinner with a sore penalty. Also deadly Night bare Nemesis (Indignation) to afflict mortal men, and after her, Deceit and Friendship and hateful Age and hard-hearted Strife.

But abhorred Strife bare painful Toil and Forgetfulness and Famine and tearful Sorrows, Fightings also, Battles, Murders, Manslaughters, Quarrels, Lying Words, Disputes, Lawlessness and Ruin, all of one nature, and Oath who most troubles men upon earth when anyone wilfully swears a false oath.

And Sea begat Nereus, the eldest of his children, who is true and lies not: and men call him the Old Man because he is trusty and gentle and does not forget the laws of righteousness, but thinks just and kindly thoughts. And yet again he got great Thaumas and proud Phorcys, being mated with Earth, and fair-cheeked Ceto and Eurybia who has a heart of flint within her.

And of Nereus and rich-haired Doris, daughter of Ocean the perfect river, were born children,[2] passing lovely amongst goddesses, Ploto, Eucrante, Sao, and Amphitrite, and Eudora, and Thetis, Galene and Glauce, Cymothoe, Speo, Thoe and lovely Halie, and Pasithea, and Erato, and rosy-armed Eunice, and gracious Melite, and Eulimene, and Agaue, Doto, Proto, Pherusa, and Dynamene, and Nisaea, and Actaea, and Protomedea, Doris, Panopea, and comely Galatea, and lovely Hippothoe, and rosy-armed Hipponoe, and Cymodoce who with Cymatolege[3] and Amphitrite easily calms the waves upon the misty sea and the blasts of raging winds, and Cymo, and Eione, and rich-crowned Alimede, and Glauconome, fond of laughter, and Pontoporea, Leagore, Euagore, and Laomedea, and Polynoe, and Autonoe, and Lysianassa, and Euarne, lovely of shape and without blemish of form, and Psamathe of charming figure and divine Menippe, Neso, Eupompe, Themisto, Pronoe, and Nemertes[4] who has the nature of her deathless father. These fifty daughters sprang from blameless Nereus, skilled in excellent crafts.

And Thaumas wedded Electra the daughter of deep-flowing Ocean, and she bare him swift Iris and the long-haired Harpies, Aello (Storm-swift) and Ocypetes (Swift-flier) who on their swift wings keep pace with the blasts of the winds and the birds; for quick as time they dart along.

---

[1] Clotho (the Spinner) is she who spins the thread of man's life; Lachesis (the Disposer of Lots) assigns to each man his destiny; Atropos (She who cannot be turned) is the 'Fury with the abhorred shears.'

[2] Many of the names which follow express various qualities or aspects of the sea: thus Galene is 'Calm', Cymothoe is the 'Wave-swift', Pherusa and Dynamene are 'She who speeds (ships)' and 'She who has power'.

[3] The 'Wave-receiver' and the 'Wave-stiller'.

[4] 'The Unerring' or 'Truthful'; cp. l. 235.

And again, Ceto bare to Phorcys the fair-cheeked Graiae, sisters grey from their birth: and both deathless gods and men who walk on earth call them Graiae, Pemphredo well-clad, and saffron-robed Enyo, and the Gorgons who dwell beyond glorious Ocean in the frontier land towards Night where are the clear-voiced Hesperides, Sthenno, and Euryale, and Medusa who suffered a woeful fate: she was mortal, but the two were undying and grew not old. With her lay the Dark-haired One[1] in a soft meadow amid spring flowers. And when Perseus cut off her head, there sprang forth great Chrysaor and the horse Pegasus who is so called because he was born near the springs (pegae) of Ocean; and that other, because he held a golden blade (aor) in his hands. Now Pegasus flew away and left the earth, the mother of flocks, and came to the deathless gods: and he dwells in the house of Zeus and brings to wise Zeus the thunder and lightning. But Chrysaor was joined in love to Callirrhoe, the daughter of glorious Ocean, and begot three-headed Geryones. Him mighty Heracles slew in sea-girt Erythea by his shambling oxen on that day when he drove the wide-browed oxen to holy Tiryns, and had crossed the ford of Ocean and killed Orthus and Eurytion the herdsman in the dim stead out beyond glorious Ocean.

And in a hollow cave she bare another monster, irresistible, in no wise like either to mortal men or to the undying gods, even the goddess fierce Echidna who is half a nymph with glancing eyes and fair cheeks, and half again a huge snake, great and awful, with speckled skin, eating raw flesh beneath the secret parts of the holy earth. And there she has a cave deep down under a hollow rock far from the deathless gods and mortal men. There, then, did the gods appoint her a glorious house to dwell in: and she keeps guard in Arima beneath the earth, grim Echidna, a nymph who dies not nor grows old all her days.

Men say that Typhaon the terrible, outrageous and lawless, was joined in love to her, the maid with glancing eyes. So she conceived and brought forth fierce offspring; first she bare Orthus the hound of Geryones, and then again she bare a second, a monster not to be overcome and that may not be described, Cerberus who eats raw flesh, the brazen-voiced hound of Hades, fifty-headed, relentless and strong. And again she bore a third, the evil-minded Hydra of Lerna, whom the goddess, white-armed Hera nourished, being angry beyond measure with the mighty Heracles. And her Heracles, the son of Zeus, of the house of Amphitryon, together with warlike Iolaus, destroyed with the unpitying sword through the plans of Athene the spoil-driver. She was the mother of Chimaera who breathed raging fire, a creature fearful, great, swift-footed and strong, who had three heads, one of a grim-eyed lion; in her hinderpart, a dragon; and in her middle, a goat, breathing forth a fearful blast of blazing fire. Her did Pegasus and noble Bellerophon slay; but Echidna was subject in love to Orthus and brought forth the deadly Sphinx which destroyed the Cadmeans, and the Nemean lion, which Hera, the good wife of Zeus, brought up and made to haunt the hills of Nemea, a plague to men. There he preyed upon the tribes of her own people and had power over Tretus of Nemea and Apesas: yet the strength of stout Heracles overcame him.

---

[1] i.e. Poseidon.

And Ceto was joined in love to Phorcys and bare her youngest, the awful snake who guards the apples all of gold in the secret places of the dark earth at its great bounds. This is the offspring of Ceto and Phorcys.

And Tethys bare to Ocean eddying rivers, Nilus, and Alpheus, and deep-swirling Eridanus, Strymon, and Meander, and the fair stream of Ister, and Phasis, and Rhesus, and the silver eddies of Achelous, Nessus, and Rhodius, Haliacmon, and Heptaporus, Granicus, and Aesepus, and holy Simois, and Peneus, and Hermus, and Caicus fair stream, and great Sangarius, Ladon, Parthenius, Euenus, Ardescus, and divine Scamander.

Also she brought forth a holy company of daughters[1] who with the lord Apollo and the Rivers have youths in their keeping—to this charge Zeus appointed them—Peitho, and Admete, and Ianthe, and Electra, and Doris, and Prymno, and Urania divine in form, Hippo, Clymene, Rhodea, and Callirrhoe, Zeuxo and Clytie, and Idyia, and Pasithoe, Plexaura, and Galaxaura, and lovely Dione, Melobosis and Thoe and handsome Polydora, Cerceis lovely of form, and soft eyed Pluto, Perseis, Ianeira, Acaste, Xanthe, Petraea the fair, Menestho, and Europa, Metis, and Eurynome, and Telesto saffron-clad, Chryseis and Asia and charming Calypso, Eudora, and Tyche, Amphirho, and Ocyrrhoe, and Styx who is the chiefest of them all. These are the eldest daughters that sprang from Ocean and Tethys; but there are many besides. For there are three thousand neat-ankled daughters of Ocean who are dispersed far and wide, and in every place alike serve the earth and the deep waters, children who are glorious among goddesses. And as many other rivers are there, babbling as they flow, sons of Ocean, whom queenly Tethys bare, but their names it is hard for a mortal man to tell, but people know those by which they severally dwell.

And Theia was subject in love to Hyperion and bare great Helius (Sun) and clear Selene (Moon) and Eos (Dawn) who shines upon all that are on earth and upon the deathless Gods who live in the wide heaven.

And Eurybia, bright goddess, was joined in love to Crius and bare great Astraeus, and Pallas, and Perses who also was eminent among all men in wisdom.

And Eos bare to Astraeus the strong-hearted winds, brightening Zephyrus, and Boreas, headlong in his course, and Notus,—a goddess mating in love with a god. And after these Erigenia[2] bare the star Eosphorus (Dawn-bringer), and the gleaming stars with which heaven is crowned.

And Styx the daughter of Ocean was joined to Pallas and bare Zelus (Emulation) and trim-ankled Nike (Victory) in the house. Also she brought forth Cratos (Strength) and Bia (Force), wonderful children. These have no house apart from Zeus, nor any dwelling nor path except that wherein God leads them, but they dwell always with Zeus the loud-

[1] Goettling notes that some of these nymphs derive their names from lands over which they preside, as Europa, Asia, Doris, Ianeira ('Lady of the Ionians'), but that most are called after some quality which their streams possessed: thus Xanthe is the 'Brown' or 'Turbid', Amphirho is the 'Surrounding' river, Ianthe is 'She who delights', and Ocyrrhoe is the 'Swift-flowing'.
[2] i.e. Eos, the 'Early-born'.

thunderer. For so did Styx the deathless daughter of Ocean plan on that day when the Olympian Lightener called all the deathless gods to great Olympus, and said that whosoever of the gods would fight with him against the Titans, he would not cast him out from his rights, but each should have the office which he had before amongst the deathless gods. And he declared that he who was without office and rights under Cronos, should be raised to both office and rights as is just. So deathless Styx came first to Olympus with her children through the wit of her dear father. And Zeus honoured her, and gave her very great gifts, for her he appointed to be the great oath of the gods, and her children to live with him always. And as he promised, so he performed fully unto them all. But he himself mightily reigns and rules.

Again, Phoebe came to the desired embrace of Coeus.

Then the goddess through the love of the god conceived and brought forth dark-gowned Leto, always mild, kind to men and to the deathless gods, mild from the beginning, gentlest in all Olympus. Also she bare Asteria of happy name, whom Perses once led to his great house to be called his dear wife. And she conceived and bare Hecate whom Zeus the son of Cronos honoured above all. He gave her splendid gifts, to have a share of the earth and the unfruitful sea. She received honour also in starry heaven, and is honoured exceedingly by the deathless gods. For to this day, whenever any one of men on earth offers rich sacrifices and prays for favour according to custom, he calls upon Hecate. Great honour comes full easily to him whose prayers the goddess receives favourably, and she bestows wealth upon him; for the power surely is with her. For as many as were born of Earth and Ocean amongst all these she has her due portion. The son of Cronos did her no wrong nor took anything away of all that was her portion among the former Titan gods: but she holds, as the division was at the first from the beginning, privilege both in earth, and in heaven, and in sea. Also, because she is an only child, the goddess receives not less honour, but much more still, for Zeus honours her. Whom she will she greatly aids and advances: she sits by worshipful kings in judgement, and in the assembly whom she will is distinguished among the people. And when men arm themselves for the battle that destroys men, then the goddess is at hand to give victory and grant glory readily to whom she will. Good is she also when men contend at the games, for there too the goddess is with them and profits them: and he who by might and strength gets the victory wins the rich prize easily with joy, and brings glory to his parents. And she is good to stand by horsemen, whom she will: and to those whose business is in the grey discomfortable sea, and who pray to Hecate and the loud-crashing Earth-Shaker, easily the glorious goddess gives great catch, and easily she takes it away as soon as seen, if so she will. She is good in the byre with Hermes to increase the stock. The droves of kine and wide herds of goats and flocks of fleecy sheep, if she will, she increases from a few, or makes many to be less. So, then, albeit her mother's only child,[1] she is honoured amongst all the deathless gods. And the son of Cronos made her a nurse of the

---

[1] Van Lennep explains that Hecate, having no brothers to support her claim, might have been slighted.

young who after that day saw with their eyes the light of all-seeing Dawn. So from the beginning she is a nurse of the young, and these are her honours.

But Rhea was subject in love to Cronos and bare splendid children, Hestia,[1] Demeter, and gold-shod Hera and strong Hades, pitiless in heart, who dwells under the earth, and the loud-crashing Earth-Shaker, and wise Zeus, father of gods and men, by whose thunder the wide earth is shaken. These great Cronos swallowed as each came forth from the womb to his mother's knees with this intent, that no other of the proud sons of Heaven should hold the kingly office amongst the deathless gods. For he learned from Earth and starry Heaven that he was destined to be overcome by his own son, strong though he was, through the contriving of great Zeus.[2] Therefore he kept no blind outlook, but watched and swallowed down his children: and unceasing grief seized Rhea. But when she was about to bear Zeus, the father of gods and men, then she besought her own dear parents, Earth and starry Heaven, to devise some plan with her that the birth of her dear child might be concealed, and that retribution might overtake great, crafty Cronos for his own father and also for the children whom he had swallowed down. And they readily heard and obeyed their dear daughter, and told her all that was destined to happen touching Cronos the king and his stout-hearted son. So they sent her to Lyetus, to the rich land of Crete, when she was ready to bear great Zeus, the youngest of her children. Him did vast Earth receive from Rhea in wide Crete to nourish and to bring up. Thither came Earth carrying him swiftly through the black night to Lyctus first, and took him in her arms and hid him in a remote cave beneath the secret places of the holy earth on thick-wooded Mount Aegeum; but to the mightily ruling son of Heaven, the earlier king of the gods, she gave a great stone wrapped in swaddling clothes. Then he took it in his hands and thrust it down into his belly: wretch! he knew not in his heart that in place of the stone his son was left behind, unconquered and untroubled, and that he was soon to overcome him by force and might and drive him from his honours, himself to reign over the deathless gods.

After that, the strength and glorious limbs of the prince increased quickly, and as the years rolled on, great Cronos the wily was beguiled by the deep suggestions of Earth, and brought up again his offspring, vanquished by the arts and might of his own son, and he vomited up first the stone which he had swallowed last. And Zeus set it fast in the wide-pathed earth at goodly Pytho under the glens of Parnassus, to be a sign thenceforth and a marvel to mortal men.[3] And he set free from their deadly bonds the brothers of his father, sons of Heaven whom his father in his foolishness had bound. And they remembered to be

[1] The goddess of the hearth (the Roman "Vesta"), and so of the house.
[2] The variant reading 'of his father' (sc. Heaven) rests on inferior MS. authority and is probably an alteration due to the difficulty stated by a Scholiast: 'How could Zeus, being not yet begotten, plot against his father?' The phrase is, however, part of the prophecy. The whole line may well be spurious, and is rejected by Heyne, Wolf, Gaisford and Guyet.
[3] Pausanias (x. 24.6) saw near the tomb of Neoptolemus 'a stone of no great size', which the Delphians anointed every day with oil, and which he says was supposed to be the stone given to Cronos.

grateful to him for his kindness, and gave him thunder and the glowing thunderbolt and lightening: for before that, huge Earth had hidden these. In them he trusts and rules over mortals and immortals.

Now Iapetus took to wife the neat-ankled mad Clymene, daughter of Ocean, and went up with her into one bed. And she bare him a stout-hearted son, Atlas: also she bare very glorious Menoetius and clever Prometheus, full of various wiles, and scatter-brained Epimetheus who from the first was a mischief to men who eat bread; for it was he who first took of Zeus the woman, the maiden whom he had formed.[1] But Menoetius was outrageous, and far-seeing Zeus struck him with a lurid thunderbolt and sent him down to Erebus because of his mad presumption and exceeding pride. And Atlas through hard constraint upholds the wide heaven with unwearying head and arms, standing at the borders of the earth before the clear-voiced Hesperides; for this lot wise Zeus assigned to him. And ready-witted Prometheus he bound with inextricable bonds, cruel chains, and drove a shaft through his middle, and set on him a long-winged eagle, which used to eat his immortal liver; but by night the liver grew as much again everyway as the long-winged bird devoured in the whole day. That bird Heracles, the valiant son of shapely-ankled Alcmene, slew; and delivered the son of Iapetus from the cruel plague, and released him from his affliction—not without the will of Olympian Zeus who reigns on high, that the glory of Heracles the Theban-born might be yet greater than it was before over the plenteous earth. This, then, he regarded, and honoured his famous son; though he was angry, he ceased from the wrath which he had before because Prometheus matched himself in wit with the almighty son of Cronos. For when the gods and mortal men had a dispute at Mecone, even then Prometheus was forward to cut up a great ox and set portions before them, trying to befool the mind of Zeus. Before the rest he set flesh and inner parts thick with fat upon the hide, covering them with an ox paunch; but for Zeus he put the white bones dressed up with cunning art and covered with shining fat. Then the father of men and of gods said to him:

'Son of Iapetus, most glorious of all lords, good sir, how unfairly you have divided the portions!'

So said Zeus whose wisdom is everlasting, rebuking him. But wily Prometheus answered him, smiling softly and not forgetting his cunning trick:

'Zeus, most glorious and greatest of the eternal gods, take which ever of these portions your heart within you bids.' So he said, thinking trickery. But Zeus, whose wisdom is everlasting, saw and failed not to perceive the trick, and in his heart he thought mischief against mortal men which also was to be fulfilled. With both hands he took up the white fat and was angry at heart, and wrath came to his spirit when he saw the white ox-bones craftily tricked out: and because of this the tribes of men upon earth burn white bones to the

---

[1] i.e., Pandora; Hesiod tells more of the myth on the next page but does not name her explicitly until *Works and Days*. (EGW)

deathless gods upon fragrant altars. But Zeus who drives the clouds was greatly vexed and said to him:

'Son of Iapetus, clever above all! So, sir, you have not yet forgotten your cunning arts!'

So spake Zeus in anger, whose wisdom is everlasting; and from that time he was always mindful of the trick, and would not give the power of unwearying fire to the Melian[1] race of mortal men who live on the earth. But the noble son of Iapetus outwitted him and stole the far-seen gleam of unwearying fire in a hollow fennel stalk. And Zeus who thunders on high was stung in spirit, and his dear heart was angered when he saw amongst men the far-seen ray of fire. Forthwith he made an evil thing for men as the price of fire; for the very famous Limping God formed of earth the likeness of a shy maiden as the son of Cronos willed. And the goddess bright-eyed Athene girded and clothed her with silvery raiment, and down from her head she spread with her hands a broidered veil, a wonder to see; and she, Pallas Athene, put about her head lovely garlands, flowers of new-grown herbs. Also she put upon her head a crown of gold which the very famous Limping God made himself and worked with his own hands as a favour to Zeus his father. On it was much curious work, wonderful to see; for of the many creatures which the land and sea rear up, he put most upon it, wonderful things, like living beings with voices: and great beauty shone out from it.

But when he had made the beautiful evil to be the price for the blessing, he brought her out, delighting in the finery which the bright-eyed daughter of a mighty father had given her, to the place where the other gods and men were. And wonder took hold of the deathless gods and mortal men when they saw that which was sheer guile, not to be withstood by men.

For from her is the race of women and female kind: of her is the deadly race and tribe of women who live amongst mortal men to their great trouble, no helpmeets in hateful poverty, but only in wealth. And as in thatched hives bees feed the drones whose nature is to do mischief—by day and throughout the day until the sun goes down the bees are busy and lay the white combs, while the drones stay at home in the covered skeps and reap the toil of others into their own bellies—even so Zeus who thunders on high made women to be an evil to mortal men, with a nature to do evil. And he gave them a second evil to be the price for the good they had: whoever avoids marriage and the sorrows that women cause, and will not wed, reaches deadly old age without anyone to tend his years, and though he at least has no lack of livelihood while he lives, yet, when he is dead, his kinsfolk divide his possessions amongst them. And as for the man who chooses the lot of marriage and takes a good wife suited to his mind, evil continually contends with good; for whoever happens to have mischievous children, lives always with unceasing grief in his spirit and heart within him; and this evil cannot be healed.

---

[1] A Scholiast explains: 'Either because they (men) sprang from the Melian nymphs (cp. l. 187); or because, when they were born (?), they cast themselves under the ash-trees, that is, the trees.' The reference may be to the origin of men from ash-trees.

So it is not possible to deceive or go beyond the will of Zeus; for not even the son of Iapetus, kindly Prometheus, escaped his heavy anger, but of necessity strong bands confined him, although he knew many a wile.

But when first their father was vexed in his heart with Obriareus and Cottus and Gyes, he bound them in cruel bonds, because he was jealous of their exceeding manhood and comeliness and great size: and he made them live beneath the wide-pathed earth, where they were afflicted, being set to dwell under the ground, at the end of the earth, at its great borders, in bitter anguish for a long time and with great grief at heart. But the son of Cronos and the other deathless gods whom rich-haired Rhea bare from union with Cronos, brought them up again to the light at Earth's advising. For she herself recounted all things to the gods fully, how that with these they would gain victory and a glorious cause to vaunt themselves. For the Titan gods and as many as sprang from Cronos had long been fighting together in stubborn war with heart-grieving toil, the lordly Titans from high Othyrs, but the gods, givers of good, whom rich-haired Rhea bare in union with Cronos, from Olympus. So they, with bitter wrath, were fighting continually with one another at that time for ten full years, and the hard strife had no close or end for either side, and the issue of the war hung evenly balanced. But when he had provided those three with all things fitting, nectar and ambrosia which the gods themselves eat, and when their proud spirit revived within them all after they had fed on nectar and delicious ambrosia, then it was that the father of men and gods spoke amongst them:

'Hear me, bright children of Earth and Heaven, that I may say what my heart within me bids. A long while now have we, who are sprung from Cronos and the Titan gods, fought with each other every day to get victory and to prevail. But do you show your great might and unconquerable strength, and face the Titans in bitter strife; for remember our friendly kindness, and from what sufferings you are come back to the light from your cruel bondage under misty gloom through our counsels.'

So he said. And blameless Cottus answered him again: 'Divine one, you speak that which we know well: nay, even of ourselves we know that your wisdom and understanding is exceeding, and that you became a defender of the deathless ones from chill doom. And through your devising we are come back again from the murky gloom and from our merciless bonds, enjoying what we looked not for, O lord, son of Cronos. And so now with fixed purpose and deliberate counsel we will aid your power in dreadful strife and will fight against the Titans in hard battle.'

So he said: and the gods, givers of good things, applauded when they heard his word, and their spirit longed for war even more than before, and they all, both male and female, stirred up hated battle that day, the Titan gods, and all that were born of Cronos together with those dread, mighty ones of overwhelming strength whom Zeus brought up to the light from Erebus beneath the earth. An hundred arms sprang from the shoulders of all alike, and each had fifty heads growing upon his shoulders upon stout limbs. These, then, stood against the Titans in grim strife, holding huge rocks in their strong hands. And on the other part the

Titans eagerly strengthened their ranks, and both sides at one time showed the work of their hands and their might. The boundless sea rang terribly around, and the earth crashed loudly: wide Heaven was shaken and groaned, and high Olympus reeled from its foundation under the charge of the undying gods, and a heavy quaking reached dim Tartarus and the deep sound of their feet in the fearful onset and of their hard missiles. So, then, they launched their grievous shafts upon one another, and the cry of both armies as they shouted reached to starry heaven; and they met together with a great battle-cry.

Then Zeus no longer held back his might; but straight his heart was filled with fury and he showed forth all his strength. From Heaven and from Olympus he came forthwith, hurling his lightning: the bolts flew thick and fast from his strong hand together with thunder and lightning, whirling an awesome flame. The life-giving earth crashed around in burning, and the vast wood crackled loud with fire all about. All the land seethed, and Ocean's streams and the unfruitful sea. The hot vapour lapped round the earthborn Titans: flame unspeakable rose to the bright upper air: the flashing glare of the thunder-stone and lightning blinded their eyes for all that there were strong. Astounding heat seized Chaos: and to see with eyes and to hear the sound with ears it seemed even as if Earth and wide Heaven above came together; for such a mighty crash would have arisen if Earth were being hurled to ruin, and Heaven from on high were hurling her down; so great a crash was there while the gods were meeting together in strife. Also the winds brought rumbling earthquake and duststorm, thunder and lightning and the lurid thunderbolt, which are the shafts of great Zeus, and carried the clangour and the warcry into the midst of the two hosts. An horrible uproar of terrible strife arose: mighty deeds were shown and the battle inclined. But until then, they kept at one another and fought continually in cruel war.

And amongst the foremost Cottus and Briareos and Gyes insatiate for war raised fierce fighting: three hundred rocks, one upon another, they launched from their strong hands and overshadowed the Titans with their missiles, and buried them beneath the wide-pathed earth, and bound them in bitter chains when they had conquered them by their strength for all their great spirit, as far beneath the earth to Tartarus. For a brazen anvil falling down from heaven nine nights and days would reach the earth upon the tenth: and again, a brazen anvil falling from earth nine nights and days would reach Tartarus upon the tenth. Round it runs a fence of bronze, and night spreads in triple line all about it like a neck-circlet, while above grow the roots of the earth and unfruitful sea. There by the counsel of Zeus who drives the clouds the Titan gods are hidden under misty gloom, in a dank place where are the ends of the huge earth. And they may not go out; for Poseidon fixed gates of bronze upon it, and a wall runs all round it on every side. There Gyes and Cottus and great-souled Obriareus live, trusty warders of Zeus who holds the aegis.

And there, all in their order, are the sources and ends of gloomy earth and misty Tartarus and the unfruitful sea and starry heaven, loathsome and dank, which even the gods abhor.

It is a great gulf, and if once a man were within the gates, he would not reach the floor until a whole year had reached its end, but cruel blast upon blast would carry him this way and that. And this marvel is awful even to the deathless gods.

There stands the awful home of murky Night wrapped in dark clouds. In front of it the son of Iapetus[1] stands immovably upholding the wide heaven upon his head and unwearying hands, where Night and Day draw near and greet one another as they pass the great threshold of bronze: and while the one is about to go down into the house, the other comes out at the door.

And the house never holds them both within; but always one is without the house passing over the earth, while the other stays at home and waits until the time for her journeying come; and the one holds all-seeing light for them on earth, but the other holds in her arms Sleep the brother of Death, even evil Night, wrapped in a vaporous cloud.

And there the children of dark Night have their dwellings, Sleep and Death, awful gods. The glowing Sun never looks upon them with his beams, neither as he goes up into heaven, nor as he comes down from heaven. And the former of them roams peacefully over the earth and the sea's broad back and is kindly to men; but the other has a heart of iron, and his spirit within him is pitiless as bronze: whomsoever of men he has once seized he holds fast: and he is hateful even to the deathless gods.

There, in front, stand the echoing halls of the god of the lower-world, strong Hades, and of awful Persephone. A fearful hound guards the house in front, pitiless, and he has a cruel trick. On those who go in he fawns with his tail and both his ears, but suffers them not to go out back again, but keeps watch and devours whomsoever he catches going out of the gates of strong Hades and awful Persephone.

And there dwells the goddess loathed by the deathless gods, terrible Styx, eldest daughter of back-flowing[2] Ocean. She lives apart from the gods in her glorious house vaulted over with great rocks and propped up to heaven all round with silver pillars. Rarely does the daughter of Thaumas, swift-footed Iris, come to her with a message over the sea's wide back.

But when strife and quarrel arise among the deathless gods, and when any of them who live in the house of Olympus lies, then Zeus sends Iris to bring in a golden jug the great oath of the gods from far away, the famous cold water which trickles down from a high and beetling rock. Far under the wide-pathed earth a branch of Oceanus flows through the dark night out of the holy stream, and a tenth part of his water is allotted to her. With nine silver-swirling streams he winds about the earth and the sea's wide back, and then falls into the

---

[1] sc. Atlas, the Shu of Egyptian mythology: cp. note on line 177.
[2] Oceanus is here regarded as a continuous stream enclosing the earth and the seas, and so as flowing back upon himself.

main;[1] but the tenth flows out from a rock, a sore trouble to the gods. For whoever of the deathless gods that hold the peaks of snowy Olympus pours a libation of her water is forsworn, lies breathless until a full year is completed, and never comes near to taste ambrosia and nectar, but lies spiritless and voiceless on a strewn bed: and a heavy trance overshadows him. But when he has spent a long year in his sickness, another penance and an harder follows after the first. For nine years he is cut off from the eternal gods and never joins their councils of their feasts, nine full years. But in the tenth year he comes again to join the assemblies of the deathless gods who live in the house of Olympus. Such an oath, then, did the gods appoint the eternal and primaeval water of Styx to be: and it spouts through a rugged place.

And there, all in their order, are the sources and ends of the dark earth and misty Tartarus and the unfruitful sea and starry heaven, loathsome and dank, which even the gods abhor.

And there are shining gates and an immoveable threshold of bronze having unending roots and it is grown of itself.[2] And beyond, away from all the gods, live the Titans, beyond gloomy Chaos. But the glorious allies of loud-crashing Zeus have their dwelling upon Ocean's foundations, even Cottus and Gyes; but Briareos, being goodly, the deep-roaring Earth-Shaker made his son-in-law, giving him Cymopolea his daughter to wed.

But when Zeus had driven the Titans from heaven, huge Earth bare her youngest child Typhoeus of the love of Tartarus, by the aid of golden Aphrodite. Strength was with his hands in all that he did and the feet of the strong god were untiring. From his shoulders grew an hundred heads of a snake, a fearful dragon, with dark, flickering tongues, and from under the brows of his eyes in his marvellous heads flashed fire, and fire burned from his heads as he glared. And there were voices in all his dreadful heads which uttered every kind of sound unspeakable; for at one time they made sounds such that the gods understood, but at another, the noise of a bull bellowing aloud in proud ungovernable fury; and at another, the sound of a lion, relentless of heart; and at another, sounds like whelps, wonderful to hear; and again, at another, he would hiss, so that the high mountains re-echoed. And truly a thing past help would have happened on that day, and he would have come to reign over mortals and immortals, had not the father of men and gods been quick to perceive it. But he thundered hard and mightily: and the earth around resounded terribly and the wide heaven above, and the sea and Ocean's streams and the nether parts of the earth. Great Olympus reeled beneath the divine feet of the king as he arose and earth groaned thereat. And through the two of them heat took hold on the dark-blue sea, through the thunder and lightning, and through the fire from the monster, and the scorching winds and blazing thunderbolt. The

---

[1] The conception of Oceanus is here different: he has nine streams which encircle the earth and then flow out into the 'main' which appears to be the waste of waters on which, according to early Greek and Hebrew cosmology, the disk-like earth floated.

[2] i.e. the threshold is of 'native' metal, and not artificial.

whole earth seethed, and sky and sea: and the long waves raged along the beaches round and about, at the rush of the deathless gods: and there arose an endless shaking. Hades trembled where he rules over the dead below, and the Titans under Tartarus who live with Cronos, because of the unending clamour and the fearful strife. So when Zeus had raised up his might and seized his arms, thunder and lightning and lurid thunderbolt, he leaped from Olympus and struck him, and burned all the marvellous heads of the monster about him. But when Zeus had conquered him and lashed him with strokes, Typhoeus was hurled down, a maimed wreck, so that the huge earth groaned. And flame shot forth from the thunder-stricken lord in the dim rugged glens of the mount,[1] when he was smitten. A great part of huge earth was scorched by the terrible vapour and melted as tin melts when heated by men's art in channelled[2] crucibles; or as iron, which is hardest of all things, is softened by glowing fire in mountain glens and melts in the divine earth through the strength of Hephaestus.[3] Even so, then, the earth melted in the glow of the blazing fire. And in the bitterness of his anger Zeus cast him into wide Tartarus.

And from Typhoeus come boisterous winds which blow damply, except Notus and Boreas and clear Zephyr. These are a god-sent kind, and a great blessing to men; but the others blow fitfully upon the seas. Some rush upon the misty sea and work great havoc among men with their evil, raging blasts; for varying with the season they blow, scattering ships and destroying sailors. And men who meet these upon the sea have no help against the mischief. Others again over the boundless, flowering earth spoil the fair fields of men who dwell below, filling them with dust and cruel uproar.

But when the blessed gods had finished their toil, and settled by force their struggle for honours with the Titans, they pressed far-seeing Olympian Zeus to reign and to rule over them, by Earth's prompting. So he divided their dignities amongst them.

Now Zeus, king of the gods, made Metis his wife first, and she was wisest among gods and mortal men. But when she was about to bring forth the goddess bright-eyed Athene, Zeus craftily deceived her with cunning words and put her in his own belly, as Earth and starry Heaven advised. For they advised him so, to the end that no other should hold royal sway over the eternal gods in place of Zeus; for very wise children were destined to be born of her, first the maiden bright-eyed Tritogeneia, equal to her father in strength and in wise understanding; but afterwards she was to bear a son of overbearing spirit, king of gods and men. But Zeus put her into his own belly first, that the goddess might devise for him both good and evil.

Next he married bright Themis who bare the Horae (Hours), and[4] Eunomia (Order), Dike (Justice), and blooming Eirene (Peace), who mind the works of mortal men, and the

---

[1] According to Homer Typhoeus was overwhelmed by Zeus amongst the Arimi in Cilicia. Pindar represents him as buried under Aetna, and Tzetzes reads Aetna in this passage.

[2] The epithet (which means literally 'well-bored') seems to refer to the spout of the crucible.

[3] The fire god. There is no reference to volcanic action: iron was smelted on Mount Ida.

[4] This "and" does not belong here—Eunomia, Dike, and Eirene *were* the Horae. (EGW)

Moerae (Fates) to whom wise Zeus gave the greatest honour, Clotho, and Lachesis, and Atropos who give mortal men evil and good to have.[1]

And Eurynome, the daughter of Ocean, beautiful in form, bare him three fair-cheeked Charites (Graces), Aglaea, and Euphrosyne, and lovely Thaleia, from whose eyes as they glanced flowed love that unnerves the limbs: and beautiful is their glance beneath their brows.

Also he came to the bed of all-nourishing Demeter, and she bare white-armed Persephone whom Aidoneus carried off from her mother; but wise Zeus gave her to him.

And again, he loved Mnemosyne with the beautiful hair: and of her the nine gold-crowned Muses were born who delight in feasts and the pleasures of song.

And Leto was joined in love with Zeus who holds the aegis, and bare Apollo and Artemis delighting in arrows, children lovely above all the sons of Heaven.

Lastly, he made Hera his blooming wife: and she was joined in love with the king of gods and men, and brought forth Hebe and Ares and Eileithyia.

But Zeus himself gave birth from his own head to bright-eyed Tritogeneia,[2] the awful, the strife-stirring, the host-leader, the unwearying, the queen, who delights in tumults and wars and battles. But Hera without union with Zeus—for she was very angry and quarrelled with her mate—bare famous Hephaestus, who is skilled in crafts more than all the sons of Heaven.

[3]But Hera was very angry and quarrelled with her mate. And because of this strife she bare without union with Zeus who holds the aegis a glorious son, Hephaestus, who excelled all the sons of Heaven in crafts. But Zeus lay with the fair-cheeked daughter of Ocean and Tethys apart from Hera....[4]....deceiving Metis (Thought) although she was full wise. But he seized her with his hands and put her in his belly, for fear that she might bring forth something stronger than his thunderbolt: therefore did Zeus, who sits on high and dwells in the aether, swallow her down suddenly. But she straightway conceived Pallas Athene: and the father of men and gods gave her birth by way of his head on the banks of the river Trito. And she remained hidden beneath the inward parts of Zeus, even Metis, Athena's mother, worker of righteousness, who was wiser than gods and mortal men. There the goddess (Athena) received that[5] whereby she excelled in strength all the deathless ones who dwell in Olympus, she who made the host-scaring weapon of Athena. And with it (Zeus) gave her birth, arrayed in arms of war.

---

[1] This contradicts what Hesiod says earlier, naming the Moirae as daughters of Nyx. (EGW)

[2] i.e. Athena, who was born 'on the banks of the river Trito' (cp. l. 929l)

[3] Restored by Peppmuller. The nineteen following lines from another recension of lines 889-900, 924-9 are quoted by Chrysippus (in Galen).

[4] This part of the text is missing. (EGW)

[5] sc. the aegis. Line 929s is probably spurious, since it disagrees with l. 929q and contains a suspicious reference to Athens.

And of Amphitrite and the loud-roaring Earth-Shaker was born great, wide-ruling Triton, and he owns the depths of the sea, living with his dear mother and the lord his father in their golden house, an awful god.

Also Cytherea bare to Ares the shield-piercer Panic and Fear, terrible gods who drive in disorder the close ranks of men in numbing war, with the help of Ares, sacker of towns: and Harmonia whom high-spirited Cadmus made his wife.

And Maia, the daughter of Atlas, bare to Zeus glorious Hermes, the herald of the deathless gods, for she went up into his holy bed.

And Semele, daughter of Cadmus was joined with him in love and bare him a splendid son, joyous Dionysus,—a mortal woman an immortal son. And now they both are gods.

And Alcmena was joined in love with Zeus who drives the clouds and bare mighty Heracles.

And Hephaestus, the famous Lame One, made Aglaea, youngest of the Graces, his buxom wife.

And golden-haired Dionysus made brown-haired Ariadne, the daughter of Minos, his buxom wife: and the son of Cronos made her deathless and unageing for him.

And mighty Heracles, the valiant son of neat-ankled Alcmena, when he had finished his grievous toils, made Hebe the child of great Zeus and gold-shod Hera his shy wife in snowy Olympus. Happy he! For he has finished his great works and lives amongst the undying gods, untroubled and unageing all his days.

And Perseis, the daughter of Ocean, bare to unwearying Helios Circe and Aeetes the king. And Aeetes, the son of Helios who shows light to men, took to wife fair-cheeked Idyia, daughter of Ocean the perfect stream, by the will of the gods: and she was subject to him in love through golden Aphrodite and bare him neat-ankled Medea.

And now farewell, you dwellers on Olympus and you islands and continents and thou briny sea within. Now sing the company of goddesses, sweet-voiced Muses of Olympus, daughter of Zeus who holds the aegis,—even those deathless one who lay with mortal men and bare children like unto gods.

Demeter, bright goddess, was joined in sweet love with the hero Iasion in a thrice-ploughed fallow in the rich land of Crete, and bare Plutus, a kindly god who goes everywhere over land and the sea's wide back, and him who finds him and into whose hands he comes he makes rich, bestowing great wealth upon him.

And Harmonia, the daughter of golden Aphrodite, bare to Cadmus Ino and Semele and fair-cheeked Agave and Autonoe whom long haired Aristaeus wedded, and Polydorus also in rich-crowned Thebe.

And the daughter of Ocean, Callirrhoe was joined in the love of rich Aphrodite with stout hearted Chrysaor and bare a son who was the strongest of all men, Geryones, whom mighty Heracles killed in sea-girt Erythea for the sake of his shambling oxen.

And Eos bare to Tithonus brazen-crested Memnon, king of the Ethiopians, and the Lord Emathion. And to Cephalus she bare a splendid son, strong Phaethon, a man like the gods, whom, when he was a young boy in the tender flower of glorious youth with childish thoughts, laughter-loving Aphrodite seized and caught up and made a keeper of her shrine by night, a divine spirit.

And the son of Aeson by the will of the gods led away from Aeetes the daughter of Aeetes the heaven-nurtured king, when he had finished the many grievous labours which the great king, over bearing Pelias, that outrageous and presumptuous doer of violence, put upon him. But when the son of Aeson had finished them, he came to Iolcus after long toil bringing the coy-eyed girl with him on his swift ship, and made her his buxom wife. And she was subject to Iason, shepherd of the people,[1] and bare a son Medeus whom Cheiron the son of Philyra brought up in the mountains. And the will of great Zeus was fulfilled.

But of the daughters of Nereus, the Old man of the Sea, Psamathe the fair goddess, was loved by Aeacus through golden Aphrodite and bare Phocus.[2] And the silver-shod goddess Thetis was subject to Peleus and brought forth lion-hearted Achilles,[3] the destroyer of men.

And Cytherea with the beautiful crown was joined in sweet love with the hero Anchises and bare Aeneas[4] on the peaks of Ida with its many wooded glens.

And Circe the daughter of Helius, Hyperion's son, loved steadfast Odysseus and bare Agrius and Latinus who was faultless and strong: also she brought forth Telegonus by the will of golden Aphrodite. And they ruled over the famous Tyrenians, very far off in a recess of the holy islands.

And the bright goddess Calypso was joined to Odysseus in sweet love, and bare him Nausithous and Nausinous.

These are the immortal goddesses who lay with mortal men and bare them children like unto gods.

But now, sweet-voiced Muses of Olympus, daughters of Zeus who holds the aegis, sing of the company of women.

---

[1] This is the same Jason who went after the Golden Fleece, of which Medea was guardian; you may know that story from *Jason and the Argonauts*. (EGW)

[2] One of two mythical figures for whom the region of Phocis was said to be named; this Phocus is said to have been killed by his jealous mortal half-brothers, though various sources differ widely in the details. (EGW)

[3] Chief hero of the *Iliad*. Thetis dipped the infant Achilles in the River Styx to make him invulnerable, but the water failed to reach the part of his heel where she was holding onto him, so his heel remained his one weak spot. From this legend we get both the term *Achilles' heel* for a fatal weakness and the *Achilles tendon*, the tendon that attaches the muscles of the back of the leg to the heel bone; a person whose Achilles tendon ruptures or is severed will be unable to walk on that leg unless and until the tendon is surgically repaired. (EGW)

[4] The Trojan hero Aeneas is far more important to Roman mythology, as seen in the *Aeneid*, than to the Greeks. (EGW)

Virgil
from The Aeneid[1]
Translated by John Dryden

Book I

Arms, and the man I sing, who, forc'd by fate,
And haughty Juno's unrelenting hate,
Expell'd and exil'd, left the Trojan shore.
Long labors, both by sea and land, he bore,
And in the doubtful war, before he won
The Latian realm, and built the destin'd town;[2]
His banish'd gods restor'd to rites divine,
And settled sure succession in his line,
From whence the race of Alban fathers come,
And the long glories of majestic Rome.

O Muse! the causes and the crimes relate;
What goddess was provok'd, and whence her hate;
For what offense the Queen of Heav'n began
To persecute so brave, so just a man;
Involv'd his anxious life in endless cares,
Expos'd to wants, and hurried into wars!
Can heav'nly minds such high resentment show,
Or exercise their spite in human woe?

Against the Tiber's mouth, but far away,
An ancient town was seated on the sea;
A Tyrian colony;[3] the people made
Stout for the war, and studious of their trade:
Carthage the name; belov'd by Juno more
Than her own Argos, or the Samian shore.

---

[1] Notes on this text will primarily use the Roman names for the gods.
[2] i.e., Rome
[3] Dido was reputed to be from Sidon and to have founded Carthage after escaping from Tyre, where her homicidal brother was king. More of her story appears later in Book 1. (She was probably more contemporaneous with Solomon than with Aeneas, but Virgil clearly is not one to let facts stand in the way of a good story.)

Here stood her chariot; here, if Heav'n were kind,
The seat of awful empire she design'd.
Yet she had heard an ancient rumor fly,
(Long cited by the people of the sky,)
That times to come should see the Trojan race
Her Carthage ruin, and her tow'rs deface;
Nor thus confin'd, the yoke of sov'reign sway
Should on the necks of all the nations lay.
She ponder'd this, and fear'd it was in fate;[1]
Nor could forget the war she wag'd of late
For conqu'ring Greece against the Trojan state.
Besides, long causes working in her mind,
And secret seeds of envy, lay behind;
Deep graven in her heart the doom remain'd
Of partial Paris, and her form disdain'd;[2]
The grace bestow'd on ravish'd Ganymed,[3]
Electra's glories, and her injur'd bed.[4]
Each was a cause alone; and all combin'd
To kindle vengeance in her haughty mind.
For this, far distant from the Latian coast
She drove the remnants of the Trojan host;
And sev'n long years th' unhappy wand'ring train
Were toss'd by storms, and scatter'd thro' the main.
Such time, such toil, requir'd the Roman name,
Such length of labor for so vast a frame.

Now scarce the Trojan fleet, with sails and oars,
Had left behind the fair Sicilian shores,
Ent'ring with cheerful shouts the wat'ry reign,
And plowing frothy furrows in the main;

---

[1] While not as apocalyptic and fatalistic as Teutonic mythology, as seen particularly in "Balder the Beautiful," Greco-Roman mythology did adhere to the notion that even the gods were subject to fortune and fate.

[2] Jupiter called upon Paris, prince of Troy, to judge a beauty contest between Juno, Minerva, and Venus—but Venus cheated by promising to give Paris the most beautiful woman in the world, Helen of Sparta (better known now as Helen of Troy). Unfortunately, Helen was already married to the Spartan king, Menelaus, who rallied the armies of all the Greek states to wage war on Troy to get Helen back. Juno sided with the Greeks.

[3] Ganymede was a Phrygian boy with whom Jupiter fell in love; Jupiter abducted him, made him eternally young, and installed him as the cupbearer of the gods. Phrygia was near Troy and allied with Troy during the Trojan War.

[4] Not to be confused with Electra of Argos, this Electra was one of the Pleiades and another of Jupiter's sexual conquests; her son by Jupiter was Dardanus, of whom Aeneas was a direct descendant.

When, lab'ring still with endless discontent,
The Queen of Heav'n did thus her fury vent:

"Then am I vanquish'd? must I yield?" said she,
"And must the Trojans reign in Italy?
So Fate will have it, and Jove adds his force;
Nor can my pow'r divert their happy course.
Could angry Pallas, with revengeful spleen,
The Grecian navy burn, and drown the men?[1]
She, for the fault of one offending foe,
The bolts of Jove himself presum'd to throw:[2]
With whirlwinds from beneath she toss'd the ship,
And bare expos'd the bosom of the deep;
Then, as an eagle gripes the trembling game,
The wretch, yet hissing with her father's flame,
She strongly seiz'd, and with a burning wound
Transfix'd, and naked, on a rock she bound.
But I, who walk in awful[3] state above,
The majesty of heav'n, the sister wife of Jove,
For length of years my fruitless force employ
Against the thin remains of ruin'd Troy!
What nations now to Juno's pow'r will pray,
Or off'rings on my slighted altars lay?"

Thus rag'd the goddess; and, with fury fraught.
The restless regions of the storms she sought,
Where, in a spacious cave of living stone,
The tyrant Aeolus,[4] from his airy throne,
With pow'r imperial curbs the struggling winds,
And sounding tempests in dark prisons binds.
This way and that th' impatient captives tend,

---

[1] Ajax, prince of Locris (also known as Ajax the Lesser), had raped Cassandra in the temple of Minerva during the sack of Troy. The Greeks failed to punish him, so Minerva sent a storm to wreck the fleet and kill Ajax.

[2] When Neptune helped Ajax escape the wreck on a rock, Minerva tried to kill him with a thunderbolt; according to the *Odyssey*, Neptune protected Ajax again, but then Ajax made a blasphemous boast that prompted Neptune to split the rock and hurl Ajax into the sea.

[3] In the older sense of "full of awe."

[4] In the earliest Greek myths, Aeolus was the mortal king of a floating island called Aeolia; later myths conflated him with a son of Neptune who had the same name and considered him a god. In almost every case, he is considered the ruler of the winds.

And, pressing for release, the mountains rend.
High in his hall th' undaunted monarch stands,
And shakes his scepter, and their rage commands;
Which did he not, their unresisted sway
Would sweep the world before them in their way;
Earth, air, and seas thro' empty space would roll,
And heav'n would fly before the driving soul.
In fear of this, the Father of the Gods
Confin'd their fury to those dark abodes,
And lock'd 'em safe within, oppress'd with mountain loads;
Impos'd a king, with arbitrary sway,
To loose their fetters, or their force allay.
To whom the suppliant queen her pray'rs address'd,
And thus the tenor of her suit express'd:

"O Aeolus! for to thee the King of Heav'n
The pow'r of tempests and of winds has giv'n;
Thy force alone their fury can restrain,
And smooth the waves, or swell the troubled main-
A race of wand'ring slaves, abhorr'd by me,
With prosp'rous passage cut the Tuscan sea;
To fruitful Italy their course they steer,
And for their vanquish'd gods design new temples there.
Raise all thy winds; with night involve the skies;
Sink or disperse my fatal enemies.
Twice sev'n, the charming daughters of the main,
Around my person wait, and bear my train:
Succeed my wish, and second my design;
The fairest, Deiopeia, shall be thine,[1]
And make thee father of a happy line."

To this the god: "'T is yours, O queen, to will
The work which duty binds me to fulfil.
These airy kingdoms, and this wide command,
Are all the presents of your bounteous hand:
Yours is my sov'reign's grace; and, as your guest,
I sit with gods at their celestial feast;

---

[1] This is the only mention of Deiopeia potentially marrying Aeolus in any of the myths that I can find.

Raise tempests at your pleasure, or subdue;
Dispose of empire, which I hold from you."

He said, and hurl'd against the mountain side
His quiv'ring spear, and all the god applied.
The raging winds rush thro' the hollow wound,
And dance aloft in air, and skim along the ground;
Then, settling on the sea, the surges sweep,
Raise liquid mountains, and disclose the deep.
South, East, and West with mix'd confusion roar,
And roll the foaming billows to the shore.
The cables crack; the sailors' fearful cries
Ascend; and sable night involves the skies;
And heav'n itself is ravish'd from their eyes.
Loud peals of thunder from the poles ensue;
Then flashing fires the transient light renew;
The face of things a frightful image bears,
And present death in various forms appears.
Struck with unusual fright, the Trojan chief,
With lifted hands and eyes, invokes relief;
And, "Thrice and four times happy those," he cried,
"That under Ilian walls before their parents died!
Tydides,[1] bravest of the Grecian train!
Why could not I by that strong arm be slain,
And lie by noble Hector[2] on the plain,
Or great Sarpedon,[3] in those bloody fields
Where Simois[4] rolls the bodies and the shields
Of heroes, whose dismember'd hands yet bear
The dart aloft, and clench the pointed spear!"

Thus while the pious prince his fate bewails,
Fierce Boreas drove against his flying sails,
And rent the sheets; the raging billows rise,
And mount the tossing vessels to the skies:
Nor can the shiv'ring oars sustain the blow;

---

[1] i.e. Diomedes, king of Argos, second only to Achilles among the Greek heroes of the Trojan War.
[2] Crown prince of Troy and Aeneas' second cousin. Although Hector had dueled several times with Diomedes, he was actually killed by Achilles.
[3] Son of Zeus, grandson of Bellerophon, and king of Lycia.
[4] A river on the Trojan plain.

The galley gives her side, and turns her prow;
While those astern, descending down the steep,
Thro' gaping waves behold the boiling deep.
Three ships were hurried by the southern blast,
And on the secret shelves with fury cast.
Those hidden rocks th' Ausonian sailors knew:
They call'd them Altars, when they rose in view,
And show'd their spacious backs above the flood.
Three more fierce Eurus, in his angry mood,
Dash'd on the shallows of the moving sand,
And in mid ocean left them moor'd aland.
Orontes' bark, that bore the Lycian crew,
(A horrid sight!) ev'n in the hero's view,
From stem to stern by waves was overborne:
The trembling pilot, from his rudder torn,
Was headlong hurl'd; thrice round the ship was toss'd,
Then bulg'd at once, and in the deep was lost;
And here and there above the waves were seen
Arms, pictures, precious goods, and floating men.
The stoutest vessel to the storm gave way,
And suck'd thro' loosen'd planks the rushing sea.
Ilioneus was her chief: Alethes old,
Achates faithful, Abas young and bold,[1]
Endur'd not less; their ships, with gaping seams,
Admit the deluge of the briny streams.

Meantime imperial Neptune heard the sound
Of raging billows breaking on the ground.
Displeas'd, and fearing for his wat'ry reign,
He rear'd his awful head above the main,
Serene in majesty; then roll'd his eyes
Around the space of earth, and seas, and skies.
He saw the Trojan fleet dispers'd, distress'd,
By stormy winds and wintry heav'n oppress'd.
Full well the god his sister's envy knew,
And what her aims and what her arts pursue.
He summon'd Eurus and the western blast,

---

[1] The Trojans mentioned in this stanza appear only in the *Aeneid*, although some of them share names with other mythical figures.

And first an angry glance on both he cast;
Then thus rebuk'd: "Audacious winds! from whence
This bold attempt, this rebel insolence?
Is it for you to ravage seas and land,
Unauthoriz'd by my supreme command?
To raise such mountains on the troubled main?
Whom I—but first 't is fit the billows to restrain;
And then you shall be taught obedience to my reign.
Hence! to your lord my royal mandate bear—
The realms of ocean and the fields of air
Are mine, not his. By fatal lot to me
The liquid empire fell, and trident of the sea.
His pow'r to hollow caverns is confin'd:
There let him reign, the jailer of the wind,
With hoarse commands his breathing subjects call,
And boast and bluster in his empty hall."
He spoke; and, while he spoke, he smooth'd the sea,
Dispell'd the darkness, and restor'd the day.
Cymothoe, Triton, and the sea-green train
Of beauteous nymphs, the daughters of the main,
Clear from the rocks the vessels with their hands:
The god himself with ready trident stands,
And opes the deep, and spreads the moving sands;
Then heaves them off the shoals. Where'er he guides
His finny coursers and in triumph rides,
The waves unruffle and the sea subsides.
As, when in tumults rise th' ignoble crowd,
Mad are their motions, and their tongues are loud;
And stones and brands in rattling volleys fly,
And all the rustic arms that fury can supply:
If then some grave and pious man appear,
They hush their noise, and lend a list'ning ear;
He soothes with sober words their angry mood,
And quenches their innate desire of blood:
So, when the Father of the Flood appears,
And o'er the seas his sov'reign trident rears,
Their fury falls: he skims the liquid plains,
High on his chariot, and, with loosen'd reins,
Majestic moves along, and awful peace maintains.
The weary Trojans ply their shatter'd oars

To nearest land, and make the Libyan shores.
Within a long recess there lies a bay:
An island shades it from the rolling sea,
And forms a port secure for ships to ride;
Broke by the jutting land, on either side,
In double streams the briny waters glide.
Betwixt two rows of rocks a sylvan scene
Appears above, and groves for ever green:
A grot is form'd beneath, with mossy seats,
To rest the Nereids, and exclude the heats.
Down thro' the crannies of the living walls
The crystal streams descend in murm'ring falls:
No haulsers need to bind the vessels here,
Nor bearded anchors; for no storms they fear.
Sev'n ships within this happy harbor meet,
The thin remainders of the scatter'd fleet.
The Trojans, worn with toils, and spent with woes,
Leap on the welcome land, and seek their wish'd repose.

First, good Achates, with repeated strokes
Of clashing flints, their hidden fire provokes:
Short flame succeeds; a bed of wither'd leaves
The dying sparkles in their fall receives:
Caught into life, in fiery fumes they rise,
And, fed with stronger food, invade the skies.
The Trojans, dropping wet, or stand around
The cheerful blaze, or lie along the ground:
Some dry their corn, infected with the brine,
Then grind with marbles, and prepare to dine.
Aeneas climbs the mountain's airy brow,
And takes a prospect of the seas below,
If Capys thence, or Antheus he could spy,
Or see the streamers of Caicus fly.
No vessels were in view; but, on the plain,
Three beamy stags command a lordly train
Of branching heads: the more ignoble throng
Attend their stately steps, and slowly graze along.
He stood; and, while secure they fed below,
He took the quiver and the trusty bow
Achates us'd to bear: the leaders first

He laid along, and then the vulgar pierc'd;
Nor ceas'd his arrows, till the shady plain
Sev'n mighty bodies with their blood distain.
For the sev'n ships he made an equal share,
And to the port return'd, triumphant from the war.
The jars of gen'rous wine (Acestes'[1] gift,
When his Trinacrian shores the navy left)
He set abroach, and for the feast prepar'd,
In equal portions with the ven'son shar'd.
Thus while he dealt it round, the pious chief
With cheerful words allay'd the common grief:
"Endure, and conquer! Jove will soon dispose
To future good our past and present woes.
With me, the rocks of Scylla[2] you have tried;
Th' inhuman Cyclops[3] and his den defied.
What greater ills hereafter can you bear?
Resume your courage and dismiss your care,
An hour will come, with pleasure to relate
Your sorrows past, as benefits of Fate.
Thro' various hazards and events, we move
To Latium and the realms foredoom'd by Jove.
Call'd to the seat (the promise of the skies)
Where Trojan kingdoms once again may rise,
Endure the hardships of your present state;
Live, and reserve yourselves for better fate."

These words he spoke, but spoke not from his heart;
His outward smiles conceal'd his inward smart.
The jolly crew, unmindful of the past,
The quarry share, their plenteous dinner haste.
Some strip the skin; some portion out the spoil;
The limbs, yet trembling, in the caldrons boil;
Some on the fire the reeking entrails broil.
Stretch'd on the grassy turf, at ease they dine,
Restore their strength with meat, and cheer their souls with wine.

---

[1] Son of a Trojan woman who had been exiled to Sicily.

[2] Scylla and Charybdis were monsters that lived on opposite sides of an almost impossibly narrow strait; trying to steer clear of Scylla would bring a ship dangerously close to Charybdis and vice versa.

[3] Polyphemus, son of Neptune—no relation (well, only distant relation) to the sons of Caelus and Terra Mater.

Their hunger thus appeas'd, their care attends
The doubtful fortune of their absent friends:
Alternate hopes and fears their minds possess,
Whether to deem 'em dead, or in distress.
Above the rest, Aeneas mourns the fate
Of brave Orontes, and th' uncertain state
Of Gyas, Lycus, and of Amycus.[1]
The day, but not their sorrows, ended thus.

When, from aloft, almighty Jove surveys
Earth, air, and shores, and navigable seas,
At length on Libyan realms he fix'd his eyes—
Whom, pond'ring thus on human miseries,
When Venus saw, she with a lowly look,
Not free from tears, her heav'nly sire[2] bespoke:

"O King of Gods and Men! whose awful hand
Disperses thunder on the seas and land,
Disposing all with absolute command;
How could my pious son thy pow'r incense?
Or what, alas! is vanish'd Troy's offense?
Our hope of Italy not only lost,
On various seas by various tempests toss'd,
But shut from ev'ry shore, and barr'd from ev'ry coast.
You promis'd once, a progeny divine
Of Romans, rising from the Trojan line,
In after times should hold the world in awe,
And to the land and ocean give the law.
How is your doom revers'd, which eas'd my care
When Troy was ruin'd in that cruel war?
Then fates to fates I could oppose; but now,
When Fortune still pursues her former blow,
What can I hope? What worse can still succeed?
What end of labors has your will decreed?
Antenor,[3] from the midst of Grecian hosts,

---

[1] These Trojans also appear only in the *Aeneid*.

[2] Contrary to Hesiod, Homer has Aphrodite as the daughter of Zeus and Dione.

[3] Trojan elder who tried to convince Paris to send Helen back to Menelaus. Some writers later than Homer considered him a traitor who collaborated with the Greeks.

Could pass secure, and pierce th' Illyrian coasts,[1]
Where, rolling down the steep, Timavus[2] raves
And thro' nine channels disembogues his waves.
At length he founded Padua's happy seat,
And gave his Trojans a secure retreat;
There fix'd their arms, and there renew'd their name,
And there in quiet rules, and crown'd with fame.
But we,[3] descended from your sacred line,
Entitled to your heav'n and rites divine,
Are banish'd earth; and, for the wrath of one,
Remov'd from Latium and the promis'd throne.
Are these our scepters? these our due rewards?
And is it thus that Jove his plighted faith regards?"

To whom the Father of th' immortal race,
Smiling with that serene indulgent face,
With which he drives the clouds and clears the skies,
First gave a holy kiss; then thus replies:

"Daughter, dismiss thy fears; to thy desire
The fates of thine are fix'd, and stand entire.
Thou shalt behold thy wish'd Lavinian walls;
And, ripe for heav'n, when fate Aeneas calls,
Then shalt thou bear him up, sublime, to me:
No councils have revers'd my firm decree.
And, lest new fears disturb thy happy state,
Know, I have search'd the mystic rolls of Fate:
Thy son (nor is th' appointed season far)
In Italy shall wage successful war,
Shall tame fierce nations in the bloody field,
And sov'reign laws impose, and cities build,
Till, after ev'ry foe subdued, the sun
Thrice thro' the signs his annual race shall run:
This is his time prefix'd. Ascanius then,

---

[1] The Illyrians lived mostly in the Balkans, but some lived on the other side of the Adriatic in southeastern Italy.
[2] Known today as the Timavo, a river near Trieste.
[3] Here Venus is identifying herself with her son Aeneas and his companions.

Now call'd Iulus,[1] shall begin his reign.
He thirty rolling years the crown shall wear,
Then from Lavinium shall the seat transfer,
And, with hard labor, Alba Longa build.
The throne with his succession shall be fill'd
Three hundred circuits more: then shall be seen
Ilia the fair, a priestess and a queen,
Who, full of Mars, in time, with kindly throes,
Shall at a birth two goodly boys disclose.
The royal babes a tawny wolf shall drain:[2]
Then Romulus his grandsire's throne shall gain,
Of martial tow'rs the founder shall become,
The people Romans call, the city Rome.
To them no bounds of empire I assign,
Nor term of years to their immortal line.
Ev'n haughty Juno, who, with endless broils,
Earth, seas, and heav'n, and Jove himself turmoils;
At length aton'd, her friendly pow'r shall join,
To cherish and advance the Trojan line.
The subject world shall Rome's dominion own,
And, prostrate, shall adore the nation of the gown.
An age is ripening in revolving fate
When Troy shall overturn the Grecian state,[3]
And sweet revenge her conqu'ring sons shall call,
To crush the people that conspir'd her fall.
Then Caesar from the Julian stock shall rise,
Whose empire ocean, and whose fame the skies
Alone shall bound; whom, fraught with eastern spoils,
Our heav'n, the just reward of human toils,
Securely shall repay with rites divine;
And incense shall ascend before his sacred shrine.
Then dire debate and impious war shall cease,
And the stern age be soften'd into peace:

---

[1] Ascanius is Aeneas' son, founder of Alba Longa, ancestor of Romulus and Remus, and purported ancestor of the Gens Julia, a revered patrician family that included both Julius Caesar and his great-nephew Octavian, better known to us as Caesar Augustus.
[2] After being abandoned by their great-uncle, who had usurped the throne from his brother and feared that they would depose him, Romulus and Remus were saved by the river-god Tiberinus and were suckled by a she-wolf until being adopted by a shepherd.
[3] "Troy" here meaning the Trojans' descendants in Rome.

Then banish'd Faith shall once again return,
And Vestal fires in hallow'd temples burn;
And Remus with Quirinus[1] shall sustain
The righteous laws, and fraud and force restrain.
Janus[2] himself before his fane shall wait,
And keep the dreadful issues of his gate,
With bolts and iron bars: within remains
Imprison'd Fury, bound in brazen chains;
High on a trophy rais'd, of useless arms,
He sits, and threats the world with vain alarms."

He said, and sent Cyllenius[3] with command
To free the ports, and ope the Punic land
To Trojan guests; lest, ignorant of fate,
The queen might force them from her town and state.
Down from the steep of heav'n Cyllenius flies,
And cleaves with all his wings the yielding skies.
Soon on the Libyan shore descends the god,
Performs his message, and displays his rod:
The surly murmurs of the people cease;
And, as the fates requir'd, they give the peace:
The queen herself suspends the rigid laws,
The Trojans pities, and protects their cause.

Meantime, in shades of night Aeneas lies:
Care seiz'd his soul, and sleep forsook his eyes.
But, when the sun restor'd the cheerful day,
He rose, the coast and country to survey,
Anxious and eager to discover more.
It look'd a wild uncultivated shore;
But, whether humankind, or beasts alone
Possess'd the new-found region, was unknown.
Beneath a ledge of rocks his fleet he hides:
Tall trees surround the mountain's shady sides;
The bending brow above a safe retreat provides.

---

[1] Possibly once a Sabine god of war, but Plutarch recounts a legend that Romulus was deified as Quirinus.
[2] Roman god of doors and transitions, most frequently depicted with two faces; he has no Greek counterpart. The doors of his temple near the Forum were opened in times of war and closed in times of peace, which is why Jupiter refers to it in the following lines as imprisoning Fury.
[3] Mercury

Arm'd with two pointed darts, he leaves his friends,
And true Achates on his steps attends.
Lo! in the deep recesses of the wood,
Before his eyes his goddess mother stood:
A huntress in her habit and her mien;
Her dress a maid, her air confess'd a queen.
Bare were her knees, and knots her garments bind;
Loose was her hair, and wanton'd[1] in the wind;
Her hand sustain'd a bow; her quiver hung behind.
She seem'd a virgin of the Spartan blood:
With such array Harpalyce[2] bestrode
Her Thracian courser and outstripp'd the rapid flood.
"Ho, strangers! have you lately seen," she said,
"One of my sisters, like myself array'd,
Who cross'd the lawn, or in the forest stray'd?
A painted quiver at her back she bore;
Varied with spots, a lynx's hide she wore;
And at full cry pursued the tusky boar."

Thus Venus: thus her son replied again:
"None of your sisters have we heard or seen,
O virgin! or what other name you bear
Above that style—O more than mortal fair!
Your voice and mien celestial birth betray!
If, as you seem, the sister of the day,
Or one at least of chaste Diana's train,
Let not an humble suppliant sue in vain;
But tell a stranger, long in tempests toss'd,
What earth we tread, and who commands the coast?
Then on your name shall wretched mortals call,
And offer'd victims at your altars fall."
"I dare not," she replied, "assume the name
Of goddess, or celestial honors claim:
For Tyrian virgins bows and quivers bear,
And purple buskins o'er their ankles wear.
Know, gentle youth, in Libyan lands you are—
A people rude in peace, and rough in war.

---

[1] Blown about wantonly

[2] Daughter of a king of Thrace, raised as a warrior and noted for her speed as a runner.

The rising city, which from far you see,
Is Carthage, and a Tyrian colony.
Phoenician Dido rules the growing state,
Who fled from Tyre, to shun her brother's hate.
Great were her wrongs, her story full of fate;
Which I will sum in short. Sichaeus, known
For wealth, and brother to the Punic throne,
Possess'd fair Dido's bed; and either heart
At once was wounded with an equal dart.
Her father gave her, yet a spotless maid;
Pygmalion then the Tyrian scepter sway'd:
One who condemn'd divine and human laws.
Then strife ensued, and cursed gold the cause.
The monarch, blinded with desire of wealth,
With steel invades his brother's[1] life by stealth;
Before the sacred altar made him bleed,
And long from her conceal'd the cruel deed.
Some tale, some new pretense, he daily coin'd,
To soothe his sister, and delude her mind.
At length, in dead of night, the ghost appears
Of her unhappy lord: the specter stares,
And, with erected eyes, his bloody bosom bares.
The cruel altars and his fate he tells,
And the dire secret of his house reveals,
Then warns the widow, with her household gods,
To seek a refuge in remote abodes.
Last, to support her in so long a way,
He shows her where his hidden treasure lay.
Admonish'd thus, and seiz'd with mortal fright,
The queen provides companions of her flight:
They meet, and all combine to leave the state,
Who hate the tyrant, or who fear his hate.
They seize a fleet, which ready rigg'd they find;
Nor is Pygmalion's treasure left behind.
The vessels, heavy laden, put to sea
With prosp'rous winds; a woman leads the way.
I know not, if by stress of weather driv'n,
Or was their fatal course dispos'd by Heav'n;

---

[1] Brother-in-law—Pygmalion was Dido's brother; Sichaeus was their uncle.

At last they landed, where from far your eyes
May view the turrets of new Carthage rise;
There bought a space of ground, which (Byrsa call'd,
From the bull's hide)[1] they first inclos'd, and wall'd.
But whence are you? what country claims your birth?
What seek you, strangers, on our Libyan earth?"

To whom, with sorrow streaming from his eyes,
And deeply sighing, thus her son replies:
"Could you with patience hear, or I relate,
O nymph, the tedious annals of our fate!
Thro' such a train of woes if I should run,
The day would sooner than the tale be done!
From ancient Troy, by force expell'd, we came—
If you by chance have heard the Trojan name.
On various seas by various tempests toss'd,
At length we landed on your Libyan coast.
The good Aeneas am I call'd—a name,
While Fortune favor'd, not unknown to fame.
My household gods, companions of my woes,
With pious care I rescued from our foes.
To fruitful Italy my course was bent;
And from the King of Heav'n is my descent.
With twice ten sail I cross'd the Phrygian sea;
Fate and my mother goddess led my way.
Scarce sev'n, the thin remainders of my fleet,
From storms preserv'd, within your harbor meet.
Myself distress'd, an exile, and unknown,
Debarr'd from Europe, and from Asia thrown,
In Libyan desarts wander thus alone."

His tender parent could no longer bear;
But, interposing, sought to soothe his care.
"Whoe'er you are—not unbelov'd by Heav'n,
Since on our friendly shore your ships are driv'n—
Have courage: to the gods permit the rest,

---

[1] The story goes that Dido, upon landing in North Africa, asked the local Berber king for as much land as she could surround with a bull's hide; she then cut the hide into strips and used it to surround an area large enough to become the city of Carthage.

And to the queen expose your just request.
Now take this earnest of success, for more:
Your scatter'd fleet is join'd upon the shore;
The winds are chang'd, your friends from danger free;
Or I renounce my skill in augury.
Twelve swans behold in beauteous order move,
And stoop with closing pinions from above;
Whom late the bird of Jove had driv'n along,
And thro' the clouds pursued the scatt'ring throng:
Now, all united in a goodly team,
They skim the ground, and seek the quiet stream.
As they, with joy returning, clap their wings,
And ride the circuit of the skies in rings;
Not otherwise your ships, and ev'ry friend,
Already hold the port, or with swift sails descend.
No more advice is needful; but pursue
The path before you, and the town in view."

Thus having said, she turn'd, and made appear
Her neck refulgent, and dishevel'd hair,
Which, flowing from her shoulders, reach'd the ground.
And widely spread ambrosial scents around:
In length of train descends her sweeping gown;
And, by her graceful walk, the Queen of Love is known.
The prince pursued the parting deity
With words like these: "Ah! whither do you fly?
Unkind and cruel! to deceive your son
In borrow'd shapes, and his embrace to shun;
Never to bless my sight, but thus unknown;
And still to speak in accents not your own."
Against the goddess these complaints he made,
But took the path, and her commands obey'd.
They march, obscure; for Venus kindly shrouds
With mists their persons, and involves in clouds,
That, thus unseen, their passage none might stay,
Or force to tell the causes of their way.
This part perform'd, the goddess flies sublime
To visit Paphos and her native clime;
Where garlands, ever green and ever fair,
With vows are offer'd, and with solemn pray'r:

A hundred altars in her temple smoke;
A thousand bleeding hearts her pow'r invoke.

They climb the next ascent, and, looking down,
Now at a nearer distance view the town.
The prince with wonder sees the stately tow'rs,
Which late were huts and shepherds' homely bow'rs,
The gates and streets; and hears, from ev'ry part,
The noise and busy concourse of the mart.
The toiling Tyrians on each other call
To ply their labor: some extend the wall;
Some build the citadel; the brawny throng
Or dig, or push unwieldly stones along.
Some for their dwellings choose a spot of ground,
Which, first design'd, with ditches they surround.
Some laws ordain; and some attend the choice
Of holy senates, and elect by voice.
Here some design a mole, while others there
Lay deep foundations for a theater;
From marble quarries mighty columns hew,
For ornaments of scenes, and future view.
Such is their toil, and such their busy pains,
As exercise the bees in flow'ry plains,
When winter past, and summer scarce begun,
Invites them forth to labor in the sun;
Some lead their youth abroad, while some condense
Their liquid store, and some in cells dispense;
Some at the gate stand ready to receive
The golden burthen, and their friends relieve;
All with united force, combine to drive
The lazy drones from the laborious hive:
With envy stung, they view each other's deeds;
The fragrant work with diligence proceeds.
"Thrice happy you, whose walls already rise!"
Aeneas said, and view'd, with lifted eyes,
Their lofty tow'rs; then, entiring at the gate,
Conceal'd in clouds (prodigious to relate)
He mix'd, unmark'd, among the busy throng,
Borne by the tide, and pass'd unseen along.

Full in the center of the town there stood,
Thick set with trees, a venerable wood.
The Tyrians, landing near this holy ground,
And digging here, a prosp'rous omen found:
From under earth a courser's head they drew,
Their growth and future fortune to foreshew.
This fated sign their foundress Juno gave,
Of a soil fruitful, and a people brave.
Sidonian Dido here with solemn state
Did Juno's temple build, and consecrate,
Enrich'd with gifts, and with a golden shrine;
But more the goddess made the place divine.
On brazen steps the marble threshold rose,
And brazen plates the cedar beams inclose:
The rafters are with brazen cov'rings crown'd;
The lofty doors on brazen hinges sound.
What first Aeneas this place beheld,
Reviv'd his courage, and his fear expell'd.
For while, expecting there the queen, he rais'd
His wond'ring eyes, and round the temple gaz'd,
Admir'd the fortune of the rising town,
The striving artists, and their arts' renown;
He saw, in order painted on the wall,
Whatever did unhappy Troy befall:
The wars that fame around the world had blown,
All to the life, and ev'ry leader known.
There Agamemnon, Priam here, he spies,[1]
And fierce Achilles, who both kings defies.
He stopp'd, and weeping said: "O friend! ev'n here
The monuments of Trojan woes appear!
Our known disasters fill ev'n foreign lands:
See there, where old unhappy Priam stands!
Ev'n the mute walls relate the warrior's fame,
And Trojan griefs the Tyrians' pity claim."
He said (his tears a ready passage find),
Devouring what he saw so well design'd,
And with an empty picture fed his mind:

---

[1] Agamemnon, king of Mycenae, was Menelaus' brother; Priam, king of Troy, was Hector's father and Aeneas' first cousin once removed.

For there he saw the fainting Grecians yield,
And here the trembling Trojans quit the field,
Pursued by fierce Achilles thro' the plain,
On his high chariot driving o'er the slain.
The tents of Rhesus next his grief renew,
By their white sails betray'd to nightly view;[1]
And wakeful Diomede, whose cruel sword
The sentries slew, nor spar'd their slumb'ring lord,
Then took the fiery steeds, ere yet the food
Of Troy they taste, or drink the Xanthian flood.
Elsewhere he saw where Troilus[2] defied
Achilles, and unequal combat tried;
Then, where the boy disarm'd, with loosen'd reins,
Was by his horses hurried o'er the plains,
Hung by the neck and hair, and dragg'd around:
The hostile spear, yet sticking in his wound,
With tracks of blood inscrib'd the dusty ground.
Meantime the Trojan dames, oppress'd with woe,
To Pallas' fane in long procession go,
In hopes to reconcile their heav'nly foe.[3]
They weep, they beat their breasts, they rend their hair,
And rich embroider'd vests for presents bear;
But the stern goddess stands unmov'd with pray'r.
Thrice round the Trojan walls Achilles drew
The corpse of Hector, whom in fight he slew.[4]
Here Priam sues; and there, for sums of gold,

---

[1] Rhesus was a king of Thrace who allied with the Trojans. According to Epidurus' play *Rhesus*, which expands on Homer's account in the *Iliad*, the Thracians had been delayed in coming to Troy by war with Scythia, but the bombastic Rhesus got off on the wrong foot with Hector by boasting that he would best the Greeks in one battle. That very night, Diomedes and Odysseus captured one of Hector's messengers, who not only gave away the positions of the Trojans and all their allies *and* the fact that only the Trojans kept watchfires burning but also informed the Greeks of Rhesus' grand arrival. Thereupon Diomedes and Odysseus sneaked into the Thracian camp, killed Rhesus and twelve of his retainers in their sleep, and stole Rhesus' fine white horses.

[2] One of the protagonists of *Troilus and Cressida*, which was later retold by both Chaucer and Shakespeare, Troilus was another of Priam's sons.

[3] The women of Troy offered impressive sacrifices to Minerva, including the most beautiful robe they had, if she would abandon the Greeks. Minerva refused.

[4] Because Hector had killed Achilles' armor-bearer (and probable lover) Patroclus, the enraged Achilles not only killed Hector but abused the corpse by dragging it behind his chariot—according to the *Iliad*, for twelve days straight—until Iris and Thetis finally made him stop and allow Priam to ransom his son's remains. (The *Iliad*'s first line proclaims its theme to be the rage of Achilles.)

The lifeless body of his son is sold.
So sad an object, and so well express'd,
Drew sighs and groans from the griev'd hero's breast,
To see the figure of his lifeless friend,
And his old sire his helpless hand extend.
Himself he saw amidst the Grecian train,
Mix'd in the bloody battle on the plain;
And swarthy Memnon in his arms he knew,
His pompous ensigns, and his Indian crew.
Penthisilea[1] there, with haughty grace,
Leads to the wars an Amazonian race:
In their right hands a pointed dart they wield;
The left, for ward, sustains the lunar shield.
Athwart her breast a golden belt she throws,
Amidst the press alone provokes a thousand foes,
And dares her maiden arms to manly force oppose.

Thus while the Trojan prince employs his eyes,
Fix'd on the walls with wonder and surprise,
The beauteous Dido, with a num'rous train
And pomp of guards, ascends the sacred fane.
Such on Eurotas'[2] banks, or Cynthus'[3] height,
Diana seems; and so she charms the sight,
When in the dance the graceful goddess leads
The choir of nymphs, and overtops their heads:
Known by her quiver, and her lofty mien,
She walks majestic, and she looks their queen;
Latona sees her shine above the rest,
And feeds with secret joy her silent breast.
Such Dido was; with such becoming state,
Amidst the crowd, she walks serenely great.
Their labor to her future sway she speeds,
And passing with a gracious glance proceeds;
Then mounts the throne, high plac'd before the shrine:

---

[1] One of the queens of the Amazons, Penthisilea had accidentally killed her sister Hippolyta and, driven by remorse to seek death in battle, agreed to bring the Amazons to Troy's aid. Achilles killed her in battle but expressed immediate remorse upon removing her helmet and discovering she was a woman.
[2] River in Laconia.
[3] Mountain on the island of Delos where Apollo and Diana were born, whence they bore the epithets Cynthius and Cynthia.

In crowds around, the swarming people join.
She takes petitions, and dispenses laws,
Hears and determines ev'ry private cause;
Their tasks in equal portions she divides,
And, where unequal, there by lots decides.
Another way by chance Aeneas bends
His eyes, and unexpected sees his friends,
Antheus, Sergestus[1] grave, Cloanthus strong,
And at their backs a mighty Trojan throng,
Whom late the tempest on the billows toss'd,
And widely scatter'd on another coast.
The prince, unseen, surpris'd with wonder stands,
And longs, with joyful haste, to join their hands;
But, doubtful of the wish'd event, he stays,
And from the hollow cloud his friends surveys,
Impatient till they told their present state,
And where they left their ships, and what their fate,
And why they came, and what was their request;
For these were sent, commission'd by the rest,
To sue for leave to land their sickly men,
And gain admission to the gracious queen.
Ent'ring, with cries they fill'd the holy fane;
Then thus, with lowly voice, Ilioneus began:

"O queen! indulg'd by favor of the gods
To found an empire in these new abodes,
To build a town, with statutes to restrain
The wild inhabitants beneath thy reign,
We wretched Trojans, toss'd on ev'ry shore,
From sea to sea, thy clemency implore.
Forbid the fires our shipping to deface!
Receive th' unhappy fugitives to grace,
And spare the remnant of a pious race!
We come not with design of wasteful prey,
To drive the country, force the swains away:
Nor such our strength, nor such is our desire;
The vanquish'd dare not to such thoughts aspire.

---

[1] Fictional ancestor of the Gens Sergia, another of Rome's oldest patrician families.

A land there is, Hesperia[1] nam'd of old;
The soil is fruitful, and the men are bold—
Th' Oenotrians[2] held it once—by common fame
Now call'd Italia, from the leader's name.
To that sweet region was our voyage bent,
When winds and ev'ry warring element
Disturb'd our course, and, far from sight of land,
Cast our torn vessels on the moving sand:
The sea came on; the South, with mighty roar,
Dispers'd and dash'd the rest upon the rocky shore.
Those few you see escap'd the Storm, and fear,
Unless you interpose, a shipwreck here.
What men, what monsters, what inhuman race,
What laws, what barb'rous customs of the place,
Shut up a desart shore to drowning men,
And drive us to the cruel seas again?
If our hard fortune no compassion draws,
Nor hospitable rights, nor human laws,
The gods are just, and will revenge our cause.
Aeneas was our prince: a juster lord,
Or nobler warrior, never drew a sword;
Observant of the right, religious of his word.
If yet he lives, and draws this vital air,
Nor we, his friends, of safety shall despair;
Nor you, great queen, these offices repent,
Which he will equal, and perhaps augment.
We want not cities, nor Sicilian coasts,
Where King Acestes Trojan lineage boasts.
Permit our ships a shelter on your shores,
Refitted from your woods with planks and oars,
That, if our prince be safe, we may renew
Our destin'd course, and Italy pursue.
But if, O best of men, the Fates ordain
That thou art swallow'd in the Libyan main,
And if our young Iulus be no more,
Dismiss our navy from your friendly shore,

---

[1] Greek name for the Italian peninsula.
[2] Apparently historical tribe that lived for a time in southern Italy; their name may have derived from the rich vineyards there.

That we to good Acestes may return,
And with our friends our common losses mourn."
Thus spoke Ilioneus: the Trojan crew
With cries and clamors his request renew.

The modest queen a while, with downcast eyes,
Ponder'd the speech; then briefly thus replies:
"Trojans, dismiss your fears; my cruel fate,
And doubts attending an unsettled state,
Force me to guard my coast from foreign foes.
Who has not heard the story of your woes,
The name and fortune of your native place,
The fame and valor of the Phrygian race?
We Tyrians are not so devoid of sense,
Nor so remote from Phoebus' influence.
Whether to Latian shores your course is bent,
Or, driv'n by tempests from your first intent,
You seek the good Acestes' government,
Your men shall be receiv'd, your fleet repair'd,
And sail, with ships of convoy for your guard:
Or, would you stay, and join your friendly pow'rs
To raise and to defend the Tyrian tow'rs,
My wealth, my city, and myself are yours.
And would to Heav'n, the Storm, you felt, would bring
On Carthaginian coasts your wand'ring king.
My people shall, by my command, explore
The ports and creeks of ev'ry winding shore,
And towns, and wilds, and shady woods, in quest
Of so renown'd and so desir'd a guest."

Rais'd in his mind the Trojan hero stood,
And long'd to break from out his ambient cloud:
Achates found it, and thus urg'd his way:
"From whence, O goddess-born, this long delay?
What more can you desire, your welcome sure,
Your fleet in safety, and your friends secure?
One only wants; and him we saw in vain
Oppose the Storm, and swallow'd in the main.
Orontes in his fate our forfeit paid;
The rest agrees with what your mother said."

Scarce had he spoken, when the cloud gave way,
The mists flew upward and dissolv'd in day.

The Trojan chief appear'd in open sight,
August in visage, and serenely bright.
His mother goddess, with her hands divine,
Had form'd his curling locks, and made his temples shine,
And giv'n his rolling eyes a sparkling grace,
And breath'd a youthful vigor on his face;
Like polish'd ivory, beauteous to behold,
Or Parian marble,[1] when enchas'd in gold:
Thus radiant from the circling cloud he broke,
And thus with manly modesty he spoke:

"He whom you seek am I; by tempests toss'd,
And sav'd from shipwreck on your Libyan coast;
Presenting, gracious queen, before your throne,
A prince that owes his life to you alone.
Fair majesty, the refuge and redress
Of those whom fate pursues, and wants oppress,
You, who your pious offices employ
To save the relics of abandon'd Troy;
Receive the shipwreck'd on your friendly shore,
With hospitable rites relieve the poor;
Associate in your town a wand'ring train,
And strangers in your palace entertain:
What thanks can wretched fugitives return,
Who, scatter'd thro' the world, in exile mourn?
The gods, if gods to goodness are inclin'd;
If acts of mercy touch their heav'nly mind,
And, more than all the gods, your gen'rous heart.
Conscious of worth, requite its own desert!
In you this age is happy, and this earth,
And parents more than mortal gave you birth.
While rolling rivers into seas shall run,
And round the space of heav'n the radiant sun;
While trees the mountain tops with shades supply,
Your honor, name, and praise shall never die.

---

[1] High-quality semi-translucent marble quarried on the island of Paros, prized by Greek sculptors.

Whate'er abode my fortune has assign'd,
Your image shall be present in my mind."
Thus having said, he turn'd with pious haste,
And joyful his expecting friends embrac'd:
With his right hand Ilioneus was grac'd,
Serestus with his left; then to his breast
Cloanthus and the noble Gyas press'd;
And so by turns descended to the rest.

The Tyrian queen stood fix'd upon his face,
Pleas'd with his motions, ravish'd with his grace;
Admir'd his fortunes, more admir'd the man;
Then recollected stood, and thus began:
"What fate, O goddess-born; what angry pow'rs
Have cast you shipwrack'd on our barren shores?
Are you the great Aeneas, known to fame,
Who from celestial seed your lineage claim?

The same Aeneas whom fair Venus bore
To fam'd Anchises on th' Idaean shore?
It calls into my mind, tho' then a child,
When Teucer came, from Salamis exil'd,[1]
And sought my father's aid, to be restor'd:
My father Belus then with fire and sword
Invaded Cyprus, made the region bare,
And, conqu'ring, finish'd the successful war.
From him the Trojan siege I understood,
The Grecian chiefs, and your illustrious blood.
Your foe himself the Dardan valor prais'd,
And his own ancestry from Trojans rais'd.
Enter, my noble guest, and you shall find,
If not a costly welcome, yet a kind:
For I myself, like you, have been distress'd,

---

[1] Half-brother of Ajax the Great, Teucer was also related to the Trojan royal family but fought on the Greek side of the war as an archer. After Achilles' death, Ajax and Odysseus argued over who should get Achilles' armor, which had been made by Vulcan himself; Odysseus won, whereupon Ajax took out his wrath on the Greeks' captured livestock and then committed suicide. Teucer and Odysseus persuaded Agamemnon and Menelaus to let Ajax be buried properly, but when Teucer returned to Salamis, his father exiled him for failing to bring Ajax's body and arms home. As Dido recounts, Teucer then turned to Phoenicia and joined Belus in a war against Cyprus; having conquered it, Belus gave the island to Teucer, who founded the city of Salamis there.

Till Heav'n afforded me this place of rest;
Like you, an alien in a land unknown,
I learn to pity woes so like my own."
She said, and to the palace led her guest;
Then offer'd incense, and proclaim'd a feast.
Nor yet less careful for her absent friends,
Twice ten fat oxen to the ships she sends;
Besides a hundred boars, a hundred lambs,
With bleating cries, attend their milky dams;
And jars of gen'rous wine and spacious bowls
She gives, to cheer the sailors' drooping souls.
Now purple hangings clothe the palace walls,
And sumptuous feasts are made in splendid halls:
On Tyrian carpets, richly wrought, they dine;
With loads of massy plate the sideboards shine,
And antique vases, all of gold emboss'd
(The gold itself inferior to the cost),
Of curious work, where on the sides were seen
The fights and figures of illustrious men,
From their first founder to the present queen.

The good Aeneas, paternal care
Iulus' absence could no longer bear,
Dispatch'd Achates to the ships in haste,
To give a glad relation of the past,
And, fraught with precious gifts, to bring the boy,
Snatch'd from the ruins of unhappy Troy:
A robe of tissue, stiff with golden wire;
An upper vest, once Helen's rich attire,
From Argos by the fam'd adultress brought,
With golden flow'rs and winding foliage wrought,
Her mother Leda's present, when she came
To ruin Troy and set the world on flame;
The scepter Priam's eldest daughter bore,
Her orient necklace, and the crown she wore
Of double texture, glorious to behold,
One order set with gems, and one with gold.
Instructed thus, the wise Achates goes,
And in his diligence his duty shows.

But Venus, anxious for her son's affairs,
New counsels tries, and new designs prepares:
That Cupid should assume the shape and face
Of sweet Ascanius, and the sprightly grace;
Should bring the presents, in her nephew's stead,
And in Eliza's[1] veins the gentle poison shed:
For much she fear'd the Tyrians, double-tongued,
And knew the town to Juno's care belong'd.
These thoughts by night her golden slumbers broke,
And thus alarm'd, to winged Love she spoke:
"My son, my strength, whose mighty pow'r alone
Controls the Thund'rer on his awful throne,
To thee thy much-afflicted mother flies,
And on thy succor and thy faith relies.
Thou know'st, my son, how Jove's revengeful wife,
By force and fraud, attempts thy brother's life;
And often hast thou mourn'd with me his pains.
Him Dido now with blandishment detains;
But I suspect the town where Juno reigns.
For this 't is needful to prevent her art,
And fire with love the proud Phoenician's heart:
A love so violent, so strong, so sure,
As neither age can change, nor art can cure.
How this may be perform'd, now take my mind:
Ascanius by his father is design'd
To come, with presents laden, from the port,
To gratify the queen, and gain the court.
I mean to plunge the boy in pleasing sleep,
And, ravish'd, in Idalian bow'rs to keep,
Or high Cythera, that the sweet deceit
May pass unseen, and none prevent the cheat.
Take thou his form and shape. I beg the grace
But only for a night's revolving space:
Thyself a boy, assume a boy's dissembled face;
That when, amidst the fervor of the feast,
The Tyrian hugs and fonds thee on her breast,
And with sweet kisses in her arms constrains,
Thou may'st infuse thy venom in her veins."

---

[1] Elissa (or Eliza, as here) is another name given for Dido and might be closer to her Phoenician given name.

The God of Love obeys, and sets aside
His bow and quiver, and his plumy pride;
He walks Iulus in his mother's sight,
And in the sweet resemblance takes delight.

The goddess then to young Ascanius flies,
And in a pleasing slumber seals his eyes:
Lull'd in her lap, amidst a train of Loves,
She gently bears him to her blissful groves,
Then with a wreath of myrtle crowns his head,
And softly lays him on a flow'ry bed.
Cupid meantime assum'd his form and face,
Foll'wing Achates with a shorter pace,
And brought the gifts. The queen already sate
Amidst the Trojan lords, in shining state,
High on a golden bed: her princely guest
Was next her side; in order sate the rest.
Then canisters with bread are heap'd on high;
Th' attendants water for their hands supply,
And, having wash'd, with silken towels dry.
Next fifty handmaids in long order bore
The censers, and with fumes the gods adore:
Then youths, and virgins twice as many, join
To place the dishes, and to serve the wine.
The Tyrian train, admitted to the feast,
Approach, and on the painted couches rest.
All on the Trojan gifts with wonder gaze,
But view the beauteous boy with more amaze,
His rosy-color'd cheeks, his radiant eyes,
His motions, voice, and shape, and all the god's disguise;
Nor pass unprais'd the vest and veil divine,
Which wand'ring foliage and rich flow'rs entwine.
But, far above the rest, the royal dame,
(Already doom'd to love's disastrous flame,)
With eyes insatiate, and tumultuous joy,
Beholds the presents, and admires the boy.
The guileful god about the hero long,
With children's play, and false embraces, hung;
Then sought the queen: she took him to her arms
With greedy pleasure, and devour'd his charms.

Unhappy Dido little thought what guest,
How dire a god, she drew so near her breast;
But he, not mindless of his mother's pray'r,
Works in the pliant bosom of the fair,
And molds her heart anew, and blots her former care.
The dead is to the living love resign'd;
And all Aeneas enters in her mind.

Now, when the rage of hunger was appeas'd,
The meat remov'd, and ev'ry guest was pleas'd,
The golden bowls with sparkling wine are crown'd,
And thro' the palace cheerful cries resound.
From gilded roofs depending lamps display
Nocturnal beams, that emulate the day.
A golden bowl, that shone with gems divine,
The queen commanded to be crown'd with wine:
The bowl that Belus us'd, and all the Tyrian line.
Then, silence thro' the hall proclaim'd, she spoke:
"O hospitable Jove! we thus invoke,
With solemn rites, thy sacred name and pow'r;
Bless to both nations this auspicious hour!
So may the Trojan and the Tyrian line
In lasting concord from this day combine.
Thou, Bacchus, god of joys and friendly cheer,
And gracious Juno, both be present here!
And you, my lords of Tyre, your vows address
To Heav'n with mine, to ratify the peace."
The goblet then she took, with nectar crown'd
(Sprinkling the first libations on the ground,)
And rais'd it to her mouth with sober grace;
Then, sipping, offer'd to the next in place.
'T was Bitias whom she call'd, a thirsty soul;
He took challenge, and embrac'd the bowl,
With pleasure swill'd the gold, nor ceas'd to draw,
Till he the bottom of the brimmer saw.
The goblet goes around: Iopas brought
His golden lyre, and sung what ancient Atlas taught:
The various labors of the wand'ring moon,
And whence proceed th' eclipses of the sun;
Th' original of men and beasts; and whence

The rains arise, and fires their warmth dispense,
And fix'd and erring stars dispose their influence;
What shakes the solid earth; what cause delays
The summer nights and shortens winter days.
With peals of shouts the Tyrians praise the song:
Those peals are echo'd by the Trojan throng.
Th' unhappy queen with talk prolong'd the night,
And drank large draughts of love with vast delight;
Of Priam much enquir'd, of Hector more;
Then ask'd what arms the swarthy Memnon wore,
What troops he landed on the Trojan shore;
The steeds of Diomede varied the discourse,
And fierce Achilles, with his matchless force;
At length, as fate and her ill stars requir'd,
To hear the series of the war desir'd.
"Relate at large, my godlike guest," she said,
"The Grecian stratagems, the town betray'd:
The fatal issue of so long a war,
Your flight, your wand'rings, and your woes, declare;
For, since on ev'ry sea, on ev'ry coast,
Your men have been distress'd, your navy toss'd,
Sev'n times the sun has either tropic view'd,
The winter banish'd, and the spring renew'd."[1]

Balder the Beautiful
As told by Donald A. Mackenzie

Balder the Beautiful was the most noble and pious of the gods in Asgard. The whitest flower upon earth is called Balder's brow, because the countenance of the god was snow-white and shining. Like fine gold was his hair, and his eyes were radiant and blue. He was well loved by all the gods, save evil Loke, who cunningly devised his death.

Balder, the summer sun-god, was Odin's fairest son; his mother was Frigg, goddess of fruitful earth and sister of Njord. His brother was blind Hodur. On Balder's tongue were runes graven, so that he had great eloquence. He rode a brightly shining horse, and his ships, which men called "billow falcons", were the sunbeams that sailed through the drifting

---

[1] Part of what follows in Book 2 appears in a recast form in Act 2 of *Hamlet*.

cloudways. For wife he was given Nanna, the moon maid, the brave one who fought with him the light battles. On a bright horse she rode also, and tender was she and very fair.

There came a time when Odin and Balder went forth to journey through a wood. A dread omen forewarned them of disaster, because the leg was sprained of Balder's horse — the horse from whose hoofmarks bubbled forth clear wells. Charms were sung over the sun-god by Nanna and by her fair sister Sunna, the sun maid. Frigg also sang, and then Fulla her sister. Odin uttered magic runes to protect him from evil.

But soon after Balder began to languish. The light went from his eyes, care sat on his forehead, and melancholy were his lips. To him came the gods beseeching to know what ailed him, and he told that nightly he dreamed fearsome dreams which boded ill, and revealed to him, alas! that his life was in dire peril.

Now Frigg, who had fore-knowledge of all things save Balder's fate, sent forth her maid-servants to take oaths from all creatures living, from plants and metals, and from stones, not to do any hurt unto the god Balder. To her, in due time, the maidens returned, and she received from them the compacts and vows that were given. All things promised to spare him, save the mistletoe, slender and harmless, from which no vow was asked, for it clung, as was its need, to a strong tree for protection. Then was Frigg's heart filled with comfort, and no longer did she fear the fate of her noble son.

But the heart of Odin was filled with foreboding. He mounted his horse Sleipner, and went over Bif-rost towards the north, and descended unto darksome Nifelhel, where dwelt the spirits of the great giants who were crushed in the World-mill. On the borders of Hela, as he rode speedily, a great and fierce hel-dog came after him. There was blood on its breast, and in the darkness it barked loudly. When it could go no farther, it howled long with gaping jaws.

Over a long green plain went Odin, while the hoofs of Sleipner rang fast and clear, until he came to a high dwelling, the name of which is Heljar-ran, of which the keeper is Delling, the Red Elf of Dawn. Therein have their Hela-home the fair Asmegir—Lif and Lifthraser and their descendants who shall come at Time's new dawn that shall follow Ragnarok to regenerate the world of men.

To the eastern gate went Odin, where he knew there was the grave of a Vala (prophetess). Dismounting from Sleipner, he chanted over her death chamber strange magic songs. He looked towards the north; he uttered runes; he pronounced a spell, and demanded sure response. Then rose the Vala, and from the grave chamber her ghostly voice spake forth and said:

"What unknown man cometh to disturb my rest? Snow has covered me in its deeps; by cold rains have I been beaten and by many dews made wet. . . . Long indeed have I lain dead."

Odin answered: "My name is Vegtam and my sire was Valtam. Tell me, O Vala," he cried, "for whom are the benches of Delling's hall strewn with rings, and for whom are the rooms decked with fine gold?"

The Vala answered and said: "Here stands for Balder mead prepared, pure drink indeed. Over the cup shields are laid. Impatiently do the Asmegir await him and to make merry . . . . Alas! by compulsion hast thou made me to speak . . . . Now must I be silent."

Odin said: "Silent thou must not be until I know who shall slay Balder—who shall bereave Odin's son of life."

The Vala answered: "Hodur shall send his brother hither, for Balder shall he slay, and Odin's son bereave of life. . . . Alas! by compulsion hast thou made me speak. . . . Now must I be silent."

Odin said: "Silent thou must not be until I know who shall avenge the deed on Hodur, who shall raise Balder's slayer on the funeral pyre."

The Vala answered: "A son, Vale, shall Rhind bear in the halls of Winter. He shall not wash his hands nor comb his hair until to the funeral pyre he beareth Balder's foe. Alas! by compulsion hast thou made me to speak. Now must I be silent."

Odin said: "Silent thou shalt not be until I know who are the maidens that sorrow and throw high their veils with grief. Sleep not until thou dost answer."

The Vala spake and said: "Thou art not Vegtam, as I deemed, but Odin, ruler of all."

Odin said: "No Vala art thou, but the mother of three giants."

Then cried the Vala: "Return, O Odin, unto Asgard. Never again shall I be called upon until Loke escapes from bonds and the world-devastating Dusk of the Gods is at hand."

To Asgard did Odin return; but there was no sorrow there nor foreboding, because of the vows which Frigg had taken from all creatures and all things that are, so that no harm might be done unto her fair son. And of this had the gods full proof. Balder they made to stand amidst a rain of javelins that harmed him not. Some flung at him stones, others smote him with their swords; yet was he not injured. Of Balder were they all proud because he was charmed against wounds. To honour him did they make fruitless attack on his fair body.

Evil there was in the heart of Loke, and in woman's guise he went unto Frigg, who spake and said: "Why do the gods thus assail my fair son Balder?"

Loke answered: "It is in sport they fling at him javelins and stones and strike him with swords, because they know full well that they can do him no hurt."

Frigg said: "By neither metal, nor wood, nor stone, can he be injured because of the world-vows which I have received."

"Have all things indeed sworn to protect Balder?" Loke asked with downcast eyes.

"All things save the mistletoe," answered Frigg, "and so slender and weak is the mistletoe that from it no vow was demanded."

Then Loke went from Frigg and plucked a mistletoe sprig, which he carried to a cunning elf-smith named Hlebard, whom he robbed of his understanding. With the mistletoe twig the smith shaped a magic arrow—a deadly arrow of pain. . . . Loke made haste with it to Asgard, and he went to the green place where the gods assailed Balder and made merry. He saw blind Hodur standing apart, and to him he went and spake thus:

"Why, O Hodur, dost thou not join the game and cast a missile at Balder also?"

"Alas!" cried Hodur; "am I not blind? I can see not my fair brother, nor have I aught which I can throw."

"Come and do honour unto Balder like the others," Loke urged him. "I shall give thee an arrow for thy bow, and hold thine arm so that thou mayest know where he stands."

Hodur then took from Loke the magic arrow which the elf-smith had made and placed it in his bow. Then raised he his left arm, while evil Loke took certain aim.

"Thou canst now share in the sport," said the Evil One unto the blind god, and went to a place apart.

The gods beheld Hodur standing with bent bow, and paused in their game. . . . Then did the arrow dart forth. . . . It struck Balder; it pierced his fair body, and he fell dead upon the sward.

In horror, and frozen with silence, the gods stood around. . . . Where there had been joy and merrymaking, dumb grief prevailed. . . . Alone stood Hodur wondering and in mute amaze.

But ere long angry cries broke forth, and the gods sought to slay Death's blind archer; but the sward on which they stood was consecrated to peace, and unwillingly were their hands withheld.

Then a loud voice cried through Asgard: "Balder is dead! . . . . Balder the Beautiful is dead! . . . ."

Every voice was hushed and every face turned pale because of the disaster which had befallen the gods in that black hour.

Thereafter arose the sound of loud lamentations, and a tempest of grief swept over the Celestial City. Frigg wept in silence and alone. Odin grieved inwardly, and more than the rest he realized the great disaster which Balder's death would bring unto the Asa-gods. The spirit of Balder descended to the Lower World and crossed the golden bridge over the River Gjoll.

The Asmegir in their gold-decked hall awaited him, for they desired that he should be their ruler until the dawn of the world's new age.

But Frigg would not suffer that Balder should remain in Hela. She went forth when the gods ceased to cry aloud in their sorrow and said:

"Who among thee hath longing to win my gratitude and my love? For such shall be given unto him who rideth to Hela to find Balder. It is my heart's desire, in this my hour of grief, that a great ransom be offered unto Urd, Queen of Death, so that she may permit my fair son to return unto me again."

Forth stepped Heimdal the Young. He was a messenger of the gods and a son of Odin. He spake forth and said: "Unto Hela shall I go, O Queen of Asgard, as thou desirest, to find Balder and to offer great ransom unto Urd, so that she may permit him to return unto thee once again."

Then was Sleipner taken forth for Hermod, who leapt nimbly into the saddle. Swift as the wind he went over the gate bridge, and through the air and across the seas he sped and descended unto Nifel-hel towards the north to search for Balder.

The gods bore Balder's body unto the bleak shore of Ocean, where lay his great ship, Hringhorn. On its deck they built a pyre covered with much treasure, and then they sought to launch it.

But that they were unable to do, because the keel stuck fast in the sand and would not be moved seaward. So they sent unto Jotun-heim for the storm-giantess, Hyrrokin, who was Angerboda, that ancient-cold Vala of the east, who sweeps wind-tossed ships into the very jaws of Æger. On a great wolf she came and the bridle was a writhing snake. She leapt on the beach and with disdain regarded the gods. To four giants were given the keeping of the wolf. Then went she to the ship and thrust it speedily into the sea. Fire blazed from the rollers and the earth shook.

Angry was Thor when he beheld the Hag, and he swung his hammer to strike her down; but him did the gods restrain, for they sought not bloodshed in that hour.

Then was Balder's body carried to the ship and laid upon the pyre, and his steed beside him. Beautiful was he in death. In white robes was Balder clad, and round his head lay a wreath of radiant flowers.

On the shore were gathered the gods and goddesses of Asgard. Odin was there, and he went first. His ravens hovered over the ship, and his wolf-dogs wailed. Beside him was wise Frigg, who was wont to spin golden cloud-threads from her jewelled wheel. Queen of Asgard was she and goddess of Maternal Love. She was robed in black who was erstwhile attired in cloudy whiteness; on her golden head were the heron plumes of silence; a golden girdle clasped her waist and on her feet were golden shoes. Tall was she and stately and surpassing fair.

Dark-browed Thor was nigh to Odin, and Brage and Tyr also. Njord, black-bearded, and clad in green, strode his stately way. With his golden-bristled boar came Frey, and Heimdal, horsed on Gulltop, shone fair as sunshine. Beauteous Freyja, veiled in tears, rode her chariot drawn by great cats, and fair Idun was there also, and Sith with harvest hair. Loke stood apart with tearless eyes.

The valkyries leaned on their spears. Frigg's maids were nigh the Queen of Asgard, and these were Fulla, her sister; Hlin, who carries to Frigg the prayers of mortals; Gna, the speedy messenger who passes to and fro over the earth, beholding and remembering; Lofn, guardian of lovers, in whose name vows are made; Vjofr, the peacemaker, who unites lovers, and husbands and wives who have quarrelled; Syn, the wise doorkeeper; and Gefjon, guardian of maids who shall never wed.

White elves were assembled on that sad shore to sorrow, and even black elves were there. Many Frost-giants and Mountain-giants gathered around, for there was sadness everywhere because Balder was dead.

But none mourned more than Nanna, Balder's wife. Silent was she; her heart wept, and fire burned in her eyes.

Then Odin mounted the pyre. On Balder's breast he laid the gold ring Draupner, and bending low he whispered in Balder's ear. . . .

From that hour have gods and men wondered what said Odin in his son's ear.

> When Odin whispered
>> In Balder's ear,
> Nor god nor man
>> Was nigh to hear.
> What Odin whispered,
>> Bending low,
> No man knoweth
>> Or e'er shall know.

In silence Odin returned to the shore, and then Thor consecrated the pyre with his hammer. A dwarf named Littur, who ran past him, he kicked into the boat, where he was burned with Balder.

So ended the ceremony of grief, and the torch was placed to the pyre. High as heaven leapt the flames, and the faces of the gods were made ruddy in the glow. . . . Nanna cried aloud in grief, and her heart burst within her, and she fell dead upon the cold sea strand. Seaward swept the burning ship. . . . The whole world sorrowed for Balder. . . .

Meanwhile Hermod made his darksome way through Nifel-hel towards Hela's glittering plains. Nine days and nine nights he rode on Sleipner through misty blackness and in bitter cold over high mountains and along ridges where chasms yawn vast and bottomless. On Hela's borders the terrible wolf dog of the giant Offotes followed him, barking in the black mist. . . . Then Hermod reached the rivers. Over Slid, full of daggers, he went, and over Kormet and Ormet, and the two rivers Kerlogar, through which Thor wades when he goes to the Lower Thingstead of the gods. He crossed shining Leipter, by whose holy waters men swear oaths that bind. At length he came to the River Gjoll and its golden bridge.

Modgud, the elf maid who watches the bridge, cried aloud: "Whence cometh thou who hath not yet died?"

Of her did Hermod ask who had crossed before him. Impatient was he to brook delay.

"But five days since," she said, "there passed five troops of warriors who rode over with valkyries, yet made they less noise than thee alone. . . . Whom seekest thou?"

Hermod answered and said: "Balder, my brother, son of Odin and Frigg, do I seek. If thou hast seen him, speak forth and tell me whither he hath gone."

In silence did Modgud point towards the north, whereat Hermod spurred Sleipner and went on. . . . Soon he came to Hela's great stone gate. Strongly barred it was and very high, and guarded by a great armed sentinel. To none was given entry save the dead who are brought to judgment.

Hermod leapt to the ground. He tightened the girths of Sleipner. He remounted again. Then he spurred Odin's horse towards the gate, and with a great bound it leapt over, nor ceased to go onward when it came down. . . . Swiftly rode Hermod until he came to the palace in which Balder dwelt with the Asmegir.

From the saddle he leapt and went within. . . . There in a golden hall he saw Balder seated on a throne of gold. Wan was his face and careworn, for the gloom of death had not yet passed from him. On his brow was a wreath of faded flowers, and on his breast the ring Draupner. He sat listening, as if he still heard the voice of Odin whispering in his ear. Before him stood a goblet of mead, which he had touched not. Nanna sat by his side, and her cheeks were pale.

Hermod beheld nigh unto them Urd, the queen of Hela. In cold grandeur she stood, silent and alone. Deathly white was her face, and hard and stern, and she looked downward. On her dark robe gleamed great diamonds and ornaments of fine gold. . . .

To Balder spoke Hermod, and said: "For thee have I been sent hither, O my brother. In Asgard there is deep mourning for thee, and thy queen mother beseecheth thy speedy return."

Sadly did Balder shake his head, and to Nanna he pointed. But she leaned towards him and whispered: "Love is stronger than death, nor can the grave destroy it. . . . With thee, O Balder, shall I ever remain . . . .."

They would have wept, but in Hela there are no tears.

Throughout the night did Hermod hold converse with the twain, and when morning came he besought Urd to release Balder from death's bonds.

With eyes still looking downwards she heard him speak.

"In Asgard," Hermod said, "the gods sorrow for Balder, and on earth is he also mourned. All who have being and all things with life weep for Balder, and beseech thee that he may return again."

Urd made answer coldly: "If all who have being and all things with life weep for Balder and beseech his return, then must he be restored again. . . . But if one eye is without tears, then must he remain in Hela forever."

Hermod bowed himself before Urd in silence, and turned again to Balder and to Nanna, who went with him to the door. . . . Ere their sad farewells were spoken, Balder gave Hermod the ring Draupner to carry back unto Odin, for in Hela the ring was without fertility. Her veil Nanna did send unto Frigg, and a bride's gold ring she gave for Fulla.

To Asgard did Hermod make speedy return, bearing the gifts of Balder and of Nanna, and unto gods and goddesses assembled together he made known the stern decree of Hela's queen.

Over all the world did Frigg then send messengers to beseech all who have being and all things with life to weep for Balder, so that he might be restored again. Then did sorrow indeed prevail. The frost of grief was broken, and the sound of weeping was heard like to falling streams. Men wept, as did also every animal, peaceful and wild. Stones had tears, and metals were made wet. On trees and plants and on every grass blade were dewdrops of mourning for Balder.

But as the messengers of Frigg were returning to Asgard, they came to a deep dark cavern in which sat Gulveig-Hoder, the Hag of Ironwood, in the guise of Thok (darkness). Her they besought to weep, so that Balder might return. She spake coldly and said:

"Thok shall weep tears of fire only because Balder is dead. No joy hath he ever given unto me living or dead. . . . Let Hela's queen hold what is her own."

Great was the sorrow in Asgard because that the Hag would weep not and free Balder from death's bonds. Upon Loke was laid the blame, because he never ceased to work evil among the gods. But not afar off was the day of his doom.

∞∞

"The Coming of the Tuatha de Danaan"
from Gods and Fighting Men
Translated by Lady Gregory

Chapter I
The Fight with the Firbolgs

It was in a mist the Tuatha de Danaan, the people of the gods of Dana, or as some called them, the Men of Dea, came through the air and the high air to Ireland.[1]

It was from the north they came; and in the place they came from they had four cities, where they fought their battle for learning: great Falias, and shining Gorias, and Finias, and rich Murias that lay to the south. And in those cities they had four wise men to teach their young men skill and knowledge and perfect wisdom: Senias in Murias; and Arias, the fair-haired poet, in Finias; and Urias of the noble nature in Gorias; and Morias in Falias itself. And they brought from those four cities their four treasures: a Stone of Virtue from Falias, that was called the Lia Fail, the Stone of Destiny; and from Gorias they brought a Sword; and from Finias a Spear of Victory; and from Murias the fourth treasure, the Cauldron that no company ever went away from unsatisfied.

It was Nuada was king of the Tuatha de Danaan at that time, but Manannan, son of Lir, was greater again. And of the others that were chief among them were Ogma, brother to the king, that taught them writing, and Diancecht, that understood healing, and Neit, a god of battle, and Credenus the Craftsman, and Goibniu the Smith. And the greatest among their women were Badb, a battle goddess; and Macha, whose mast-feeding was the heads of men

---

[1] Lady Gregory uses Irish Gaelic syntax in her English translations, and this sentence structure ("It was x that y") is one of the most common in Gaelic.

killed in battle; and the Morrigu,[1] the Crow of Battle; and Eire and Fodla and Banba, daughters of the Dagda, that all three gave their names to Ireland afterwards; and Eadon, the nurse of poets; and Brigit, that was a woman of poetry, and poets worshipped her, for her sway was very great and very noble. And she was a woman of healing along with that, and a woman of smith's work, and it was she first made the whistle for calling one to another through the night. And the one side of her face was ugly, but the other side was very comely. And the meaning of her name was Breo-saighit, a fiery arrow. And among the other women there were many shadow-forms and great queens; but Dana, that was called the Mother of the Gods, was beyond them all.

And the three things they put above all others were the plough and the sun and the hazel-tree, so that it was said in the time to come that Ireland was divided between those three, Coll the hazel, and Cecht the plough, and Grian the sun.

And they had a well below the sea where the nine hazels of wisdom were growing; that is, the hazels of inspiration and of the knowledge of poetry. And their leaves and their blossoms would break out in the same hour, and would fall on the well in a shower that raised a purple wave. And then the five salmon that were waiting there would eat the nuts, and their colour would come out in the red spots of their skin, and any person that would eat one of those salmon would know all wisdom and all poetry. And there were seven streams of wisdom that sprang from that well and turned back to it again; and the people of many arts have all drank from that well.

It was on the first day of Beltaine, that is called now May Day, the Tuatha de Danaan came, and it was to the north-west of Connacht they landed. But the Firbolgs, the Men of the Bag, that were in Ireland before them, and that had come from the South, saw nothing but a mist, and it lying on the hills.

Eochaid, son of Erc, was king of the Firbolgs at that time, and messengers came to him at Teamhair,[2] and told him there was a new race of people come into Ireland, but whether from the earth or the skies or on the wind was not known, and that they had settled themselves at Magh Rein.

They thought there would be wonder on Eochaid when he heard that news;[3] but there was no wonder on him, for a dream had come to him in the night, and when he asked his Druids the meaning of the dream, it is what they said, that it would not be long till there would be a strong enemy coming against him.

Then King Eochaid took counsel with his chief advisers, and it is what they agreed, to send a good champion of their own to see the strangers and to speak with them. So they chose out Sreng, that was a great fighting man, and he rose up and took his strong red-brown

---

[1] Also known as the Morrigan.

[2] Pronounced *Tyower*, this name has become corrupted over the centuries to *Tara*.

[3] In Irish, an attribute or emotion is said to be on that person. The Irish for "My name is Seamus" literally means "Seamus is the name that is on me," for example, and "I am hungry" is "It is hunger that is on me."

shield, and his two thick-handled spears, and his sword, and his head-covering, and his thick iron club, and he set out from Teamhair, and went on towards the place the strangers were, at Magh Rein.

But before he reached it, the watchers of the Tuatha de Danaan got sight of him, and they sent out one of their own champions, Bres, with his shield and his sword and his two spears, to meet him and to talk with him.

So the two champions went one towards the other slowly, and keeping a good watch on one another, and wondering at one another's arms, till they came near enough for talking; and then they stopped, and each put his shield before his body and struck it hard into the ground, and they looked at one another over the rim. Bres was the first to speak, and when Sreng heard it was Irish he was talking, his own tongue, he was less uneasy, and they drew nearer, and asked questions as to one another's family and race.

And after a while they put their shields away, and it was what Sreng said, that he had raised his in dread of the thin, sharp spears Bres had in his hand. And Bres said he himself was in dread of the thick-handled spears he saw with Sreng, and he asked were all the arms of the Firbolgs of the same sort. And Sreng took off the tyings of his spears to show them better, and Bres wondered at them, being so strong and so heavy, and so sharp at the sides though they had no points. And Sreng told him the name of those spears was Craisech, and that they would break through shields and crush flesh and bones, so that their thrust was death or wounds that never healed. And then he looked at the sharp, thin, hard-pointed spears that were with Bres. And in the end they made an exchange of spears, the way the fighters on each side would see the weapons the others were used to. And it is the message Bres sent to the Firbolgs, that if they would give up one half of Ireland, his people would be content to take it in peace; but if they would not give up that much, there should be a battle. And he and Sreng said to one another that whatever might happen in the future, they themselves would be friends.

Sreng went back then to Teamhair and gave the message and showed the spear; and it is what he advised his people, to share the country and not to go into battle with a people that had weapons so much better than their own. But Eochaid and his chief men consulted together, and they said in the end: "We will not give up the half of the country to these strangers; for if we do," they said, "they will soon take the whole."

Now as to the Men of Dea, when Bres went back to them, and showed them the heavy spear, and told them of the strong, fierce man he had got it from, and how sturdy he was and well armed, they thought it likely there would soon be a battle. And they went back from where they were to a better place, farther west in Connacht, and there they settled themselves, and made walls and ditches on the plain of Magh Nia, where they had the great mountain, Belgata, in their rear. And while they were moving there and putting up their walls, three queens of them, Badb and Macha and the Morrigu, went to Teamhair where the Firbolgs were making their plans. And by the power of their enchantments they brought mists and clouds of darkness over the whole place, and they sent showers of fire and of blood over the people, the way they could not see or speak with one another through the length of three days. But at the end of that time, the three Druids of the Firbolgs, Cesarn and Gnathach and Ingnathach, broke the enchantment.

The Firbolgs gathered their men together then, and they came with their eleven battalions and took their stand at the eastern end of the plain of Magh Nia.

And Nuada, king of the Men of Dea, sent his poets to make the same offer he made before, to be content with the half of the country if it was given up to him. King Eochaid bade the poets to ask an answer of his chief men that were gathered there; and when they heard the offer they would not consent. So the messengers asked them when would they begin the battle. "We must have a delay," they said; "for we want time to put our spears and our armour in order, and to brighten our helmets and to sharpen our swords, and to have spears made like the ones you have. And as to yourselves," they said, "you will be wanting to have spears like our Craisechs made for you." So they agreed then to make a delay of a quarter of a year for preparation.

It was on a Midsummer day they began the battle. Three times nine hurlers of the Tuatha de Danaan went out against three times nine hurlers of the Firbolgs, and they were beaten, and every one of them was killed. And the king, Eochaid, sent a messenger to ask would they have the battle every day or every second day. And it is what Nuada answered that they would have it every day, but there should be just the same number of men fighting on each side. Eochaid agreed to that, but he was not well pleased, for there were more men of the Firbolgs than of the Men of Dea.

So the battle went on for four days, and there were great feats done on each side, and a great many champions came to their death. But for those that were alive at evening, the physicians on each side used to make a bath of healing, with every sort of healing plant or herb in it, the way they would be strong and sound for the next day's fight.

And on the fourth day the Men of Dea got the upper hand, and the Firbolgs were driven back. And a great thirst came on Eochaid, their king, in the battle, and he went off the field looking for a drink, and three fifties of his men protecting him; but three fifties of the Tuatha de Danaan followed after them till they came to the strand that is called Traigh Eothaile, and they had a fierce fight there, and at the last King Eochaid fell, and they buried him there, and they raised a great heap of stones over his grave.

And when there were but three hundred men left of the eleven battalions of the Firbolgs, and Sreng at the head of them, Nuada offered them peace, and their choice among the five provinces of Ireland. And Sreng said they would take Connacht; and he and his people lived there and their children after them. It is of them Ferdiad came afterwards that made such a good fight against Cuchulain, and Erc, son of Cairbre, that gave him his death.[1]

---

[1] The stories featuring Cuchulain of Muirthemne are part of the legend cycle known as the Red Branch of Ulster and include the tale *Bricriu's Feast*, which introduces elements found in *Sir Gawain and the Green Knight*.

And that battle, that was the first fought in Ireland by the Men of Dea, was called by some the first battle of Magh Tuireadh.

And the Tuatha de Danaan took possession of Teamhair, that was sometimes called Druim Cain, the Beautiful Ridge, and Liathdruim, the Grey Ridge, and Druim na Descan, the Ridge of the Outlook, all those names were given to Teamhair. And from that time it was above all other places, for its king was the High King over all Ireland. The king's rath lay to the north, and the Hill of the Hostages to the north-east of the High Seat, and the Green of Teamhair to the west of the Hill of the Hostages. And to the north-east, in the Hill of the Sidhe, was a well called Nemnach, and out of it there flowed a stream called Nith, and on that stream the first mill was built in Ireland.

And to the north of the Hill of the Hostages was the stone, the Lia Fail, and it used to roar under the feet of every king that would take possession of Ireland. And the Wall of the Three Whispers was near the House of the Women that had seven doors to the east, and seven doors to the west; and it is in that house the feasts of Teamhair used to be held. And there was the Great House of a Thousand Soldiers, and near it, to the south, the little Hill of the Woman Soldiers.

Chapter II
The Reign of Bres

But if Nuada won the battle, he lost his own arm in it, that was struck off by Sreng; and by that loss there came troubles and vexation on his people.

For it was a law with the Tuatha de Danaan that no man that was not perfect in shape should be king. And after Nuada had lost the battle he was put out of the kingship on that account.

And the king they chose in his place was Bres, that was the most beautiful of all their young men, so that if a person wanted to praise any beautiful thing, whether it was a plain, or a dun, or ale, or a flame, or a woman, or a man, or a horse, it is what he would say, "It is as beautiful as Bres." And he was the son of a woman of the Tuatha de Danaan, but who his father was no one knew but herself.

But in spite of Bres being so beautiful, his reign brought no great good luck to his people; for the Fomor, whose dwelling-place was beyond the sea, or as some say below the sea westward, began putting tribute on them, the way they would get them under their own rule.

It was a long time before that the Fomor came first to Ireland; dreadful they were to look at, and maimed, having but one foot or one hand, and they under the leadership of a giant and his mother. There never came to Ireland an army more horrible or more dreadful than that army of the Fomor. And they were friendly with the Firbolgs and content to leave Ireland to them, but there was jealousy between them and the Men of Dea.

And it was a hard tax they put on them, a third part of their corn they asked, and a third part of their milk, and a third part of their children, so that there was not smoke rising from a roof in Ireland but was under tribute to them. And Bres made no stand against them, but let them get their way.

And as to Bres himself, he put a tax on every house in Ireland of the milk of hornless dun cows, or of the milk of cows of some other single colour, enough for a hundred men. And one time, to deceive him, Nechtan singed all the cows of Ireland in a fire of fern, and then he smeared them with the ashes of flax seed, the way they were all dark brown. He did that by the advice of the Druid Findgoll, son of Findemas. And another time they made three hundred cows of wood with dark brown pails in place of udders, and the pails were filled with black bog stuff. Then Bres came to look at the cows, and to see them milked before him, and Cian, father of Lugh, was there. And when they were milked it was the bog stuff that was squeezed out; and Bres took a drink of it thinking it to be milk, and he was not the better of it for a long time.

And there was another thing against Bres; he was no way open-handed, and the chief men of the Tuatha de Danaan grumbled against him, for their knives were never greased in his house, and however often they might visit him there was no smell of ale on their breath.[1] And there was no sort of pleasure or merriment in his house, and no call for their poets, or singers, or harpers, or pipers, or horn-blowers, or jugglers, or fools. And as to the trials of strength they were used to see between their champions, the only use their strength was put to now was to be doing work for the king. Ogma himself, the shining poet, was under orders to bring firing to the palace every day for the whole army from the Islands of Mod; and he so weak for want of food that the sea would sweep away two-thirds of his bundle every day. And as to the Dagda, he was put to build raths, for he was a good builder, and he made a trench round Rath Brese. And he used often to be tired at the work, and one time he nearly gave in altogether for want of food, and this is the way that happened. He used to meet in the house an idle blind man, Cridenbel his name was, that had a sharp tongue, and that coveted the Dagda's share of food, for he thought his own to be small beside it. So he said to him: "For the sake of your good name let the three best bits of your share be given to me." And the Dagda gave in to that every night; but he was the worse of it, for what the blind man called a bit would be the size of a good pig, and with his three bits he would take a full third of the whole.

But one day, as the Dagda was in the trench, he saw his son, Angus Og, coming to him. "That is a good meeting," said Angus; "but what is on you, for you have no good appearance to-day?" "There is a reason for that," said the Dagda, "for every evening, Cridenbel, the blind man, makes a demand for the three best bits of my share of food, and

---

[1] Among both the Celts and the Germanic tribes, one of the marks of a good king was how well he treated his guests, especially by giving them gifts, feasting them liberally, and tending to their weapons.

takes them from me." "I will give you an advice," said Angus. He put his hand in his bag then, and took out three pieces of gold and gave them to him.

"Put these pieces of gold into the three bits you will give this evening to Cridenbel," he said, "and they will be the best bits in the dish, and the gold will turn within him the way he will die."

So in the evening the Dagda did that; and no sooner had Cridenbel swallowed down the gold than he died. Some of the people said then to the king: "The Dagda has killed Cridenbel, giving him some deadly herb." The king believed that, and there was anger on him against the Dagda, and he gave orders he should be put to death. But the Dagda said: "You are not giving the right judgment of a prince." And he told all that had happened, and how Cridenbel used to say, "Give me the three best bits before you, for my own share is not good to-night." "And on this night," he said, "the three pieces of gold were the best things before me, and I gave them to him, and he died."

The king gave orders then to have the body cut open. And they found the gold inside it, and they knew it was the truth the Dagda had told.

And Angus came to him again the next day, and he said: "Your work will soon be done, and when you are given your wages, take nothing they may offer you till the cattle of Ireland are brought before you, and choose out a heifer then, black and black-maned, that I will tell you the signs of."

So when the Dagda had brought his work to an end, and they asked him what reward he wanted, he did as Angus had bidden him. And that seemed folly to Bres; he thought the Dagda would have asked more than a heifer of him.

There came a day at last when a poet came to look for hospitality at the king's house, Corpre, son of Etain, poet of the Tuatha de Danaan. And it is how he was treated, he was put in a little dark narrow house where there was no fire, or furniture, or bed; and for a feast three small cakes, and they dry, were brought to him on a little dish. When he rose up on the morrow he was no way thankful, and as he was going across the green, it is what he said: "Without food ready on a dish; without milk enough for a calf to grow on; without shelter; without light in the darkness of night; without enough to pay a story-teller; may that be the prosperity of Bres."

And from that day there was no good luck with Bres, but it is going down he was for ever after. And that was the first satire ever made in Ireland.

Now as to Nuada: after his arm being struck off, he was in his sickness for a while, and then Diancecht, the healer, made an arm of silver for him, with movement in every finger of it, and put it on him. And from that he was called Nuada Argat-lamh, of the Silver Hand, for ever after.

Now Miach, son of Diancecht, was a better hand at healing than his father, and had done many things. He met a young man, having but one eye, at Teamhair one time, and the young man said: "If you are a good physician you will put an eye in the place of the eye I lost." "I could put the eye of that cat in your lap in its place," said Miach. "I would like that well," said the young man. So Miach put the cat's eye in his head; but he would as soon have been without it after, for when he wanted to sleep and take his rest, it is then the eye would start at the squeaking of the mice, or the flight of the birds, or the movement of the rushes; and when he was wanting to watch an army or a gathering, it is then it was sure to be in a deep sleep.

And Miach was not satisfied with what his father had done to the king, and he took Nuada's own hand that had been struck off, and brought it to him and set it in its place, and he said: "Joint to joint, and sinew to sinew." Three days and three nights he was with the king; the first day he put the hand against his side, and the second day against his breast, till it was covered with skin, and the third day he put bulrushes that were blackened in the fire on it, and at the end of that time the king was healed.

But Diancecht was vexed when he saw his son doing a better cure than himself, and he threw his sword at his head, that it cut the flesh, but the lad healed the wound by means of his skill. Then Diancecht threw it a second time, that it reached the bone, but the lad was able to cure the wound. Then he struck him the third time and the fourth, till he cut out the brain, for he knew no physician could cure him after that blow; and Miach died, and he buried him.

And herbs grew up from his grave, to the number of his joints and sinews, three hundred and sixty-five. And Airmed, his sister, came and spread out her cloak and laid out the herbs in it, according to their virtue. But Diancecht saw her doing that, and he came and mixed up the herbs, so that no one knows all their right powers to this day.

Then when the Tuatha de Danaan saw Nuada as well as he was before, they gathered together to Teamhair, where Bres was, and they bade him give up the kingship, for he had held it long enough. So he had to give it up, though he was not very willing, and Nuada was put back in the kingship again.

There was great vexation on Bres then, and he searched his mind to know how could he be avenged on those that had put him out, and how he could gather an army against them; and he went to his mother, Eri, daughter of Delbaith, and bade her tell him what his race was.

"I know that well," she said; and she told him then that his father was a king of the Fomor, Elathan, son of Dalbaech, and that he came to her one time over a level sea in some great vessel that seemed to be of silver, but she could not see its shape, and he himself having the appearance of a young man with yellow hair, and his clothes sewed with gold, and five rings of gold about his neck. And she that had refused the love of all the young men of her own people, gave him her love, and she cried when he left her. And he gave her a ring from his hand, and bade her give it only to the man whose finger it would fit, and he went away then the same way as he had come.

And she brought out the ring then to Bres, and he put it round his middle finger, and it fitted him well. And they went then together to the hill where she was the time she saw the silver vessel coming, and down to the strand, and she and Bres and his people set out for the country of the Fomor.

And when they came to that country they found a great plain with many gatherings of people on it, and they went to the gathering that looked the best, and the people asked where did they come from, and they said they were come from Ireland. "Have you hounds with you?" they asked them then, for it was the custom at that time, when strangers came to a gathering, to give them some friendly challenge. "We have hounds," said Bres. So the hounds were matched against one another, and the hounds of the Tuatha de Danaan were better than the hounds of the Fomor. "Have you horses for a race?" they asked then. "We have," said Bres. And the horses of the Tuatha de Danaan beat the horses of the Fomor.

Then they asked was any one among them a good hand with the sword, and they said Bres was the best. But when he put his hand to his sword, Elathan, his father, that was among them, knew the ring, and he asked who was this young man. Then his mother answered him and told the whole story, and that Bres was his own son.

There was sorrow on his father then, and he said: "What was it drove you out of the country you were king over?" And Bres said: "Nothing drove me out but my own injustice and my own hardness; I took away their treasures from the people, and their jewels, and their food itself. And there were never taxes put on them before I was their king."

"That is bad," said his father; "it is of their prosperity you had a right to think more than of your own kingship. And their good-will would be better than their curses," he said; "and what is it you are come to look for here?" "I am come to look for fighting men," said Bres, "that I may take Ireland by force." "You have no right to get it by injustice when you could not keep it by justice," said his father. "What advice have you for me then?" said Bres.

And Elathan bade him go to the chief king of the Fomor, Balor of the Evil Eye, to see what advice and what help would he give him.

❧❧

from Myths of the Cherokee
As told by James Mooney

How the World Was Made

The earth is a great island floating in a sea of water, and suspended at each of the four cardinal points by a cord hanging down from the sky vault, which is of solid rock. When the world grows old and worn out, the people will die and the cords will break and let the earth sink down into the ocean, and all will be water again. The Indians are afraid of this.

When all was water, the animals were above in Gälûñ'läti, beyond the arch; but it was very much crowded, and they were wanting more room. They wondered what was below the water, and at last Dâyuni'sï, "Beaver's Grandchild," the little Water-beetle, offered to go and see if it could learn. It darted in every direction over the surface of the water, but could find no firm place to rest. Then it dived to the bottom and came up with some soft mud, which began to grow and spread on every side until it became the island which we call the earth. It was afterward fastened to the sky with four cords, but no one remembers who did this.

At first the earth was flat and very soft and wet. The animals were anxious to get down, and sent out different birds to see if it was yet dry, but they found no place to alight and came back again to Gälûñ'lätï. At last it seemed to be time, and they sent out the Buzzard and told him to go and make ready for them. This was the Great Buzzard, the father of all the buzzards we see now. He flew all over the earth, low down near the ground, and it was still soft. When he reached the Cherokee country, he was very tired, and his wings began to flap and strike the ground, and wherever they struck the earth there was a valley, and where they turned up again there was a mountain. When the animals above saw this, they were afraid that the whole world would be mountains, so they called him back, but the Cherokee country remains full of mountains to this day.

When the earth was dry and the animals came down, it was still dark, so they got the sun and set it in a track to go every day across the island from east to west, just overhead. It was too hot this way, and Tsiska'gïlï', the Red Crawfish, had his shell scorched a bright red, so that his meat was spoiled; and the Cherokee do not eat it. The conjurers put the sun another hand-breadth higher in the air, but it was still too hot. They raised it another time, and another, until it was seven handbreadths high and just under the sky arch. Then it was right, and they left it so. This is why the conjurers call the highest place Gûlkwâ'gine Di'gälûñ'lätiyûñ', "the seventh height," because it is seven hand-breadths above the earth. Every day the sun goes along under this arch, and returns at night on the upper side to the starting place.

There is another world under this, and it is like ours in everything—animals, plants, and people—save that the seasons are different. The streams that come down from the mountains are the trails by which we reach this underworld, and the springs at their heads are the doorways by which we enter it, but to do this one must fast and go to water and have one of the underground people for a guide. We know that the seasons in the underworld are different from ours, because the water in the springs is always warmer in winter and cooler in summer than the outer air.

When the animals and plants were first made—we do not know by whom—they were told to watch and keep awake for seven nights, just as young men now fast and keep awake when they pray to their medicine. They tried to do this, and nearly all were awake through the first night, but the next night several dropped off to sleep, and the third night others were asleep, and then others, until, on the seventh night, of all the animals only the owl, the panther, and one or two more were still awake. To these were given the power to see and to go about in the dark, and to make prey of the birds and animals which must sleep at night.

Of the trees only the cedar, the pine, the spruce, the holly, and the laurel were awake to the end, and to them it was given to be always green and to be greatest for medicine, but to the others it was said: "Because you have not endured to the end you shall lose your hair every winter."

Men came after the animals and plants. At first there were only a brother and sister until he struck her with a fish and told her to multiply, and so it was. In seven days a child was born to her, and thereafter every seven days another, and they increased very fast until there was danger that the world could not keep them. Then it was made that a woman should have only one child in a year, and it has been so ever since.

Origin of Disease and Medicine

In the old days the beasts, birds, fishes, insects, and plants could all talk, and they and the people lived together in peace and friendship. But as time went on the people increased so rapidly that their settlements spread over the whole earth, and the poor animals found themselves beginning to be cramped for room. This was bad enough, but to make it worse Man invented bows, knives, blowguns, spears, and hooks, and began to slaughter the larger animals, birds, and fishes for their flesh or their skins, while the smaller creatures, such as the frogs and worms, were crushed and trodden upon without thought, out of pure carelessness or contempt. So the animals resolved to consult upon measures for their common safety.

The Bears were the first to meet in council in their townhouse under Kuwâ'hï mountain, the "Mulberry place," and the old White Bear chief presided. After each in turn had complained of the way in which Man killed their friends, ate their flesh, and used their skins for his own purposes, it was decided to begin war at once against him. Some one asked what weapons Man used to destroy them. "Bows and arrows, of course, cried all the Bears in chorus. "And what are they made of?" was the next question. "The bow of wood, and the string of our entrails," replied one of the Bears. It was then proposed that they make a bow and some arrows and see if they could not use the same weapons against Man himself. So one Bear got a nice piece of locust wood and another sacrificed himself for the good of the rest in order to furnish a piece of his entrails for the string. But when everything was ready and the first Bear stepped up to make the trial, it was found that in letting the arrow fly after drawing back the bow, his long claws caught the string and spoiled the shot. This was annoying, but some one suggested that they might trim his claws, which was accordingly done, and on a second trial it was found that the arrow went straight to the mark. But here the chief, the old White Bear, objected, saying it was necessary that they should have long claws in order to be able to climb trees. "One of us has already died to furnish the bowstring, and if we now cut off our claws we must all starve together. It is better to trust to the teeth and claws that nature gave us, for it is plain that man's weapons were not intended for us."

No one could think of any better plan, so the old chief dismissed the council and the Bears dispersed to the woods and thickets without having concerted any way to prevent the increase of the human race. Had the result of the council been otherwise, we should now be at war with the Bears, but as it is, the hunter does not even ask the Bear's pardon when he kills one.

The Deer next held a council under their chief, the Little Deer, and after some talk decided to send rheumatism to every hunter who should kill one of them unless he took care to ask their pardon for the offense. They sent notice of their decision to the nearest settlement of Indians and told them at the same time what to do when necessity forced them to kill one of the Deer tribe. Now, whenever the hunter shoots a Deer, the Little Deer, who is swift as the wind and can not be wounded, runs quickly up to the spot and, bending over the blood-stains, asks the spirit of the Deer if it has heard the prayer of the hunter for pardon. If the reply be "Yes," all is well, and the Little Deer goes on his way; but if the reply be "No," he follows on the trail of the hunter, guided by the drops of blood on the ground, until he arrives at his cabin in the settlement, when the Little Deer enters invisibly and strikes the hunter with rheumatism, so that he becomes at once a helpless cripple. No hunter who has regard for his health ever fails to ask pardon of the Deer for killing it, although some hunters who have not learned the prayer may try to turn aside the Little Deer from his pursuit by building a fire behind them in the trail.

Next came the Fishes and Reptiles, who had their own complaints against Man. They held their council together and determined to make their victims dream of snakes twining about them in slimy folds and blowing foul breath in their faces, or to make them dream of eating raw or decaying fish, so that they would lose appetite, sicken, and die. This is why people dream about snakes and fish.

Finally the Birds, Insects, and smaller animals came together for the same purpose, and the Grubworm was chief of the council. It was decided that each in turn should give an opinion, and then they would vote on the question as to whether or not Man was guilty. Seven votes should be enough to condemn him. One after another denounced Man's cruelty and injustice toward the other animals and voted in favor of his death. The Frog spoke first, saying: "We must do something to check the increase of the race, or people will become so numerous that we shall be crowded from off the earth. See how they have kicked me about because I'm ugly, as they say, until my back is covered with sores;" and here he showed the spots on his skin. Next came the Bird—no one remembers now which one it was—who condemned Man "because he burns my feet off," meaning the way in which the hunter barbecues birds by impaling them on a stick set over the fire, so that their feathers and tender feet are singed off. Others followed in the same strain. The Ground-squirrel alone ventured to say a good word for Man, who seldom hurt him because he was so small, but this made the others so angry that they fell upon the Ground-squirrel and tore him with their claws, and the stripes are on his back to this day.

They began then to devise and name so many new diseases, one after another, that had not their invention at last failed them, no one of the human race would have been able to survive. The Grubworm grew constantly more pleased as the name of each disease was called off, until at last they reached the end of the list, when some one proposed to make menstruation sometimes fatal to women. On this he rose-up in his place and cried: "*Wadâñ'!* [Thanks!] I'm glad some more of them will die, for they are getting so thick that they tread on me." The thought fairly made him shake with joy, so that he fell over backward and could not get on his feet again, but had to wriggle off on his back, as the Grubworm has done ever since.

When the Plants, who were friendly to Man, heard what had been done by the animals, they determined to defeat the latter's evil designs. Each Tree, Shrub, and Herb, down even to the Grasses and Mosses, agreed to furnish a cure for some one of the diseases named, and each said: "I shall appear to help Man when he calls upon me in his need." Thus came medicine; and the plants, every one of which has its use if we only knew it, furnish the remedy to counteract the evil wrought by the revengeful animals. Even weeds were made for some good purpose, which we must find out for ourselves. When the doctor does not know what medicine to use for a sick man the spirit of the plant tells him.

The Deluge

A long time ago a man had a dog, which began to go down to the river every day and look at the water and howl. At last the man was angry and scolded the dog, which then spoke to him and said: "Very soon there is going to be a great freshet and the water will come so high that everybody will be drowned; but if you will make a raft to get upon when the rain comes you can be saved, but you must first throw me into the water." The man did not believe it, and the dog said, "If you want a sign that I speak the truth, look at the back of my neck." He looked and saw that the dog's neck had the skin worn off so that the bones stuck out.

Then he believed the dog, and began to build a raft. Soon the rain came and he took his family, with plenty of provisions and they all got upon it. It rained for a long time, and the water rose until the mountains were covered and all the people in the world were drowned. Then the rain stopped and the waters went down again, until at last it was safe to come off the raft. Now there was no one alive but the man and his family, but one day they heard a sound of dancing and shouting on the other side of the ridge. The man climbed to the top and looked over; everything was still, but all along the valley he saw great piles of bones of the people who had been drowned, and then he knew that the ghosts had been dancing.

The Dream of the Rood
Translated by James M. Garnett

Lo! choicest of dreams I will relate,
What dream I dreamt in middle of night
When mortal men reposed in rest.
Methought I saw a wondrous wood
Tower aloft with light bewound,
Brightest of trees; that beacon was all
Begirt with gold; jewels were standing
Four at surface of earth, likewise were there five[1]
Above on the shoulder-brace. All angels of God beheld it,[2]
Fair through future ages; 'twas no criminal's cross indeed,
But holy spirits beheld it there,
Men upon earth, all this glorious creation.
Strange was that victor-tree, and stained with sins was I,
With foulness defiled. I saw the glorious tree
With vesture adorned winsomely shine,
Begirt with gold; bright gems had there
Worthily decked the tree of the Lord.
Yet through that gold I might perceive
Old strife of the wretched, that first it gave
Blood on the stronger [right] side.[3] With sorrows was I oppressed,
Afraid for that fair sight; I saw the ready beacon
Change in vesture and hue; at times with moisture covered,
Soiled with course of blood; at times with treasure adorned.
Yet lying there a longer while,
Beheld I sad the Saviour's tree
Until I heard that words it uttered;
The best of woods gan[4] speak these words:

---

[1] Students have asked in the past what these gems represent, which is a somewhat tricky question because four and five have a wide variety of meanings in medieval number symbolism. They probably represent the four Gospels and the five wounds of Christ—and possibly much more than that.

[2] This is a mistranslation; better would be "The Lord's angel all beheld there"—the *Rood* is the angel in the sense of being God's messenger to the Dreamer.

[3] *Swætan*, the actual verb used here, can mean both "sweat" and "bleed," and the Gospels state that there was "a great flow of blood and water" when Jesus' heart was pierced. Medieval art typically portrays that wound on Jesus' right side. If one does interpret *swætan* as "bleed," however, it creates the curious image of the Rood itself suffering the wounds.

[4] began (to)

"'Twas long ago (I remember it still)
That I was hewn at end of a grove,
Stripped from off my stem; strong foes laid hold of me there,
Wrought for themselves a show, bade felons raise me up;
Men bore me on their shoulders, till on a mount they set me;
Fiends many fixed me there. Then saw I mankind's Lord
Hasten with mickle[1] might, for He would sty[2] upon me.
There durst I not 'gainst word of the Lord
Bow down or break, when saw I tremble
The surface of earth; I might then all
My foes have felled, yet fast I stood.
The Hero young begirt Himself, Almighty God was He,
Strong and stern of mind; He stied on the gallows high,
Bold in sight of many, for man He would redeem.
I shook when the Hero clasped me, yet durst not bow to earth,
Fall to surface of earth, but firm I must there stand.
A rood was I upreared; I raised the mighty King,
The Lord of Heaven; I durst not bend me.
They drove their dark nails through me; the wounds are seen upon me,
The open gashes of guile; I durst harm none of them.
They mocked us both together; all moistened with blood was I,
Shed from side of the man, when forth He sent His spirit.
Many have I on that mount endured
Of cruel fates; I saw the Lord of Hosts
Strongly outstretched; darkness had then
Covered with clouds the corse of the Lord,
The brilliant brightness; the shadow continued,
Wan[3] 'neath the welkin.[4] There wept all creation,
Bewailed the King's death; Christ was on the cross.
Yet hastening thither they came from afar
To the Son of the King: that all I beheld.
Sorely with sorrows was I oppressed; yet I bowed 'neath the hands of men,
Lowly with mickle might. Took they there Almighty God,
Him raised from the heavy torture; the battle-warriors left me
To stand bedrenched with blood; all wounded with darts was I.

---

[1] much
[2] mount
[3] pale
[4] sky

There laid they the weary of limb, at head of His corse they stood,
Beheld the Lord of Heaven, and He rested Him there awhile,
Worn from the mickle war. Began they an earth-house to work,
Men in the murderers' sight, carved it of brightest stone,
Placed therein victories' Lord. Began sad songs to sing
The wretched at eventide; then would they back return
Mourning from the mighty prince; all lonely[1] rested He there.
Yet weeping we then a longer while
Stood at our station: the [voice][2] arose
Of battle-warriors; the corse grew cold,
Fair house of life. Then one gan fell
Us[3] all to earth; 'twas a fearful fate!
One buried us in deep pit, yet of me the thanes of the Lord,
His friends, heard tell; [from earth they raised me],[4]
And me begirt with gold and silver.
Now thou mayst hear, my dearest man,
That bale of woes have I endured,
Of sorrows sore. Now the time is come,
That me shall honor both far and wide
Men upon earth, and all this mighty creation
Will pray to this beacon.[5] On me God's Son
Suffered awhile; so glorious now
I tower to Heaven, and I may heal
Each one of those who reverence me;
Of old I became the hardest of pains,
Most loathsome to ledes [nations], the way of life,
Right way, I prepared for mortal men.
Lo! the Lord of Glory honored me then
Above the grove, the guardian of Heaven,
As He His mother, even Mary herself,
Almighty God before all men
Worthily honored above all women.

---

[1] Lit. "with a small troop"—this is the poetic device the Greeks called *litotes*, where the poet takes an image that is contrary to fact and then understates it. The same image, with the same meaning, appears again at the end of the poem.

[2] There is a word missing in the manuscript here; most scholars fill the gap with *stefn* (voice).

[3] i.e., the three crosses.

[4] In the manuscript, there is only half a line here. Garnett, following one of his sources, treats it as a lacuna and fills it this way, but most scholars view it as unnecessary.

[5] This view of the Cross may arise from the similarity in shape to Thor's hammer.

Now thee I bid, my dearest man,
That thou this sight shalt say to men,
Reveal in words, 'tis the tree of glory,
On which once suffered Almighty God
For the many sins of all mankind,
And also for Adam's misdeeds of old.
Death tasted He there; yet the Lord arose
With His mickle might for help to men.
Then stied He to Heaven; again shall come
Upon this mid-earth to seek mankind
At the day of doom the Lord Himself,
Almighty God, and His angels with Him;
Then He will judge, who hath right of doom,
Each one of men as here before
In this vain life he hath deserved.
No one may there be free from fear
In view of the word that the Judge will speak.
He will ask 'fore the crowd, where is the man
Who for name of the Lord would bitter death
Be willing to taste, as He did on the tree.
But then they will fear, and few will bethink them
What they to Christ may venture to say.
Then need there no one be filled with fear
Who bears in his breast the best of beacons;
But through the rood a kingdom shall seek
From earthly way each single soul
That with the Lord thinketh to dwell."
Then I prayed to the tree with joyous heart,
With mickle might, when I was alone
With small attendance; the thought of my mind
For the journey was ready; I've lived through many
Hours of longing. Now 'tis hope of my life
That the victory-tree I am able to seek,
Oftener than all men I alone may
Honor it well; my will to that
Is mickle in mind, and my plea for protection
To the rood is directed. I've not many mighty
Of friends on earth; but hence went they forth
From joys of the world, sought glory's King;
Now live they in Heaven with the Father on high,

In glory dwell, and I hope for myself
On every day when the rood of the Lord,
Which here on earth before I viewed,
In this vain life may fetch me away
And bring me then, where bliss is mickle,
Joy in the Heavens, where the folk of the Lord
Is set at the feast, where bliss is eternal;
And may He then set me where I may hereafter
In glory dwell, and well with the saints
Of joy partake. May the Lord be my friend,
Who here on earth suffered before
On the gallows-tree for the sins of man!
He us redeemed, and gave to us life,
A heavenly home. Hope was renewed,
With blessing and bliss, for the sufferers of burning.
The Son was victorious on that fateful journey,
Mighty and happy, when He came with a many,
With a band of spirits to the kingdom of God,
The Ruler Almighty, for joy to the angels
And to all the saints, who in Heaven before
In glory dwelt, when their Ruler came,
Almighty God, where was His home.

Arthuriana

Geoffrey of Monmouth
from The History of the Kings of Britain
Translated by J. A. Giles[1]

Book VI.
Chap. V.
Constantine, being made king of Britain, leaves three sons.

When they had made all necessary preparations, they embarked, and arrived at the port of Totness;[2] and then without delay assembled together the youth that was left in the island, and encountered the enemy; over whom, by the merit of the holy prelate, they obtained the victory. After this the Britons, before dispersed, flocked together from all parts and in a council held at Silchester, promoted Constantine to the throne, and there performed the ceremony of his coronation. They also married him to a lady, descended from a noble Roman family, whom archbishop Guethelin had educated, and by whom the king had afterwards three sons, Constans, Aurelius Ambrosius, and Uther Pendragon. Constans, who was the eldest, he delivered to the church of Amphibalus in Winchester, that he might there take upon him the monastic order.[3] But the other two, viz. Aurelius and Uther, he committed to the care of Guethelin for their education. At last, after ten years were expired, there came a certain Pict, who had entered in his service, and under pretence of holding some private discourse with him, in a nursery of young trees where nobody was present, stabbed him with a dagger.

Chap. VI.
Constans is by Vortigern crowned king of Britain.

Upon the death of Constantine, a dissension arose among the nobility, about a successor to the throne. Some were for setting up Aurelius Ambrosius; others Uther Pendragon; others

---

[1] Notes on this text will incorporate some of Giles' notes from his 1848 translation.

[2] Totnes [*sic*] is the town in modern Devonshire where Brutus, descendant of Aeneas, is said to have landed after escaping the fall of Troy, and from it he supposedly founded Britain. Brutus is almost certainly a myth—the first mention of him appears in Nennius, nearly two thousand years after the Trojan War, and appears to be intended to give Britain equal dignity with Rome—but the legend appears now and again throughout medieval romances, and Geoffrey devotes considerable space to it earlier in his *History*.

[3] Giles notes: "It is true that Constans, the son of Constantine, entered into the sacerdotal profession, but both he and his father Constantine were slain in Gaul, which they had made the seat of their empire, to the entire neglect of Britain." Constantine's folly in putting his heir in a position to learn "any thing else but state affairs" not only underscores the poor state of politics in Britain after the withdrawal of the legions but also serves as the first domino to fall in the chain that will lead to Arthur's tragic end.

again some other persons of the royal family. At last, when they could come to no conclusion, Vortigern, consul of the Gewisseans,[1] who was himself very ambitious of the crown, went to Constans the monk, and thus addressed himself to him: "You see your father is dead, and your brothers on account of their age are incapable of the government; neither do I see any of your family besides yourself, whom the people ought to promote to the kingdom. If you will therefore follow my advice, I will, on condition of your increasing my private estate, dispose the people to favour your advancement, and free you from that habit, notwithstanding that it is against the rule of your order." Constans, overjoyed at the proposal, promised, with an oath, that upon these terms he would grant him whatever he would desire. Then Vortigern took him, and investing him in his regal habiliments, conducted him to London, and made him king, though not with the free consent of the people. Archbishop Guethelin was then dead, nor was there any other that durst perform the ceremony of his unction, on account of his having quitted the monastic order. However, this proved no hindrance to his coronation, for Vortigern himself performed the ceremony instead of a bishop.[2]

Chap. VII.
Vortigern treacherously contrives to get king Constans assassinated.

Constans, being thus advanced, committed the whole government of the kingdom to Vortigern, and surrendered himself up so entirely to his counsels, that he did nothing without his order. His own incapacity for government obliged him to do this, for he had learned any thing else rather than state affairs within his cloister. Vortigern became sensible of this, and therefore began to deliberate with himself what course to take to obtain the crown, of which he had been before extremely ambitious. He saw that now was his proper time to gain his end easily, when the kingdom was wholly intrusted to his management; and Constans, who bore the title of king, was no more than the shadow of one; for he was of a soft temper, a bad judge in matters of right, and not in the least feared, either by his own people, or by the neighbouring states. And as for his two brothers, Uther Pendragon and Aurelius Ambrosius, they were only children in their cradles,[3] and therefore incapable of the government. There was likewise this farther misfortune, that all the older persons of the nobility were dead, so that Vortigern seemed to be the only man surviving, that had craft, policy, and experience in matters of state; and all the rest in a manner children, or raw youths,

---

[1] Geoffrey is not terribly scrupulous about place names; he seems not to have realized that Gewissæ was a Saxon kingdom.

[2] Another sign that Vortigern is bad news, not only taking a monk out of his cloister but also arrogating the power of consecration to himself. Geoffrey may have intended readers to recall a similar sin perpetrated by Saul in 1 Samuel 13.

[3] Actually, Ambrosius Aurelianus [sic] would have been around seven years old when Honorius pulled the legions out of Britain—still not old enough to rule, but hardly an infant.

who only inherited the honours of their parents and relations that had been killed in the former wars.[1] Vortigern, finding a concurrence of so many favourable circumstances, contrived how he might easily and cunningly depose Constans the monk, and immediately establish himself in his place. But in order to do this, he waited until he had first well established his power and interest in several countries. He therefore petitioned to have the king's treasures, and his fortified cities, in his own custody; pretending there was a rumour, that the neighbouring islanders designed an invasion of the kingdom. This being granted him, he placed his own creatures in those cities, to secure them for himself. Then having formed a scheme how to execute his treasonable designs, he went to the king, and represented to him the necessity of augmenting the number of his domestics, that he might more safely oppose the invasion of the enemy. "Have I not left all things to your disposal?" said Constans: "Do what you will as to that, so that they be but faithful to me." Vortigern replied, "I am informed that the Picts are going to bring the Dacians and Norwegians in upon us, with a design to give us very great annoyance. I would therefore advise you, and in my opinion it is the best course you can take, that you maintain some Picts in your court, who may do you good service among those of that nation. For if it is true that they are preparing to begin a rebellion, you may employ them as spies upon their countrymen in their plots and stratagems, so as easily to escape them." This was the dark treason of a secret enemy; for he did not recommend this out of regard to the safety of Constans, but because he knew the Picts to be a giddy people, and ready for all manner of wickedness; so that, in a fit of drunkenness or passion, they might easily be incensed against the king, and make no scruple to assassinate him. And such an accident, when it should happen, would make an open way for his accession to the throne, which he so often had in view. Hereupon he despatched messengers into Scotland, with an invitation to a hundred Pictish soldiers, whom accordingly he received into the king's household; and when admitted, he showed them more respect than all the rest of the domestics, by making them several presents, and allowing them a luxurious table, insomuch that they looked upon him as the king. So great was the regard they had for him, that they made songs of him about the streets, the subject of which was, that Vortigern deserved the government, deserved the sceptre of Britain; but that Constans was unworthy of it. This encouraged Vortigern to show them still more favour, in order the more firmly to engage them in his interest; and when by these practices he had made them entirely his creatures, he took an opportunity, when they were drunk, to tell them, that he was going to retire out of Britain, to see if he could get a better estate; for the small revenue he had then, he said, would not so much as enable him to maintain a retinue of fifty men. Then putting on a look of sadness, he withdrew to his own apartment, and left them drinking in the hall. The Picts at this sight were in inexpressible sorrow, as thinking

---

[1] Elsewhere, Geoffrey blasts the Roman legionary system under Maximian for causing this state of affairs, not only blaming Maximian for stealing away the best men from among the Britons but also blaming the Britons themselves for trusting the legions for protection too much and not learning to defend themselves.

what he had said was true, and murmuring said one to another, "Why do we suffer this monk to live? Why do not we kill him, that Vortigern may enjoy his crown? Who is so fit to succeed as he? A man so generous to us is worthy to rule, and deserves all the honour and dignity that we can bestow upon him."

Chap. VIII.

Aurelius Ambrosius and Uther Pendragon flee from Vortigern, and go to Lesser Britain.

After this, breaking into Constan's bed-chamber, they fell upon him and killed him, and carried his head to Vortigern. At the sight of it, he put on a mournful countenance, and burst forth into tears, though at the same time he was almost transported with joy. However, he summoned together the citizens of London, (for there the fact was committed,) and commanded all the assassins to be bound, and their heads to be cut off for this abominable parricide. In the meantime there were some who had a suspicion, that this piece of villany was wholly the contrivance of Vortigern, and that the Picts were only his instruments to execute it. Others again as positively asserted his innocence. At last the matter being left in doubt, those who had the care of the two brothers, Aurelius Ambrosius, and Uther Pendragon, fled over with them into Lesser Britain,[1] for fear of being killed by Vortigern. There they were kindly received by king Budes, who took care to give them an education suitable to their royal birth.

Chap. IX.

Vortigern makes himself king of Britain.

Now Vortigern, seeing nobody to rival him in the kingdom, placed the crown on his own head, and thus gained the preeminence over all the rest of the princes. At last his treason being discovered, the people of the adjacent islands, whom the Picts had brought into Albania,[2] made insurrection against him. For the Picts were enraged on account of the death of their fellow soldiers, who had been slain for the murder of Constans, and endeavoured to revenge that injury upon him. Vortigern therefore was daily in great distress, and lost a considerable part of his army in a war with them. He had likewise no less trouble from another quarter, for fear of Aurelius Ambrosius, and his brother Uther Pendragon, who, as we said before, had fled, on his account, into Lesser Britain. For he heard it rumoured, day after day, that they had now arrived at man's estate, and had built a vast fleet, with a design to return back to the kingdom, which was their undoubted right.

---

[1] This probably refers to the region of Brittany in modern France.
[2] "Albania" here refers to *Albion*, the Celtic name for northern Britain, especially modern Scotland.

Chap. X.

Vortigern takes the Saxons that were new-comers, to his assistance.

In the meantime there arrived in Kent three brigandines, or long galleys, full of armed men, under the command of two brothers, Horsa and Hengist.[1] Vortigern was then at Dorobernia, now Canterbury, which city he used often to visit; and being informed of the arrival of some tall strangers in large ships, he ordered that they should be received peaceably, and conducted into his presence. As soon as they were brought before him, he cast his eyes upon the two brothers, who excelled all the rest both in nobility and gracefulness of person; and having taken a view of the whole company, asked them of what country they were, and what was the occasion of their coming into his kingdom. To whom Hengist (whose years and wisdom entitled him to a precedence), in the name of the rest, made the following answer:—

"Most noble king, Saxony, which is one of the countries of Germany, was the place of our birth; and the occasion of our coming was to offer our service to you or some other prince. For we were driven out of our native country, for no other reason, but that the laws of the kingdom required it. It is customary among us, that when we come to be overstocked with people, our princes from all the provinces meet together, and command all the youths of the kingdom to assemble before them; then casting lots, they make choice of the strongest and ablest of them, to go into foreign nations, to procure themselves a subsistence, and free their native country from a superfluous multitude of people. Our country, therefore, being of late overstocked, our princes met, and after having cast lots, made choice of the youth which you see in your presence, and have obliged us to obey the custom which has been established of old. And us two brothers, Hengist and Horsa, they made generals over them, out of respect to our ancestors, who enjoyed the same honour. In obedience, therefore, to the laws so long established, we put out to sea, and under the good guidance of Mercury have arrived in your kingdom."

The king, at the name of Mercury, looking earnestly upon them, asked them what religion they professed. "We worship," replied Hengist, "our country's gods, Saturn and Jupiter, and the other deities that govern the world, but especially Mercury, whom in our language we call Woden, and to whom our ancestors consecrated the fourth day of the week, still called after his name Wodensday.[2] Next to him we worship the powerful goddess, Frea, to whom they also dedicated the sixth day, which after her name we call Friday." Vortigern replied, "For your credulity, or rather incredulity, I am much grieved, but I rejoice at your arrival, which, whether by God's providence or some other agency, happens very seasonably for me in my present difficulties. For I am oppressed by my enemies on every side, and if

---

[1] The *Anglo-Saxon Chronicle* dates this event in AD 449; Nennius dates it in 447. Scholars differ on the historicity of the brothers, but the kings of Kent traced their lineage to Hengist, which suggests that Hengist and Horsa were Jutes rather than Saxons.

[2] Geoffrey, writing in Latin, uses some very unreliable parallels—including this one—between the Roman gods and the Saxon gods. Odin (Woden) is much closer to Jupiter and Prometheus than to Mercury.

you will engage with me in my wars, I will entertain you honourably in my kingdom, and bestow upon you lands and other possessions." The barbarians readily accepted his offer, and the agreement between them being ratified, they resided at his court. Soon after this, the Picts, issuing forth from Albania, with a very great army, began to lay waste the northern parts of the island. When Vortigern had information of it, he assembled his forces, and went to meet them beyond the Humber. Upon their engaging, the battle proved very fierce on both sides, though there was but little occasion for the Britons to exert themselves, for the Saxons fought so bravely, that the enemy, formerly so victorious, were speedily put to flight.

Chap. XI.
Hengist brings over great numbers of Saxons into Britain: his crafty petition to Vortigern.

Vortigern, therefore, as he owed the victory to them, increased his bounty to them, and gave their general, Hengist, large possessions of land in Lindesia, for the subsistence of himself and his fellow soldiers. Hereupon Hengist, who was a man of experience and subtilty, finding how much interest he had with the king, addressed him in this manner:—"Sir, your enemies give you disturbance from all quarters, and few of your subjects love you. They all threaten you, and say, they are going to bring over Aurelius Ambrosius from Armorica,[1] to depose you, and make him king. If you please, let us send to our country to invite over some more soldiers, that with our forces increased we may be better able to oppose them. But there is one thing which I would desire of your clemency, if I did not fear a refusal." Vortigern made answer, "Send your messengers to Germany, and invite over whom you please, and you shall have no refusal from me in whatever you shall desire." Hengist, with a low bow, returned to him thanks, and said, "The possessions which you have given me in land and houses are very large, but you have not yet done me that honour which becomes my station and birth, because, among other things, I should have had some town or city granted me, that I might be entitled to greater esteem among the nobility of your kingdom. I ought to have been made a consul or prince, since my ancestors enjoyed both those dignities." "It is not in my power," replied Vortigern, "to do you so much honour, because you are strangers and pagans; neither am I yet so far acquainted with your manners and customs, as to set you upon a level with my natural born subjects. And, indeed, if I did esteem you as my subjects, I should not be forward to do so, because the nobility of my kingdom would strongly dissuade me from it." "Give your servant," said Hengist, "only so much ground in the place you have assigned me, as I can encompass with a leathern thong, for to build a fortresss upon, as a place of retreat if occasion should require. For I will always be faithful to you, as I have been hitherto, and pursue no other design in the request which I have made." With these words the king was prevailed upon to grant him his petition; and ordered him to despatch messengers into Germany, to invite more men over speedily to his assistance.

---

[1] Brittany

Hengist immediately executed his orders, and taking a bull's hide, made one thong out of the whole, with which he encompassed a rocky place that he had carefully made choice of, and within that circuit began to build a castle, which, when finished, took its name from the thong wherewith it had been measured; for it was afterwards called, in the British tongue, Kaercorrei; in Saxon, Thancastre, that is, Thong Castle.[1]

[*Vortigern falls in love with Hengist's daughter Rowen and marries her, which scandalizes his sons and countrymen. Hengist convinces Vortigern to send for two other Saxon princes and their armies, but the Britons have had enough and depose Vortigern in favor of his son Vortimer, who routs the new arrivals and begins restoring what the Saxons have damaged or destroyed. Rowen has him poisoned.*]

Chap. XV.
Hengist, having wickedly murdered the princes of Britain, keeps Vortigern prisoner.

Vortigern, after the death of his son, was again restored to the kingdom, and at the request of his wife sent messengers into Germany to Hengist, with an invitation to return into Britain, but privately, and with a small retinue, to prevent a quarrel between the barbarians and his subjects. But Hengist, hearing that Vortimer was dead, raised an army of no less than three hundred thousand men, and fitting out a fleet returned with them to Britain. When Vortigern and the nobility heard of the arrival of so vast a multitude, they were immoderately incensed, and, after consultation together, resolved to fight them, and drive them from their coasts. Hengist, being informed of their design by messengers sent from his daughter, immediately entered into deliberation what course to pursue against them. After several stratagems had been considered, he judged it most feasible, to impose upon the nation by making show of peace. With this view he sent ambassadors to the king, to declare to him, that he had not brought so great a number of men for the purpose either of staying with him, or offering any violence to the country. But the reason why he brought them, was because he thought Vortimer was yet living, and that he should have occasion for them against him, in case of an assault. But now since he no longer doubted of his being dead, he submitted himself and his people to the disposal of Vortigern; so that he might retain as many of them as he should think fit, and whomsoever he rejected Hengist would allow to return back without delay to Germany. And if these terms pleased Vortigern, he desired him to appoint a time and place for their meeting, and adjusting matters according to his pleasure. When these things were represented to the king, he was mightily pleased, as being very unwilling to part with Hengist; and at last ordered his subjects and the Saxons to meet upon the kalends of May,

---

[1] Giles connects this location with Caistor, Lincolnshire, which is indeed in West Lindsey; but Caistor is so named because it had been the site of a Roman *castrum* (fortress). The only reference to it as Thancastre that I can find is in this very sentence. Hengist's trick with the bull's hide is the same trick Dido supposedly used to gain the land to found Carthage, however, so Geoffrey might be plagiarizing from the *Aeneid*.

which were now very near, at the monastery of Ambrius,[1] for the settling of the matters above mentioned. The appointment being agreed to on both sides, Hengist, with a new design of villany in his head, ordered his soldiers to carry every one of them a long dagger under their garments; and while the conference should be held with the Britons, who would have no suspicion of them, he would give them this word of command, *"Nemet oure Saxas;"* at which moment they were all to be ready to seize boldly every one his next man, and with his drawn dagger stab him. Accordingly they all met at the time and place appointed, and began to treat of peace; and when a fit opportunity offered for executing his villany, Hengist cried out, *"Nemet oure Saxas,"* and the same instant seized Vortigern, and held him by his cloak. The Saxons, upon the signal given, drew their daggers, and falling upon the princes, who little suspected any such design, assassinated them to the number of four hundred and sixty barons and consuls; to whose bodies St. Eldad afterwards gave Christian burial; not far from Kaercaradauc, now Salisbury, in a burying-place near the monastery of Ambrius, the abbat, who was the founder of it. For they all came without arms, having no thoughts of anything but treating of peace; which gave the others a fairer opportunity of exercising their villainous design against them. But the pagans did not escape unpunished while they acted this wickedness; a great number of them being killed during this massacre of their enemies. For the Britons, taking up clubs and stones from the ground, resolutely defended themselves, and did good execution upon the traitors.

Chap. XVI.

Eldol's valiant exploit. Hengist forces Vortigern to yield up the strongest fortifications in Britain, in consideration of his release.

There was present one Eldol, consul of Gloucester, who, at the sight of this treachery, took up a stake which he happened to find, and with that made his defence. Every blow he gave carried death along with it; and by breaking either the head, arms, shoulders, or legs of a great many, he struck no small terror into the traitors, nor did he move from the spot before he had killed with that weapon seventy men. But being no longer able to stand his ground against such numbers, he made his escape from them, and retired to his own city. Many fell on both sides, but the Saxons got the victory; because the Britons, having no suspicion of treachery, came unarmed, and therefore made a weaker defence. After the commission of this detestable villany, the Saxons would not kill Vortigern; but having threatened him with death and bound him, demanded his cities and fortified places in consideration of their

---

[1] The Night of the Long Knives, which is being described in this chapter, actually took place at Stonehenge, which is two miles west of Amesbury and eight miles north of Salisbury. Geoffrey later has Uther and Merlin go to Ireland to bring back a monument called the Giant's Dance and erect it over the graves of the nobles slain during the Night of the Long Knives, which is nonsense—there are indeed graves at Stonehenge, but the site dates from Neolithic times. The present-day Amesbury Abbey, which is near Stonehenge, was not founded until around 979; however, it was built on the ruins of what might have been another monastery.

granting him his life. He, to secure himself, denied them nothing; and when they had made him confirm his grants with an oath, they released him from his chains, and then marched first to London, which they took, as they did afterwards York, Lincoln, and Winchester; wasting the countries through which they passed, and destroying the people, as wolves do sheep when left by their shepherds. When Vortigern saw the desolation which they made, he retired into the parts of Cambria, not knowing what to do against so barbarous a people.

Chap. XVII.
Vortigern, after consultation with magicians, orders a youth to be brought that never had a father.

At last he had recourse to magicians for their advice, and commanded them to tell him what course to take. They advised him to build a very strong tower for his own safety, since he had lost all his other fortified places. Accordingly he made a progress about the country, to find out a convenient situation, and came at last to Mount Erir, where he assembled workmen from several countries, and ordered them to build the tower. The builders, therefore, began to lay the foundation; but whatever they did one day the earth swallowed up the next, so as to leave no appearance of their work. Vortigern being informed of this again consulted with his magicians concerning the cause of it, who told him that he must find out a youth that never had a father, and kill him, and then sprinkle the stones and cement with his blood; for by those means, they said, he would have a firm foundation. Hereupon messengers were despatched away over all the provinces, to inquire out such a man. In their travels they came to a city, called afterwards Kaermerdin, where they saw some young men, playing before the gate, and went up to them; but being weary with their journey, they sat down in the ring, to see if they could meet with what they were in quest of. Towards evening, there happened on a sudden quarrel between two of the young men, whose names were Merlin and Dabutius. In the dispute, Dabutius said to Merlin: "You fool, do you presume to quarrel with me? Is their any equality in our birth? I am descended of royal race, both by my father and mother's side. As for you, nobody knows what you are, for you never had a father." At that word the messengers looked earnestly upon Merlin, and asked the by-standers who he was. They told him, it was not known who was his father; but that his mother was daughter to the king of Dimetia, and that she lived in St. Peter's church among the nuns of that city.

Chap. XVIII.
Vortigern inquires of Merlin's mother concerning her conception of him.

Upon this the messengers hastened to the governor of the city, and ordered him, in the king's name, to send Merlin and his mother to the king. As soon as the governor understood the occasion of their message, he readily obeyed the order, and sent them to Vortigern to complete his design. When they were introduced into the king's presence, he received the mother in a very respectful manner, on account of her noble birth; and began to inquire of her by what man she had conceived. "My sovereign lord," said she, "by the life of your soul and mine, I know nobody that begot him of me. Only this I know, that as I was once with my companions in our chambers, there appeared to me a person in the shape of a most beautiful young man, who often embraced me eagerly in his arms, and kissed me; and when he had stayed a little time, he suddenly vanished out of my sight. But many times after this he would talk with me when I sat alone, without making any visible appearance. When he had a long time haunted me in this manner, he at last lay with me several times in the shape of a man, and left me with child. And I do affirm to you, my sovereign lord, that excepting that young man, I know no body that begot him of me." The king full of admiration at this account, ordered Maugantius to be called, that he might satisfy him as to the possibility of what the woman had related. Maugantius, being introduced, and having the whole matter repeated to him, said to Vortigern: "In the books of our philosophers, and in a great many histories, I have found that several men have had the like original. For, as Apuleius informs us in his book concerning the Demon of Socrates, between the moon and the earth inhabit those spirits, which we will call incubuses. These are of the nature partly of men, and partly of angels, and whenever they please assume human shapes, and lie with women. Perhaps one of them appeared to this woman, and begot that young man of her."

Chap. XIX.
Merlin's speech to the king's magicians, and advice about the building of the tower.

Merlin in the meantime was attentive to all that had passed, and then approached the king, and said to him, "For what reason am I and my mother introduced into your presence?" — "My magicians," answered Vortigern, "advised me to seek out a man that had no father, with whose blood my building is to be sprinkled, in order to make it stand." — "Order your magicians," said Merlin, "to come before me, and I will convict them of a lie." The king was surprised at his words, and presently ordered the magicians to come, and sit down before Merlin, who spoke to them after this manner: "Because you are ignorant what it is that hinders the foundation of the tower, you have recommended the shedding of my blood for cement to it, as if that would presently make it stand. But tell me now, what is there under the foundation? For something there is that will not suffer it to stand." The magicians at this began to be afraid, and made him no answer. Then said Merlin, who was also called Ambrose, "I entreat your majesty would command your workmen to dig into the ground, and you will find a pond which causes the foundations to sink." This accordingly was done, and then presently they found a pond deep under ground, which had made it give way. Merlin after this went again to the magicians, and said, "Tell me ye false sycophants, what is there under the pond." But they were silent. Then said he again to the king, "Command the pond to be drained, and at the bottom you will see two hollow stones, and in them two dragons asleep." The king made no scruple of believing him, since he had found true what he said of the pond, and therefore ordered it to be drained: which done, he found as Merlin had said; and now was possessed with the greatest admiration of him. Nor were the rest that were present less amazed at his wisdom, thinking it to be no less than divine inspiration.

Book VIII.

[*Aurelius gains the kingship and drives the Saxons back with Uther's help. Then Aurelius falls ill, and the Saxons send one of their number in the guise of a monk to poison him. Aurelius dies alone, but a comet ("a star of wonderful magnitude and brightness, darting forth a ray, at the end of which was a globe of fire in form of a dragon") appears the same night, which Merlin interprets as a sign of Aurelius' death and Uther's impending ascension. Uther thus takes the dragon as his badge and earns the name "Pendragon," the Dragon's Head.*]

Chap. XIX.
Uther, falling in love with Igerna, enjoys her by the assistance of Merlin's magical operations.

After this victory Uther repaired to the city of Alclud, where he settled the affairs of that province, and restored peace everywhere. He also made a progress round all the countries of the Scots, and tamed the fierceness of that rebellious people, by such a strict administration of justice, as none of his predecessors had exercised before: so that in his time offenders were everywhere under great terror, since they were sure of being punished without mercy. At last, when he had established peace in the northern provinces, he went to London, and commanded Octa and Eosa to be kept in prison there. The Easter following he ordered all the nobility of the kingdom to meet at that city, in order to celebrate that great festival; in honour of which he designed to wear his crown. The summons was everywhere obeyed, and there was a great concourse from all cities to celebrate the day. So the king observed the festival with great solemnity, as he had designed, and very joyfully entertained his nobility, of whom there was a very great muster, with their wives and daughters, suitably to the magnificence of the banquet prepared for them. And having been received with joy by the king, they also expressed the same in their deportment before him. Among the rest was present Gorlois, duke of Cornwall, with his wife Igerna, the greatest beauty in all Britain. No sooner had the king cast his eyes upon her among the rest of the ladies, than he fell passionately in love with her, and little regarding the rest, made her the subject of all his thoughts. She was the only lady that he continually served with fresh dishes, and to whom he sent golden cups by his confidants; on her he bestowed all his smiles, and to her he addressed all his discourse. The husband, discovering this, fell into a great rage, and retired from the court without taking leave: nor was there any body that could stop him, while he was under fear of losing the chief object of his delight. Uther, therefore, in great wrath commanded him to return back to court, to make him satisfaction for this affront. But Gorlois refused to obey; upon which the king was highly incensed, and swore he would destroy his country, if he did not speedily compound for his offence. Accordingly, without delay, while their anger was hot against each other, the king got together a great army, and marched into Cornwall, the cities and towns whereof he set on fire. But Gorlois durst not engage with him, on account of the inferiority of his numbers; and thought it a wiser course to fortify his towns, till he could get succour from Ireland. And as he was under more concern for his wife than himself, he put her into the town of Tintagel, upon the sea-shore, which he looked upon as a place of great safety.[1] But he himself entered the castle of Dimilioc, to prevent their being both at once involved in the same danger, if any should happen. The king, informed of this, went to the town where Gorlois was, which he besieged, and shut up all the avenues to it. A whole week was now past, when, retaining in mind his love to Igerna, he said to one of his confidants, named Ulfin de Ricaradoch: "My passion for Igerna is such, that I can neither have ease of mind, nor health of body, till I obtain her: and if you cannot assist me with your advice how to accomplish my desire, the inward torments I endure will kill me." — "Who can advise you in this matter," said Ulfin, "when no force will enable us to have access to her in the town of Tintagel? For it is situated upon the sea, and on every side surrounded by it; and there is but one entrance into it, and that through a straight rock, which three men shall be able to defend against the whole power of the kingdom. Notwithstanding, if the prophet Merlin would in earnest set about this attempt, I am of opinion, you might with his advice obtain your wishes." The king readily believed what he was so well inclined to, and ordered Merlin, who was also come to the siege, to be called. Merlin, therefore, being introduced into the king's presence, was commanded to give his advice, how the king might accomplish his desire with respect to Igerna. And he, finding the great anguish of the king, was moved by such excessive love, and said, "To accomplish your desire, you must make use of such arts as have not been heard of in your time. I know how, by the force of my medicines, to give you the exact likeness of Gorlois, so that in all respects you shall seem to be no other than himself. If you will therefore obey my prescriptions, I will metamorphose you into the true semblance of Gorlois, and Ulfin into Jordan of Tintagel, his familiar friend; and I myself, being transformed into another shape, will make the third in the adventure; and in this disguise you may go safely to the town where Igerna is, and have admittance to her." The king complied with the proposal, and acted with great caution in this affair; and when he had committed the care of the siege to his intimate friends, underwent the medical applications of Merlin, by whom he was transformed into the likeness of Gorlois; as was Ulfin also into Jordan, and Merlin himself into Bricel; so that nobody could see any remains now of their former likeness. They then set forward on their way to Tintagel, at which they arrived in the evening twilight, and forthwith signified to the porter, that the consul was come; upon which the gates were opened, and the men let in. For what room could there be for suspicion, when Gorlois himself seemed to be there present? The king therefore stayed

---

[1] The town of Tintagel, on the northern coast of Cornwall, survives to this day. The ruins of Tintagel Castle, as Giles notes, show that it was heavily fortified, so Gorlois' opinion here makes perfect sense.

that night with Igerna, and had the full enjoyment of her, for she was deceived with the false disguise which he had put on, and the artful and amorous discourses wherewith he entertained her. He told her he had left his own place besieged, purely to provide for the safety of her dear self, and the town she was in; so that believing all that he said, she refused him nothing which he desired. The same night therefore she conceived of the most renowned Arthur, whose heroic and wonderful actions have justly rendered his name famous to posterity.

Chap. XX.
Gorlois being killed, Uther marries Igerna.

In the meantime, as soon as the king's absence was discovered at the siege, his army unadvisedly made an assault upon the walls, and provoked the besieged count to a battle; who himself also, acting as inconsiderately as they, sallied forth with his men, thinking with such a small handful to oppose a powerful army; but happened to be killed in the very first brunt of the fight, and had all his men routed. The town also was taken; but all the riches of it were not shared equally among the besiegers, but every one greedily took what he could get, according as fortune or his own strength favoured him. After this bold attempt, came messengers to Igerna, with the news both of the duke's death, and of the event of the siege. But when they saw the king in the likeness of the consul, sitting close by her, they were struck with shame and astonishment at his safe arrival there, whom they had left dead at the siege; for they were wholly ignorant of the miracles which Merlin had wrought with his medicines. The king therefore smiled at the news, and embracing the countess, said to her: "Your own eyes may convince you that I am not dead, but alive. But notwithstanding, the destruction of the town, and the slaughter of my men, is what very much grieves me; so that there is reason to fear the king's coming upon us, and taking us in this place. To prevent which, I will go out to meet him, and make my peace with him, for fear of a worse disaster." Accordingly, as soon as he was out of the town, he went to his army, and having put off the disguise of Gorlois, was now Uther Pendragon again. When he had a full relation made to him how matters had succeeded, he was sorry for the death of Gorlois, but rejoiced that Igerna was now at liberty to marry again. Then he returned to the town of Tintagel, which he took, and in it, what he impatiently wished for, Igerna herself. After this they continued to live together with much affection for each other, and had a son and daughter, whose names were Arthur and Anne.

[*Uther, like Aurelius, starts a campaign against the Saxons but falls ill. This time the Saxons poison a well and kill not only Uther but a number of other Britons before the survivors close up the well.*]

Book IX.
Chap. I.
Arthur succeeds Uther his father in the kingdom of Britain, and besieges Colgrin.

Uther Pendragon being dead, the nobility from several provinces assembled together at Silchester, and proposed to Dubricius, archbishop of Legions,[1] that he should consecrate Arthur, Uther's son, to be their king. For they were now in great straits, because, upon hearing of the king's death, the Saxons had invited over their countrymen from Germany, and, under the command of Colgrin, were attempting to exterminate the whole British race. They had also entirely subdued all that part of the island which extends from the Humber to the sea of Caithness. Dubricius, therefore, grieving for the calamities of his country, in conjunction with the other bishops, set the crown upon Arthur's head. Arthur was then fifteen years old, but a youth of such unparalleled courage and generosity, joined with that sweetness of temper and innate goodness, as gained him universal love. When his coronation was over, he, according to the usual custom, showed his bounty and munificence to the people. And such a number of soldiers flocked to him upon it, that his treasury as not able to answer that vast expense. But such a spirit of generosity, joined with valour, can never long want means to support itself. Arthur, therefore, the better to keep up his munificence, resolved to make use of his courage, and to fall upon the Saxons, that he might enrich his followers with their wealth. To this he was also moved by the justice of the cause, since the entire monarchy of Britain belonged to him by hereditary right. Hereupon assembling the youth under his command, he marched to York, of which, when Colgrin had intelligence, he met him with a very great army, composed of Saxons, Scots, and Picts, by the river Duglas; where a battle happened, with the loss of the greater part of both armies. Notwithstanding, the victory fell to Arthur, who pursued Colgrin to York, and there besieged him. Baldulph, upon the news of his brother's flight, went towards the siege with a body of six thousand men, to his relief; for at the time of the battle he was upon the sea-coast, waiting the arrival of duke Cheldric with succours from Germany. And being now no more than ten miles distant from the city, his purpose was to make a speedy march in the night-time, and fall upon the enemy by way of surprise. But Arthur, having intelligence of his design, sent a detachment of six hundred horse, and three thousand foot, under the command of Cador, duke of Cornwall, to meet him the same night. Cador, therefore, falling into the same road along which the enemy was passing, made a sudden assault upon them, and entirely defeated the Saxons, and put them to flight. Baldulph was excessively grieved at this disappointment in the relief which he intended for his brother, and began to think of some other stratagem to gain access to him; in which if he could but succeed, he thought they might concert measures together for their safety. And since he had no other way for it, he shaved his head and beard, and put on the habit of a jester with a harp, and in this disguise

---

[1] Probably Caerleon, Wales, given Geoffrey's later description of it.

walked up and down in the camp, playing upon his instrument as if he had been a harper. He thus passed unsuspected, and by a little and little went up to the walls of the city, where he was at last discovered by the besieged, who thereupon drew him up with cords, and conducted him to his brother. At this unexpected, though much desired meeting, they spent some time in joyfully embracing each other, and then began to consider various stratagems for their delivery. At last, just as they were considering their case desperate, the ambassadors returned from Germany, and brought with them to Albania a fleet of six hundred sail, laden with brave soldiers, under the command of Cheldric. Upon this news, Arthur was dissuaded by his council from continuing the siege any longer, for fear of hazarding a battle with so powerful and numerous an army.

Chap. II.
Hoel sends fifteen thousand men to Arthur's assistance.

Arthur complied with their advice, and made his retreat to London, where he called an assembly of all the clergy and nobility of the kingdom, to ask their advice, what course to take against the formidable power of the pagans. After some deliberation, it was agreed that ambassadors should be despatched into Armorica, to king Hoel, to represent to him the calamitous state of Britain. Hoel was the son of Arthur's sister by Dubricius, king of the Armorican Britons; so that, upon advice of the disturbances his uncle was threatened with, he ordered his fleet to be got ready, and, having assembled fifteen thousand men, he arrived with the first fair wind at Hamo's Port,[1] and was received with all suitable honour by Arthur, and most affectionately embraced by him.

Chap. III.
Arthur makes the Saxons his tributaries.

After a few days they went to relieve the city Kaerliudcoit, that was besieged by the pagans; which being situated upon a mountain, between two rivers in the province of Lindisia,[2] is called by another name Lindocolinum.[3] As soon as they arrived there with all their forces, they fought with the Saxons, and made a grievous slaughter of them, to the number of six thousand; part of whom were drowned in the rivers, part fell by the hands of the Britons. The rest in a great consternation quitted the siege and fled, but were closely pursued by Arthur, till they came to the wood of Celidon,[4] where they endeavoured to form themselves into a body again, and make a stand. And here they again joined battle with the Britons, and

---

[1] Modern Southampton.

[2] Lindsey

[3] Lincoln (the name *Kaerliudcoit* seems to be Geoffrey's dubious invention)

[4] Caledonian Forest, which at the time covered most of modern Scotland

made a brave defence, whilst the trees that were in the place secured them against the enemies' arrows. Arthur, seeing this, commanded the trees that were in that part of the wood to be cut down, and the trunks to be placed quite round them, so as to hinder their getting out; resolving to keep them pent up here till he could reduce them by famine. He then commanded his troops to besiege the wood, and continued three days in that place. The Saxons, having now no provisions to sustain them, and being just ready to starve with hunger, begged for leave to go out; in consideration whereof they offered to leave all their gold and silver behind them, and return back to Germany with nothing but their empty ships. They promised also that they would pay him tribute from Germany, and leave hostages with him. Arthur, after consultation, about it, granted their petition; allowing them only leave to depart, and retaining all their treasures, as also hostages for payment of the tribute. But as they were under sail on their return home, they repented of their bargain, and tacked about again towards Britain, and went on shore at Totness. No sooner were they landed, than they made an utter devastation of the country as far as the Severn sea, and put all the peasants to the sword. From thence they pursued their furious march to the town of Bath, and laid siege to it. When the king had intelligence of it, he was beyond measure surprised at their proceedings, and immediately gave orders for the execution of the hostages. And desisting from an attempt which he had entered upon to reduce the Scots and Picts, he marched with the utmost expedition to raise the siege; but laboured under very great difficulties, because he had left his nephew Hoel sick at Alclud. At length, having entered the province of Somerset, and beheld how the siege was carried on, he addressed himself to his followers in these words: "Since these impious and detestable Saxons have disdained to keep faith with me, I, to keep faith with God, will endeavour to revenge the blood of my countrymen this day upon them. To arms, soldiers, to arms, and courageously fall upon the perfidious wretches, over whom we shall, with Christ assisting us, undoubtedly obtain the victory."

Chap. IV.

Dubricius's speech against the treacherous Saxons. Arthur with his own hand kills four hundred and seventy Saxons in one battle. Colgrin and Baldulph are killed in the same.

When he had done speaking, St. Dubricius, archbishop of Legions, going to the top of a hill, cried out with a loud voice, "You that have the honour to profess the Christian faith, keep fixed in your minds the love which you owe to your country and fellow subjects, whose sufferings by the treachery of the pagans will be an everlasting reproach to you, if you do not courageously defend them. It is your country which you fight for, and for which you should, when required, voluntarily suffer death; for that itself is victory and the curse of the soul. For he that shall die for his brethren, offers himself a living sacrifice to God, and has Christ for his example, who condescended to lay down his life for his brethren. If therefore any of you shall be killed in this war, that death itself, which is suffered in so glorious a cause, shall be to him for penance and absolution of all his sins." At these words, all of them, encouraged with the benediction of the holy prelate, instantly armed themselves, and prepared to obey his orders.[1] Also Arthur himself, having put on a coat of mail suitable to the grandeur of so powerful a king, placed a golden helmet upon his head, on which was engraven the figure of a dragon; and on his shoulders his shield called Priwen; upon which the picture of the blessed Mary, mother of God, was painted, in order to put him frequently in mind of her. Then girding on his Caliburn, which was an excellent sword made in the isle of Avallon, he graced his right hand with his lance, named Ron, which was hard, broad, and fit for slaughter. After this, having placed his men in order, he boldly attacked the Saxons, who were drawn out in the shape of a wedge, as their manner was. And they, notwithstanding that the Britons fought with great eagerness, made a noble defence all that day; but at length, towards sunsetting, climbed up the next mountain, which served them for a camp: for they desired no larger extent of ground, since they confided very much in their numbers. The next morning Arthur, with his army, went up the mountain, but lost many of his men in the ascent, by the advantage which the Saxons had in their station on the top, from whence they could pour down upon him with much greater speed, than he was able to advance against them. Notwithstanding, after a very hard struggle, the Britons gained the summit of the hill, and quickly came to a close engagement with the enemy, who again gave them a warm reception, and made a vigorous defence. In this manner was a great part of that day also spent; whereupon Arthur, provoked to see the little advantage he had yet gained, and that victory still continued in suspense, drew out his Caliburn, and, calling upon the name of the blessed Virgin, rushed forward with great fury into the thickest of the enemy's ranks; of whom (such was the merit of his prayers) not one escaped alive that felt the fury of his sword; neither did he give over the fury of his assault until he had, with his Caliburn alone, killed four hundred and seventy men. The Britons, seeing this, followed their leader in great multitudes, and made slaughter on all sides; so that Colgrin, and Baldulph his brother, and many thousands more, fell before them. But Cheldric, in this imminent danger of his men, betook himself to flight.

Chap. VIII.
Arthur restores York to its ancient beauty, especially as to its churches.

The king, after his general pardon granted to the Scots, went to York to celebrate the feast of Christ's nativity, which was now at hand. On entering the city, he beheld with grief the desolation of the churches; for upon the expulsion of the holy Archbishop Sanxo, and of all the clergy there, the temples which were half burned down, had no longer divine service

---

[1] What follows is an account of the Battle of Badon Hill, one of the few battles connected with Arthur from the beginning. Gildas, writing around AD 540, states that it took place forty-four years earlier, which would put it—and the historical Arthur, assuming he did exist—within living memory for Gildas' immediate audience.

performed in them: so much had the impious rage of the pagans prevailed. After this, in an assembly of the clergy and people, he appointed Pyramus his chaplain metropolitan of that see. The churches that lay level with the ground, be rebuilt, and (which was their chief ornament) saw them filled with assemblies of devout persons of both sexes. Also the nobility that were driven out by the disturbances of the Saxons, he restored to their country.

Chap. XII.

Arthur summons a great many kings, princes, archbishops, &c. to a solemn assembly at the City of Legions.

Upon the approach of the feast of Pentecost, Arthur, the better to demonstrate his joy after such triumphant success, and for the more solemn observation of that festival, and reconciling the minds of the princes that were now subject to him, resolved, during that season, to hold a magnificent court, to place the crown upon his head, and to invite all the kings and dukes under his subjection, to the solemnity. And when he had communicated his design to his familiar friends, he pitched upon the City of Legions as a proper place for his purpose. For besides its great wealth above the other cities, its situation, which was in Glamorganshire upon the river Uske, near the Severn sea, was most pleasant, and fit for so great a solemnity. For on one side it was washed by that noble river, so that the kings and princes from the countries beyond the seas might have the convenience of sailing up to it. On the other side, the beauty of the meadows and groves, and magnificence of the royal palaces with lofty gilded roofs that adorned it, made it even rival the grandeur of Rome. It was also famous for two churches; whereof one was built in honour of the martyr Julius, and adorned with a choir of virgins, who had devoted themselves wholly to the service of God; but the other, which was founded in memory of St. Aaron, his companion, and maintained a convent of canons, was the third metropolitan church of Britain. Besides, there was a college of two hundred philosophers, who, being learned in astronomy and the other arts, were diligent in observing the courses of the stars, and gave Arthur true predictions of the events that would happen at that time. In this place, therefore, which afforded such delights, were preparations made for the ensuing festival. Ambassadors were then sent into several kingdoms, to invite to court the princes both of Gaul and all the adjacent islands. [. . .] Besides these, there remained no prince of any consideration on this side of Spain, who came not upon this invitation. And no wonder, when Arthur's munificence, which was celebrated over the whole world, made him beloved by all people.

Chap. XV
A letter from Lucius Tiberius, general of the Romans, to Arthur being read, they consult about an answer to it.

But St. Dubricius, from a pious desire of leading a hermit's life, made a voluntary resignation of his archiepiscopal dignity; and in his room was consecrated David, the king's uncle, whose life was a perfect example of that goodness which by his doctrine he taught. In place of St. Samson, archbishop of Dole, was appointed, with the consent of Hoel, king of the Armorican Britons, Chelianus [Kilian] a priest of Llandaff, a person highly recommended for his good life and character. The Bishopric of Silchester was conferred upon Mauganius, that of Winchester upon Diwanius, and that of Alclud upon Eledanius. While he was disposing of these preferments upon them, it happened that twelve men of an advanced age, and venerable aspect, and bearing olive branches in their right hands, for a token that they were come upon an embassy, appeared before the king, moving towards him with a slow pace, and speaking with a soft voice; and after their compliments paid, presented him with a letter from Lucius Tiberius,[1] in these words:—

"Lucius, procurator of the commonwealth, to Arthur, king of Britain, according to his desert. The insolence of your tyranny is what fills me with the highest admiration, and the injuries you have done to Rome still increase my wonder. But it is provoking to reflect, that you are grown so much above yourself, as wilfully to avoid seeing this: nor do you consider what it is to have offended by unjust deeds a senate, to whom you cannot be ignorant the whole world owes vassalage. For the tribute of Britain, which the senate had enjoined you to pay, and which used to be paid to the Roman emperors successively from the time of Julius Caesar, you have had the presumption to withhold, in contempt of their imperial authority. You have seized upon the province of the Allobroges, and all the islands of the ocean, whose kings, while the Roman power prevailed in those parts, paid tribute to our ancestors. And because the senate have decreed to demand justice of you for such repeated injuries, I command you to appear at Rome before the middle of August the next year, there to make satisfaction to your masters, and undergo such sentence as they shall in justice pass upon you. Which if you refuse to do, I shall come to you, and endeavour to recover with my sword, what you in your madness have robbed us of."

As soon as the letter was read in the presence of the kings and consuls, Arthur withdrew with them into the Giant's Tower, which was at the entrance of the palace, to think what answer was fit to be returned to such an insolent message. As they were going up the stairs, Cador, duke of Cornwall, who was a man of a merry disposition, said to the king in a jocose manner: "I have been till now under fear, lest the easy life which the Britons lead, by

[1] There is *zero* historical precedent for this part of the story. Scholars have long debated whether Geoffrey shoehorned in an unrelated legend, as he did with most of the material about Merlin, or whether he made it up out of whole cloth.

enjoying a long peace, might make them cowards, and extinguish the fame of their gallantry, by which they have raised their name above all other nations. For where the exercise of arms is wanting, and the pleasures of women, dice, and other diversions take place, no doubt, what remains of virtue, honour, courage, and thirst of praise, will be tainted with the rust of idleness. For now almost five years have passed, since we have been abandoned to these delights, and have had no exercise of war. Therefore, to deliver us from sloth, God has stirred up this spirit of the Romans, to restore our military virtues to their ancient state." [...]

Chap. XIX.
They unanimously agree upon a war with the Romans.

To the same effect spoke all the rest, and promised each of them their full quota of forces; so that besides those promised by the duke of Armorica, the number of men from the island of Britain alone was sixty thousand, all completely armed. But the kings of the other islands, as they had not been accustomed to any cavalry, promised their quota of infantry; and, from the six provincial islands, viz. Ireland, Iceland, Gothland, the Orkneys, Norway, and Dacia, were reckoned a hundred and twenty thousand. From the duchies of Gaul, that is, of the Ruteni, the Portunians, the Estrusians, the Cenomanni, the Andegavians, and Pictavians, were eighty thousand. From the twelve consulships of those who came along with Guerinus Carnotensis, twelve hundred. All together made up a hundred and eighty-three thousand two hundred, besides foot which did not easily fall under number.

Chap. XX.
Arthur prepares for a war, and refuses to pay tribute to the Romans.

King Arthur, seeing all unanimously ready for his service, ordered them to return back to their countries with speed, and get ready the forces which they had promised, and to hasten to the general rendezvous upon the kalends of August, at the mouth of the river Barba, that from thence they might advance with them to the borders of the Allobroges, to meet the Romans. Then he sent word to the emperors by their ambassadors; that as to paying them tribute, he would in no wise obey their commands; and that the journey he was about to make to Rome, was not to stand the award of their sentence, but to demand of them what they had judicially decreed to demand of him. With this answer the ambassadors departed; and at the same time also departed all the kings and noblemen, to perform with all expedition the orders that had been given them.

Book X.
Chap. I.
Lucius Tiberius calls together the eastern kings against the Britons.

Lucius Tiberius, on receiving this answer, by order of the senate published a decree, for the eastern kings to come with their forces, and assist in the conquest of Britain. In obedience to which there came in a very short time, Epistrophius, king of the Grecians; Mustensar, king of the Africans; Alifantinam, king of Spain; Hirtacius, king of the Parthians; Boccus, of the Medes; Sertorius, of Libya; Teucer, king of Phrygia; Serses, king of the Itureans; Pandrasus, king of Egypt; Micipsa, king of Babylon; Polytetes, duke of Bithynia; Teucer, duke of Phrygia; Evander, of Syria; æthion, of Boeotia; Hippolytus, of Crete, with the generals and nobility under them. Of the senatorian order also came, Lucius Catellus, Marius Lepidus, Caius Metellus Cotta, Quintus Milvius Catulus, Quintas Carutius, and as many others as made up the number of forty thousand one hundred and sixty.

Chap. II.
Arthur commits to his nephew Modred the government of Britain. His dream at Hamo's Port.

After the necessary dispositions were made, upon the kalends of August, they began their march towards Britain, which when Arthur had intelligence of, he committed the government of the kingdom to his nephew Modred, and queen Guanhumara, and marched with his army to Hamo's Port, where the wind stood fair for him. But while he, surrounded with all his numerous fleet, was sailing joyfully with a brisk gale, it happened that about midnight he fell into a very sound sleep, and in a dream saw a bear flying in the air, at the noise of which all the shores trembled; also a terrible dragon flying from the west, which enlightened the country with the brightness of its eyes. When these two met, they began a dreadful fight; but the dragon with its fiery breath burned the bear which often assaulted him, and threw him down scorched to the ground. Arthur upon this awaking, related his dream to those that stood about him, who took upon them to interpret it, and told him that the dragon signified himself, but the bear, some giant that should encounter with him; and that the fight portended the duel that would be between them, and the dragon's victory the same that would happen to himself. But Arthur conjectured it portended something else, and that the vision was applicable to himself and the emperor. As soon as the morning after this night's sail appeared, they found themselves arrived at the mouth of the river Barba. And there they pitched their tents, to wait the arrival of the kings of the islands and the generals of the other provinces.

Chap. IX.

A battle between Arthur and Lucius Tiberius.

And now the Britons and the Romans stood presenting their arms at one another; when forthwith at the sound of the trumpets, the company that was headed by the king of Spain and Lucius Catellus, boldly rushed forward against that which the king of Scotland and duke of Cornwall led, but were not able to make the least breach in their firm ranks. So that while these stood their ground, up came Guerinus and Boso with a body of horse upon their full speed, broke through the party that began the assault, and met with another which the king of the Parthians was leading up against Aschillius, king of Dacia. After this first onset, there followed a general engagement of both armies with great violence, and several breaches were made on each side. The shouts, the slaughter, the quantity of blood spilled, and the agonies of the dying, made a dreadful scene of horror. At first, the Britons sustained a great loss, by having Bedver the butler killed, and Caius the sewer mortally wounded. For, as Bedver met Boccus, king of the Medes, he fell dead by a stab of his lance amidst the enemies' troops. And Caius, in endeavouring to revenge his death, was surrounded by the Median troops, and there received a mortal wound; yet as a brave soldier he opened himself a way with the wing which he led, killed and dispersed the Medes, and would have made a safe retreat with all his men, had he not met the king of Libya with the forces under him, who put his whole company into disorder; yet not so great, but that he was still able to get off with a few, and flee with Bedver's corps to the golden dragon. The Neustrians grievously lamented at the sight of their leader's mangled body; and so did the Andegavians, when they beheld their consul wounded. But there was now no room for complaints, for the furious and bloody shocks of both armies made it necessary to provide for their own defence. Therefore Hirelgas, the nephew of Bedver, being extremely enraged at his death, called up to him three hundred men, and like a wild boar amongst a pack of dogs, broke through the enemies' ranks with his horse, making towards the place where he had seen the standard of the king of the Medes; little regarding what might befall him, if he could but revenge the loss of his uncle. At length he reached the place, killed the king, brought off his body to his companions, and laid it by that of his uncle, where he mangled it in the same manner. Then calling with a loud voice to his countrymen, he animated their troops, and vehemently pressed them to exert themselves to the utmost, now that their spirits were raised, and the enemy disheartened; and especially as they had the advantage of them in being placed in better order, and so might the more grievously annoy them. Encouraged with this exhortation, they began a general assault upon the enemy, which was attended with a terrible slaughter on both sides. For on the part of the Romans, besides many others, fell Alifantinam, king of Spain, Micipsa of Babylon, as also Quintus Milvius and Marius Lepidus, senators. On the part of the Britons, Holdin, king of the Ruteni, Leodegarius of Bolonia, and three consuls of Britain, Cursalem of Caicester, Galluc of Salisbury, and Urbgennius of Bath. So that the troops which they commanded, being extremely weakened, retreated till they came to the army of the Armorican Britons, commanded by Hoel and Walgan. But these, being inflamed at the retreat of their friends, encouraged them to stand their ground, and caused them with the help of their own forces to put their pursuers to flight. While they continued this pursuit, they beat down and killed several of them, and gave them no respite, till they came to the general's troop; who, seeing the distress of his companions, hastened to their assistance.

Chap. X.
Hoel and Walgan signalize their valour in the fight.

And now in this latter encounter the Britons were worsted, with the loss of Kimarcoc, consul of Trigeria, and two thousand with him; besides three famous noblemen, Richomarcus, Bloccovius, and Jagivius of Bodloan, who, had they but enjoyed the dignity of princes, would have been celebrated for their valour through all succeeding ages. For, during this assault which they made in conjunction with Hoel and Walgan, there was not an enemy within their reach that could escape the fury of their sword or lance. But upon their falling in among Lucius's party, they were surrounded by them, and suffered the same fate with the consul and the other men. The loss of these men made those matchless heroes, Hoel and Walgan, much more eager to assault the general's ranks, and to try on all sides where to make the greatest impression. But Walgan, whose valour was never to be foiled, endeavoured to gain access to Lucius himself, that he might encounter him, and with this view beat down and killed all that stood in his way. And Hoel, not inferior to him, did no less service in another part, by spiriting up his men, and giving and receiving blows among the enemy with the same undaunted courage. It was hard to determine, which of them was the stoutest soldier.

Chap. XI.
Lucius Tiberius being killed, the Britons obtain the victory.

But Walgan, by forcing his way through the enemy's troops, as we said before, found at last (what he had wished for) access to the general, and immediately encountered him. Lucius, being then in the flower of his youth, and a person of great courage and vigour, desired nothing more than to engage with such a one as might put his strength to its full trial. Putting himself, therefore, into a posture of defence, he received Walgan with joy, and was not a little proud to try his courage with one of whom he had heard such great things. The fight continued between them a long time, with great force of blows, and no less dexterity in warding them off, each being resolved upon the other's destruction. During this sharp conflict between them, the Romans, on a sudden, recovering their courage, made an assault upon the Armoricans, and having relieved their general, repulsed Hoel and Walgan, with their troops, till they found themselves unawares met by Arthur and the forces under him. For he, hearing of the slaughter that was a little before made of his men, had speedily advanced with his legion, and drawing out his Caliburn, spoke to them, with a loud voice, after this manner: "What are you doing, soldiers? Will you suffer these effeminate wretches to escape? Let not one of them get off alive. Remember the force of your arms, that have reduced thirty kingdoms under my subjection. Remember your ancestors, whom the Romans, when at the height of their power, made tributary. Remember your liberties, which these pitiful fellows, that are much your inferiors, attempt to deprive you of. Let none of them escape alive. What are you doing?" With these expostulations, he rushed upon the enemy, made terrible havoc among them, and not a man did he meet but at one blow he laid either him or his horse dead upon the ground. They, therefore, in astonishment fled from him, as a flock of sheep from a fierce lion, whom raging hunger provokes to devour whatever happens to come near him. Their arms were no manner of protection to them against the force with which this valiant prince wielded his Caliburn. Two kings, Sertorius of Libya, and Polytetes of Bithynia, unfortunately felt its fury, and had their heads cut off by it. The Britons, when they saw the king performing such wonders, took courage again. With one consent they assaulted the Romans, kept close together in their ranks, and while they assailed the foot in one part, endeavoured to beat down and pierce through the horse in another. Notwithstanding, the Romans made a brave defence, and at the instigation of Lucius laboured to pay back their slaughter upon the Britons. The eagerness and force that were now shown on both sides were as great as if it was the beginning of the battle. Arthur continued to do great execution with his own hand, and encouraged the Britons to maintain the fight; as Lucius Tiberius did the Romans, and made them perform many memorable exploits. He himself, in the meantime, was very active in going from place to place, and suffered none to escape with life that happened to come within the reach of his sword or lance. The slaughter that was now made on both sides was very dreadful, and the turns of fortune various, sometimes the Britons prevailing, sometimes the Romans. At last, while this sharp dispute continued, Morvid, consul of Gloucester, with his legion, which, as we said before, was placed between the hills, came up with speed upon the rear of the enemy, and to their great surprise assaulted, broke through, and dispersed them with great slaughter. This last and decisive blow proved fatal to many thousands of Romans, and even to the general Lucius himself, who was killed among the crowds with a lance by an unknown hand. But the Britons, by long maintaining the fight, at last with great difficulty gained the victory.

Chap. XIII.
The bodies of the slain are decently buried, each in their respective countries.

Arthur, after he had completed his victory, gave orders for separating the bodies of his nobility from those of the enemy, and preparing a pompous funeral for them; and that, when ready, they should be carried to the abbeys of their repective countries, there to be honourably buried. [. . .] But at the beginning of the following summer, as he was on his march towards Rome, and was beginning to pass the Alps, he had news brought him that his nephew Modred, to whose care he had entrusted Britain, had by tyrannical and treasonable practices set the crown upon his own head; and that queen Guanhumara, in violation of her first marriage, had wickedly married him.

Book XI.
Chap. I.
Modred makes a great slaughter of Arthur's men, but is beaten, and flees to Winchester.

Of the matter now to be treated of, most noble consul, Geoffrey of Monmouth shall be silent; but will, nevertheless, though in a mean style, briefly relate what he found in the British book above mentioned, and heard from that most learned historian, Walter, archdeacon of Oxford, concerning the wars which this renowned king, upon his return to Britain after this victory, waged against his nephew. As soon, therefore, as the report, of this flagrant wickedness reached him, he immediately desisted from his enterprise against Leo, king of the Romans; and having sent away Hoel, duke of the Armoricans, with the army of Gaul, to restore peace in those parts, returned back with speed to Britain, attended only by the kings of the islands, and their armies. But the wicked traitor, Modred, had sent Cheldric, the Saxon leader, into Germany, there to raise all the forces he could find, and return with all speed: and in consideration of this service, had promised him all that part of the island, which reaches from the Humber to Scotland, and whatever Hengist and Horsa had possessed of Kent in the time of Vortigern. So that he, in obedience to his commands, had arrived with eight hundred ships filled with pagan soldiers, and had entered into covenant to obey the traitor as his sovereign; who had also drawn to his assistance the Scots, Picts, Irish, and all others whom he knew to be enemies to his uncle. His whole army, taking pagans and Christians together, amounted to eighty thousand men; with the help of whom he met Arthur just after his landing at the port of Rutupi, and joining battle with him, made a very great slaughter of his men. For the same day fell Augusel, king of Albania, and Walgan, the king's nephew, with innumerable others. Augusel was succeeded in his kingdom by Eventus, his brother Urian's son, who afterwards performed many famous exploits in those wars. After they had at last, with much difficulty, got ashore, they paid back the slaughter, and put Modred and his army to flight. For, by long practice in war, they had learned an excellent way of ordering their forces; which was so managed, that while their foot were employed either in an assault or upon the defensive, the horse would come in at full speed obliquely, break through the enemy's ranks, and so force them to flee. Nevertheless, this perjured usurper got his forces together again, and the night following entered Winchester. As soon as queen Guanhumara heard this, she immediately, despairing of success, fled from York to the City of Legions, where she resolved to lead a chaste life among the nuns in the church of Julius the Martyr, and entered herself one of their order.

Chap. II.

Modred, after being twice besieged and routed, is killed. Arthur, being wounded, gives up the kingdom to Constantine.

But Arthur, whose anger was now much more inflamed, upon the loss of so many hundreds of his fellow soldiers, after he had buried his slain, went on the third day to the city, and there besieged the traitor, who, notwithstanding, was unwilling to desist from his enterprise, but used all methods to encourage his adherents, and marching out with his troops prepared to fight his uncle. In the battle that followed hereupon, great numbers lost their lives on both sides; but at last Modred's army suffered most, so that he was forced to quit the field shamefully. From hence he made a precipitate flight, and, without taking any care for the burial of his slain, marched in haste towards Cornwall. Arthur, being inwardly grieved that he should so often escape, forthwith pursued him into that country as far as the river Cambula, where the other was expecting his coming. And Modred, as he was the boldest of men, and always the quickest at making an attack, immediately placed his troops in order, resolving either to conquer or to die, rather than continue his flight any longer. He had yet remaining with him sixty thousand men, out of whom he composed three bodies, which contained each of them six thousand six hundred and sixty-six men: but all the rest he joined in one body; and having assigned to each of the other parties their leaders, he took the command of this upon himself. After he had made this disposition of his forces, he endeavoured to animate them, and promised them the estates of their enemies if they came off with victory. Arthur, on the other side, also marshalled his army, which he divided into nine square companies, with a right and left wing; and having appointed to each of them their commanders, exhorted them to make a total rout of those robbers and perjured villains, who, being brought over into the island from foreign countries at the instance of the arch-traitor, were attempting to rob them of all their honours. He likewise told them that a mixed army composed of barbarous people of so many different countries, and who were all raw soldiers and inexperienced in war, would never be able to stand against such brave veteran troops as they were, provided they did their duty. After this encouragement given by each general to his fellow soldiers, the battle on a sudden began with great fury; wherein it would be both grievous and tedious to relate the slaughter, the cruel havoc, and the excess of fury that was to be seen on both sides. In this manner they spent a good part of the day, till Arthur at last made a push with his company, consisting of six thousand six hundred and sixty-six men, against that in which he knew Modred was; and having opened a way with their swords, they pierced quite through it, and made a grievous slaughter. For in this assault fell the wicked traitor himself, and many thousands with him. But notwithstanding the loss of him, the rest did not flee, but running together from all parts of the field maintained their ground with undaunted courage. The fight now grew more furious than ever, and proved fatal to almost all the commanders and their forces. For on Modred's side fell Cheldric, Elasius, Egbrict, and Bunignus, Saxons; Gillapatric, Gillamor, Gistafel, and Gillarius, Irish;

also the Scots and Picts, with almost all their leaders: on Arthur's side Olbrict, king of Norway; Aschillus, king of Dacia; Cador Limenic Cassibellaun, with many thousands of others, as well Britons as foreigners, that he had brought with him. And even the renowned king Arthur himself was mortally wounded; and being carried thence to the isle of Avallon to be cured of his wounds, he gave up the crown of Britain to his kinsman Constantine, the son of Cador, duke of Cornwall, in the five hundred and forty-second year of our Lord's incarnation.

❧✦☙

Laȝamon
from Brut
Translated by Eugene Mason

Arthur marched to Cornwall, with an immense army. Modred heard that, and advanced against him with innumerable folk—there were many fated! Upon the Tambre they came together; the place hight[1] Camelford, evermore lasted the same word. And at Camelford was assembled sixty thousand men, and more thousands thereto; Modred was their chief. Then thitherward gan[2] ride Arthur the mighty, with innumerable folk—fated though it were! Upon the Tambre they encountered together; elevated their standards; advanced together; drew their long swords, and smote on the helms; fire out sprang; spears splintered; shields gan shiver; shafts brake in pieces! There fought all together innumerable folk! Tambre was in flood with blood to excess; there might no man in the fight know any warrior, nor who did worse, nor who did better, so was the conflict mingled! For each slew downright, were he swain, were he knight. There was Modred slain, and deprived of life-day, and all his knights slain in the fight. There were slain all the brave, Arthur's warriors, high and low, and all the Britons of Arthur's board, and all his dependents, of many kingdoms. And Arthur himself wounded with a broad slaughter-spear; fifteen dreadful wounds he had; in the least one might thrust two gloves! Then was there no more remained in the fight, of two hundred thousand men that there lay hewed in pieces,[3] except Arthur the king alone, and two of his knights.

Arthur was wounded wondrously much. There came to him a lad, who was of his kindred; he was Cador's son, the Earl of Cornwall; Constantine the lad hight, he was dear to the king. Arthur looked on him, where he lay on the ground, and said these words, with

---

[1] was called

[2] began (to)

[3] For scale: roughly 180,000 soldiers took part in the Battle of Gettysburg, the largest and bloodiest battle of the American Civil War. The battle resulted in a combined estimate of at most 51,000 casualties—and that number includes wounded, missing, captured, and dead. (Laȝamon is clearly exaggerating here.)

sorrowful heart: "Constantine, thou art welcome; thou wert Cador's son. I give thee here my kingdom, and defend thou my Britons ever in thy life, and maintain them all the laws that have stood in my days, and all the good laws that in Uther's days stood. And I will fare to Avalun, to the fairest of all maidens, to Argante the queen, an elf most fair, and she shall make my wounds all sound; make me all whole with healing draughts. And afterwards I will come again to my kingdom, and dwell with the Britons with mickle[1] joy."

Even with the words there approached from the sea that was a short boat, floating with the waves; and two women therein, wondrously formed; and they took Arthur anon, and bare him quickly, and laid him softly down, and forth they gan depart.

Then was it accomplished that Merlin whilom[2] said, that mickle care should be of[3] Arthur's departure. The Britons believe yet that he is alive, and dwelleth in Avalun with the fairest of all elves; and the Britons ever yet expect when Arthur shall return. Was never the man born, of ever any lady chosen, that knoweth of the sooth, to say more of Arthur. But whilom was a sage hight Merlin; he said with words—his sayings were sooth—that an Arthur should yet come to help the English.

❧❧

Marie de France
Sir Launfal
Translated by Jessie L. Weston

This is the adventure of the rich and noble knight Sir Launfal, even as the Breton lay recounts it.

The valiant and courteous King, Arthur, was sojourning at Carduel, because of the Picts and the Scots who had greatly destroyed the land, for they were in the kingdom of Logres[4] and often wrought mischief therein.

In Carduel, at Pentecost, the King held his summer court, and gave rich gifts to the counts, the barons, and all the knights of the Round Table. Never before in all the world were such gifts given. Honours and lands he shared forth to all, save to one alone, of those who served him.

This was Sir Launfal; of him and his the King thought not; and yet all men loved him, for worthy he was, free of hand, very valiant, and fair to look upon. Had any ill happened to this knight, his fellows would have been but ill-pleased.

---

[1] much
[2] formerly
[3] caused by
[4] Britain/England

Launfal was son to a king of high descent, but his heritage was far hence in a distant land; he was of the household of King Arthur, but all his money was spent, for the King gave him nothing, and nothing would Launfal ask from him. But now Sir Launfal was much perplexed, very sorrowful, and heavy of heart. Nor need ye wonder at it, for one who is a stranger and without counsel is but sorrowful in a foreign land when he knows not where to seek for aid.

This knight of whom I tell ye, who had served the King so well, one day mounted his horse and rode forth for diversion. He left the city behind him, and came all alone into a fair meadow through which ran a swift water. As he rode downwards to the stream, his horse shivered beneath him. Then the knight dismounted, and loosening the girth let the steed go free to feed at its will on the grass of the meadow. Then folding his mantle beneath his head he laid himself down; but his thoughts were troubled by his ill fortune, and as he lay on the grass he knew nothing that might pleasure him.

Suddenly, as he looked downward towards the bank of the river, he saw two maidens coming towards him; never before had he seen maidens so fair. They were richly clad in robes of purple grey, and their faces were wondrous beautiful. The elder bore in her hands a basin of gold finely wrought (indeed it is but truth I tell you); the other held a snow-white towel.

They came straight to where the knight was lying, and Launfal, who was well taught in courteous ways, sprang to his feet in their presence. Then they saluted him, and delivered to him their message. "Sir Launfal," said the elder, "my lady, who is most fair and courteous, has sent us to you, for she wills that you shall return with us. See, her pavilion is near at hand, we will lead you thither in all safety."

Then Launfal went with them, taking no thought for his steed, which was grazing beside him in the meadow. The maidens led him to the tent, rich it was and well placed. Not even the Queen Semiramis[1] in the days of her greatest wealth and power and wisdom, nor the Emperor Octavian, could have equalled from their treasures the drapery alone.

Above the tent was an eagle of gold, its worth I know not how to tell you; neither can I tell that of the silken cords and shining lances which upheld the tent; there is no king under heaven who could purchase its equal, let him offer what he would for it.

Within this pavilion was a maiden, of beauty surpassing even that of the lily and the new-blown rose, when they flower in the fair summer-tide. She lay upon a rich couch, the covering of which was worth the price of a castle, her fair and gracious body clothed only in a simple vest. Her costly mantle of white ermine, covered with purple of Alexandria,[2] had she cast from her for the heat, and face and throat and neck were whiter than flower of the

---

[1] Legendary queen of Babylon, probably based on the real Queen Sammu-Ramat of Assyria, who ruled as regent for her son in the years 811-806 BC.

[2] Ermine is a type of weasel with a white winter coat distinguished by a black tip on the tail. Ermine fur was used only for the garments of high officials and nobility because of its cost. Purple, too, was an extremely expensive dye, especially used on fabric—probably silk here—imported from Egypt.

thorn. Then the maiden called the knight to her, and he came near and seated himself beside the couch.

"Launfal," she said, "fair friend, for you have I come forth from my own land; even from Lains have I come to seek you. If you be of very truth valiant and courteous then neither emperor, count nor king have known such joy as shall be yours, for I love you above all things."

Then Love smote him swiftly, and seized and kindled his heart, and he answered:

"Fair lady, if it so please you, and such joy may be my portion that you deign to love me, then be the thing folly or wisdom you can command nothing that I will not do to the utmost of my power. All your wishes will I fulfil, for you I will renounce my folk and my land, nor will I ever ask to leave you, if that be what you most desire of me."

When the maiden heard him whom she could love well speak thus she granted him all her heart and her love.

And now was Launfal in the way to good fortune. A gift the lady bestowed upon him: there should be nothing so costly but that it might be his if he so willed it. Let him give or spend as freely as he would he should always have enough for his need. Happy indeed was Launfal, for the more largely he spent the more gold and silver should he have.

"Friend," said the maiden, "of one thing must I now warn you, nay more, I command and pray you, reveal this your adventure to no man. The reason will I tell you; if this our love be known you would lose me for ever, never again might you look upon me, never again embrace me."

Then he answered that he would keep faithfully all that she should command him.

Thus were the two together even till the vesper-tide,[1] and if his lady would have consented fain would Launfal have remained longer.

"Friend," said she, "rise up, no longer may you linger here, you must go and I must remain. But one thing will I tell you, when you wish to speak with me (and I would that may ever be when a knight may meet his lady without shame and without reproach) I shall be ever there at your will, but no man save you shall see me, or hear me speak."

When the knight heard that he was joyful, and he kissed his lady and rose up, and the maidens who had led him to the tent brought him new and rich garments, and when he was clad in them there was no fairer knight under heaven. Then they brought him water for his hands, and a towel whereon to dry them, and laid food before him, and he supped with his lady. Courteously were they served, and great was the joy of Sir Launfal, for ever and again his love kissed him and he embraced her tenderly.

When they were risen from supper his horse was brought to him, saddled and bridled; right well had they tended it. Then the knight took leave of his lady, and mounted and rode towards the city; but often he looked behind him, for he marvelled greatly at all that had

---

[1] Around dusk.

befallen him, and he rode ever thinking of his adventure, amazed and half-doubting, for he scarcely knew what the end thereof should be.

Then he entered his hostel and found all his men well clad, and he held great state but knew not whence the money came to him. In all the city there was no knight that had need of lodging but Launfal made him come unto him and gave him rich service. Launfal gave costly gifts; Launfal ransomed prisoners; Launfal clothed the minstrels; Launfal lavished wealth and honours; there was neither friend nor stranger to whom he gave not gifts. Great were his joy and gladness, for whether by day or by night he might full often look upon his lady, and all things were at his commandment.

Now in the self-same year, after the feast of St. John, thirty of the knights went forth to disport themselves in a meadow, below the tower wherein the queen had her lodging. With them went Sir Gawain and his cousin, the gallant Iwein. Then said Gawain, the fair and courteous, who was loved of all: "Pardieu,[1] my lords, we do ill in that we have not brought with us our companion, Sir Launfal, who is so free-handed and courteous, and son to so rich a king." Then they turned back to his hostelry, and by their prayers persuaded Launfal to come with them.

It so chanced that the queen leant forth from an open casement, and three of her chosen ladies with her. She looked upon Sir Launfal and knew him. Then she called one of her ladies, and bade her command the fairest and most graceful of her maidens to make ready and come forth with her to the meadow. Thirty or more she took with her, and descended the stairway of the tower. The knights were joyful at their coming, and hastened to meet them, and took them by the hand with all courtesy. But Sir Launfal went apart from the others, for the time seemed long to him ere he could see his lady, kiss her, and hold her in his arms. All other joys were but small to him if he had not that one delight of his heart.

When the queen saw him alone she went straight towards him, and seated herself beside him; then, calling him by his name, she opened her heart to him.

"Launfal," she said, "greatly have I honoured, cherished and loved you. All my love is yours if you will have it, and if I thus grant you my favour, then ought you to be joyful indeed."

"Lady," said the knight, "let me be; I have small desire of your love. Long have I served King Arthur; I will not now deny my faith. Neither for you nor for your love will I betray my liege lord."

The queen was angry, and in her wrath she spoke scoffingly. "They but spake the truth," she said, "who told me that you knew not how to love. Coward and traitor, false knight, my lord has done ill to suffer you so long about him; he loses much by it, to my thinking."

When Sir Launfal heard that he was wroth, and answered her swiftly, and by misfortune he said that of which he afterwards repented sorely. "Lady," he said, "you have

---

[1] By God (later also *Perdie*)

been ill-advised. I love and I am loved by one who deserves the prize of beauty above all whom I know. One thing I will tell you, hear and mark it well; one of her serving maidens, even the meanest among them, is worth more than you, my lady queen, in face and figure, in beauty, wisdom, and goodness."

Then the queen rose up and went weeping to her chamber, shamed and angered that Launfal should have thus insulted her. She laid herself down on her bed as if sick; never, she said, would she arise off it till the king did justice on the plaint she would lay before him.

King Arthur came back from the woods after a fair day's hunting and sought the queen's chamber. When she saw him she cried out, and fell at his feet, beseeching his favour, and saying that Sir Launfal had shamed her, for he had asked her love, and when she refused him had mocked and insulted her, for he had boasted of his lady that she was so fair, so noble, and so proud that even the lowest of her waiting women was worth more than the queen.

At this King Arthur fell into a rage, and swore a solemn oath that unless the knight could defend himself well and fully in open court, he should be hanged or burnt.

Forth from the chamber went the king, and called three of his barons to him, and bade them fetch Sir Launfal, who indeed was now sad and sorry enough. He had returned to his hostelry, but alas! he learnt all too soon that he had lost his lady, since he had revealed the secret of their love. He was all alone in his chamber, full of anguish. Again and again he called upon his love, but it availed him nothing. He wept and sighed, and once and again fell on the ground in his despair. A hundred times he besought her to have mercy on him, and to speak once more to her true knight. He cursed his heart and his mouth that had betrayed him; 'twas a marvel he did not slay himself. But neither cries nor blows nor lamentations sufficed to awaken her pity, and make her show herself to his eyes.

Alas, what comfort might there be for the unhappy knight who had thus made an enemy of his king? The barons came and bade him follow them to court without delay, for the queen had accused him, and the king, by their mouth, commanded his presence. Launfal followed them, sorrowing greatly; had they slain him it would have pleased him well. He stood before the king, mute and speechless, his countenance changed for sorrow.

The king spoke in anger: "Vassal," he said, "you have greatly wronged me; an evil excuse have you found to shame and injure me, and insult the queen. Foolish was your boast, and foolish must be your lady to hold that her maid-servant is fairer than my queen."

Sir Launfal denied that he had dishonoured himself or insulted his liege lord. Word by word he repeated what the queen had said to him; but of the words he himself had spoken, and the boast he had made concerning his love, he owned the truth; sorrowful enough he was, since by so doing he had lost her. And for this speech he would make amends, as the court might require.

The king was sorely enraged against him, and conjured his knights to say what might rightfully be done in such a case, and how Launfal should be punished. And the knights did as he bade them, and some spake fair, and some spake ill. Then they all took counsel together and decreed that judgment should be given on a fixed day; and that Sir Launfal should give pledges to his lord that he would return to his hostelry and await the verdict. Otherwise, he should be held a prisoner till the day came. The barons returned to the king, and told him what they had agreed upon; and King Arthur demanded pledges, but Launfal was alone, a stranger in a strange land, without friend or kindred.

Then Sir Gawain came near, with all his companions, and said to the king: "Take pledges of all ye hold of mine and these my friends, fiefs or lands, each for himself." And when they had thus given pledges for him who had nothing of his own, he was free to go to his hostelry. The knights bore Sir Launfal company, chiding him as they went for his grief, and cursing the mad love that had brought him to this pass. Every day they visited him that they might see if he ate and drank, for they feared much that he would go mad for sorrow.

At the day they had named the barons were all assembled, the king was there, and the queen, and the sureties delivered up Launfal. Very sorrowful they were for him. I think there were even three hundred of them who had done all in their power without being able to deliver him from peril. Of a great offence did they accuse him, and the king demanded that sentence should be given according to the accusation and the defence.

Then the barons went forth to consider their judgment, heavy at heart, many of them, for the gallant stranger who was in such stress among them. Others, indeed, were ready to sacrifice Launfal to the will of their seigneur.

Then spoke the Duke of Cornwall, for the right was his, whoever might weep or rage, to him it pertained to have the first word, and he said:

"The king lays his plea against a vassal, Launfal ye call him, of felony and misdeed he accuses him in the matter of a love of which he boasted himself, thus making my lady, the queen, wrathful. None, save the king, has aught against him; therefore do ye as I say, for he who would speak the truth must have respect unto no man, save only such honour as shall be due to his liege lord. Let Launfal be put upon his oath (the king will surely have naught against it) and if he can prove his words, and bring forward his lady, and that which he said and which so angered the queen be true, then he shall be pardoned; 'twas no villainy that he spake. But if he cannot bring proof of his word, then shall we make him to know that the king no longer desires his service and gives him dismissal from his court."

Then they sent messengers to the knight, and spake, and made clear to him that he must bring forth his lady that his word might be proved, and he held guiltless. But he told them that was beyond his power, never through her might succour come to him. Then the messengers returned to the judges, who saw there was no chance of aid, for the king pressed them hard, urged thereto by the queen, who was weary of awaiting their judgment.

But as they arose to seek the king they saw two maidens come riding on white palfreys.[1] Very fair they were to look upon, clad in green sendal[2] over their white skin. The knights beheld them gladly, and Gawain, with three others, hastened to Sir Launfal and told him what had chanced, and bade him look upon the maidens; and they prayed him eagerly to say whether one of the twain were his lady, but he answered them nay.

The two, so fair to look upon, had gone forward to the palace, and dismounted before the daïs[3] whereon King Arthur was seated. If their beauty was great, so also was their speech courteous.

"King," they said, "command that chambers be assigned to us, fair with silken hangings, wherein our mistress can fitly lodge, for with you will she sojourn awhile."

They said no more, and the king called two knights, and bade them lead the maidens to the upper chambers.

Then the king demanded from his barons their judgment and their verdict, and said he was greatly wroth with them for their long delay.

"Sire," they answered, "we were stayed by the coming of the damsels. Our decision is not yet made, we go but now to take counsel together." Then they reassembled, sad and thoughtful, and great was the clamour and strife among them.

While they were yet in perplexity, they saw, descending the street, two maidens of noble aspect, clad in robes broidered with gold, and mounted on Spanish mules. Then all the knights were very joyful, and said each to the other: "Surely now shall Sir Launfal, the valiant and courteous, be safe."

Gawain and six companions went to seek the knight. "Sir," they said, "be of good courage, for the love of God speak to us. Hither come two damsels, most beautiful, and richly clad, one of them must of a truth be your lady!" But Launfal answered simply; "Never before to-day have I looked upon, or known, or loved them."

Meantime, the maidens had come to the palace and stood before the king. Many praised them for their beauty and bright colour, and some deemed them fairer even than the queen.

The elder was wise and courteous, and she delivered her message gracefully. "King," she said, "bid your folk give us chambers wherein we may lodge with our lady; she comes hither to speak with you."

Then the king commanded that they should be led to their companions who had come before them. Nor as yet was the judgment spoken. So when the maidens had left the hall, he commanded his barons to deliver their verdict, their judgment already tarried too long, and the queen waxed wrathful for their delay.

---

[1] A palfrey was generally smaller and had an easier gait than a destrier (war-horse), making it more suitable for a lady to ride.
[2] Sendal was a thin silk used for fine clothes and vestments.
[3] Raised platform on which a throne was set.

But even as they sought the king, through the city came riding a maiden, in all the world was none so fair. She rode a white palfrey, that bore her well and easily. Well shaped were its head and neck, no better trained steed was there in all the world. Costly were the trappings of that palfrey, under heaven was there no king rich enough to purchase the like, save that he sold or pledged his land.

And thus was the lady clad: her raiment was all of white, laced on either side. Slender was her shape, and her neck whiter than snow on the bough. Her eyes were blue, her skin fair. Straight was her nose, and lovely her mouth. Her eyebrows were brown, her forehead white, and her hair fair and curling. Her mantle was of purple, and the skirts were folded about her; on her hand she bare a hawk, and a hound followed behind her.

In all the Burg[1] there was no one, small nor great, young nor old, but was eager to look upon her as she passed. She came riding swiftly, and her beauty was no mere empty boast, but all men who looked upon her held her for a marvel, and not one of those who beheld her but felt his heart verily kindled with love.

Then those who loved Sir Launfal went to him, and told him of the maiden who came, if by the will of heaven she might deliver him. "Sir knight and comrade, hither comes one, no nutbrown maid is she, but the fairest of all fair women in this world." And Launfal heard, and sighed, for well he knew her. He raised his head and the blood flew to his cheek as he made swift answer: "Of a faith," he said, "this is my lady! Now let them slay me if they will and she has no mercy on me. I am whole if I do but see her."

The maiden reached the palace; fairer was she than any who had entered there. She dismounted before the king that all might behold her; she had let her mantle fall that they might the better see her beauty. King Arthur, in his courtesy, had risen to meet her, and all around him sprang to their feet, and were eager to offer their service. When they had looked well upon her, and praised her beauty, she spoke in these words, for no will had she to delay:

"King Arthur, I have loved one of your knights, behold him there, seigneur, Sir Launfal. He hath been accused at your court, but it is not my will that harm shall befall him. Concerning that which he said, know that the queen was in the wrong; never on any day did he pray her for her love. Of the boast that he hath made, if he may by me be acquitted, then shall your barons speak him free, as they have rightfully engaged to do."

The king granted that so it might be, nor was there a single voice but declared that Launfal was guiltless of wrong, for their own eyes had acquitted him.

And the maiden departed; in vain did the king pray her to remain; and many there were who would fain have served her. Without the hall was there a great block of grey marble, from which the chief knights of the king's court were wont to mount their steeds; on this Launfal took his stand, and when the maiden rode forth from the palace he sprang swiftly upon the palfrey behind her. Thus, as the Bretons tell us, he departed with her for

---

[1] castle

that most fair island, Avalon; thither the fairy maiden had carried her knight, and none hath heard man speak further of Sir Launfal. Nor know I more of his story.

✌✌

Chrétien de Troyes
from Lancelot
or, The Knight of the Cart
Translated by William Wistar Comfort[1]

Since my lady of Champagne wishes me to undertake to write a romance,[2] I shall very gladly do so, being so devoted to her service as to do anything in the world for her, without any intention of flattery. But if one were to introduce any flattery upon such an occasion, he might say, and I would subscribe to it, that this lady surpasses all others who are alive, just as the south wind which blows in May or April is more lovely than any other wind. But upon my word, I am not one to wish to flatter my lady. I will simply say: "The Countess is worth as many queens as a gem is worth of pearls and sards." Nay I shall make no comparison, and yet it is true in spite of me; I will say, however, that her command has more to do with this work than any thought or pains that I may expend upon it. Here Chrétien begins his book about the Knight of the Cart. The material and the treatment of it are given and furnished to him by the Countess, and he is simply trying to carry out her concern and intention. Here he begins the story.

Upon a certain Ascension Day King Arthur had come from Caerleon, and had held a very magnificent court at Camelot as was fitting on such a day.[3] After the feast the King did not quit his noble companions, of whom there were many in the hall. The Queen was present, too, and with her many a courteous lady able to converse in French. And Kay, who had furnished the meal, was eating with the others who had served the food. While Kay was sitting there at meat, behold there came to court a knight, well equipped and fully armed, and thus the knight appeared before the King as he sat among his lords. He gave him no greeting, but spoke out thus: "King Arthur, I hold in captivity knights, ladies, and damsels who belong to thy dominion and household; but it is not because of any intention to restore

---

[1] Unless denoted otherwise, notes on this text are taken from Comfort's 1913 translation, which incorporates notes from Prof. Wendelin Foerster's edition of the text; the latter are denoted with "(F.)" at the end of the note.

[2] Marie, daughter of Louis VII. of France and Eleanor of Aquitaine, married in 1164, Henri I., Count of Champagne. On the poet's own statement below, she furnished him with the subject matter ("*maitere*") and the manner of treatment ("*san*") of this romance. (F.)

[3] The situation of Camelot has not been certainly determined. Foerster places it in Somersetshire, while F. Paris identified it with Colchester in Essex. (F.)

them to thee that I make reference to them here; rather do I wish to proclaim and serve thee notice that thou hast not the strength or the resources to enable thee to secure them again. And be assured that thou shalt die before thou canst ever succour them."

The King replies that he must needs endure what he has not the power to change; nevertheless, he is filled with grief. Then the knight makes as if to go away, and turns about, without tarrying longer before the King; but after reaching the door of the hall, he does not go down the stairs, but stops and speaks from there these words: "King, if in thy court there is a single knight in whom thou hast such confidence that thou wouldst dare to entrust to him the Queen that he might escort her after me out into the woods whither I am going, I will promise to await him there, and will surrender to thee all the prisoners whom I hold in exile in my country if he is able to defend the Queen and if he succeeds in bringing her back again."

Many who were in the palace heard this challenge, and the whole court was in an uproar. Kay, too, heard the news as he sat at meat with those who served. Leaving the table, he came straight to the King, and as if greatly enraged, he began to say: "O King, I have served thee long, faithfully, and loyally; now I take my leave, and shall go away, having no desire to serve thee more."

The King was grieved at what he heard, and as soon as he could, he thus replied to him: "Is this serious, or a joke?"

And Kay replied: "O King, fair sire, I have no desire to jest, and I take my leave quite seriously. No other reward or wages do I wish in return for the service I have given you. My mind is quite made up to go away immediately."

"Is it in anger or in spite that you wish to go?" the King inquired; "seneschal, remain at court, as you have done hitherto, and be assured that I have nothing in the world which I would not give you at once in return for your consent to stay."

"Sire," says Kay, "no need of that. I would not accept for each day's pay a measure of fine pure gold."

Thereupon, the King in great dismay went off to seek the Queen. "My lady," he says, "you do not know the demand that the seneschal makes of me. He asks me for leave to go away, and says he will no longer stay at court; the reason of this I do not know. But he will do at your request what he will not do for me. Go to him now, my lady dear. Since he will not consent to stay for my sake, pray him to remain on your account, and if need be, fall at his feet, for I should never again be happy if I should lose his company."[1]

The King sends the Queen to the seneschal, and she goes to him. Finding him with the rest, she went up to him, and said: "Kay, you may be very sure that I am greatly troubled by the news I have heard of you. I am grieved to say that I have been told it is your intention to leave the King. How does this come about? What motive have you in your mind? I cannot

---

[1] The high value here set upon Kay by king Arthur is worth noting in view of the unfavourable light in which Chrétien usually portrays him.

think that you are so sensible or courteous as usual. I want to ask you to remain: stay with us here, and grant my prayer."

"Lady," he says, "I give you thanks; nevertheless, I shall not remain."

The Queen again makes her request, and is joined by all the other knights. And Kay informs her that he is growing tired of a service which is unprofitable. Then the Queen prostrates herself at full length before his feet. Kay beseeches her to rise, but she says that she will never do so until he grants her request. Then Kay promises her to remain, provided the King and she will grant in advance a favour he is about to ask.

"Kay," she says, "he will grant it, whatever it may be. Come now, and we shall tell him that upon this condition you will remain." So Kay goes away with the Queen to the King's presence. The Queen says: "I have had hard work to detain Kay; but I have brought him here to you with the understanding that you will do what he is going to ask." The King sighed with satisfaction, and said that he would perform whatever request he might make.

"Sire," says Kay, "hear now what I desire, and what is the gift you have promised me. I esteem myself very fortunate to gain such a boon with your consent. Sire, you have pledged your word that you would entrust to me my lady here, and that we should go after the knight who awaits us in the forest."

Though the King is grieved, he trusts him with the charge, for he never went back upon his word. But it made him so ill-humoured and displeased that it plainly showed in his countenance. The Queen, for her part, was sorry too, and all those of the household say that Kay had made a proud, outrageous, and mad request. Then the King took the Queen by the hand, and said: "My lady, you must accompany Kay without making objection."

And Kay said: "Hand her over to me now, and have no fear, for I shall bring her back perfectly happy and safe."

The King gives her into his charge, and he takes her off. After them all the rest go out, and there is not one who is not sad. You must know that the seneschal was fully armed, and his horse was led into the middle of the courtyard, together with a palfrey, as is fitting, for the Queen. The Queen walked up to the palfrey, which was neither restive nor hard-mouthed. Grieving and sad, with a sigh the Queen mounts, saying to herself in a low voice, so that no one could hear: "Alas, alas, if you only knew it, I am sure you would never allow me without interference to be led away a step."[1] She thought she had spoken in a very low tone; but Count Guinable heard her, who was standing by when she mounted.

When they started away, as great a lament was made by all the men and women present as if she already lay dead upon a bier. They do not believe that she will ever in her life come back. The seneschal in his impudence takes her where that other knight is awaiting her.

---

[1] This enigmatic exclamation is addressed to the absent Lancelot, who is the secret lover of Guinevere, and who, though he long remains anonymous as "the Knight of the Cart", is really the hero of the poem.

But no one was so much concerned as to undertake to follow him; until at last my lord Gawain thus addressed the King his uncle: "Sire," he says, "you have done a very foolish thing, which causes me great surprise; but if you will take my advice, while they are still near by, I and you will ride after them, and all those who wish to accompany us. For my part, I cannot restrain myself from going in pursuit of them at once. It would not be proper for us not to go after them, at least far enough to learn what is to become of the Queen, and how Kay is going to comport himself."

"Ah, fair nephew," the King replied, "you have spoken courteously. And since you have undertaken the affair, order our horses to be led out bridled and saddled that there may be no delay in setting out."

The horses are at once brought out, all ready and with the saddles on. First the King mounts, then my lord Gawain, and all the others rapidly. Each one, wishing to be of the party, follows his own will and starts away. Some were armed, but there were not a few without their arms. My lord Gawain was armed, and he bade two squires lead by the bridle two extra steeds. And as they thus approached the forest, they saw Kay's horse running out; and they recognised him, and saw that both reins of the bridle were broken. The horse was running wild, the stirrup-straps all stained with blood, and the saddle-bow was broken and damaged. Every one was chagrined at this, and they nudged each other and shook their heads. My lord Gawain was riding far in advance of the rest of the party, and it was not long before he saw coming slowly a knight on a horse that was sore, painfully tired, and covered with sweat. The knight first saluted my lord Gawain, and his greeting my lord Gawain returned. Then the knight, recognising my lord Gawain, stopped and thus spoke to him: "You see, sir, my horse is in a sweat and in such case as to be no longer serviceable. I suppose that those two horses belong to you now, with the understanding that I shall return the service and the favour, I beg you to let me have one or the other of them, either as a loan or outright as a gift."

And he answers him: "Choose whichever you prefer."

Then he who was in dire distress did not try to select the better or the fairer or the larger of the horses, but leaped quickly upon the one which was nearer to him, and rode him off. Then the one he had just left fell dead, for he had ridden him hard that day, so that he was used up and overworked. The knight without delay goes pricking through the forest, and my lord Gawain follows in pursuit of him with all speed, until he reaches the bottom of a hill. And when he had gone some distance, he found the horse dead which he had given to the knight, and noticed that the ground had been trampled by horses, and that broken shields and lances lay strewn about, so that it seemed that there had been a great combat between several knights, and he was very sorry and grieved not to have been there. However, he did not stay there long, but rapidly passed on until he saw again by chance the knight all alone on foot, completely armed, with helmet laced, shield hanging from his neck, and with his sword girt on. He had overtaken a cart. In those days such a cart served the same purpose as does a pillory now; and in each good town where there are more than three thousand such carts nowadays, in those times there was only one, and this, like our pillories, had to do service for all those who commit murder or treason, and those who are guilty of any delinquency, and for thieves who have stolen others' property or have forcibly seized it on the roads. Whoever was convicted of any crime was placed upon a cart and dragged through all the streets, and he lost henceforth all his legal rights, and was never afterward heard, honoured, or welcomed in any court. The carts were so dreadful in those days that the saying was then first used: "When thou dost see and meet a cart, cross thyself and call upon God, that no evil may befall thee."

The knight on foot, and without a lance, walked behind the cart, and saw a dwarf sitting on the shafts, who held, as a driver does, a long goad in his hand. Then he cries out: "Dwarf, for God's sake, tell me now if thou hast seen my lady, the Queen, pass by here." The miserable, low-born dwarf would not give him any news of her, but replied: "If thou wilt get up into the cart I am driving thou shalt hear to-morrow what has happened to the Queen." Then he kept on his way without giving further heed.

The knight hesitated only for a couple of steps before getting in. Yet, it was unlucky for him that he shrank from the disgrace, and did not jump in at once; for he will later rue his delay. But common sense, which is inconsistent with love's dictates, bids him refrain from getting in, warning him and counselling him to do and undertake nothing for which he may reap shame and disgrace. Reason, which dares thus speak to him, reaches only his lips, but not his heart; but love is enclosed within his heart, bidding him and urging him to mount at once upon the cart. So he jumps in, since love will have it so, feeling no concern about the shame, since he is prompted by love's commands. And my lord Gawain presses on in haste after the cart, and when he finds the knight sitting in it, his surprise is great.

"Tell me," he shouted to the dwarf, "if thou knowest anything of the Queen." And he replied: "If thou art so much thy own enemy as is this knight who is sitting here, get in with him, if it be thy pleasure, and I will drive thee along with him."

When my lord Gawain heard that, he considered it great foolishness, and said that he would not get in, for it would be dishonourable to exchange a horse for a cart: "Go on, and wherever thy journey lies, I will follow after thee."

Thereupon they start ahead, one mounted on his horse, the other two riding in the cart, and thus they proceed in company. Late in the afternoon they arrive at a town, which, you must know, was very rich and beautiful. All three entered through the gate; the people are greatly amazed to see the knight borne upon the cart, and they take no pains to conceal their feelings, but small and great and old and young shout taunts at him in the streets, so that the knight hears many vile and scornful words at his expense.[1] They all inquire: "To what punishment is this knight to be consigned? Is he to be rayed, or hanged, or drowned,

---

[1] It was not uncommon in old French romances and epic poems for knights to be subjected to the mockery and raillery of the vulgar townspeople.

or burned upon a fire of thorns? Tell us, thou dwarf, who art driving him, in what crime was he caught? Is he convicted of robbery? Is he a murderer, or a criminal?"

And to all this the dwarf made no response, vouchsafing to them no reply. He conducts the knight to a lodging-place; and Gawain follows the dwarf closely to a tower, which stood on the same level over against the town. Beyond there stretched a meadow, and the tower was built close by, up on a lofty eminence of rock, whose face formed a sharp precipice. Following the horse and cart, Gawain entered the tower. In the hall they met a damsel elegantly attired, than whom there was none fairer in the land, and with her they saw coming two fair and charming maidens. As soon as they saw my lord Gawain, they received him joyously and saluted him, and then asked news about the other knight: "Dwarf, of what crime is this knight guilty, whom thou dost drive like a lame man?" He would not answer her question, but he made the knight get out of the cart, and then he withdrew, without their knowing whither he went. Then my lord Gawain dismounts, and valets come forward to relieve the two knights of their armour. The damsel ordered two green mantles to be brought, which they put on. When the hour for supper came, a sumptuous repast was set. The damsel sat at table beside my lord Gawain. They would not have changed their lodging-place to seek any other, for all that evening the damsel showed them gear honour, and provided them with fair and pleasant company.

When they had sat up long enough, two long, high beds were prepared in the middle of the hall; and there was another bed alongside, fairer and more splendid than the rest; for, as the story testifies, it possessed all the excellence that one could think of in a bed. When the time came to retire, the damsel took both the guests to whom she had offered her hospitality; she shows them the two fine, long, wide beds, and says: "These two beds are set up here for the accommodation of your bodies; but in that one yonder no one ever lay who did not merit it: it was not set up to be used by you."

The knight who came riding on the cart replies at once: "Tell me," he says, "for what cause this bed is inaccessible."

Being thoroughly informed of this, she answers unhesitatingly: "It is not your place to ask or make such an inquiry. Any knight is disgraced in the land after being in a cart, and it is not fitting that he should concern himself with the matter upon which you have questioned me; and most of all it is not right that he should lie upon the bed, for he would soon pay dearly for his act. So rich a couch has not been prepared for you, and you would pay dearly for ever harbouring such a thought."

He replies: "You will see about that presently."

"Am I to see it?"

"Yes."

"It will soon appear."

"By my head," the knight replies, "I know not who is to pay the penalty. But whoever may object or disapprove, I intend to lie upon this bed and repose there at my ease." Then he at once disrobed in the bed, which was long and raised half an ell above the other two, and was covered with a yellow cloth of silk and a coverlet with gilded stars. The furs were not of skinned vair[1] but of sable; the covering he had on him would have been fitting for a king. The mattress was not made of straw or rushes or of old mats. At midnight there descended from the rafters suddenly a lance, as with the intention of pinning the knight through the flanks to the coverlet and the white sheets where he lay. To the lance there was attached a pennon all ablaze. The coverlet, the bedclothes, and the bed itself all caught fire at once. And the tip of the lance passed so close to the knight's side that it cut the skin a little, without seriously wounding him. Then the knight got up, put out the fire and, taking the lance, swung it in the middle of the hall, all this without leaving his bed; rather did he lie down again and slept as securely as at first.

In the morning, at daybreak, the damsel of the tower had Mass celebrated on their account, and had them rise and dress. When Mass had been celebrated for them, the knight who had ridden in the cart sat down pensively at a window, which looked out upon the meadow, and he gazed upon the fields below. The damsel came to another window close by, and there my lord Gawain conversed with her privately for a while about something, I know not what. I do not know what words were uttered, but while they were leaning on the window-sill they saw carried along the river through the fields a bier, upon which there lay a knight,[2] and alongside three damsels walked, mourning bitterly. Behind the bier they saw a crowd approaching, with a tall knight in front, leading a fair lady by the horse's rein. The knight at the window knew that it was the Queen. He continued to gaze at her attentively and with delight as long as she was visible. And when he could no longer see her, he was minded to throw himself out and break his body down below.

And he would have let himself fall out had not my lord Gawain seen him, and drawn him back, saying: "I beg you, sire, be quiet now. For God's sake, never think again of committing such a mad deed. It is wrong for you to despise your life."

"He is perfectly right," the damsel says; "for will not the news of his disgrace be known everywhere? Since he has been upon the cart, he has good reason to wish to die, for he would be better dead than alive. His life henceforth is sure to be one of shame, vexation, and unhappiness."

Then the knights asked for their armour, and armed themselves, the damsel treating them courteously, with distinction and generosity; for when she had joked with the knight and ridiculed him enough, she presented him with a horse and lance as a token of her goodwill. The knights then courteously and politely took leave of the damsel, first saluting her, and then going off in the direction taken by the crowd they had seen. Thus they rode out from the town without addressing them. They proceeded quickly in the direction they

---

[1] A particular type of squirrel skin. The blue-grey fur was prized for decoration, but it was hardly as luxurious as sable, which comes from a dark-furred species of marten native to Russia. Sable fur, especially the longer winter coat, is unique because it remains soft and smooth even when rubbed against the grain. (EGW)

[2] The wounded knight is the defeated seneschal.

had seen taken by the Queen, but they did not overtake the procession, which had advanced rapidly. After leaving the fields, the knights enter an enclosed place, and find a beaten road. They advanced through the woods until it might be six o'clock,[1] and then at a crossroads they met a damsel, whom they both saluted, each asking and requesting her to tell them, if she knows, whither the Queen has been taken.

Replying intelligently, she said to them: "If you would pledge me your word, I could set you on the right road and path, and I would tell you the name of the country and of the knight who is conducting her; but whoever would essay to enter that country must endure sore trials, for before he could reach there he must suffer much."

Then my lord Gawain replies: "Damsel, so help me God, I promise to place all my strength at your disposal and service, whenever you please, if you will tell me now the truth." And he who had been on the cart did not say that he would pledge her all his strength; but he proclaims, like one whom love makes rich, powerful and bold for any enterprise, that at once and without hesitation he will promise her anything she desires, and he puts himself altogether at her disposal.

"Then I will tell you the truth," says she. Then the damsel relates to them the following story: "In truth, my lords, Meleagant, a tall and powerful knight, son of the King of Gorre, has taken her off into the kingdom whence no foreigner returns, but where he must perforce remain in servitude and banishment." Then they ask her: "Damsel, where is this country? Where can we find the way thither?" She replies: "That you shall quickly learn; but you may be sure that you will meet with many obstacles and difficult passages, for it is not easy to enter there except with the permission of the king, whose name is Bademagu; however, it is possible to enter by two very perilous paths and by two very difficult passage-ways. One is called the water-bridge, because the bridge is under water, and there is the same amount of water beneath it as above it, so that the bridge is exactly in the middle; and it is only a foot and a half in width and in thickness. This choice is certainly to be avoided, and yet it is the less dangerous of the two. In addition there are a number of other obstacles of which I will say nothing. The other bridge is still more impracticable and much more perilous, never having been crossed by man. It is just like a sharp sword, and therefore all the people call it 'the sword-bridge'. Now I have told you all the truth I know."

But they ask of her once again: "Damsel, deign to show us these two passages."

To which the damsel makes reply: "This road here is the most direct to the water-bridge, and that one yonder leads straight to the sword-bridge." Then the knight, who had been on the cart, says: "Sire, I am ready to share with you without prejudice: take one of these two routes, and leave the other one to me; take whichever you prefer." "In truth," my lord Gawain replies, "both of them are hard and dangerous: I am not skilled in making such

---

[1] Mediaeval knights were such early risers as to cause us astonishment! (To be fair, daybreak usually falls between 4 and 5 a.m. GMT in England in the summer. – EGW)

a choice, and hardly know which of them to take; but it is not right for me to hesitate when you have left the choice to me: I will choose the water-bridge."

The other answers: "Then I must go uncomplainingly to the sword-bridge, which I agree to do."

Thereupon, they all three part, each one commending the others very courteously to God. And when she sees them departing, she says: "Each one of you owes me a favour of my choosing, whenever I may choose to ask it. Take care not to forget that."

"We shall surely not forget it, sweet friend," both the knights call out. Then each one goes his own way, and he of the cart is occupied with deep reflections, like one who has no strength or defence against love which holds him in its sway. His thoughts are such that he totally forgets himself, and he knows not whether he is alive or dead, forgetting even his own name, not knowing whether he is armed or not, or whither he is going or whence he came. Only one creature he has in mind, and for her his thought is so occupied that he neither sees nor hears aught else.[1] And his horse bears him along rapidly, following no crooked road, but the best and the most direct; and thus proceeding unguided, he brings him into an open plain.

[*Lancelot meets a lady who tries and fails to seduce him, then asks him to let her accompany him for a while, with the ulterior motive of using Lancelot to drive off a knight she doesn't want to marry.*]

Thereupon the damsel departs, and he rides on alone until it grew very late. After vespers, about compline, as he pursued his way, he saw a knight returning from the wood where he had been hunting. With helmet unlaced, he rode along upon his big grey hunter, to which he had tied the game which God had permitted him to take. This gentleman came quickly to meet the knight, offering him hospitality. "Sire," he says, "night will soon be here. It is time for you to be reasonable and seek a place to spend the night. I have a house of mine near at hand, whither I shall take you. No one ever lodged you better than I shall do, to the extent of my resources: I shall be very glad, if you consent."

"For my part, I gladly accept," he says.

The gentleman at once sends his son ahead, to prepare the house and start the preparations for supper. The lad willingly executes his command forthwith, and goes off at a rapid pace, while the others, who are in no haste, follow the road leisurely until they arrive at the house. The gentleman's wife was a very accomplished lady; and he had five sons, whom he dearly loved, three of them mere lads, and two already knights; and he had two fair and charming daughters, who were still unmarried. They were not natives of the land, but were there in durance, having been long kept there as prisoners away from their native land of Logres. When the gentleman led the knight into his yard, the lady with her sons and daughters jumped up and ran to meet them, vying in their efforts to do him honour, as they

[1] Lancelot has constantly in mind the Queen, for whose sake he is enduring all this pain and shame.

greeted him and helped him to dismount. Neither the sisters nor the five brothers paid much attention to their father, for they knew well enough that he would have it so. They honoured the knight and welcomed him; and when they had relieved him of his armour, one of his host's two daughters threw her own mantle about him, taking it from her own shoulders and throwing it about his neck. I do not need to tell how well he was served at supper; but when the meal was finished, they felt no further hesitation in speaking of various matters. First, the host began to ask him who he was, and from what land, but he did not inquire about his name.

The knight promptly answered him: "I am from the kingdom of Logres, and have never been in this land before."

And when the gentleman heard that, he was greatly amazed, as were his wife and children too, and each one of them was sore distressed. Then they began to say to him: "Woe that you have come here, fair sire, for only trouble will come of it! For, like us, you will be reduced to servitude and exile."

"Where do you come from, then?" he asked. "Sire, we belong in your country. Many men from your country are held in servitude in this land. Cursed be the custom, together with those who keep it up! No stranger comes here who is not compelled to stay here in the land where he is detained. For whoever wishes may come in, but once in, he has to stay. About your own fate, you may be at rest, you will doubtless never escape from here."

He replies: "Indeed, I shall do so, if possible."

To this the gentleman replies: "How? Do you think you can escape?"

"Yes, indeed, if it be God's will; and I shall do all within my power." "In that case, doubtless all the rest would be set free; for, as soon as one succeeds in fairly escaping from this durance, then all the rest may go forth unchallenged."

Then the gentleman recalled that he had been told and informed that a knight of great excellence was making his way into the country to seek for the Queen, who was held by the king's son, Meleagant; and he said to himself: "Upon my word, I believe it is he, and I'll tell him so." So he said to him: "Sire, do not conceal from me your business, if I promise to give you the best advice I know. I too shall profit by any success you may attain. Reveal to me the truth about your errand, that it may be to your advantage as well as mine. I am persuaded that you have come in search of the Queen into this land and among these heathen people, who are worse than the Saracens."

And the knight replies: "For no other purpose have I come. I know not where my lady is confined, but I am striving hard to rescue her, and am in dire need of advice. Give me any counsel you can."

And he says: "Sire, you have undertaken a very grievous task. The road you are travelling will lead you straight to the sword-bridge.[1] You surely need advice. If you would

---

[1] The topography of the kingdom of Gorre, the land where dwell the captives held by King Bademagu, is much confused. One would suppose at first that the stream traversed by the two perilous bridges formed the frontier

heed my counsel, you would proceed to the sword-bridge by a surer way, and I would have you escorted thither."

Then he, whose mind is fixed upon the most direct way, asks him: "Is the road of which you speak as direct as the other way?"

"No, it is not," he says; "it is longer, but more sure."

Then he says: "I have no use for it; tell me about this road I am following!"

"I am ready to do so," he replies; "but I am sure you will not fare well if you take any other than the road I recommend. To-morrow you will reach a place where you will have trouble: it is called 'the stony passage'. Shall I tell you how bad a place it is to pass? Only one horse can go through at a time; even two men could not pass abreast, and the passage is well guarded and defended. You will meet with resistance as soon as you arrive. You will sustain many a blow of sword and lance, and will have to return full measure before you succeed in passing through."

And when he had completed the account, one of the gentleman's sons, who was a knight, stepped forward, saying: "Sire, if you do not object, I will go with this gentleman."

Then one of the lads jumps up, and says: "I too will go."

And the father gladly gives them both consent. Now the knight will not have to go alone, and he expresses his gratitude, being much pleased with the company. [. . .]

At the end of this very difficult bridge they dismount from their steeds and gaze at the wicked-looking stream, which is as swift and raging, as black and turgid, as fierce and terrible as if it were the devil's stream; and it is so dangerous and bottomless that anything failing into it would be as completely lost as if it fell into the salt sea. And the bridge, which spans it, is different from any other bridge; for there never was such a one as this. If any one asks of me the truth, there never was such a bad bridge, nor one whose flooring was so bad. The bridge across the cold stream consisted of a polished, gleaming sword; but the sword was stout and stiff, and was as long as two lances. At each end there was a tree-trunk in which the sword was firmly fixed. No one need fear to fall because of its breaking or bending, for its excellence was such that it could support a great weight. But the two knights who were with the third were much discouraged; for they surmised that two lions or two leopards would be found tied to a great rock at the other end of the bridge. The water and the bridge and the lions combine so to terrify them that they both tremble with fear, and say: "Fair sire, consider well what confronts you; for it is necessary and needful to do so. This bridge is badly made and built, and the construction of it is bad. If you do not change your mind in time, it will be too late to repent. You must consider which of several alternatives you will choose. Suppose that you once get across (but that cannot possibly come to pass, any more

---

of the kingdom. But here (v.2102), before reaching such a frontier, the captives are already met. Foerster suggests that we may be here at a sort of foreground or borderland which is defended by the knight at the ford (v. 735 f.), and which, though not within the limits of the kingdom, is nevertheless beneath the sway of Bademagu. In the sequel the stream with the perilous bridges is placed immediately before the King's palace.

than one could hold in the winds and forbid them to blow, or keep the birds from singing, or re-enter one's mother's womb and be born again—all of which is as impossible as to empty the sea of its water); but even supposing that you got across, can you think and suppose that those two fierce lions that are chained on the other side will not kill you, and suck the blood from your veins, and eat your flesh and then gnaw your bones? For my part, I am bold enough, when I even dare to look and gaze at them. If you do not take care, they will certainly devour you. Your body will soon be torn and rent apart, for they will show you no mercy. So take pity on us now, and stay here in our company! It would be wrong for you to expose yourself intentionally to such mortal peril."

And he, laughing, replies to them: "Gentlemen, receive my thanks and gratitude for the concern you feel for me: it comes from your love and kind hearts. I know full well that you would not like to see any mishap come to me; but I have faith and confidence in God, that He will protect me to the end. I fear the bridge and stream no more than I fear this dry land; so I intend to prepare and make the dangerous attempt to cross. I would rather die than turn back now." The others have nothing more to say; but each weeps with pity and heaves a sigh. Meanwhile he prepares, as best he may, to cross the stream, and he does a very marvellous thing in removing the armour from his feet and hands. He will be in a sorry state when he reaches the other side. He is going to support himself with his bare hands and feet upon the sword, which was sharper than a scythe, for he had not kept on his feet either sole or upper or hose. But he felt no fear of wounds upon his hands or feet; he preferred to maim himself rather than to fall from the bridge and be plunged in the water from which he could never escape. In accordance with this determination, he passes over with great pain and agony, being wounded in the hands, knees, and feet. But even this suffering is sweet to him: for Love, who conducts and leads him on, assuages and relieves the pain. Creeping on his hands, feet, and knees, he proceeds until he reaches the other side.

Then he recalls and recollects the two lions which he thought he had seen from the other side; but, on looking about, he does not see so much as a lizard or anything else to do him harm. He raises his hand before his face and looks at his ring,[1] and by this test he proves that neither of the lions is there which he thought he had seen, and that he had been enchanted and deceived; for there was not a living creature there. When those who had remained behind upon the bank saw that he had safely crossed, their joy was natural; but they do not know of his injuries. He, however, considers himself fortunate not to have suffered anything worse. The blood from his wounds drips on his shirt on all sides. Then he sees before him a tower, which was so strong that never had he seen such a strong one before: indeed, it could not have been a better tower. At the window there sat King Bademagu, who was very scrupulous and precise about matters of honour and what was right, and who was careful to observe and practise loyalty above all else; and beside him stood his son, who always did precisely the opposite so far as possible, for he found his pleasure in disloyalty,

---

[1] A ring given to Lancelot by the Lady of the Lake, able to reveal whether or not something is an illusion. (EGW)

and never wearied of villainy, treason, and felony. From their point of vantage they had seen the knight cross the bridge with trouble and pain. Meleagant's colour changed with the rage and displeasure he felt; for he knows now that he will be challenged for the Queen; but his character was such that he feared no man, however strong or formidable. If he were not base and disloyal, there could no better knight be found; but he had a heart of wood, without gentleness and pity. What enraged his son and roused his ire, made the king happy and glad. The king knew of a truth that he who had crossed the bridge was much better than any one else. For no one would dare to pass over it in whom there dwelt any of that evil nature which brings more shame upon those who possess it than prowess brings of honour to the virtuous. For prowess cannot accomplish so much as wickedness and sloth can do: it is true beyond a doubt that it is possible to do more evil than good.

I could say more on these two heads, if it did not cause me to delay. But I must turn to something else and resume my subject, and you shall hear how the king speaks profitably to his son: "Son," he says, "it was fortunate that thou and I came to look out this window; our reward has been to witness the boldest deed that ever entered the mind of man. Tell me now if thou art not well disposed toward him who has performed such a marvellous feat. Make peace and be reconciled with him, and deliver the Queen into his hands. Thou shalt gain no glory in battle with him, but rather mayst thou incur great loss. Show thyself to be courteous and sensible, and send the Queen to meet him before he sees thee. Show him honour in this land of thine, and before he asks it, present to him what he has come to seek. Thou knowest well enough that he has come for the Queen Guinevere. Do not act so that people will take thee to be obstinate, foolish, or proud. If this man has entered thy land alone, thou shouldst bear him company, for one gentleman ought not to avoid another, but rather attract him and honour him with courtesy. One receives honour by himself showing it; be sure that the honour will be thine, if thou doest honour and service to him who is plainly the best knight in the world."

And he replies: "May God confound me, if there is not as good a knight, or even a better one than he!" It was too bad that he did not mention himself, of whom he entertains no mean opinion. And he adds: "I suppose you wish me to clasp my hands and kneel before him as his liegeman, and to hold my lands from him? So help me God, I would rather become his man than surrender to him the Queen! God forbid that in such a fashion I should deliver her to him! She shall never be given up by me, but rather contested and defended against all who are so foolish as to dare to come in quest of her."

Then again the king says to him: "Son, thou wouldst act very courteously to renounce this pretension. I advise thee and beg thee to keep the peace. Thou knowest well that the honour will belong to the knight, if he wins the Queen from thee in battle. He would doubtless rather win her in battle than as a gift, for it will thus enhance his fame. It is my opinion that he is seeking her, not to receive her peaceably, but because he wishes to win her by force of arms. So it would be wise on thy part to deprive him of the satisfaction of fighting thee. I am sorry to see thee so foolish; but if thou dost not heed my advice, evil will come of it, and the ensuing misfortune will be worse for thee. For the knight need fear no hostility from any one here save thee. On behalf of myself and all my men, I will grant him a truce and security. I have never yet done a disloyal deed or practised treason and felony, and I shall not begin to do so now on thy account any more than I would for any stranger. I do not wish to flatter thee, for I promise that the knight shall not lack any arms, or horse or anything else he needs, in view of the boldness he has displayed in coming thus far. He shall be securely guarded and well defended against all men here excepting thee. I wish him clearly to understand that, if he can maintain himself against thee, he need have no fear of any one else."

"I have listened to you in silence long enough," says Meleagant, "and you may say what you please. But little do I care for all you say. I am not a hermit, nor so compassionate and charitable, and I have no desire to be so honourable as to give him what I most love. His task will not be performed so quickly or so lightly; rather will it turn out otherwise than as you and he expect. You and I need not quarrel because you aid him against me. Even if he enjoys peace and a truce with you and all your men, what matters that to me? My heart does not quail on that account; rather, so help me God, I am glad that he need not feel concern for any one here but me; I do not wish you to do on my account anything which might be construed as disloyalty or treachery. Be as compassionate as you please, but let me be cruel."

"What? Wilt thou not change thy mind?"

"No," he says.

"Then I will say nothing more. I will leave thee alone to do thy best and will go now to speak with the knight. I wish to offer and present to him my aid and counsel in all respects; for I am altogether on his side."

Then the king goes down and orders them to bring his horse. A large steed is brought to him, upon which he springs by the stirrup, and he rides off with some of his men: three knights and two squires he bade to go with him. They did not stop their ride downhill until they came to the bridge, where they see him stanching his wounds and wiping the blood from them. The king expects to keep him as his guest for a long time while his wounds are healing; but he might as well expect to drain the sea. The king hastens to dismount, and he who was grievously wounded, stood up at once to meet him, though he did not know him, and he gave no more evidence of the pain he felt in his feet and hands than if he had been actually sound. The king sees that he is exerting himself, and quickly runs to greet him with the words: "Sire, I am greatly amazed that you have fallen upon us in this land. But be welcome, for no one will ever repeat the attempt: it never happened in the past, and it will never happen in the future that any one should perform such a hardy feat or expose himself to such peril. And know that I admire you greatly for having executed what no one before ever dared to conceive. You will find me very kindly disposed, and loyal and courteous toward you. I am the king of this land, and offer you freely all my counsel and service; and I think I know pretty well what you have come here to seek. You come, I am sure, to seek the Queen."

"Sire," he replies, "your surmise is correct; no other cause brings me here."

"Friend, you must suffer hardship to obtain her," he replies; "and you are sorely wounded, as I see by the wounds and the flowing blood. You will not find him who brought her hither so generous as to give her up without a struggle; but you must tarry, and have your wounds cared for until they are completely healed. I will give you some of 'the three Marys' ointment,[1] and something still better, if it can be found, for I am very solicitous about your comfort and your recovery. And the Queen is so confined that no mortal man has access to her—not even my son, who brought her here with him and who resents such treatment, for never was a man so beside himself and so desperate as he. But I am well disposed toward you, and will gladly give you, so help me God, all of which you stand in need. My son himself will not have such good arms but that I will give you some that are just as good, and a horse, too, such as you will need, though my son will be angry with me. Despite the feelings of any one, I will protect you against all men. You will have no cause to fear any one excepting him who brought the Queen here. No man ever menaced another as I have menaced him, and I came near driving him from my land, in my displeasure because he will not surrender her to you. To be sure, he is my son; but feel no concern, for unless he defeats you in battle, he can never do you the slightest harm against my will."

"Sire," he says, "I thank you. But I am losing time here which I do not wish to waste. I have no cause to complain, and have no wound which is paining me. Take me where I can find him; for with such arms as I have, I am ready to divert myself by giving and receiving blows."

"Friend, you had better wait two or three weeks until your wounds are healed, for it would be well for you to tarry here at least two weeks, and not on any account could I allow it, or look on, while you fought in my presence with such arms and with such an outfit."

And he replies: "With your permission, no other arms would be used than these, for I should prefer to fight with them, and I should not ask for the slightest postponement, adjournment or delay. However, in deference to you, I will consent to wait until to-morrow; but despite what any one may say, longer I will not wait."

Then the king assured him that all would be done as he wished; then he has the lodging-place prepared, and insistently requests his men, who are in the company, to serve him, which they do devotedly. And the king, who would gladly have made peace, had it been possible, went at once to his son and spoke to him like one who desires peace and harmony, saying: "Fair son, be reconciled now with this knight without a fight! He has not come here to disport himself or to hunt or chase, but he comes in search of honour and to increase his fame and renown, and I have seen that he stands in great need of rest. If he had taken my advice, he would not have rashly undertaken, either this month or the next, the battle which he so greatly desires. If thou makest over the Queen to him, dost thou fear any

---

[1] The legendary origin of this ointment, named after Mary Magdalene, Mary the mother of James, and Mary Salome, is mentioned in the epic poem "Mort Aimeri de Narbonne" (ed. "Anciens Textes", p. 86). (F.)

dishonour in the deed? Have no fear of that, for no blame can attach to thee; rather is it wrong to keep that to which one has no rightful claim. He would gladly have entered the battle at once, though his hands and feet are not sound, but cut and wounded."

Meleagant answers his father thus: "You are foolish to be concerned. By the faith I owe St. Peter, I will not take your advice in this matter. I should deserve to be drawn apart with horses, if I heeded your advice. If he is seeking his honour, so do I seek mine; if he is in search of glory, so am I; if he is anxious for the battle, so am I a hundred times more so than he."

"I see plainly," says the king, "that thou art intent upon thy mad enterprise, and thou shalt have thy fill of it. Since such is thy pleasure, to-morrow thou shalt try thy strength with the knight."

"May no greater hardship ever visit me than that!" Meleagant replies; "I would much rather it were to-day than to-morrow. Just see how much more downcast I am than is usual! My eyes are wild, and my face is pale! I shall have no joy or satisfaction or any cause for happiness until I am actually engaged with him."

The king understands that further advice and prayers are of no avail, so reluctantly he leaves his son and, taking a good, strong horse and handsome arms, he sends them to him who well deserves them, together with a surgeon who was a loyal and Christian man. There was in the world no more trusty man, and he was more skilled in the cure of wounds than all the doctors of Montpellier.[1] That night he treated the knight as best he could, in accordance with the king's command. Already the news was known by the knights and damsels, the ladies and barons of all the country-side, and all through the night until daybreak strangers and friends were making long journeys from all the country round. When morning came, there was such a press before the castle that there was not room to move one's foot. And the king, rising early in his distress about the battle, goes directly to his son, who had already laced upon his head the helmet which was of Poitiers make. No delay or peace is possible, for though the king did his best, his efforts are of no effect. In the middle of the castle-square, where all the people are assembled, the battle will be fought in compliance with the king's wish and command. The king sends at once for the stranger knight, and he is conducted to the grounds which were filled with people from the kingdom of Logres. For just as people are accustomed to go to church to hear the organ on the annual feast-days of Pentecost or Christmas, so they had all assembled now. All the foreign maidens from King Arthur's realm had fasted three days and gone barefoot in their shifts, in order that God might endow with strength and courage the knight who was to fight his adversary on behalf of the captives.

---

[1] The universities of Montpellier and of Salerno were the chief centres of medical study in the Middle Ages.

Very early, before prime had yet been sounded,[1] both of the knights fully armed were led to the place, mounted upon two horses equally protected. Meleagant was very graceful, alert, and shapely; the hauberk with its fine meshes, the helmet, and the shield hanging from his neck—all these became him well. All the spectators, however, favoured the other knight, even those who wished him ill, and they say that Meleagant is worth nothing compared with him. As soon as they were both on the ground, the king comes and detains them as long as possible in an effort to make peace between them, but he is unable to persuade his son. Then he says to them: "Hold in your horses until I reach the top of the tower. It will be only a slight favour, if you will wait so long for me."

Then in sorrowful mood he leaves them and goes directly to the place where he knew he would find the Queen. She had begged him the evening before to place her where she might have an unobstructed view of the battle; he had granted her the boon, and went now to seek and fetch her, for he was very anxious to show her honour and courtesy. He placed her at one window, and took his place at another window on her right. Beside them, there were gathered there many knights and prudent dames and damsels, who were natives of that land; and there were many others, who were captives, and who were intent upon their orisons and prayers. Those who were prisoners were praying for their lord, for to God and to him they entrusted their succour and deliverance. Then the combatants without delay make all the people stand aside; then they clash the shields with their elbows, and thrust their arms into the straps, and spur at each other so violently that each sends his lance two arms' length through his opponent's shield, causing the lance to split and splinter like a flying spark. And the horses meet head on, clashing breast to breast, and the shields and helmets crash with such a noise that it seems like a mighty thunder-clap; not a breast-strap, girth, rein or surcingle remains unbroken, and the saddle-bows, though strong, are broken to pieces. The combatants felt no shame in falling to earth, in view of their mishaps, but they quickly spring to their feet, and without waste of threatening words rush at each other more fiercely than two wild boars, and deal great blows with their swords of steel like men whose hate is violent. Repeatedly they trim the helmets and shining hauberks so fiercely that after the sword the blood spurts out. They furnished an excellent battle, indeed, as they stunned and wounded each other with their heavy, wicked blows. Many fierce, hard, long bouts they sustained with equal honour, so that the onlookers could discern no advantage on either side. But it was inevitable that he who had crossed the bridge should be much weakened by his wounded hands. The people who sided with him were much dismayed, for they notice that his strokes are growing weaker, and they fear he will get the worst of it; it seemed to

---

[1] The hours of the Divine Office (the daily liturgy followed especially by monks) were Lauds, said at daybreak; Prime, the first hour of the day (around 6 a.m.); Terce, the third (9 a.m.); Sext, the sixth (noon); None, the ninth (3 p.m.); Vespers, at dusk; Compline, in the late evening; and Matins, at midnight. The precise time of each service varied with the seasons, but a bell tolled to call the monks to prayer each time. This fight is thus probably taking place around 5 a.m. (EGW)

them that he was weakening, while Meleagant was triumphing, and they began to murmur all around.

But up at the window of the tower there was a wise maiden who thought within herself that the knight had not undertaken the battle either on her account or for the sake of the common herd who had gathered about the list, but that his only incentive had been the Queen; and she thought that, if he knew that she was at the window seeing and watching him, his strength and courage would increase. And if she had known his name, she would gladly have called to him to look about him. Then she came to the Queen and said: "Lady, for God's sake and your own as well as ours, I beseech you to tell me, if you know, the name of yonder knight, to the end that it may be of some help to him."

"Damsel," the Queen replies, "you have asked me a question in which I see no hate or evil, but rather good intent; the name of the knight, I know, is Lancelot of the Lake."[1]

"God, how happy and glad at heart I am!" the damsel says. Then she leans forward and calls to him by name so loudly that all the people hear: "Lancelot, turn about and see who is here taking note of thee!"

When Lancelot heard his name, he was not slow to turn around: he turns and sees seated up there at the window of the tower her whom he desired most in the world to see. From the moment he caught sight of her, he did not turn or take his eyes and face from her, defending himself with backhand blows. And Meleagant meanwhile attacked him as fiercely as he could, delighted to think that the other cannot withstand him now; and they of the country are well pleased too, while the foreigners are so distressed that they can no longer support themselves, and many of them fall to earth either upon their knees or stretched out prone; thus some are glad, and some distressed. Then the damsel cried again from the window: "Ah, Lancelot, how is it that thou dost now conduct thyself so foolishly? Once thou wert the embodiment of prowess and of all that is good, and I do not think God ever made a knight who could equal thee in valour and in worth. But now we see thee so distressed that thou dealest back-hand blows and fightest thy adversary, behind thy back. Turn, so as to be on the other side, and so that thou canst face toward this tower, for it will help thee to keep it in view."

Then Lancelot is so ashamed and mortified that he hates himself, for he knows full well that all have seen how, for some time past, he has had the worst of the fight. Thereupon he leaps backward and so manoeuvres as to force Meleagant into a position between him and the tower. Meleagant makes every effort to regain his former position. But Lancelot rushes upon him, and strikes him so violently upon his body and shield whenever he tries to get around him, that he compels him to whirl about two or three times in spite of himself. Lancelot's strength and courage grow, partly because he has love's aid, and partly because he never hated any one so much as him with whom he is engaged. Love and mortal hate, so fierce that never before was such hate seen, make him so fiery and bold that Meleagant ceases

---

[1] The hero of the poem is here first mentioned by name.

to treat it as a jest and begins to stand in awe of him, for he had never met or known so doughty a knight, nor had any knight ever wounded or injured him as this one does. He is glad to get away from him, and he winces and sidesteps, fearing his blows and avoiding them. And Lancelot does not idly threaten him, but drives him rapidly toward the tower where the Queen was stationed on the watch. There upon the tower he did her the homage of his blows until he came so close that, if he advanced another step, he would lose sight of her. Thus Lancelot drove him back and forth repeatedly in whatever direction he pleased, always stopping before the Queen, his lady, who had kindled the flame which compels him to fix his gaze upon her. And this same flame so stirred him against Meleagant that he was enabled to lead and drive him wherever he pleased. In spite of himself he drives him on like a blind man or a man with a wooden leg.

The king sees his son so hard pressed that he is sorry for him and he pities him, and he will not deny him aid and assistance if possible; but if he wishes to proceed courteously, he must first beg the Queen's permission. So he began to say to her: "Lady, since I have had you in my power, I have loved you and faithfully served and honoured you. I never consciously left anything undone in which I saw your honour involved; now repay me for what I have done. For I am about to ask you a favour which you should not grant unless you do so willingly. I plainly see that my son is getting the worst of this battle; I do not speak so because of the chagrin I feel, but in order that Lancelot, who has him in his power, may not kill him. Nor ought you to wish to see him killed; not because he has not wronged both you and him, but because I make the request of you: so tell him, please, to stop beating him. If you will, you can thus repay me for what I have done for you."

"Fair sire, I am willing to do so at your request," the Queen replies; "had I mortal hatred for your son, whom it is true I do not love, yet you have served me so well that, to please you, I am quite willing that he should desist."

These words were not spoken privately, but Lancelot and Meleagrant heard what was said. The man who is a perfect lover is always obedient and quickly and gladly does his mistress' pleasure. So Lancelot was constrained to do his Lady's will, for he loved more than Pyramus,[1] if that were possible for any man to do. Lancelot heard what was said, and as soon as the last word had issued from her mouth, "since you wish him to desist, I am willing that he should do so," Lancelot would not have touched him or made a movement for anything, even if the other had killed him. He does not touch him or raise his hand. But Meleagant, beside himself with rage and shame when he hears that it has been necessary to intercede in his behalf, strikes him with all the strength he can muster. And the king went down from the tower to upbraid his son, and entering the list he addressed him thus: "How now? Is this

---

[1] The classic love-story of Pyramus and Thisbe, told by Ovid et al., was a favourite in the Middle Ages. (Much like Romeo and Juliet, Pyramus and Thisbe were lovers whose parents forbade them to marry. When they tried to elope, Thisbe reached the rendezvous point first but was scared away by a lioness, which caught her veil. Pyramus arrived, assumed the worst, and killed the lioness and then himself; Thisbe returned just as he was dying and killed herself in turn. —EGW)

becoming, to strike him when he is not touching thee? Thou art too cruel and savage, and thy prowess is now out of place! For we all know beyond a doubt that he is thy superior."

Then Meleagant, choking with shame, says to the king: "I think you must be blind! I do not believe you see a thing. Any one must indeed be blind to think I am not better than he."

"Seek some one to believe thy words!" the king replies, "for all the people know whether thou speakest the truth or a lie. All of us know full well the truth." Then the king bids his barons lead his son away, which they do at once in execution of his command: they led away Meleagant. But it was not necessary to use force to induce Lancelot to withdraw, for Meleagant might have harmed him grievously, before he would have sought to defend himself. Then the king says to his son: "So help me God, now thou must make peace and surrender the Queen. Thou must cease this quarrel once for all and withdraw thy claim."

"That is great nonsense you have uttered! I hear you speak foolishly. Stand aside! Let us fight, and do not mix in our affairs!"

But the king says he will take a hand, for he knows well that, were the fight to continue, Lancelot would kill his son.

"He kill me! Rather would I soon defeat and kill him, if you would leave us alone and let us fight."

Then the king says: "So help me God, all that thou sayest is of no avail."

"Why is that?" he asks.

"Because I will not consent. I will not so trust in thy folly and pride as to allow thee to be killed. A man is a fool to court death, as thou dost in thy ignorance. I know well that thou hatest me because I wish to save thy life. God will not let me see and witness thy death, if I can help it, for it would cause me too much grief." He talks to him and reproves him until finally peace and good-will are restored. The terms of the peace are these: he will surrender the Queen to Lancelot, provided that the latter without reluctance will fight them again within a year of such time as he shall choose to summon him: this is no trial to Lancelot. When peace is made, all the people press about, and it is decided that the battle shall be fought at the court of King Arthur, who holds Britain and Cornwall in his sway: there they decide that it shall be. And the Queen has to consent, and Lancelot has to promise, that if Meleagant can prove him recreant, she shall come back with him again without the interference of any one. When the Queen and Lancelot had both agreed to this, the arrangement was concluded, and they both retired and removed their arms.

Now the custom in the country was that when one issued forth, all the others might do so too. All called down blessings upon Lancelot: and you may know that he must have felt great joy, as in truth he did. All the strangers assemble and rejoice over Lancelot, speaking so as to be heard by him: "Sire, in truth we were joyful as soon as we heard your name, for we felt sure at once that we should all be set free." There was a great crowd present at this glad scene, as each one strives and presses forward to touch him if possible. Any one who succeeded in touching him was more delighted than he could tell. There was plenty of joy, and of sorrow too; those who were now set free rejoiced unrestrainedly; but Meleagant and his followers have not anything they want, but are pensive, gloomy, and downcast.

The king turns away from the list, taking with him Lancelot, who begs him to take him to the Queen. "I shall not fail to do so," the king replies; "for it seems to me the proper thing to do. And if you like, I will show you Kay the seneschal." At this Lancelot is so glad that he almost falls at his feet. Then the king took him at once into the hall, where the Queen had come to wait for him.

When the Queen saw the king holding Lancelot by the hand, she rose before the king, but she looked displeased with clouded brow, and she spoke not a word. "Lady, here is Lancelot come to see you," says the king; "you ought to be pleased and satisfied."

"I, sire? He cannot please me. I care nothing about seeing him."

"Come now, lady," says the king who was very frank and courteous, "what induces you to act like this? You are too scornful toward a man who has served you so faithfully that he has repeatedly exposed his life to mortal danger on this journey for your sake, and who has defended and rescued you from my son Meleagant who had deeply wronged you."

"Sire, truly he has made poor use of his time. I shall never deny that I feel no gratitude toward him."

Now Lancelot is dumbfounded; but he replies very humbly like a polished lover: "Lady, certainly I am grieved at this, but I dare not ask your reason."

The Queen listened as Lancelot voiced his disappointment, but in order to grieve and confound him, she would not answer a single word, but returned to her room. And Lancelot followed her with his eyes and heart until she reached the door; but she was not long in sight, for the room was close by. His eyes would gladly have followed her, had that been possible; but the heart, which is more lordly and masterful in its strength, went through the door after her, while the eyes remained behind weeping with the body.

And the king said privily to him: "Lancelot, I am amazed at what this means: and how it comes about that the Queen cannot endure the sight of you, and that she is so unwilling to speak with you. If she is ever accustomed to speak with you, she ought not to be niggardly now or avoid conversation with you, after what you have done for her. Now tell me, if you know, why and for what misdeed she has shown you such a countenance."

"Sire, I did not notice that just now; but she will not look at me or hear my words, and that distresses and grieves me much." "Surely," says the king, "she is in the wrong, for you have risked your life for her. Come away now, fair sweet friend, and we shall go to speak with the seneschal."

"I shall be glad to do so," he replies. Then they both go to the seneschal.

As soon as Lancelot came where he was, the seneschal's first exclamation was: "How thou hast shamed me!"

"I? How so?" Lancelot inquires; "tell me what disgrace have I brought upon you?"

"A very great disgrace, for thou hast carried out what I could not accomplish, and thou hast done what I could not do."

Then the king left them together in the room, and went out alone. And Lancelot inquires of the seneschal if he has been badly off.

"Yes," he answers, "and I still am so. I was never more wretched than I am now. And I should have died a long time ago, had it not been for the king, who in his compassion has shown me so much gentleness and kindness that he willingly let me lack nothing of which I stood in need; but I was furnished at once with everything that I desired. But opposed to the kindness which he showed me, was Meleagant his son, who is full of wickedness, and who summoned the physicians to him and bade them apply such ointments as would kill me. Such a father and stepfather have I had! For when the king had a good plaster applied to my wounds in his desire that I should soon be cured, his treacherous son, wishing to put me to death, had it promptly taken off and some harmful salve applied. But I am very sure that the king was ignorant of this; he would not tolerate such base and murderous tricks. But you do not know how courteous he has been to my lady: no frontier tower since the time that Noah built the ark was ever so carefully guarded, for he has guarded her so vigilantly that, though his son chafed under the restraint, he would not let him see her except in the presence of the king himself. Up to the present time the king in his mercy has shown her all the marks of consideration which she herself proposed. She alone had the disposition of her affairs. And the king esteemed her all the more for the loyalty she showed. But is it true, as I am told, that she is so angry with you that she has publicly refused to speak with you?"

"You have been told the exact truth," Lancelot replies, "but for God's sake, can you tell me why she is so displeased with me?"

He replies that he does not know, and that he is greatly surprised at it.

"Well, let it be as she pleases," says Lancelot, feeling his helplessness; "I must now take my leave, and I shall go to seek my lord Gawain who has entered this land, and who arranged with me that he would proceed directly to the waterbridge." Then, leaving the room, he appeared before the king and asked for leave to proceed in that direction. And the king willingly grants him leave to go. Then those whom Lancelot had set free and delivered from prison ask him what they are to do.

And he replies: "All those who desire may come with me, and those who wish to stay with the Queen may do so: there is no reason why they should accompany me." Then all those, who so desire, accompany him, more glad and joyous than is their wont. With the Queen remain her damsels who are light of heart, and many knights and ladies too. But there is not one of those who stay behind, who would not have preferred to return to his own country to staying there. But on my lord Gawain's account, whose arrival is expected, the Queen keeps them, saying that she will never stir until she has news of him.

[*Due to a serious misunderstanding, Bademagu's subjects capture Lancelot, and rumors fly that they've killed him and that Guinevere has killed herself in grief. Once both sides find out that's not true, Lancelot's captors escort him back to the king.*]

Then the king leaves her, and the Queen yearns ardently for the arrival of her lover and her joy. She has no desire this time to bear him any grudge. But rumour, which never rests but runs always unceasingly, again reaches the Queen to the effect that Lancelot would have killed himself for her sake, if he had had the chance. She is happy at the thought that this is true, but she would not have had it happen so for anything, for her sorrow would have been too great. Thereupon Lancelot arrived in haste.[1] As soon as the king sees him, he runs to kiss and embrace him. He feels as if he ought to fly, borne along by the buoyancy of his joy. But his satisfaction is cut short by those who had taken and bound his guest, and the king tells them they have come in an evil hour, for they shall all be killed and confounded. Then they made answer that they thought he would have it so.

"It is I whom you have insulted in doing your pleasure. He has no reason to complain," the king replies; "you have not shamed him at all, but only me who was protecting him. However you look at it, the shame is mine. But if you escape me now, you will see no joke in this."

When Lancelot hears his wrath, he puts forth every effort to make peace and adjust matters; when his efforts have met with success, the king takes him away to see the Queen. This time the Queen did not lower her eyes to the ground, but she went to meet him cheerfully, honouring him all she could, and making him sit down by her side. Then they talked together at length of all that was upon their hearts, and love furnished them with so much to say that topics did not lack.

And when Lancelot sees how well he stands, and that all he says finds favour with the Queen, he says to her in confidence: "Lady, I marvel greatly why you received me with such a countenance when you saw me the day before yesterday, and why you would not speak a word to me: I almost died of the blow you gave me, and I had not the courage to dare to question you about it, as I now venture to do. I am ready now, lady, to make amends, when you have told me what has been the crime which has caused me such distress."

Then the Queen replies: "What? Did you not hesitate for shame to mount the cart? You showed you were loath to get in, when you hesitated for two whole steps. That is the reason why I would neither address nor look at you."

"May God save me from such a crime again," Lancelot replies, "and may God show me no mercy, if you were not quite right! For God's sake, lady, receive my amends at once, and tell me, for God's sake, if you can ever pardon me."

"Friend, you are quite forgiven," the Queen replies; "I pardon you willingly."

"Thank you for that, lady," he then says; "but I cannot tell you here all that I should like to say; I should like to talk with you more at leisure, if possible."

Then the Queen indicates a window by her glance rather than with her finger, and says: "Come through the garden to-night and speak with me at yonder window, when every

---

[1] Here we have the explanation of Guinevere's cold reception of Lancelot; he had been faithless to the rigid code of courtesy when he had hesitated for even a moment to cover himself with shame for her sake.

one inside has gone to sleep. You will not be able to get in: I shall be inside and you outside: to gain entrance will be impossible. I shall be able to touch you only with my lips or hand, but, if you please, I will stay there until morning for love of you. Our bodies cannot be joined, for close beside me in my room lies Kay the seneschal, who is still suffering from his wounds. And the door is not open, but is tightly closed and guarded well. When you come, take care to let no spy catch sight of you."

"Lady," says he, "if I can help it, no spy shall see me who might think or speak evil of us." Then, having agreed upon this plan, they separate very joyfully.

[*Lancelot manages to break in and spend the night with Guinevere, but his wounded hands leave blood on the sheets. Meleagant finds the bloody sheets in the morning and accuses Kay of sleeping with her, but Guinevere sends for Lancelot to defend them. Meleagant and Lancelot agree to a trial by combat.*]

When the oaths had been taken, their horses were brought forward, which were fair and good in every way. Each man mounts his own horse, and they ride at once at each other as fast as the steeds can carry them; and when the horses are in mid-career, the knights strike each other so fiercely that there is nothing left of the lances in their hands. Each brings the other to earth; however, they are not dismayed, but they rise at once and attack each other with their sharp drawn swords. The burning sparks fly in the air from their helmets. They assail each other so bitterly with the drawn swords in their hands that, as they thrust and draw, they encounter each other with their blows and will not pause even to catch their breath. The king in his grief and anxiety called the Queen, who had gone up in the tower to look out from the balcony: he begged her for God's sake, the Creator, to let them be separated.

"Whatever is your pleasure is agreeable to me," the Queen says honestly: "I shall not object to anything you do."

Lancelot plainly heard what reply the Queen made to the king's request, and from that time he ceased to fight and renounced the struggle at once. But Meleagant does not wish to stop, and continues to strike and hew at him. But the king rushes between them and stops his son, who declares with an oath that he has no desire for peace. He wants to fight, and cares not for peace.

Then the king says to him: "Be quiet, and take my advice, and be sensible. No shame or harm shall come to thee, if thou wilt do what is right and heed my words. Dost thou not remember that thou hast agreed to fight him at King Arthur's court? And dost thou not suppose that it would be a much greater honour for thee to defeat him there than anywhere else?" The king says this to see if he can so influence him as to appease him and separate them.

[*Lancelot leaves to look for Gawain but is led away from his company by a treacherous dwarf. His companions find Gawain and rescue him from drowning, but no one can find Lancelot. Finally, a message comes to Bademagu that Lancelot is safely back in Camelot, so Gawain and Kay lead Guinevere and all the captives home—only to discover that the message was a forgery. No one knows that Lancelot is being held captive by Meleagant's seneschal. Lancelot persuades the seneschal's wife to let him escape long enough to take part in a tournament at Camelot, but when he returns victorious, the seneschal, at Meleagant's order, locks Lancelot in an escape-proof tower. Meleagant goes to Camelot at the appointed time to fight Lancelot, but since Lancelot is still missing, Gawain vows to either find Lancelot within a year's time or fight the duel himself. Meleagant agrees but goes home to boast to his father; his sister, overhearing Bademagu's surmise that Lancelot must be either dead or captured, goes off to find Lancelot. Eventually she happens upon his tower and helps him escape, admitting that she's the maiden whose unwanted suitor he drove off before he arrived at Bademagu's court.]*

Lancelot was so glad to be on the road that, if I should take an oath, I could not possibly describe the joy he felt at having escaped from his trap. But he said to himself repeatedly that woe was the traitor, the reprobate, whom now he has tricked and ridiculed, "for in spite of him I have escaped." Then he swears by the heart and body of Him who made the world that not for all the riches and wealth from Babylon to Ghent would he let Meleagant escape, if he once got him in his power: for he has him to thank for too much harm and shame! But events will soon turn out so as to make this possible; for this very Meleagant, whom he threatens and presses hard, had already come to court that day without being summoned by any one; and the first thing he did was to search until he found my lord Gawain. Then the rascally proven traitor asks him about Lancelot, whether he had been seen or found, as if he himself did not know the truth. As a matter of fact, he did not know the truth, although he thought he knew it well enough. And Gawain told him, as was true, that he had not been seen, and that he had not come.

"Well, since I don't find him," says Meleagant, "do you come and keep the promise you made me: I shall not longer wait for you."

Then Gawain makes answer: "I will keep presently my word with you, if it please God in whom I place my trust. I expect to discharge my debt to you. But if it comes to throwing dice for points, and I should throw a higher number than you, so help me God and the holy faith, I'll not withdraw, but will keep on until I pocket all the stakes."[1]

Then without delay Gawain orders a rug to be thrown down and spread before him. There was no snivelling or attempt to run away when the squires heard this command, but without grumbling or complaint they execute what he commands. They bring the rug and spread it out in the place indicated; then he who had sent for it takes his seat upon it and gives orders to be armed by the young men who were standing unarmed before him. There were two of them, his cousins or nephews, I know not which, but they were accomplished and knew what to do. They arm him so skilfully and well that no one could find any fault in

---

[1] The figure is, of course, taken from the game of throwing dice for high points.

the world with them for any mistake in what they did. When they finished arming him, one of them went to fetch a Spanish steed able to cross the fields, woods, hills, and valleys more swiftly than the good Bucephalus.[1] Upon a horse such as you have heard Gawain took his seat—the admired and most accomplished knight upon whom the sign of the Cross was ever made. Already he was about to seize his shield, when he saw Lancelot dismount before him, whom he was not expecting to see. He looked at him in amazement, because he had come so unexpectedly; and, if I am not wrong, he was as much surprised as if he had fallen from the clouds. However, no business of his own can detain him, as soon as he sees Lancelot, from dismounting and extending his arms to him, as he embraces, salutes and kisses him. Now he is happy and at ease, when he has found his companion.

Now I will tell you the truth, and you must not think I lie, that Gawain would not wish to be chosen king, unless he had Lancelot with him. The King and all the rest now learn that, in spite of all, Lancelot, for whom they so long have watched, has come back quite safe and sound. Therefore they all rejoice, and the court, which so long has looked for him, comes together to honour him. Their happiness dispels and drives away the sorrow which formerly was theirs. Grief takes flight and is replaced by an awakening joy.

And how about the Queen? Does she not share in the general jubilee? Yes, verily, she first of all. How so? For God's sake, where, then, could she be keeping herself? She was never so glad in her life as she was for his return. And did she not even go to him? Certainly she did; she is so close to him that her body came near following her heart. Where is her heart, then? It was kissing and welcoming Lancelot. And why did the body conceal itself? Why is not her joy complete? Is it mingled with anger or hate? No, certainly, not at all; but it may be that the King or some of the others who are there, and who are watching what takes place, would have taken the whole situation in, if, while all were looking on, she had followed the dictates of her heart. If common-sense had not banished this mad impulse and rash desire, her heart would have been revealed and her folly would have been complete. Therefore reason closes up and binds her fond heart and her rash intent, and made it more reasonable, postponing the greeting until it shall see and espy a suitable and more private place where they would fare better than here and now.

The King highly honoured Lancelot, and after welcoming him, thus spoke: "I have not heard for a long time news of any man which were so welcome as news of you; yet I am much concerned to learn in what region and in what land you have tarried so long a time. I have had search made for you up and down, all the winter and summer through, but no one could find a trace of you."

"Indeed, fair sire," says Lancelot, "I can inform you in a few words exactly how it has fared with me. The miserable traitor Meleagant has kept me in prison ever since the hour of the deliverance of the prisoners in his land, and has condemned me to a life of shame in a tower of his beside the sea. There he put me and shut me in, and there I should still be

---

[1] Alexander's horse.

dragging out my weary life, if it were not for a friend of mine, a damsel for whom I once performed a slight service. In return for the little favour I did her, she has repaid me liberally: she has bestowed upon me great honour and blessing. But I wish to repay without delay him for whom I have no love, who has sought out and devised for me this shame and injury. He need not wait, for the sum is all ready, principal and interest; but God forbid that he find in it cause to rejoice!"

Then Gawain said to Lancelot: "Friend, it will be only a slight favour for me, who am in your debt, to make this payment for you. Moreover, I am all ready and mounted, as you see. Fair, sweet friend, do not deny me the boon I desire and request."

But Lancelot replies that he would rather have his eye plucked out, or even both of them, than be persuaded to do this: he swears it shall never be so. He owes the debt and he will pay it himself: for with his own hand he promised it. Gawain plainly sees that nothing he can say is of any avail, so he loosens and takes off his hauberk from his back, and completely disarms himself. Lancelot at once arms himself without delay; for he is impatient to settle and discharge his debt.

Meleagant, who is amazed beyond measure at what he sees, has reached the end of his good fortunes, and is about to receive what is owing him. He is almost beside himself and comes near fainting. "Surely I was a fool," he says, "not to go, before coming here, to see if I still held imprisoned in my tower him who now has played this trick on me. But, God, why should I have gone? What cause had I to think that he could possibly escape? Is not the wall built strong enough, and is not the tower sufficiently strong and high? There was no hole or crevice in it, through which he could pass, unless he was aided from outside. I am sure his hiding-place was revealed. If the wall were worn away and had fallen into decay, would he not have been caught and injured or killed at the same time? Yes, so help me God, if it had fallen down, he would certainly have been killed. But I guess, before that wall gives away without being torn down, that all the water in the sea will dry up without leaving a drop and the world will come to an end. No, that is not it: it happened otherwise: he was helped to escape, and could not have got out otherwise: I have been outwitted through some trickery. At any rate, he has escaped; but if I had been on my guard, all this would never have happened, and he would never have come to court. But it's too late now to repent. The rustic, who seldom errs, pertinently remarks that it is too late to close the stable when the horse is out. I know I shall now be exposed to great shame and humiliation, if indeed I do not suffer and endure something worse. What shall I suffer and endure? Rather, so long as I live, I will give him full measure, if it please God, in whom I trust." Thus he consoles himself, and has no other desire than to meet his antagonist on the field.

And he will not have long to wait, I think, for Lancelot goes in search of him, expecting soon to conquer him. But before the assault begins, the King bids them go down into the plain where the tower stands, the prettiest place this side of Ireland for a fight. So they did, and soon found themselves on the plain below. The King goes down too, and all the rest, men and women in crowds. No one stays behind; but many go up to the windows of the tower, among them the Queen, her ladies and damsels, of whom she had many with her who were fair.

In the field there stood a sycamore as fair as any tree could be; it was wide-spread and covered a large area, and around it grew a fine border of thick fresh grass which was green at all seasons of the year. Under this fair and stately sycamore, which was planted back in Abel's time, there rises a clear spring of water which flows away hurriedly. The bed of the spring is beautiful and as bright as silver, and the channel through which the water flows is formed, I think, of refined and tested gold, and it stretches away across the field down into a valley between the woods. There it pleases the King to take his seat where nothing unpleasant is in sight. After the crowd has drawn back at the King's command, Lancelot rushes furiously at Meleagant as at one whom he hates cordially, but before striking him, he shouted with a loud and commanding voice: "Take your stand, I defy you! And take my word, this time you shall not be spared." Then he spurs his steed and draws back the distance of a bow-shot. Then they drive their horses toward each other at top speed, and strike each other so fiercely upon their resisting shields that they pierced and punctured them. But neither one is wounded, nor is the flesh touched in this first assault. They pass each other without delay, and come back at the top of their horses: speed to renew their blows on the strong, stout shields. Both of the knights are strong and brave, and both of the horses are stout and fast. So mighty are the blows they deal on the shields about their necks that the lances passed clean through, without breaking or splintering, until the cold steel reached their flesh. Each strikes the other with such force that both are borne to earth, and no breast-strap, girth, or stirrup could save them from falling backward over their saddle-bow, leaving the saddle without an occupant. The horses run riderless over hill and dale, but they kick and bite each other, thus showing their mortal hatred.

As for the knights who fell to earth, they leaped up as quickly as possible and drew their swords, which were engraved with chiselled lettering. Holding their shields before the face, they strive to wound each other with their swords of steel. Lancelot stands in no fear of him, for he knew half as much again about fencing as did his antagonist, having learned it in his youth. Both dealt such blows on the shield slung from their necks, and upon their helmets barred with gold, that they crushed and damaged them. But Lancelot presses him hard and gives him a mighty blow upon his right arm which, though encased in mail, was unprotected by the shield, severing it with one clean stroke.

And when he felt the loss of his right arm, he said that it should be dearly sold. If it is at all possible, he will not fail to exact the price; he is in such pain and wrath and rage that he is well-nigh beside himself, and he has a poor opinion of himself, if he cannot score on his rival now. He rushes at him with the intent to seize him, but Lancelot forestalls his plan, for with his trenchant sword he deals his body such a cut as he will not recover from until April and May be passed. He smashes his nose-guard against his teeth, breaking three of them in his mouth. And Meleagant's rage is such that he cannot speak or say a word; nor does he deign to cry for mercy, for his foolish heart holds tight in such constraint that even now it deludes him still. Lancelot approaches and, unlacing his helmet, cuts off his head. Never more will this man trouble him; it is all over with him as he falls dead. Not a soul who was present there felt any pity at the sight. The King and all the others there are jubilant and express their joy. Happier than they ever were before, they relieve Lancelot of his arms, and lead him away exultingly.

My lords, if I should prolong my tale, it would be beside the purpose, and so I will conclude. Godefroi de Leigni, the clerk, has written the conclusion of "the Cart"; but let no one find fault with him for having embroidered on Chrétien's theme, for it was done with the consent of Chrétien who started it. Godefroi has finished it from the point where Lancelot was imprisoned in the tower. So much he wrote; but he would fain add nothing more, for fear of disfiguring the tale.

୬୬

Sir Thomas Malory
Le Morte D'Arthur[1]

Book XIII.

Chapter I.
How at the vigil of the Feast of Pentecost entered into the hall before King Arthur a damosel, and desired Sir Launcelot for to come and dub a knight, and how he went with her.

At the vigil of Pentecost, when all the fellowship of the Round Table were come unto Camelot and there heard their service, and the tables were set ready to the meat, right so entered into the hall a full fair gentlewoman on horseback, that had ridden full fast, for her horse was all besweated. Then she there alighted, and came before the king and saluted him; and he said: "Damosel, God thee bless." "Sir," said she, "for God's sake say me where Sir Launcelot is." "Yonder ye may see him," said the king. Then she went unto Launcelot and said: "Sir Launcelot, I salute you on King Pelles' behalf, and I require you come on with me hereby into a forest." Then Sir Launcelot asked her with whom she dwelled. "I dwell," said she, "with King Pelles." "What will ye with me?" said Launcelot. "Ye shall know, said she, when ye come thither." "Well," said he, "I will gladly go with you." So Sir Launcelot bade his squire saddle his horse and bring his arms; and in all haste he did his commandment.

Then came the queen unto Launcelot, and said: "Will ye leave us at this high feast?" "Madam," said the gentlewoman, "wit ye well he shall be with you to-morn by dinner time."

---

[1] Notes on this text incorporate notes from Alfred W. Pollard's 1900 edition, marked with "(P)" at the end. I have also added quotation marks and italics for greater ease of reading.

"If I wist," said the queen, "that he should not be with us here to-morn he should not go with you by my good will." Right so departed Sir Launcelot with the gentlewoman, and rode until that he came into a forest and into a great valley, where they saw an abbey of nuns; and there was a squire ready and opened the gates, and so they entered and descended off their horses; and there came a fair fellowship about Sir Launcelot, and welcomed him, and were passing glad of his coming. And then they led him unto the Abbess's chamber and unarmed him; and right so he was ware upon a bed lying two of his cousins, Sir Bors and Sir Lionel, and then he waked them; and when they saw him they made great joy. "Sir," said Sir Bors unto Sir Launcelot, "what adventure hath brought you hither, for we weened to-morn to have found you at Camelot?" "As God me help," said Sir Launcelot, "a gentlewoman brought me hither, but I know not the cause."

In the meanwhile that they thus stood talking together, therein came twelve nuns that brought with them Galahad, the which was passing fair and well made, that unnethe[1] in the world men might not find his match: and all those ladies wept. "Sir," said they all, "we bring you here this child the which we have nourished, and we pray you to make him a knight, for of a more worthier man's hand may he not receive the order of knighthood."[2] Sir Launcelot beheld the young squire and saw him seemly and demure as a dove, with all manner of good features, that he weened of his age never to have seen so fair a man of form. Then said Sir Launcelot: "Cometh this desire of himself?" He and all they said yea. "Then shall he," said Sir Launcelot, "receive the high order of knighthood as to-morn at the reverence of the high feast." That night Sir Launcelot had passing good cheer; and on the morn at the hour of prime, at Galahad's desire, he made him knight and said: "God make him a good man, for of beauty faileth you not as any that liveth."

Chapter II.
How the letters were found written in the Siege Perilous[3] and of the marvellous adventure of the sword in a stone.

"Now fair sir," said Sir Launcelot, "will ye come with me unto the court of King Arthur?" "Nay," said he,[4] "I will not go with you as at this time." Then he[5] departed from them and

---

[1] Hardly, scarcely (i.e., it would be almost impossible to find Galahad's equal anywhere in the world)

[2] Galahad is in fact Lancelot's son.

[3] Thanks to Merlin's spellwork, the various seats (here called *sieges* from the French) around the Round Table were magically assigned to each knight—all except the Siege Perilous, which was reserved for the best knight in the world and would kill any other knight who sat in it. The knight who can sit in the Siege Perilous is also the knight who will complete the quest for the Holy Grail, which is foretold early in the *Morte D'Arthur* but does not appear as an actual adventure until this book. In this arc, the knights are about to learn the identity of the knight for whom the Siege Perilous is reserved.

[4] Galahad

[5] Lancelot

took his two cousins with him, and so they came unto Camelot by the hour of underne[1] on Whitsunday.[2] By that time the king and the queen were gone to the minster to hear their service. Then the king and the queen were passing glad of Sir Bors and Sir Lionel, and so was all the fellowship. So when the king and all the knights were come from service, the barons espied in the sieges of the Round Table all about, written with golden letters: *Here ought to sit he, and he ought to sit here.* And thus they went so long till that they came to the Siege Perilous, where they found letters newly written of gold which said: *Four hundred winters and four and fifty accomplished after the passion of our Lord Jesu Christ ought this siege to be fulfilled.*[3] Then all they said: "This is a marvellous thing and an adventurous." "In the name of God," said Sir Launcelot; and then accompted[4] the term of the writing from the birth of our Lord unto that day. "It seemeth me," said Sir Launcelot, "this siege ought to be fulfilled this same day, for this is the feast of Pentecost after the four hundred and four and fifty year; and if it would please all parties, I would none of these letters were seen this day, till he be come that ought to enchieve[5] this adventure." Then made they to ordain a cloth of silk, for to cover these letters in the Siege Perilous.

Then the king bade haste unto dinner. "Sir," said Sir Kay the Steward, "if ye go now unto your meat ye shall break your old custom of your court, for ye have not used on this day to sit at your meat or that ye have seen some adventure."[6] "Ye say sooth," said the king, "but I had so great joy of Sir Launcelot and of his cousins, which be come to the court whole and sound, so that I bethought me not of mine old custom." So, as they stood speaking, in came a squire and said unto the king: "Sir, I bring unto you marvellous tidings." "What be they?" said the king. "Sir, there is here beneath at the river a great stone which I saw fleet[7] above the water, and therein I saw sticking a sword." The king said: "I will see that marvel." So all the knights went with him, and when they came to the river they found there a stone fleeting, as it were of red marble, and therein stuck a fair rich sword, and in the pommel thereof were precious stones wrought with subtle letters of gold. Then the barons read the letters which said in this wise: *Never shall man take me hence, but only he by whose side I ought to hang, and he shall be the best knight of the world.*[8]

When the king had seen the letters, he said unto Sir Launcelot: "Fair Sir, this sword ought to be yours, for I am sure ye be the best knight of the world." Then Sir Launcelot

---

[1] Frustratingly, this term can be used to describe 9 a.m., noon, and late afternoon! Since the court has already gone to Mass, however, here it probably means sometime in the late morning.

[2] i.e., Pentecost.

[3] filled

[4] calculated

[5] achieve

[6] This custom had become a well-established trope in the romance tradition by this point.

[7] float

[8] Note that this is a *different* sword from the Sword in the Stone that Merlin set up to prove Arthur's right to the throne.

answered full soberly: "Certes,[1] sir, it is not my sword; also, Sir, wit ye well I have no hardiness to set my hand to it, for it longed not to hang by my side. Also, who that assayeth[2] to take the sword and faileth of it, he shall receive a wound by that sword that he shall not be whole long after. And I will that ye wit that this same day shall the adventures of the Sangreal,[3] that is called the Holy Vessel, begin."

Chapter III.
How Sir Gawaine assayed to draw out the sword, and how an old man brought in Galahad.

"Now, fair nephew," said the king unto Sir Gawaine, "assay ye, for my love." "Sir," he said, "save your good grace I shall not do that." "Sir," said the king, "assay to take the sword and at my commandment." "Sir," said Gawaine, "your commandment I will obey." And therewith he took up the sword by the handles, but he might not stir it. "I thank you," said the king to Sir Gawaine. "My lord Sir Gawaine," said Sir Launcelot, "now wit ye well this sword shall touch you so sore that ye shall will ye had never set your hand thereto for the best castle of this realm." "Sir," he said, "I might not withsay[4] mine uncle's will and commandment." But when the king heard this he repented it much, and said unto Sir Percivale that he should assay, for his love. And he said: "Gladly, for to bear Sir Gawaine fellowship." And therewith he set his hand on the sword and drew it strongly, but he might not move it. Then were there none[5] that durst be so hardy to set their hands thereto. "Now may ye go to your dinner," said Sir Kay unto the king, "for a marvellous adventure have ye seen." So the king and all went unto the court, and every knight knew his own place, and set him therein, and young men that were knights served them.

So when they were served, and all sieges fulfilled save only the Siege Perilous, anon there befell a marvellous adventure, that all the doors and windows of the palace shut by themself. Not for then the hall was not greatly darked; and therewith they were all abashed both one and other. Then King Arthur spake first and said: "By God, fair fellows and lords, we have seen this day marvels, but or[6] night I suppose we shall see greater marvels."

In the meanwhile came in a good old man, and an ancient, clothed all in white, and there was no knight knew from whence he came. And with him he brought a young knight, both on foot, in red arms, without sword or shield, save a scabbard hanging by his side. And these words he said: "Peace be with you, fair lords." Then the old man said unto Arthur: "Sir, I bring here a young knight, the which is of king's lineage, and of the kindred of Joseph

---

[1] Certainly
[2] attempts
[3] The Holy Grail
[4] oppose or show contempt for
[5] Omitted by Caxton, supplied from W. de Worde. (P)
[6] before

of Aramathie,[1] whereby the marvels of this court, and of strange realms, shall be fully accomplished."

Chapter IV.

How the old man brought Galahad to the Siege Perilous and set him therein, and how all the knights marvelled.

The king was right glad of his words, and said unto the good man: Sir, ye be right welcome, and the young knight with you. Then the old man made the young man to unarm him, and he was in a coat of red sendal, and bare a mantle upon his shoulder that was furred with ermine, and put that upon him. And the old knight said unto the young knight: "Sir, follow me." And anon he led him unto the Siege Perilous, where beside sat Sir Launcelot; and the good man lift up the cloth, and found there letters that said thus: *This is the siege of Galahad, the haut[2] prince.* "Sir," said the old knight, "wit ye well that place is yours." And then he set him down surely in that siege. And then he said to the old man: "Sir, ye may now go your way, for well have ye done that ye were commanded to do; and recommend me unto my grandsire, King Pelles, and unto my lord Petchere, and say them on my behalf, I shall come and see them as soon as ever I may." So the good man departed; and there met him twenty noble squires, and so took their horses and went their way.

Then all the knights of the Table Round marvelled greatly of Sir Galahad, that he durst sit there in that Siege Perilous, and was so tender of age; and wist not from whence he came but all only by God; and said: "This is he by whom the Sangreal shall be enchieved, for there sat never none but he, but he were mischieved."[3] Then Sir Launcelot beheld his son and had great joy of him. Then Bors told his fellows: "Upon pain of my life this young knight shall come unto great worship." This noise was great in all the court, so that it came to the queen. Then she had marvel what knight it might be that durst adventure him to sit in the Siege Perilous. Many said unto the queen he resembled much unto Sir Launcelot. "I may well suppose," said the queen, "that Sir Launcelot begat him on King Pelles' daughter, by the which he was made to lie by, by enchantment, and his name is Galahad. I would fain see him," said the queen, "for he must needs be a noble man, for so is his father that him begat, I report me unto all the Table Round."

So when the meat was done that the king and all were risen, the king yede[4] unto the Siege Perilous and lift up the cloth, and found there the name of Galahad; and then he

---

[1] Medieval legend, especially in Britain and France, held that Joseph of Arimathea was Mary's uncle, and Lancelot was by this point supposed to have been one of Joseph's direct descendants. Thus we see Guinevere stating in Chapter VII that Lancelot and Galahad have a right to be great knights because of their close blood relation to Jesus.

[2] high

[3] none but he ever sat there without coming to grief

[4] went

shewed it unto Sir Gawaine, and said: "Fair nephew, now have we among us Sir Galahad, the good knight that shall worship[1] us all; and upon pain of my life he shall enchieve the Sangreal, right as Sir Launcelot had done us to understand." Then came King Arthur unto Galahad and said: "Sir, ye be welcome, for ye shall move many good knights to the quest of the Sangreal, and ye shall enchieve that[2] never knights might bring to an end." Then the king took him by the hand, and went down from the palace to shew Galahad the adventures of the stone.

Chapter V.
How King Arthur shewed the stone hoving[3] on the water to Galahad, and how he drew out the sword.

The queen heard thereof, and came after with many ladies, and shewed them the stone where it hoved on the water. "Sir," said the king unto Sir Galahad, "here is a great marvel as ever I saw, and right good knights have assayed and failed." "Sir," said Galahad, "that is no marvel, for this adventure is not theirs but mine; and for the surety of this sword I brought none with me, for here by my side hangeth the scabbard." And anon he laid his hand on the sword, and lightly drew it out of the stone, and put it in the sheath, and said unto the king: "Now it goeth better than it did aforehand." "Sir," said the king, "a shield God shall send you." "Now have I that sword that sometime was the good knight's, Balin le Savage, and he was a passing good man of his hands; and with this sword he slew his brother Balan, and that was great pity, for he was a good knight, and either slew other through a dolorous stroke that Balin gave unto my grandfather King Pelles, the which is not yet whole, nor not shall be till I heal him."

Therewith the king and all espied where came riding down the river a lady on a white palfrey toward them. Then she saluted the king and the queen, and asked if that Sir Launcelot was there. And then he answered himself: I am here, fair lady. Then she said all with weeping: "How your great doing is changed sith this day in the morn." "Damosel, why say you so?" said Launcelot. "I say you sooth," said the damosel, "for ye were this day the best knight of the world, but who should say so now, he should be a liar, for there is now one better than ye, and well it is proved by the adventures of the sword whereto ye durst not set to your hand; and that is the change and leaving of your name. Wherefore I make unto you a remembrance, that ye shall not ween from henceforth that ye be the best knight of the world." "As touching unto that," said Launcelot, "I know well I was never the best."[4] "Yes,

---

[1] In this context: bring honor to, be a credit to

[2] what

[3] floating

[4] This statement is not just humility on Lancelot's part. Elaine of Corbenic had twice used enchantments to get him into her bed, making him believe he was sleeping with Guinevere. The first time, at Pelles' castle, was when she conceived Galahad, and he very nearly killed her for tricking him so; the second time was in Camelot,

said the damosel, that were ye, and are yet, of any sinful man of the world. And, Sir king, Nacien, the hermit, sendeth thee word, that thee shall befall the greatest worship that ever befell king in Britain; and I say you wherefore, for this day the Sangreal appeared in thy house and fed thee and all thy fellowship of the Round Table." So she departed and went that same way that she came.

Chapter VI.

How King Arthur had all the knights together for to joust in the meadow beside Camelot or they departed.

"Now," said the king, "I am sure at this quest of the Sangreal shall all ye of the Table Round depart, and never shall I see you again whole together; therefore I will see you all whole together in the meadow of Camelot to joust and to tourney, that after your death men may speak of it that such good knights were wholly together such a day." As unto that counsel and at the king's request they accorded all, and took on their harness that longed unto jousting. But all this moving of the king was for this intent, for to see Galahad proved; for the king deemed he should not lightly come again unto the court after his departing. So were they assembled in the meadow, both more and less. Then Sir Galahad, by the prayer of the king and the queen, did upon him a noble jesseraunce,[1] and also he did on his helm, but shield would he take none for no prayer of the king. And then Sir Gawaine and other knights prayed him to take a spear. Right so he did; and the queen was in a tower with all her ladies, for to behold that tournament. Then Sir Galahad dressed him in midst of the meadow, and began to break spears marvellously, that all men had wonder of him; for he there surmounted all other knights, for within a while he had defouled many good knights of the Table Round save twain, that was Sir Launcelot and Sir Percivale.

Chapter VII.

How the queen desired to see Galahad; and how after, all the knights were replenished with the Holy Sangreal, and how they avowed the enquest[2] of the same.

Then the king, at the queen's request, made him to alight and to unlace his helm, that the queen might see him in the visage. When she beheld him she said: "Soothly I dare well say

---

when Guinevere had genuinely sent for Lancelot to spend the night with her but Elaine had him intercepted. Guinevere refused to believe that Lancelot had been deceived, and her cruelty toward him caused what we would now call a dissociative fugue. Elaine had him healed with the Grail, but Lancelot was so deeply ashamed of both his conduct and his psychotic break that, in the two years since, he never even allows anyone to call him anything but *Le Chevaler Mal Fet*, the Knight Who Did Ill. He finally meets friends from Camelot and returns to court under his right name only a few months before this part of the story.

[1] put on a noble coat of armor
[2] vowed to undertake the quest

that Sir Launcelot begat him, for never two men resembled more in likeness, therefore it nis[1] no marvel though he be of great prowess." So a lady that stood by the queen said: "Madam, for God's sake ought he of right to be so good a knight?" "Yea, forsooth," said the queen, "for he is of all parties come of the best knights of the world and of the highest lineage; for Sir Launcelot is come but of the eighth degree from our Lord Jesu Christ, and Sir Galahad is of the ninth degree from our Lord Jesu Christ, therefore I dare say they be the greatest gentlemen of the world."

And then the king and all estates went home unto Camelot, and so went to evensong to the great minster, and so after upon that to supper, and every knight sat in his own place as they were toforehand.[2] Then anon they heard cracking and crying of thunder, that them thought the place should all to-drive.[3] In the midst of this blast entered a sunbeam more clearer by seven times than ever they saw day, and all they were alighted of the grace of the Holy Ghost. Then began every knight to behold other, and either saw other, by their seeming, fairer than ever they saw afore. Not for then there was no knight might speak one word a great while, and so they looked every man on other as they had been dumb.[4] Then there entered into the hall the Holy Grail covered with white samite, but there was none might see it, nor who bare it. And there was all the hall fulfilled with good odours, and every knight had such meats and drinks as he best loved in this world. And when the Holy Grail had been borne through the hall, then the holy vessel departed suddenly, that they wist not where it became:[5] then had they all breath to speak. And then the king yielded thankings to God, of His good grace that he had sent them. "Certes," said the king, "we ought to thank our Lord Jesu greatly for that he hath shewed us this day, at the reverence of this high feast of Pentecost."

"Now," said Sir Gawaine, "we have been served this day of what meats and drinks we thought on; but one thing beguiled us, we might not see the Holy Grail, it was so preciously covered. Wherefore I will make here avow, that to-morn, without longer abiding, I shall labour in the quest of the Sangreal, that I shall hold me out a twelvemonth and a day, or more if need be, and never shall I return again unto the court till I have seen it more openly than it hath been seen here; and if I may not speed I shall return again as he that may not be against the will of our Lord Jesu Christ."

When they of the Table Round heard Sir Gawaine say so, they arose up the most part and made such avows as Sir Gawaine had made. Anon as King Arthur heard this he was greatly displeased, for he wist well they might not again-say their avows.[6] "Alas," said King

---

[1] is (not a typo; *nis* is the negated form in Old and Middle English, in which a double negative was a more intense negative rather than a positive)

[2] beforehand

[3] it seemed to them that the place would be blown to pieces

[4] i.e., they were mute with wonder

[5] went

[6] The vows, in other words, are binding; the knights cannot go back on their word now.

Arthur unto Sir Gawaine, "ye have nigh slain me with the avow and promise that ye have made; for through you ye have bereft me the fairest fellowship and the truest of knighthood that ever were seen together in any realm of the world; for when they depart from hence I am sure they all shall never meet more in this world, for they shall die many in the quest. And so it forthinketh me[1] a little, for I have loved them as well as my life, wherefore it shall grieve me right sore, the departition[2] of this fellowship: for I have had an old custom to have them in my fellowship."

Chapter VIII.
How great sorrow was made of the king and the queen and ladies for the departing of the knights, and how they departed.

And therewith the tears fell in his eyes. And then he said: "Gawaine, Gawaine, ye have set me in great sorrow, for I have great doubt that my true fellowship shall never meet here more again." "Ah," said Sir Launcelot, "comfort yourself; for it shall be unto us a great honour and much more than if we died in any other places, for of death we be siker."[3] "Ah, Launcelot," said the king, "the great love that I have had unto you all the days of my life maketh me to say such doleful words; for never Christian king had never so many worthy men at his table as I have had this day at the Round Table, and that is my great sorrow."

When the queen, ladies, and gentlewomen, wist these tidings, they had such sorrow and heaviness that there might no tongue tell it, for those knights had held them in honour and chierté.[4] But among all other Queen Guenever made great sorrow. "I marvel," said she, "my lord would suffer them to depart from him." Thus was all the court troubled for the love of the departition of those knights. And many of those ladies that loved knights would have gone with their lovers; and so had they done,[5] had not an old knight come among them in religious clothing; and then he spake all on high and said: "Fair lords, which have sworn in the quest of the Sangreal, thus sendeth you Nacien, the hermit, word, that none in this quest lead lady nor gentlewoman with him, for it is not to do in so high a service as they labour in; for I warn you plain, he that is not clean of his sins he shall not see the mysteries of our Lord Jesu Christ." And for this cause they left these ladies and gentlewomen.

After this the queen came unto Galahad and asked him of whence he was, and of what country. He told her of whence he was. And son unto Launcelot, she said he was. As to that, he said neither yea nor nay. "So God me help," said the queen, "of your father ye need not to shame you, for he is the goodliest knight, and of the best men of the world come, and of the strain, of all parties, of kings. Wherefore ye ought of right to be, of your deeds, a passing

---

[1] I regret it
[2] departing
[3] certain
[4] admiration
[5] i.e., they wanted to go with their lovers and would have done so

good man; and certainly," she said, "ye resemble him much." Then Sir Galahad was a little ashamed and said: "Madam, sith ye know in certain, wherefore do ye ask it me? for he that is my father shall be known openly and all betimes." And then they went to rest them. And in the honour of the highness of Galahad he was led into King Arthur's chamber, and there rested in his own bed.[1]

And as soon as it was day the king arose, for he had no rest of all that night for sorrow. Then he went unto Gawaine and to Sir Launcelot that were arisen for to hear mass. And then the king again said: "Ah Gawaine, Gawaine, ye have betrayed me; for never shall my court be amended by you, but ye will never be sorry for me as I am for you." And therewith the tears began to run down by his visage. And therewith the king said: "Ah, knight Sir Launcelot, I require thee thou counsel me, for I would that this quest were undone, an it might be." "Sir," said Sir Launcelot, "ye saw yesterday so many worthy knights that then were sworn that they may not leave it in no manner of wise." "That wot I well," said the king, "but it shall so heavy[2] me at their departing that I wot well there shall no manner of joy remedy me." And then the king and the queen went unto the minster. So anon Launcelot and Gawaine commanded their men to bring their arms. And when they all were armed save their shields and their helms, then they came to their fellowship, which were all ready in the same wise, for to go to the minster to hear their service.

Then after the service was done the king would wit how many had undertaken the quest of the Holy Grail; and to accompt them he prayed them all. Then found they by the tale an hundred and fifty, and all were knights of the Round Table. And then they put on their helms and departed, and recommended them all wholly unto the queen; and there was weeping and great sorrow. Then the queen departed into her chamber and held her, so that no man should perceive her great sorrows. When Sir Launcelot missed the queen he went till her chamber, and when she saw him she cried aloud: "O Launcelot, Launcelot, ye have betrayed me and put me to the death, for to leave thus my lord." "Ah, madam, I pray you be not displeased, for I shall come again as soon as I may with my worship." "Alas," said she, "that ever I saw you; but he that suffered upon the cross for all mankind, he be unto you good conduct and safety, and all the whole fellowship."

Right so departed Sir Launcelot, and found his fellowship that abode his coming. And so they mounted upon their horses and rode through the streets of Camelot; and there was weeping of rich and poor, and the king turned away and might not speak for weeping. So within a while they came to a city, and a castle that hight Vagon. There they entered into the castle, and the lord of that castle was an old man that hight Vagon, and he was a good man of his living, and set open the gates, and made them all the cheer that he might. And so on

---

[1] This was standard practice in the Middle Ages: the king or lord would have multiple servants sleeping in his bedchamber, and honored guests would share the king's bed—but not in any sexual sense.

[2] grieve

the morn they were all accorded that they should depart everych[1] from other; and on the morn they departed with weeping cheer, and every knight took the way that him liked[2] best.

---

[1] "every each"—each one
[2] pleased him

The Renaissance, Enlightenment, and American Revolution

John Donne
from Holy Sonnets

X

Death, be not proud, though some have called thee
Mighty and dreadful, for thou art not so;
For those, whom thou think'st thou dost overthrow,
Die not, poor Death, nor yet canst thou kill me.
From rest and sleep, which but thy picture[s] be,
Much pleasure, then from thee much more must flow,
And soonest our best men with thee do go,
Rest of their bones, and soul's delivery.
Thou'rt slave to Fate, chance, kings, and desperate men,
And dost with poison, war, and sickness dwell,
And poppy, or charms can make us sleep as well,
And better than thy stroke; why swell'st thou then?
One short sleep past, we wake eternally,
And Death shall be no more; Death, thou shalt die.

XIV

Batter my heart, three-person'd God; for you
As yet but knock; breathe, shine, and seek to mend;
That I may rise, and stand, o'erthrow me, and bend
Your force, to break, blow, burn, and make me new.
I, like an usurp'd town, to another due,
Labour to admit you, but O, to no end.
Reason, your viceroy in me, me should defend,
But is captived, and proves weak or untrue.
Yet dearly I love you, and would be loved fain,
But am betroth'd unto your enemy;
Divorce me, untie, or break that knot again,
Take me to you, imprison me, for I,
Except you enthrall me, never shall be free,
Nor ever chaste, except you ravish me.

XV

Wilt thou love God as he thee? then digest,
My soul, this wholesome meditation,
How God the Spirit, by angels waited on
In heaven, doth make His temple in thy breast.
The Father having begot a Son most blest,
And still begetting—for he ne'er begun—
Hath deign'd to choose thee by adoption,
Co-heir to His glory, and Sabbath's endless rest.
And as a robb'd man, which by search doth find
His stolen stuff sold, must lose or buy it again,
The Sun of glory came down, and was slain,
Us whom He had made, and Satan stole, to unbind.
'Twas much, that man was made like God before,
But, that God should be made like man, much more.

George Herbert
from The Temple

Redemption

HAVING been tenant long to a rich Lord,
    Not thriving, I resolved to be bold,
    And make a suit unto him, to afford
A new small-rented lease, and cancell th' old.

In heaven at his manour I him sought:
    They told me there, that he was lately gone
    About some land, which he had dearly bought
Long since on earth, to take possession.

I straight return'd, and knowing his great birth,
    Sought him accordingly in great resorts;
    In cities, theatres, gardens, parks, and courts:
At length I heard a ragged noise and mirth

Of theeves and murderers: there I him espied,
Who straight, *Your suit is granted*, said, and died.

Easter

RISE heart; thy Lord is risen. Sing his praise
                Without delayes,
Who takes thee by the hand, that thou likewise
                With him mayst rise:
That, as his death calcined thee to dust,
His life may make thee gold, and much more just.

Awake, my lute, and struggle for thy part
                With all thy art.
The crosse taught all wood to resound his name
                Who bore the same.
His stretched sinews taught all strings, what key
Is best to celebrate this most high day.

Consort both heart and lute, and twist a song
                Pleasant and long:
Or since all music is but three parts vied,
                And multiplied;
O let thy blessed Spirit bear a part,
And make up our defects with his sweet art.

    I got me flowers to straw thy way;
    I got me boughs off many a tree:
    But thou wast up by break of day,
    And brought'st thy sweets along with thee.

    The Sunne arising in the East,
    Though he give light, and th' East perfume;
    If they should offer to contest
    With thy arising, they presume.

    Can there be any day but this,
    Though many sunnes to shine endeavour?
    We count three hundred, but we misse:
    There is but one, and that one ever.

Prayer (I)

PRAYER the Churches banquet, Angels age,
     Gods breath in man returning to his birth,
     The soul in paraphrase, heart in pilgrimage,
The Christian plummet sounding heav'n and earth;

Engine against th' Almightie, sinner's towre,
     Reversed thunder, Christ-side-piercing spear,
     The six daies world-transposing in an houre,
A kinde of tune, which all things heare and fear;

Softnesse, and peace, and joy, and love, and blisse,
     Exalted Manna, gladnesse of the best,
     Heaven in ordinarie, man well drest,
The milkie way, the bird of Paradise,

     Church-bels beyond the stars heard, the souls bloud,
     The land of spices, something understood.

Love (III)

Love bade me welcome, yet my soul drew back,
    Guilty of dust and sin.
But quick-ey'd Love, observing me grow slack
    From my first entrance in,
Drew nearer to me, sweetly questioning
    If I lack'd anything.

"A guest," I answer'd, "worthy to be here";
    Love said, "You shall be he."
"I, the unkind, the ungrateful? ah my dear,
    I cannot look on thee."
Love took my hand and smiling did reply,
    "Who made the eyes but I?"

"Truth, Lord, but I have marr'd them; let my shame
    Go where it doth deserve."
"And know you not," says Love, "who bore the blame?"
    "My dear, then I will serve."

"You must sit down," says Love, "and taste my meat."
So I did sit and eat.

❧❧

John Bunyan
from The Pilgrim's Progress

AS I walk'd through the wilderness of this world, I lighted on a certain place where was a Den, and I laid me down in that place to sleep; and as I slept, I dreamed a Dream. I dreamed, and behold I saw a Man cloathed with Rags, standing in a certain place, with his face from his own house, a Book in his hand, and a great Burden upon his back. I looked, and saw him open the Book, and read therein; and as he read, he wept and trembled; and not being able longer to contain, he brake out with a lamentable cry, saying *What shall I do?*

In this plight therefore he went home, and refrained himself as long as he could, that his Wife and Children should not perceive his distress, but he could not be silent long, because that his trouble increased: Wherefore at length he brake his mind to his Wife and Children; and thus he began to talk to them: *O my dear Wife,* said he, *and you the Children of my bowels, I your dear friend, am in myself undone by reason of a Burden that lieth hard upon me; moreover, I am for certain informed that this our City will be burned with fire from Heaven; in which fearful overthrow, both myself, with thee my Wife, and you my sweet Babes, shall miserably come to ruin, except (the which yet I see not) some way of escape can be found, whereby we may be delivered.* At this his Relations were sore amazed; not for that they believed that what he had said to them was true, but because they thought that some frenzy distemper had got into his head; therefore, it drawing towards night, and they hoping that sleep might settle his brains, with all haste they got him to bed: But the night was as troublesome to him as the day; wherefore, instead of sleeping, he spent it in sighs and tears. So, when the morning was come, they would know how he did; He told them *Worse and worse:* he also set to talking to them again, but they began to be hardened: they also thought to drive away his distemper by harsh and surly carriages to him; sometimes they would deride, sometimes they would chide, and sometimes they would quite neglect him: Wherefore he began to retire himself to his chamber, to pray for and pity them, and also to condole his own misery; he would also walk solitarily in the fields, sometimes reading, and sometimes praying: and thus for some days he spent his time.

Now, I saw upon a time, when he was walking in the fields, that he was, as he was wont, reading in his Book, and greatly distressed in his mind; and as he read, he burst out, as he had done before, crying, *What shall I do to be saved?*

I saw also that he looked this way and that way, as if he would run; yet he stood still, because, as I perceived, he could not tell which way to go. I looked then, and saw a man named *Evangelist,* coming to him, and asked, *Wherefore dost thou cry?*

He answered, Sir, I perceive by the Book in my hand, that I am condemned to die, and after that to come to Judgment, and I find that I am not willing to do the first, nor able to do the second.

> *Christian* no sooner leaves the World but meets
> *Evangelist,* who lovingly him greets
> With tidings of another: and doth shew
> Him how to mount to that from this below.

Then said *Evangelist,* Why not willing to die, since this life is attended with so many evils? The Man answered, Because I fear that this burden that is upon my back will sink me lower than the Grave, and I shall fall into *Tophet.* And, Sir, if I be not fit to go to Prison, I am not fit to go to Judgment, and from thence to Execution; and the thoughts of these things make me cry.

Then said *Evangelist,* If this be thy condition, why standest thou still? He answered, Because I know not whither to go. Then he gave him a *Parchment-roll,* and there was written within, *Fly from the wrath to come.*

The Man therefore read it, and looking upon *Evangelist* very carefully, said, Whither must I fly? Then said *Evangelist,* pointing with his finger over a very wide field, Do you see yonder *Wicket-gate?* The Man said, No. Then said the other, Do you see yonder shining Light? He said, I think I do. Then said *Evangelist,* Keep that Light in your eye, and go up directly thereto: so shalt thou see the Gate; at which, when thou knockest, it shall be told thee what thou shalt do.

So I saw in my Dream that the Man began to run.

Now he had not run far from his own door, but his Wife and Children, perceiving it, began to cry after him to return; but the Man out his fingers in his ears, and ran on, crying *Life! Life! Eternal Life!* So he looked not behind him, but fled towards the middle of the Plain.

The Neighbors also came out to see him run; and as he ran, some mocked, others threatened, and some cried after him to return; and among those that did so, there were two that resolved to fetch him back by force. The name of the one was *Obstinate,* and the name of the other *Pliable.* Now by this time the Man was got a good distance from them; but however they were resolved to pursue him, which they did, and in a little time they overtook him. Then said the Man, Neighbors, wherefore are you come? They said, To persuade you to go back with us. But he said, That can by no means be; you dwell, said he, in the City of *Destruction,* the place also where I was born, I see it to be so; and dying there, sooner or later, you will sink lower than the Grave, into a place that burns with Fire and Brimstone: be content, good Neighbors, and go along with me.

Obst. What, said *Obstinate,* and leave our friends and our comforts behind us!

Chr. Yes, said *Christian,* for that was his name, because that *all* which you shall forsake is not worthy to be compared with a *little* of that that I am seeking to enjoy; and if you will go along with me and hold it, you shall fare as I myself; for there where I go, is enough and to spare: Come away, and prove my words.

Obst. What are the things you seek, since you leave all the world to find them?

Chr. I seek an *Inheritance incorruptible, undefiled, and that fadeth not away,* and it is laid up in Heaven, and safe there, to be bestowed at the time appointed, on them that diligently seek it. Read it so, if you will, in my Book.

Obst. Tush, said *Obstinate,* away with your Book; will you go back with us or no?

Chr. No, not I, said the other, because I have laid my hand to the Plow.

Obst. Come then, Neighbor *Pliable,* let us turn again, and go home without him; there is a company of these craz'd-headed coxcombs, that, when they take a fancy by the end, are wiser in their own eyes than seven men that can render a reason.

Pli. Then said *Pliable,* Don't revile; if what the good Christian says is true, the things he looks after are better than ours; my heart inclines to go with my Neighbor.

Obst. What! more fools still? Be ruled by me, and go back; who knows whither such a brain-sick fellow will lead you? Go back, go back, and be wise.

Chr. Come with me, Neighbor Pliable; there are such things to be had which I spoke of, and many more Glories besides. If you believe not me, read here in this Book; and for the truth of what is exprest therein, behold, all is confirmed by the blood of Him that made it.

Pli. Well, Neighbor *Obstinate,* said *Pliable,* I begin to come to a point: I intend to go along with this good man, and to cast in my lot with him: but, my good companion, do you know the way to this desired place?

Chr. I am directed by a man, whose name is *Evangelist,* to speed me to a little Gate that is before us, where we shall receive instructions about the way.

Pli. Come then, good Neighbor, let us be going. Then they went both together.

Obst. And I will go back to my place, said *Obstinate;* I will be no companion of such mis-led, fantastical fellows.

Now I saw in my Dream, that when *Obstinate* was gone back, *Christian* and *Pliable* went talking over the Plain; and thus they began their discourse.

Chr. Come Neighbor *Pliable,* how do you do? I am glad you are persuaded to go along with me: Had even *Obstinate* himself but felt what I have felt of the powers and terrors of what is yet unseen, he would not thus lightly have given us the back.

Pli. Come, Neighbor *Christian,* since there are none but us two here, tell me now further what the things are, and how to be enjoyed, whither we are going?

Chr. I can better conceive of them with my Mind, than speak of them with my Tongue: but yet, since you are desirous to know, I will read of them in my Book.

Pli. And do you think that the words of your Book are certainly true?

Chr. Yes, verily; for it was made by him that cannot lye.

Pli. Well said; what things are they?

Chr. There is an endless Kingdom to be inhabited, and everlasting Life to be given us, that may inhabit that Kingdom for ever.

Pli. Well said; and what else?

Chr. There are Crowns of glory to be given us, and Garments that will make us shine like the Sun in the firmament of Heaven.

Pli. This is excellent; and what else?

Chr. There shall be no more crying, nor sorrow, for He that is owner of the place will wipe all tears from our eyes.

Pli. And what company shall we have there?

Chr. There we shall be with *Seraphims* and *Cherubins,* creatures that will dazzle your eyes to look on them: There also you shall meet with thousands and ten thousands that have gone before us to that place; none of them are hurtful, but loving and holy; every one walking in the sight of God, and standing in his presence with acceptance for ever. In a word, there we shall see the Elders with their golden Crowns, there we shall see the Holy Virgins with their golden Harps, there we shall see men that by the World were cut in pieces, burnt in flames, eaten of beasts, drowned in the seas, for the love that they bare to the Lord of the place, all well, and cloathed with Immortality as with a garment.

Pli. The hearing of this is enough to ravish one's heart; but are these things to be enjoyed? How shall we get to be sharers hereof?

Chr. The Lord, the Governor of the country, hath recorded *that* in this Book; the substance of which is, If we be truly willing to have it, he will bestow it upon us freely.

Pli. Well, my good companion, glad am I to hear of these things; come on, let us mend our pace.

Chr. I cannot go so fast as I would, by reason of this Burden that is upon my back.

Now I saw in my Dream, that just as they had ended this talk, they drew near to a very miry *Slough,* that was in the midst of the plain; and they, being heedless, did both fall suddenly into the bog. The name of the slough was *Dispond.* Here therefore they wallowed for a time, being grievously bedaubed with the dirt; and *Christian,* because of the Burden that was on his back, began to sink in the mire.

Pli. Then said *Pliable,* Ah Neighbor *Christian,* where are you now?

Chr. Truly, said *Christian,* I do not know.

Pli. At that *Pliable* began to be offended, and angerly said to his fellow, Is this the happiness you have told me all this while of? If we have such ill speed at our first setting out, what may we expect 'twixt this and our Journey's end? May I get out again with my life, you shall possess the brave Country alone for me. And with that he gave a desperate struggle or two, and got out of the mire on that side of the Slough which was next to his own house: so away he went, and *Christian* saw him no more.

Wherefore *Christian* was left to tumble in the Slough of *Dispond* alone; but still he endeavoured to struggle to that side of the Slough that was still further from his own house, and next to the Wicket-gate; the which he did, but could not get out, because of the Burden that was upon his back: But I beheld in my Dream, that a man came to him, whose name was *Help*, and asked him, *What he did there?*

Chr. Sir, said *Christian*, I was bid go this way by a man called *Evangelist*, who directed me also to yonder Gate, that I might escape the wrath to come; and as I was going thither, I fell in here.

Help. But why did you not look for the steps?

Chr. Fear followed me so hard, that I fled the next way, and fell in.

Help. Then said he, *Give me thy hand:* so he gave him his hand, and he drew him out, and set him upon sound ground, and bid him go on his way.

Then I stepped to him that pluckt him out, and said, Sir, wherefore, since over this place is the way from the City of *Destruction* to yonder Gate, is it that this plat is not mended, that poor travellers might go thither with more security? And he said unto me, This miry Slough is such a place as cannot be mended; it is the descent whither the scum and filth that attends conviction for sin doth continually run, and therefore it is called the Slough of *Dispond*; for still as the sinner is awakened about his lost condition, there ariseth in his soul many fears and doubts, and discouraging apprehensions, which all of them get together, and settle in this place: And this is the reason of the badness of this ground.

It is not the pleasure of the King that this place should remain so bad. His labourers also have, by the direction of His Majesties Surveyors, been for above these sixteen hundred years employed about this patch of ground, if perhaps it might have been mended: yea, and to my knowledge, said he, *here* hath been swallowed up at least twenty thousand cart-loads, yea, millions of wholesome instructions, that have at all seasons been brought from all places of the King's dominions (and they that can tell say they are the best materials to make good ground of the place), if so be it might have been mended, but it is the Slough of *Dispond* still, and so will be when they have done what they can.

True, there are by the direction of the Lawgiver, certain good and substantial steps, placed even through the very midst of this Slough; but at such time as this place doth much spue out its filth, as it doth against change of weather, these steps are hardly seen; or if they be, men through the dizziness of their heads, step besides; and then they are bemired to purpose, notwithstanding the steps be there; but the ground is good when they are once got in at the Gate.

Now I saw in my Dream, that by this time *Pliable* was got home to his house again. So his Neighbors came to visit him: and some of them called him wise man for coming back, and some called him fool for hazarding himself with *Christian:* others again did mock at his cowardliness; saying, Surely since you began to venture, I would not have been so base to have given out for a few difficulties. So *Pliable* sat sneaking among them. But at last he got more confidence, and then they all turned their tales, and began to deride poor *Christian* behind his back. And thus much concerning *Pliable*.

Now as *Christian* was walking solitary by himself, he espied one afar off come crossing over the field to meet him; and their hap was to meet just as they were crossing the way of each other. The gentleman's name that met him was Mr *Worldly Wiseman:* he dwelt in the Town of *Carnal Policy,* a very great Town, and also hard by from whence *Christian* came. This man then meeting with *Christian,* and having some inkling of him, — for *Christian's* setting forth from the City of *Destruction* was much noised abroad, not only in the Town where he dwelt, but also it began to be the town-talk in some other places, — Master *Worldly Wiseman* therefore, having some guess of him, by beholding his laborious going, by observing his sighs and groans, and the like, began thus to enter into some talk with *Christian*.

World. How now, good fellow, whither away after this burdened manner?

Chr. A burdened manner indeed, as ever I think poor creature had. And whereas you ask me, *Whither away?* I tell you, Sir, I am going to yonder Wicket-gate before me; for there, as I am informed, I shall be put into a way to be rid of my heavy Burden.

World. Hast thou a Wife and Children?

Chr. Yes, but I am so laden with this Burden, that I cannot take that pleasure in them as formerly; methinks I am as if I had none.

World. Wilt thou hearken to me if I give thee counsel?

Chr. If it be good, I will; for I stand in need of good counsel.

World. I would advise thee then, that thou with all speed get thyself rid of thy Burden; for thou wilt never be settled in thy mind till then; nor canst thou enjoy the benefits of the blessing which God hath bestowed upon thee till then.

Chr. That is that which I seek for, even to be rid of this heavy Burden; but get it off myself, I cannot; nor is there any man in our country that can take it off my shoulders; therefore am I going this way, as I told you, that I may be rid of my Burden.

World. Who bid thee go this way to be rid of thy Burden?

Chr. A man that appeared to me to be a very great and honorable person; his name as I remember is *Evangelist*.

World. I beshrew him for his counsel; there is not a more dangerous and troublesome way in the world than is that unto which he hath directed thee; and that thou shalt find, if thou wilt be ruled by his counsel. Thou hast met with something (as I perceive) already; for I see the dirt of the Slough of *Dispond* is upon thee; but that Slough is the beginning of the sorrows that do attend those that go on in that way: Hear me, I am older than thou; thou art like to meet with, in the way which thou goest, Wearisomeness, Painfulness, Hunger, Perils, Nakedness, Sword, Lions, Dragons, Darkness, and in a word, Death, and what not! These things are certainly true, having been confirmed by many testimonies. And why should a man so carelessly cast away himself, by giving heed to a stranger?

Chr. Why, Sir, this Burden upon my back is more terrible to me than are all these things which you have mentioned; nay, methinks I care not what I meet with in the way, so be I can also meet with deliverance from my Burden.

World. How camest thou by the Burden at first?

Chr. By reading this Book in my hand.

World. I thought so; and it is happened unto thee as to other weak men, who meddling with things too high for them, do suddenly fall into thy distractions; which distractions do not only unman men (as thine I perceive has done thee), but they run them upon desperate ventures, to obtain they know not what.

Chr. I know what I would obtain; it is ease for my heavy burden.

World. But why wilt thou seek for ease this way, seeing so many dangers attend it? Especially, since (hadst thou but patience to hear me) I could direct thee to the obtaining of what thou desirest, without the dangers that thou in this way wilt run thyself into; yea, and the remedy is at hand. Besides, I will add, that instead of those dangers, thou shalt meet with much safety, friendship, and content.

Chr. Pray Sir, open this secret to me.

World. Why in yonder Village (the village is named Morality) there dwells a Gentleman whose name is Legality, a very judicious man, and a man of very good name, that has skill to help men off with such burdens as thine are from their shoulders: yea, to my knowledge he hath done a great deal of good this way; ay, and besides, he hath skill to cure those that are somewhat crazed in their wits with their burdens. To him, as I said, thou mayest go, and be helped presently. His house is not quite a mile from this place, and if he should not be at home himself, he hath a pretty young man to his Son, whose name is *Civility*, that can do it (to speak on) as well as the old Gentleman himself; there, I say, thou mayest be eased of thy Burden; and if thou art not minded to go back to thy former habitation, as indeed I would not wish thee, thou mayest send for thy Wife and Children to thee to this village, where there are houses now stand empty, one of which thou mayest have at reasonable rates; Provision is there also cheap and good; and that which will make thy life the more happy is, to be sure there thou shalt live by honest Neighbors, in credit and good fashion.

Now was *Christian* somewhat at a stand, but presently he concluded, If this be true which this Gentleman hath said, my wisest course is to take his advice; and with that he thus farther spoke.

Chr. Sir, which is my way to this honest man's house?
World. Do you see yonder high Hill?
Chr. Yes, very well.
World. By that Hill you must go, and the first house you come at is his.

So *Christian* turned out of his way to go to Mr *Legality's* house for help; but behold, when he was got now hard by the Hill, it seemed so high, and also that side of it that was next the wayside, did hang so much over, that *Christian* was afraid to venture further, lest the Hill should fall on his head; wherefore there he stood still, and he wot not what to do. Also his Burden now seemed heavier to him than while he was in his way. There came also flashes of fire out of the Hill, that made Christian afraid that he should be burned. Here therefore he sweat and did quake for fear.

> When Christians unto Carnal Men give ear,
> Out of their way they go, and pay for 't dear;
> For Master *Worldly Wiseman* can but shew
> A Saint the way to Bondage and to Wo.

And now he began to be sorry that he had taken Mr *Worldly Wiseman's* counsel. And with that he saw *Evangelist* coming to meet him; at the sight also of whom he began to blush for shame. So *Evangelist* drew nearer and nearer; and coming up to him, he looked upon him with a severe and dreadful countenance, and thus began to reason with *Christian.*

Evan. What doest thou here, *Christian?* said he: at which words *Christian* knew not what to answer; wherefore at present he stood speechless before him. Then said *Evangelist* farther, Art not thou the man that I found crying without the walls of the City of *Destruction?*
Chr. Yes, dear Sir, I am the man.
Evan. Did not I direct thee the way to the little Wicket-gate?
Chr. Yes, dear Sir, said *Christian.*
Evan. How is it then that thou art so quickly turned aside? for thou art now out of the way.
Chr. I met with a Gentleman so soon as I had got over the Slough of *Dispond,* who persuaded me that I might, in the village before me, find a man that could take off my Burden.
Evan. What was he?
Chr. He looked like a Gentleman, and talked much to me, and got me at last to yield; so I came hither: but when I beheld this Hill, and how it hangs over the way, I suddenly made a stand, lest it should fall on my head.
Evan. What said that Gentleman to you?

Chr. Why, he asked me whither I was going; and I told him.

Evan. And what said he then?

Chr. He asked me if I had a family; and I told him. But, said I, I am so loaden with the Burden that is on my back, that I cannot take pleasure in them as formerly.

Evan. And what said he then?

Chr. He bid me with speed get rid of my Burden; and I told him 'twas ease that I sought. And, said I, I am therefore going to yonder Gate, to receive further direction how I may get to the place of deliverance. So he said that he would shew me a better way, and short, not so attended with difficulties as the way, Sir, that you set me; which way, said he, will direct you to a Gentleman's house that hath skill to take off these Burdens: So I believed him, and turned out of that way into this, if haply I might be soon eased of my Burden. But when I came to this place, and beheld things as they are, I stopped for fear (as I said) of danger: but I now know not what to do.

Evan. Then, said *Evangelist,* stand still a little, that I may shew thee the words of God. So he stood trembling. Then said *Evangelist,* See that ye refuse not him that speaketh; for if they escaped not who refused him that spake on Earth, much more shall not we escape, if we turn away from him that speaketh from Heaven. He said moreover, Now the just shall live by faith: but if any man draws back, my soul shall have no pleasure in him. He also did thus apply them, Thou art the man that art running into this misery, thou hast begun to reject the counsel of the Most High, and to draw back thy foot from the way of peace, even almost to the hazarding of thy perdition.

Then *Christian* fell down at his foot as dead, crying, *Wo is me, for I am undone:* At the sight of which, *Evangelist* caught him by the right hand, saying, All manner of sin and blasphemies shall be forgiven unto men; be not faithless, but believing. Then did *Christian* again a little revive, and stood up trembling, as at first, before *Evangelist.*

Then *Evangelist* proceeded, saying, Give more earnest heed to the things that I shall tell thee of. I will now shew thee who it was that deluded thee, and who it was also to whom he sent thee. The man that met thee is one *Worldly Wiseman,* and rightly is he so called: partly because he savoureth only the doctrine of this world, (therefore he always goes to the Town of *Morality* to church); and partly because he loveth that doctrine best, for it saveth him from the Cross. And because he is of this carnal temper, therefore he seeketh to prevent my ways, though right. Now there are three things in this man's counsel that thou must utterly abhor.

1. His turning thee out of the way.

2. His labouring to render the Cross odious to thee.

3. And his setting thy feet in that way that leadeth unto the administration of Death.

First, Thou must abhor his turning thee out of the way; yea, and thine own consenting thereto, because this is to reject the counsel of God for the sake of the counsel of a *Worldly Wiseman.* The Lord says, *Strive to enter in at the strait gate,* the gate to which I sent thee; *for strait is the gate that leadeth unto life, and few there be that find it.* From this little Wicket-gate, and from the way thereto, hath this wicked man turned thee, to the bringing of thee almost to destruction; hate therefore his turning thee out of the way, and abhor thyself for hearkening to him.

Secondly, Thou must abhor his labouring to render the Cross odious unto thee; for thou art to *prefer it before the treasures of Egypt.* Besides, the King of Glory hath told thee, that *he that will save his life shall lose it:* and He that comes after him, and hates not his father, and mother, and wife, and children, and brethren, and sisters, yea and his own life also, he cannot be my Disciple. I say therefore, for a man to labour to persuade thee, that that shall be thy death, without which, the Truth hath said, thou canst not have eternal life; This doctrine thou must abhor.

Thirdly, Thou must hate his setting of thy feet in the way that leadeth to the ministration of death. And for this thou must consider to whom he sent thee, and also how unable that person was to deliver thee from thy Burden.

He to whom thou was sent for ease, being by name *Legality,* is the Son of the Bond-woman which now is, and is in bondage with her children; and is in a mystery this Mount *Sinai,* which thou hast feared will fall on thy head. Now if she with her children are in bondage, how canst thou expect by them to be made free? This *Legality* therefore is not able to set thee free from thy Burden. No man was as yet ever rid of his Burden by him; no, nor ever is like to be: ye cannot be justified by the Works of the Law; for by the deeds of the Law no man living can be rid of his Burden: therefore, Mr *Worldly Wiseman* is an alien, and Mr *Legality* a cheat; and for his son *Civility,* notwithstanding his simpering looks, he is but a hypocrite and cannot help thee. Believe me, there is nothing in all this noise, that thou hast heard of this sottish man, but a design to beguile thee of thy Salvation, by turning thee from the way in which I had set thee. After this *Evangelist* called aloud to the Heavens for confirmation of what he had said; and with that there came words and fire out of the Mountain under which poor *Christian* stood, that made the hair of his flesh stand. The words were thus pronounced, *As many as are the works of the Law are under the curse; for it is written, Cursed is every one that continueth not in all things which are written in the Book of the Law to do them.*

Now *Christian* looked for nothing but death, and began to cry out lamentably, even cursing the time in which he met with Mr *Worldly Wiseman,* still calling himself a thousand fools for hearkening to his counsel: he also was greatly ashamed to think that this Gentleman's arguments, flowing only from the flesh, should have that prevalency with him as to cause him to forsake the right way. This done, he applied himself again to *Evangelist* in words and sense as follows.

Chr. Sir, what think you? Is there hopes? May I now go back and go up to the Wicket-gate? Shall I not be abandoned for this, and sent back from thence ashamed? I am sorry I have hearkened to this man's counsel: But may my sin be forgiven?

Evan. Then said *Evangelist* to him, Thy sin is very great, for by it thou hast committed two evils: thou hast forsaken the way that is good, to tread in forbidden paths; yet will the man at the Gate receive thee, for he has good will for men; only, said he, take heed that thou turn not aside again, lest thou perish from the way, when his wrath is kindled but a little. Then did *Christian* address himself to go back; and *Evangelist,* after he had kissed him, gave him one smile, and bid him God speed. So he went on with haste, neither spake he to any man by the way; nor if any man asked him, would he vouchsafe them an answer. He went like one that was all the while treading on forbidden ground, and could by no means think himself safe, till again he was got into the way which he left to follow Mr *Worldly Wiseman's* counsel. So in process of time *Christian* got up to the Gate. Now over the Gate there was written, *Knock and it shall be opened unto you.*

> He that will enter in must first without
> Stand knocking at the Gate, nor need he doubt
> That is a knocker but to enter in,
> For God can love him, and forgive his sin.

> He knocked therefore more than once or twice, saying,
> May I now enter here? Will he within
> Open to sorry me, though I have been
> An undeserving Rebel? Then shall I
> Not fail to sing his lasting praise on high.

At last there came a grave person to the gate named *Good-will,* who asked Who was there? and whence he came? and what he would have?

Chr. Here is a poor burdened sinner. I come from the City of *Destruction,* but am going to Mount *Zion,* that I may be delivered from the wrath to come. I would therefore, Sir, since I am informed that by this Gate is the way thither, know if you are willing to let me in.

Good-will. I am willing with all my heart, said he; and with that he opened the Gate.

So when *Christian* was stepping in, the other gave him a pull. Then said *Christian,* What means that? The other told him, A little distance from this Gate, there is erected a strong Castle, of which *Beelzebub* is the Captain; from thence both he and they that are with him shoot arrows at those that come up to this Gate, if haply they may die before they can enter in. Then said *Christian,* I rejoice and tremble. So when he was got in, the man of the Gate asked him who directed him thither?

Chr. Evangelist bid me come hither and knock (as I did); and he said that you, Sir, would tell me what I must do.

Good-will. An open door is set before thee, and no man can shut it.

Chr. Now I begin to reap the benefits of my hazards.

Good-will. But how is it that you came alone?

Chr. Because none of my Neighbors saw their danger, as I saw mine.

Good-will. Did any of them know of your coming?

Chr. Yes, my Wife and Children saw me at the first, and called after me to turn again; also some of my Neighbors stood crying and calling after me to return; but I put my fingers in my ears, and so came on my way.

Good-will. But did none of them follow you, to persuade you to go back?

Chr. Yes, both *Obstinate* and *Pliable*; but when they saw that they could not prevail, *Obstinate* went railing back, but *Pliable* came with me a little way.

Good-will. But why did he not come through?

Chr. We indeed came both together, until we came to the Slough of *Dispond,* into the which we also suddenly fell. And then was my Neighbor *Pliable* discouraged, and would not adventure further. Wherefore getting out again on that side next to his own house, he told me I should possess the brave country alone for him; so he went *his* way, and I came *mine:* he after *Obstinate,* and I to this Gate.

Good-will. Then said *Good-will,* Alas, poor man, is the cœlestial glory of so small esteem with him, that he counteth it not worth running the hazards of a few difficulties to obtain it?

Chr. Truly, said *Christian,* I have said the truth of *Pliable,* and if I should also say all the truth of myself, it before the will appear there is no betterment 'twixt him and myself. 'Tis true, he went back to his own house, but I also turned aside to go in the way of death, being persuaded thereto by the carnal arguments of one Mr *Worldly Wiseman.*

Good-will. O, did he light upon you? What! he would have had you a sought for ease at the hands of Mr *Legality.* They are both of them a very cheat: But did you take his counsel?

Chr. Yes, as far as I durst: I went to find out Mr *Legality,* until I thought that the Mountain that stands by his house would have fallen upon my head; wherefore there I was forced to stop.

Good-will. That Mountain has been the death of many, and will be the death of many more; 'tis well you escaped being by it dashed in pieces.

Chr. Why truly I do not know what had become of me there, had not *Evangelist* happily met me again, as I was musing in the midst of my dumps: but 'twas God's mercy that he came to me again, for else I had never come hither. But now I am come, such a one as I am, more fit indeed for death by that Mountain than thus to stand talking with my Lord; but O, what a favour is this to me, that yet I am admitted entrance here.

Good-will. We make no objections against any, notwithstanding all that they have done before they come hither, they in no wise are cast out; and therefore, good *Christian,* come a little way with me, and I will teach thee about the way thou must go. Look before thee; dost thou see this narrow way? THAT is the way thou must go; it was cast up by the Patriarchs, Prophets, Christ, and his Apostles; and it is as straight as a rule can make it: This is the way thou must go.

Chr. But said *Christian,* Is there no turnings nor windings, by which a Stranger may lose the way?

Good-will. Yes, there are many ways *butt* down upon this, and they are crooked and wide: But thus thou mayest distinguish the right from the wrong, the right only being straight and narrow.

Then I saw in my Dream, that *Christian* asked him further, If he could not help him off with his Burden that was upon his back; for as yet he had not got rid thereof, nor could he by any means get it off without help.

He told him, As to thy Burden, be content to bear it, until thou comest to the place of *Deliverance;* for there it will fall from back itself.

Then *Christian* began to gird up his loins, and to address himself to his Journey. So the other told him, That by that he was gone some distance from the Gate, he would come at the house of the *Interpreter,* at whose door he should knock, and he would shew him excellent things. Then *Christian* took his leave of his Friend, and he again bid him God speed.

Then he went on till he came at the house of the *Interpreter,* where he knocked over and over; at last one came to the door, and asked Who was there?

Chr. Sir, here is a Traveller, who was bid by an acquaintance of the good man of this house to call here for my profit; I would therefore speak with the Master of the house. So he called for the Master of the house, who after a little time came to *Christian,* and asked him what he would have?

Chr. Sir, said *Christian,* I am a man that am come from the City of *Destruction,* and am going to the Mount *Zion;* and I was told by the Man that stands at the Gate at the head of this way, that if I called here, you would shew me excellent things, such as would be a help to me in my Journey.

Inter. Then said the *Interpreter,* Come in, I will shew thee that which will be profitable to thee. So he commanded his man to light the Candle, and bid *Christian* follow him, so he had him into a private room, and bid his man open a door; the which when he had done, *Christian* saw the Picture of a very grave Person hang up against the wall; and this was the fashion of it. It had eyes lifted up to Heaven, the best of Books in his hand, the Law of Truth was written upon his lips, the World was behind his back. It stood as if it pleaded with men, and a Crown of Gold did hang over his head.

Chr. Then said *Christian,* What means this?

Inter. The Man whose Picture this is, is one of a thousand; he can beget children, travel in birth with children, and nurse them himself when they are born. And whereas thou seest him with his eyes lift up to Heaven, the best of Books in his hand, and the Law of Truth writ on his lips, it is to shew thee that his work is to know and unfold dark things to sinners; even as also thou seest him stand as if he pleaded with men; and whereas thou seest the World as cast behind him, and that a Crown hangs over his head, that is to shew thee that slighting and despising the things that are present, for the love that he hath to his Master's service, he is sure in the world that comes next to have Glory for his reward. Now, said the *Interpreter*, I have shewed thee this Picture first, because the Man whose Picture this is, is the only man whom the Lord of the place whither thou art going, hath authorized to be thy guide in all difficult places thou mayest meet with in the way; wherefore take good heed to what I have shewed thee, and bear well in thy mind what thou hast seen, lest in thy Journey thou meet with some that pretend to lead thee right, but their way goes down to death.

Then he took him by the hand, and led him into a very large *Parlour* that was full of dust, because never swept; the which after he had reviewed a little while, the *Interpreter* called for a man to sweep. Now when he began to sweep, the dust began so abundantly to fly about, that *Christian* had almost therewith been choaked. Then said the *Interpreter* to a *Damsel* that stood by, Bring hither the Water, and sprinkle the Room; the which when she had done, it was swept and cleansed with pleasure.

Chr. Then said *Christian*, What means this?

Inter. The *Interpreter* answered, This *parlour* is the heart of a man that was never sanctified by the sweet Grace of the Gospel: the *dust* is his Original Sin and inward Corruptions, that have defiled the whole man. He that began to sweep at first, is the Law; but she that brought water, and did sprinkle it, is the Gospel. Now, whereas thou sawest that so soon as the first began to sweep, the dust did so fly about that the Room by him could not be cleansed, but that thou wast almost choaked therewith; this is to shew thee, that the Law, instead of cleansing the heart (by its working) from sin, doth revive, put strength into, and increase it in the soul, even as it doth discover and forbid it, for it doth not give power to subdue.

Again, as thou sawest the *Damsel* sprinkle the room with Water, upon which it was cleansed with pleasure; this is to shew thee, that when the Gospel comes in the sweet and precious influences thereof to the heart, then I say, even as thou sawest the Damsel lay the dust by sprinkling the floor with Water, so is sin vanquished and subdued, and the soul made clean, through the faith of it, and consequently fit for the King of Glory to inhabit.

I saw moreover in my Dream, that the *Interpreter* took him by the hand, and had him into a little room, where sat two little Children, each one in his chair. The name of the eldest was *Passion*, and the name of the other *Patience*. *Passion* seemed to be much discontent; but *Patience* was very quiet. Then *Christian* asked, What is the reason of the discontent of *Passion*?

The *Interpreter* answered, The Governor of them would have him stay for his best things till the beginning of the next year; but he will have all now; but *Patience* is willing to wait.

Then I saw that one came to *Passion,* and brought him a bag of treasure, and poured it down at his feet, the which he took up and rejoiced therein; and withal, laughed *Patience* to scorn. But I beheld but a while, and he had lavished all away, and had nothing left him but Rags.

Chr. Then said *Christian* to the *Interpreter,* Expound this matter more fully to me.

Inter. So he said, These two Lads are figures: *Passion,* of the men of *this* world; and *Patience,* of the men of *that* which is to come; for as here thou seest, *Passion* will have all now this year, that is to say, in this world; so are the men of this world: they must have all their good things now, they cannot stay till next year, that is, until the next world, for their portion of good. That proverb, *A Bird in the Hand is worth two in the Bush,* is of more authority with them than are all the Divine testimonies of the good of the world to come. But as thou sawest that he had quickly lavished all away, and had presently left him nothing but Rags; so will it be with all such men at the end of this world.

Chr. Then said *Christian,* Now I see that *Patience* has the best wisdom, and that upon many accounts. 1. Because he stays for the best things. 2. And also because he will have the Glory of his, when the other has nothing but Rags.

Inter. Nay, you may add another, to wit, the glory of the *next* world will never wear out; but these are suddenly gone, Therefore Passion had not so much reason to laugh at *Patience,* because he had his good things first, as *Patience* will have to laugh at *Passion,* because he had his best things last; for *first* must give place to *last,* because *last* must have his time to come: but last gives place to nothing; for there is not another to succeed. He therefore that hath his portion *first,* must needs have a time to spend it; but he that hath his portion *last,* must have it lastingly; therefore it is said of *Dives, In thy lifetime thou receivedst thy good things, and likewise* Lazarus *evil things; but now he is comforted, and thou art tormented.*

Chr. Then I perceive 'tis not best to covet things that are now, but to wait for things to come.

Inter. You say truth: *For the things which are seen are* Temporal; *but the things that are not seen are* Eternal. But though this be so, yet since things present and our fleshly appetite are such near neighbors one to another; and, again, because things to come and carnal sense are such strangers one to another; therefore it is that the first of these so suddenly fell into *amity,* and that *distance* is so continued between the second.

Then I saw in my Dream that the *Interpreter* took *Christian* by the hand, and led him into a place where was a Fire burning against a wall, and one standing by it, always casting much Water upon it, to quench it; yet did the Fire burn higher and hotter.

Then said *Christian,* What means this?

184 I World Literature

The *Interpreter answered,* This Fire is the work of Grace that is wrought in the heart; he that casts Water upon it, to extinguish and put it out, is the Devil; but in that thou seest the Fire notwithstanding burn higher and hotter, thou shalt also see the reason of that. So he had him about to the backside of the wall, where he saw a man with a Vessel of Oil in his hand, of the which he did also continually cast (but secretly) into the Fire.

Then said *Christian,* What means this?

The *Interpreter answered,* This is Christ, who continually, with the Oil of his Grace, maintains the work already begun in the heart: by the means of which notwithstanding what the Devil can do, the souls of his people prove gracious still. And in that thou sawest that the man stood behind the wall to maintain the Fire, that is to teach thee that it is hard for the tempted to see how this work of Grace is maintained in the soul.

I saw also that the *Interpreter* took him again by the hand, and led him into a pleasant place, where was builded a stately Palace, beautiful to behold; at the sight of which *Christian* was greatly delighted: He saw also upon the top thereof, certain persons walking, who were cloathed all in gold.

Then said *Christian,* May we go in thither?

Then the *Interpreter* took him, and led him up toward the door of the Palace; and behold, at the door stood a great company of men, as desirous to go in, but durst not. There also sat a man at a little distance from the door, at a table-side, with a Book and his Inkhorn before him, to take the name of him that should enter therein; He saw also, that in the door-way stood many men in armour to keep it, being resolved to do the men that would enter what hurt and mischief they could. Now was *Christian* somewhat in a maze. At last, when every man started back for fear of the armed men, *Christian* saw a man of a very stout countenance come up to the man that sat there to write, saying, *Set down my name,* Sir: the which when he had done, he saw the man draw his Sword, and put an Helmet upon his head, and rush toward the door upon the armed men, who laid upon him with deadly force; but the man, not at all discouraged, fell to cutting and hacking most fiercely. So after he had received and given many wounds to those that attempted to keep him out, he cut his way through them all, and pressed forward into the Palace, at which there was a pleasant voice heard from those that were within, even of those that walked upon the top of the Palace, saying,

> Come in, Come in;
> Eternal Glory thou shalt win.

So he went in, and was cloathed with such garments as they. Then *Christian* smiled, and said, I think verily I know the meaning of this.

Now, said *Christian,* let me go hence. Nay, stay, said the *Interpreter,* till I have shewed thee a little more, and after that thou shalt go on thy way. So he took him by the hand again, and led him into a very dark room, where there sat a man in an Iron Cage.

Now the Man, to look on, seemed very sad; he sat with his eyes looking down to the ground, his hands folded together; and he sighed as if he would break his heart. Then said *Christian, What means this?* At which the *Interpreter* bid him talk with the man.

Then said *Christian* to the Man, *What art thou?* The Man answered, *I am what I was not once.*

Chr. What wast thou once?

Man. The Man said, I was once a fair and flourishing Professor, both in mine own eyes, and also in the eyes of others; I once was, as I thought, fair for the Cœlestial City, and had then even joy at the thoughts that I should get thither.

Chr. Well, but what art thou now?

Man. I am now a man of *Despair,* and am shut up in it, as in this Iron Cage. I cannot get out; O *now* I cannot.

Chr. But how camest thou in this condition?

Man. I left off to watch and be sober; I laid the reins upon the neck of my lusts; I sinned against the light of the Word and the goodness of God; I have grieved the Spirit, and he is gone; I tempted the Devil, and he is come to me; I have provoked God to anger, and he has left me; I have so hardened my heart, that I cannot repent.

Then said *Christian* to the *Interpreter,* But are there no hopes for such a man as this? Ask him, said the *Interpreter.*

Chr. Then said the *Christian,* Is there no hope, but you must be kept in the Iron Cage of Despair?

Man. No, none at all.

Chr. Why? the Son of the Blessed is very pitiful.[1]

Man. I have crucified him to myself afresh, I have despised his Person, I have despised his Righteousness, I have counted his Blood an unholy thing; I have done despite to the Spirit of Grace. Therefore I have shut myself out of all the Promises, and there now remains to me nothing but threatnings, dreadful threatnings, fearful threatnings of certain Judgment and fiery Indignation, which shall devour me as an Adversary.

Chr. For what did you bring yourself into this condition?

Man. For the Lusts, Pleasures, and Profits of this World; in the enjoyment of which I did then promise myself much delight; but now every one of those things also bite me, and gnaw me like a burning worm.

Chr. But canst thou not now repent and turn?

Man. God hath denied me repentance: his Word gives me no encouragement to believe; yea, himself hath shut me up in this Iron Cage; nor can all the men in the world let

---

[1] full of pity

me out. O Eternity! Eternity! how shall I grapple with the misery that I must meet with in Eternity!

Inter. Then said the *Interpreter* to *Christian,* Let this man's misery be remembered by thee, and be an everlasting caution to thee.

Chr. Well, said *Christian,* this is fearful; God help me to watch and be sober, and to pray that I may shun the cause of this man's misery. Sir, is it not time for me to go on my way now?

Inter. Tarry till I shall shew thee one thing more, and then thou shalt go thy way.

So he took *Christian* by the hand again, and led him into a Chamber, where there was one rising out of bed; and as he put on his raiment, he shook and trembled. Then said *Christian,* Why doth this man thus tremble? The *Interpreter* then bid him tell to Christian the reason of his so doing. So he began and said, This night, as I was in my sleep, I dreamed, and behold the Heavens grew exceeding black; also it thundred and lightned in most fearful wise, that it put me into an agony; so I looked up in my Dream, and saw the Clouds rack at an unusual rate, upon which I heard a great sound of a Trumpet, and saw also a Man sit upon a Cloud, attended with the thousands of Heaven; they were all in flaming fire, also the Heavens were in a burning flame. I heard then a Voice saying, *Arise ye dead, and come to Judgment;* and with that the Rocks rent, the Graves opened, and the Dead that were therein came forth. Some of them were exceeding glad, and looked upward; and some sought to hide themselves under the Mountains. Then I saw the Man that sat upon the Cloud open the Book, and bid the World draw near. Yet there was, by reason of a fierce flame which issued out and came from before him, a convenient distance betwixt him and them, as betwixt the Judge and the Prisoners at the bar. I heard it also proclaimed to them that attended on the Man that sat on the Cloud, *Gather together the Tares, the Chaff, and Stubble, and cast them into the burning Lake.* And with that, the bottomless pit opened, just whereabout I stood; out of the mouth of which there came in an abundant manner, smoke and coals of fire, with hideous noises. It was also said to the same persons, *Gather my Wheat into the Garner.* And with that I saw many catch'd up and carried away into the Clouds, but I was left behind. I also sought to hide myself, but I could not, for the Man that sat upon the Cloud still kept his eye upon me: my sins also came into my mind; and my Conscience did accuse me on every side. Upon this I awaked from my sleep.

Chr. But what was it that made you so afraid of this sight?

Man. Why, I thought that the day of Judgment was come, and that I was not ready for it: but this frighted me most, that the Angels gathered up several, and left me behind; also the pit of Hell opened her mouth just where I stood: my Conscience too afflicted me; and as I thought, the Judge had always his eye upon me, shewing indignation in his countenance.

Then said the *Interpreter* to *Christian, Hast thou considered all these things?*

Chr. Yes, and they put me in *hope* and *fear*.

Inter. Well, keep all things so in thy mind that they may be as a Goad in thy sides, to prick thee forward in the way thou must go. Then *Christian* began to gird up his loins, and address himself to his Journey. Then said the *Interpreter*, The Comforter be always with thee, good *Christian*, to guide thee in the way that leads to the City. So *Christian* went on his way saying,

> Here I have seen things rare and profitable;
> Things pleasant, dreadful, things to make me stable
> In what I have begun to take in hand;
> Then let me think on them, and understand
> Wherefore they shew'd me was, and let me be
> Thankful, O good Interpreter, to thee.

Now I saw in my Dream, that the highway up which *Christian* was to go, was fenced on either side with a Wall, and that Wall is called *Salvation*. Up this way therefore did burdened *Christian* run, but not without great difficulty, because of the load on his back.

He ran thus till he came at a place somewhat ascending, and upon that place stood a Cross, and a little below in the bottom, a Sepulchre. So I saw in my Dream, that just as *Christian* came up with the *Cross*, his Burden loosed from off his shoulders, and fell from off his back, and began to tumble, and so continued to do, till it came to the mouth of the Sepulchre, where it fell in, and I saw it no more.

Then was *Christian* glad and lightsome, and said with a merry heart, *He hath given me rest by his sorrow, and life by his death.* Then he stood still awhile to look and wonder; for it was very surprising to him, that the sight of the Cross should thus ease him of his Burden. He looked therefore, and looked again, even till the springs that were in his head sent the waters down his cheeks. Now as he stood looking and weeping, behold three Shining Ones came to him and saluted him with *Peace be to thee*; so the first said to him, *Thy sins be forgiven*: the second stript him of his Rags, and clothed him with Change of Raiment; the third also set a mark in his forehead, and gave him a Roll with a Seal upon it, which he bid him look on as he ran, and that he should give it in at the Cœlestial Gate. So they went their way.

> Who's this? the Pilgrim. How! 'tis very true,
> Old things are past away, all's become new.
> Strange! he's another man, upon my word,
> They be fine Feathers that make a fine Bird.

Then *Christian* gave three leaps for joy, and went on singing,

Thus far did I come laden with my sin;
Nor could aught ease the grief that I was in
Till I came hither: What a place is this!
Must here be the beginning of my bliss?
Must here the Burden fall from off my back?
Must here the strings that bound it to me crack?
Blest Cross! blest Sepulchre! blest rather be
The Man that there was put to shame for me.

❧❧

John Milton
from Paradise Lost[1]

Book 1
The Argument

This first Book proposes, first in brief, the whole Subject, *Mans disobedience, and the loss thereupon of Paradise wherein he was plac't:* Then touches *the prime cause of his fall, the Serpent, or rather* Satan *in the Serpent; who revolting from God, and drawing to his side many Legions of Angels, was by the command of God driven out of Heaven with all his Crew into the great Deep.* Which action past over, the Poem hasts into the midst of things, *presenting Satan with his Angels now fallen into Hell,* describ'd here, *not in the Center* (for Heaven and Earth may be suppos'd as yet not made, certainly not yet accurst) *but in a place of utter darkness, fitliest call'd* Chaos: *Here* Satan *with his Angels lying on the burning Lake, thunder-struck and astonisht, after a certain space recovers, as from confusion, calls up him who next in Order and Dignity lay by him; they confer of thir miserable fall.* Satan *awakens all his Legions, who lay till then in the same manner confounded; They rise, thir Numbers, array of Battel, thir chief Leaders nam'd, according to the Idols known afterwards in* Canaan *and the Countries adjoyning. To these* Satan *directs his Speech, comforts them with hope yet of regaining Heaven, but tells them lastly of a new World and new kind of Creature to be created, according to an ancient Prophesie or report in Heaven; for that Angels were long before this visible Creation, was the opinion of many ancient Fathers. To find out the truth of this Prophesie, and what to determin thereon he refers to a full Councel. What his Associates thence attempt.* Pandemonium *the Palace of Satan rises, suddenly built out of the Deep: The infernal Peers there sit in Councel.*

OF Mans First Disobedience, and the Fruit
Of that Forbidden Tree, whose mortal tast
Brought Death into the World, and all our woe,
With loss of *Eden*, till one greater Man

---

[1] I have added quotation marks to make it easier to keep up with who is speaking at any given point.

Restore us, and regain the blissful Seat,
Sing Heav'nly Muse,[1] that on the secret top
Of *Oreb*, or of *Sinai*, didst inspire
That Shepherd, who first taught the chosen Seed,
In the Beginning how the Heav'ns and Earth
Rose out of *Chaos*: Or if *Sion* Hill
Delight thee more, and *Siloa's* Brook that flow'd
Fast by the Oracle of God; I thence
Invoke thy aid to my adventrous Song,
That with no middle flight intends to soar
Above th' *Aonian* Mount, while it pursues
Things unattempted yet in Prose or Rhime.
And chiefly Thou O Spirit, that dost prefer
Before all Temples th' upright heart and pure,
Instruct me, for Thou know'st; Thou from the first
Wast present, and with mighty wings outspread
Dove-like satst brooding on the vast Abyss
And mad'st it pregnant: What in me is dark
Illumin, what is low raise and support;
That to the highth of this great Argument
I may assert Eternal Providence,
And justifie the wayes of God to men.

Say first, for Heav'n hides nothing from thy view
Nor the deep Tract of Hell, say first what cause
Mov'd our Grand Parents in that happy State,
Favour'd of Heav'n so highly, to fall off
From thir Creator, and transgress his Will
For one restraint, Lords of the World besides?
Who first seduc'd them to that foul revolt?
Th' infernal Serpent;[2] he it was, whose guile
Stird up with Envy and Revenge, deceiv'd
The Mother of Mankind, what time his Pride
Had cast him out from Heav'n, with all his Host
Of Rebel Angels, by whose aid aspiring
To set himself in Glory above his Peers,

---

[1] Notice that while Milton is using standard classical tropes in setting up his poem, the muse he invokes here is in fact the Holy Spirit.
[2] i.e., Satan

He trusted to have equal'd the most High,
If he oppos'd; and with ambitious aim
Against the Throne and Monarchy of God
Rais'd impious War in Heav'n and Battel proud
With vain attempt. Him the Almighty Power
Hurld headlong flaming from th' Ethereal Skie
With hideous ruine and combustion down
To bottomless perdition, there to dwell
In Adamantine Chains and penal Fire,
Who durst defie th' Omnipotent to Arms.
Nine times the Space that measures Day and Night
To mortal men, he with his horrid crew
Lay vanquisht, rowling in the fiery Gulfe
Confounded though immortal: But his doom
Reserv'd him to more wrath; for now the thought
Both of lost happiness and lasting pain
Torments him; round he throws his baleful eyes
That witness'd huge affliction and dismay
Mixt with obdurate pride and stedfast hate:
At once as far as Angels kenn he views
The dismal Situation waste and wilde,
A Dungeon horrible, on all sides round
As one great Furnace flam'd, yet from those flames
No light, but rather darkness visible
Serv'd onely to discover sights of woe,
Regions of sorrow, doleful shades, where peace
And rest can never dwell, hope never comes
That comes to all; but torture without end
Still urges, and a fiery Deluge, fed
With ever-burning Sulphur unconsum'd:
Such place Eternal Justice had prepar'd
For those rebellious, here thir Prison ordain'd
In utter darkness, and thir portion set
As far remov'd from God and light of Heav'n
As from the Center thrice to th' utmost Pole.
O how unlike the place from whence they fell!
There the companions of his fall, o'rewhelm'd
With Floods and Whirlwinds of tempestuous fire,
He soon discerns, and weltring by his side
One next himself in power, and next in crime,

Long after known in *Palestine,* and nam'd
Beelzebub. To whom th' Arch-Enemy,
And thence in Heav'n call'd Satan, with bold words
Breaking the horrid silence thus began.

"If thou beest he; But O how fall'n! how chang'd
From him, who in the happy Realms of Light
Cloth'd with transcendent brightness didst out-shine
Myriads though bright: If he Whom mutual league,
United thoughts and counsels, equal hope
And hazard in the Glorious Enterprize,
Joynd with me once, now misery hath joynd
In equal ruin: into what Pit thou seest
From what highth fall'n, so much the stronger prov'd
He with his Thunder: and till then who knew
The force of those dire Arms? yet not for those,
Nor what the Potent Victor in his rage
Can else inflict, do I repent or change,
Though chang'd in outward lustre; that fixt mind
And high disdain, from sence of injur'd merit,
That with the mightiest rais'd me to contend,
And to the fierce contention brought along
Innumerable force of Spirits arm'd
That durst dislike his reign, and me preferring,
His utmost power with adverse power oppos'd
In dubious Battel on the Plains of Heav'n,
And shook his throne. What though the field be lost?
All is not lost; the unconquerable Will,
And study of revenge, immortal hate,
And courage never to submit or yield:
And what is else not to be overcome?
That Glory never shall his wrath or might
Extort from me. To bow and sue for grace
With suppliant knee, and deifie his power,
Who from the terrour of this Arm so late
Doubted his Empire, that were low indeed,
That were an ignominy and shame beneath
This downfall; since by Fate the strength of Gods
And this Empyreal substance cannot fail,
Since through experience of this great event

In Arms not worse, in foresight much advanc't,
We may with more successful hope resolve
To wage by force or guile eternal Warr
Irreconcileable, to our grand Foe,
Who now triumphs, and in th' excess of joy
Sole reigning holds the Tyranny of Heav'n."

So spake th' Apostate Angel, though in pain,
Vaunting aloud, but rackt with deep despare:
And him thus answer'd soon his bold Compeer.

"O Prince, O Chief of many Throned Powers,
That led th' imbattelld Seraphim to Warr
Under thy conduct, and in dreadful deeds
Fearless, endanger'd Heav'ns perpetual King;
And put to proof his high Supremacy,
Whether upheld by strength, or Chance, or Fate,
Too well I see and rue the dire event,
That with sad overthrow and foul defeat
Hath lost us Heav'n, and all this mighty Host
In horrible destruction laid thus low,
As far as Gods and Heav'nly Essences
Can perish: for the mind and spirit remains
Invincible, and vigour soon returns,
Though all our Glory extinct, and happy state
Here swallow'd up in endless misery.
But what if he our Conquerour, (whom I now
Of force believe Almighty, since no less
Then such could hav orepow'rd such force as ours)
Have left us this our spirit and strength intire
Strongly to suffer and support our pains,
That we may so suffice his vengeful ire,
Or do him mightier service as his thralls
By right of Warr, what e're his business be
Here in the heart of Hell to work in Fire,
Or do his Errands in the gloomy Deep;
What can it then avail though yet we feel
Strength undiminisht, or eternal being
To undergo eternal punishment?"
Whereto with speedy words th' Arch-fiend reply'd.

"Fall'n Cherube, to be weak is miserable
Doing or Suffering: but of this be sure,
To do ought good never will be our task,
But ever to do ill our sole delight,
As being the contrary to his high will
Whom we resist. If then his Providence
Out of our evil seek to bring forth good,
Our labour must be to pervert that end,
And out of good still to find means of evil;
Which oft times may succeed, so as perhaps
Shall grieve him, if I fail not, and disturb
His inmost counsels from thir destind aim.
But see the angry Victor hath recall'd
His Ministers of vengeance and pursuit
Back to the Gates of Heav'n: The Sulphurous Hail
Shot after us in storm, oreblown hath laid
The fiery Surge, that from the Precipice
Of Heav'n receiv'd us falling, and the Thunder,
Wing'd with red Lightning and impetuous rage,
Perhaps hath spent his shafts, and ceases now
To bellow through the vast and boundless Deep.
Let us not slip th' occasion, whether scorn,
Or satiate fury yield it from our Foe.
Seest thou yon dreary Plain, forlorn and wilde,
The seat of desolation, voyd[1] of light,
Save what the glimmering of these livid flames
Casts pale and dreadful? Thither let us tend
From off the tossing of these fiery waves,
There rest, if any rest can harbour there,
And reassembling our afflicted Powers,
Consult how we may henceforth most offend
Our Enemy, our own loss how repair,
How overcome this dire Calamity,
What reinforcement we may gain from Hope,
If not what resolution from despare."

Thus Satan talking to his neerest Mate

---

[1] devoid

With Head up-lift above the wave, and Eyes
That sparkling blaz'd, his other Parts besides
Prone on the Flood, extended long and large
Lay floating many a rood, in bulk as huge
As whom the Fables name of monstrous size,
Titanian, or *Earth-born,* that warr'd on *Jove,*
Briareos or *Typhon,* whom the Den
By ancient *Tarsus* held, or that Sea-beast
Leviathan, which God of all his works
Created hugest that swim th' Ocean stream:
Him haply slumbring on the *Norway* foam
The Pilot of some small night-founder'd Skiff,
Deeming some Island, oft, as Sea-men tell,
With fixed Anchor in his skaly rind
Moors by his side under the Lee, while Night
Invests the Sea, and wished Morn delayes:[1]
So stretcht out huge in length the Arch-fiend lay
Chain'd on the burning Lake, nor ever thence
Had ris'n or heav'd his head, but that the will
And high permission of all-ruling Heaven
Left him at large to his own dark designs,
That with reiterated crimes he might
Heap on himself damnation, while he sought
Evil to others, and enrag'd might see
How all his malice serv'd but to bring forth
Infinite goodness, grace and mercy shewn
On Man by him seduc't, but on himself
Treble confusion, wrath and vengeance pour'd.
Forthwith upright he rears from off the Pool
His mighty Stature; on each hand the flames
Drivn backward slope thir pointing spires, and rowld
In billows, leave i'th' midst a horrid Vale.
Then with expanded wings he stears his flight
Aloft, incumbent on the dusky Air
That felt unusual weight, till on dry Land

---

[1] There are many legends of lost mariners mistaking a sea monster or whale for an island in the dark and landing on its back. One of the most colorful involves St. Brendan the Navigator, who supposedly traveled to the New World in search of the mythical land of Hy Brasil (and may in fact have reached Florida). At one point on his voyage, the story goes, he asked his companions to stop at a convenient island so that he could celebrate Mass; when the Mass was over, the island started moving—it was the back of a whale!

He lights, if it were Land that ever burn'd
With solid, as the Lake with liquid fire;
And such appear'd in hue, as when the force
Of subterranean wind transports a Hill
Torn from *Pelorus,* or the shatter'd side
Of thundring *Ætna,* whose combustible
And fewel'd entrals thence conceiving Fire,[1]
Sublim'd with Mineral fury, aid the Winds,
And leave a singed bottom all involv'd
With stench and smoak: Such resting found the sole
Of unblest feet. Him followed his next Mate,
Both glorying to have scap't the *Stygian* flood[2]
As Gods, and by thir own recover'd strength,
Not by the sufferance of supernal Power.

"Is this the Region, this the Soil, the Clime,"
Said then the lost Arch-Angel, "this the seat
That we must change for Heav'n, this mournful gloom
For that celestial light? Be it so, since he
Who now is Sovran can dispose and bid
What shall be right: fardest from him is best
Whom reason hath equald, force hath made supream
Above his equals. Farewel happy Fields
Where Joy for ever dwells: Hail horrours, hail
Infernal world, and thou profoundest Hell
Receive thy new Possessor: One who brings
A mind not to be chang'd by Place or Time.
The mind is its own place, and in it self
Can make a Heav'n of Hell, a Hell of Heav'n.
What matter where, if I be still the same,
And what I should be, all but less then he
Whom Thunder hath made greater? Here at least
We shall be free; th' Almighty hath not built
Here for his envy, will not drive us hence:
Here we may reign secure, and in my choyce
To reign is worth ambition though in Hell:
Better to reign in Hell, then serve in Heav'n.

---

[1] Mount Aetna is a volcano, and the "combustible / And fueled entrails" are the lava.
[2] *Stygian* as an adjective, especially for darkness, derives from the River Styx.

But wherefore let we then our faithful friends,
Th' associates and copartners of our loss
Lye thus astonisht on th' oblivious Pool,
And call them not to share with us their part
In this unhappy Mansion, or once more
With rallied Arms to try what may be yet
Regaind in Heav'n, or what more lost in Hell?"

So *Satan* spake, and him *Beelzebub*
Thus answer'd. "Leader of those Armies bright,
Which but th' Onmipotent none could have foyld,
If once they hear that voyce, thir liveliest pledge
Of hope in fears and dangers, heard so oft
In worst extreams, and on the perilous edge
Of battel when it rag'd, in all assaults
Thir surest signal, they will soon resume
New courage and revive, though now they lye
Groveling and prostrate on yon Lake of Fire,
As we erewhile, astounded and amaz'd,
No wonder, fall'n such a pernicious highth."[1]

He scarce had ceas't when the superiour Fiend
Was moving toward the shoar; his ponderous shield
Ethereal temper, massy, large and round,
Behind him cast; the broad circumference
Hung on his shoulders like the Moon, whose Orb
Through Optic Glass the *Tuscan* Artist views
At Ev'ning from the top of *Fesole,*
Or in *Valdarno,* to descry new Lands,
Rivers or Mountains in her spotty Globe.
His Spear, to equal which the tallest Pine
Hewn on *Norwegian* hills, to be the Mast
Of some great Ammiral,[2] were but a wand,
He walkt with to support uneasie steps
Over the burning Marle, not like those steps
On Heavens Azure, and the torrid Clime
Smote on him sore besides, vaulted with Fire;

---

[1] height
[2] admiral

Nathless[1] he so endur'd, till on the Beach
Of that inflamed Sea, he stood and call'd
His Legions, Angel Forms, who lay intrans't[2]
Thick as Autumnal Leaves that strow the Brooks
In *Vallombrosa,*[3] where th' *Etrurian*[4] shades
High overarch't imbowr; or scatterd sedge
Afloat, when with fierce Winds *Orion* arm'd
Hath vext the Red-Sea Coast, whose waves orethrew
Busiris[5] and his *Memphian* Chivalry,
While with perfidious hatred they pursu'd
The Sojourners of *Goshen,* who beheld
From the safe shore thir floating Carkases[6]
And broken Chariot Wheels, so thick bestrown
Abject and lost lay these, covering the Flood,
Under amazement of thir hideous change.
He call'd so loud, that all the hollow Deep
Of Hell resounded. "Princes, Potentates,
Warriers, the Flowr of Heav'n, once yours, now lost,
If such astonishment as this can sieze
Eternal spirits; or have ye chos'n this place
After the toyl of Battel to repose
Your wearied vertue, for the ease you find
To slumber here, as in the Vales of Heav'n?
Or in this abject posture have ye sworn
To adore the Conquerour? who now beholds
Cherube and Seraph rowling in the Flood
With scatter'd Arms and Ensigns, till anon
His swift pursuers from Heav'n Gates discern
Th' advantage, and descending tread us down
Thus drooping, or with linked Thunderbolts
Transfix us to the bottom of this Gulfe.
Awake, arise, or be for ever fall'n."

They heard, and were abasht, and up they sprung

---

[1] nonetheless

[2] entranced

[3] "Valley of Shades," located near Florence

[4] Etruscan (i.e., Italian)

[5] Greek for Pharaoh

[6] carcasses

Upon the wing, as when men wont to watch
On duty, sleeping found by whom they dread,
Rouse and bestir themselves ere well awake.
Nor did they not perceave the evil plight
In which they were, or the fierce pains not feel;
Yet to thir Generals Voyce they soon obeyd
Innumerable. As when the potent Rod
Of *Amrams* Son[1] in *Egypts* evill day
Wav'd round the Coast, up call'd a pitchy[2] cloud
Of *Locusts,* warping on the Eastern Wind,
That ore the Realm of impious *Pharaoh* hung
Like Night, and darken'd all the Land of *Nile*:
So numberless were those bad Angels seen
Hovering on wing under the Cope of Hell
'Twixt upper, nether, and surrounding Fires;
Till, as a signal giv'n, th' uplifted Spear
Of thir great Sultan waving to direct
Thir course, in even ballance down they light
On the firm brimstone, and fill all the Plain;
A multitude, like which the populous North
Pour'd never from her frozen loyns, to pass
Rhene or the *Danaw,*[3] when her barbarous Sons
Came like a Deluge on the South, and spread
Beneath *Gibralter* to the *Lybian* sands.[4]
Forthwith from every Squadron and each Band
The Heads and Leaders thither hast where stood
Thir great Commander; Godlike shapes and forms
Excelling human, Princely Dignities,
And Powers that earst in Heaven sat on Thrones;
Though of thir Names in heav'nly Records now
Be no memorial blotted out and ras'd
By thir Rebellion, from the Books of Life.
Nor had they yet among the Sons of *Eve*
Got them new Names, till wandring ore the Earth,
Through Gods high sufferance for the tryal of man,

---

[1] Moses
[2] i.e., pitch-black
[3] The Rhine or the Danube
[4] Milton makes reference here to the invasions of Germanic tribes, especially the Vandals and Goths, from north of the Alps all the way south as far as North Africa.

By falsities and lyes the greatest part
Of Mankind they corrupted to forsake
God thir Creator, and th' invisible
Glory of him that made them, to transform
Oft to the Image of a Brute, adorn'd
With gay Religions full of Pomp and Gold,
And Devils to adore for Deities:
Then were they known to men by various Names,
And various Idols through the Heathen World.[1]
Say, Muse, thir Names then known, who first, who last,
Rous'd from the slumber, on that fiery Couch,
At thir great Emperors call, as next in worth
Came singly where he stood on the bare strand,
While the promiscuous croud stood yet aloof?
The chief were those who from the Pit of Hell
Roaming to seek thir prey on earth, durst fix
Thir Seats long after next the Seat of God,
Thir Altars by his Altar, Gods ador'd
Among the Nations round, and durst abide
Jehovah thundring out of *Sion,* thron'd
Between the Cherubim; yea, often plac'd
Within his Sanctuary it self thir Shrines,
Abominations; and with cursed things
His holy Rites, and solemn Feasts profan'd,
And with thir darkness durst affront his light.
First *Moloch,* horrid King besmear'd with blood
Of human sacrifice, and parents tears,
Though for the noyse of Drums and Timbrels loud
Thir childrens cries unheard, that past through fire
To his grim Idol. Him the *Ammonite*
Worshipt in *Rabba* and her watry Plain,
In *Argob* and in *Basan,* to the stream
Of utmost *Arnon.* Nor content with such
Audacious neighbourhood, the wisest heart
Of *Solomon* he led by fraud to build
His Temple right against the Temple of God
On that opprobrious Hill, and made his Grove
The pleasant Vally of *Hinnom, Tophet* thence

---

[1] Here Milton follows the assumption that the pagan gods are in fact demons.

And black *Gehenna* call'd, the Type of Hell.
Next *Chemos*, th' obscene dread of *Moabs* Sons,
From *Aroar* to *Nebo*, and the wild
Of Southmost *Abarim*; in *Hesebon*
And *Horonaim*, *Seons* Realm, beyond
The flowry Dale of *Sibma* clad with Vines,
And *Eleale* to th' *Asphaltick* Pool.[1]
Peor his other Name, when he entic'd
Israel in *Sittim* on thir march from *Nile*
To do him wanton rites, which cost them woe.
Yet thence his lustful Orgies he enlarg'd
Even to that Hill of scandal, by the Grove
Of *Moloch* homicide, lust hard by hate;
Till good *Josiah* drove them thence to Hell.
With these came they, who from the bordring flood
Of old *Euphrates* to the Brook that parts
Egypt from *Syrian* ground, had general Names
Of *Baalim* and *Ashtaroth*, those male,
These Feminine. For Spirits when they please
Can either Sex assume, or both; so soft
And uncompounded is thir Essence pure,
Not ti'd or manacl'd with joynt or limb,
Nor founded on the brittle strength of bones,
Like cumbrous flesh; but in what shape they choose
Dilated or condens't, bright or obscure,
Can execute thir aerie purposes,
And works of love or enmity fulfill.
For those the Race of *Israel* oft forsook
Thir living strength, and unfrequented left
His righteous Altar, bowing lowly down
To bestial Gods; for which thir heads as low
Bow'd down in Battel, sunk before the Spear
Of despicable foes.[2] With these in troop
Came *Astoreth*, whom the *Phoenicians* call'd
Astarte, Queen of Heav'n, with crescent Horns;
To whose bright Image nightly by the Moon

---

[1] The Dead Sea.
[2] Milton refers here to the cycle of apostacy, judgment, repentance, and restoration that Israel followed from Judges through the days of the prophets.

Sidonian Virgins paid thir Vows and Songs,
In *Sion* also not unsung, where stood
Her Temple on th' offensive Mountain, built
By that uxorious King,[1] whose heart though large,
Beguil'd by fair Idolatresses, fell
To Idols foul. *Thammuz* came next behind,
Whose annual wound in *Lebanon* allur'd
The *Syrian* Damsels to lament his fate
In amorous dittyes all a Summers day,[2]
While smooth *Adonis*[3] from his native Rock
Ran purple to the Sea, suppos'd with blood
Of *Thammuz* yearly wounded: the Love-tale
Infected *Sions* daughters with like heat,
Whose wanton passions in the sacred Porch
Ezekiel saw, when by the Vision led
His eye survay'd the dark Idolatries
Of alienated *Judah*. Next came one
Who mourn'd in earnest, when the Captive Ark
Maim'd his brute Image, head and hands lopt off
In his own Temple, on the grunsel edge,
Where he fell flat, and sham'd his Worshipers:[4]
Dagon his Name, Sea Monster, upward Man
And downward Fish: yet had his Temple high
Rear'd in *Azotus*, dreaded through the Coast
Of *Palestine*, in *Gath* and *Ascalon*
And *Accaron* and *Gaza's* frontier bounds.
Him follow'd *Rimmon*, whose delightful Seat
Was fair *Damascus*, on the fertil Banks
Of *Abbana* and *Pharphar*, lucid streams.
He also against the house of God was bold:

---

[1] Solomon, led astray by his many foreign wives.

[2] Sumerian mythology held that Inanna (Ashtoreth) was once trapped in the underworld and Tammuz, her son and consort, offered his life in exchange for hers; he was to spend six months every year in the underworld, specifically during the hottest part of the year. Thus, beginning on the summer solstice, the pagan nations of the Ancient Near East held a ritual funeral (six days long in Babylon) for Tammuz. One of the abominations God reveals to Ezekiel in Ez. 8 is a group of Hebrew women mourning for Tammuz on the Temple Mount.

[3] Adonis is another dying and rising god, potentially derived from Tammuz, in Greek mythology; he was one of Aphrodite's lovers and was killed by a wild boar. The source of the Adonis River (or Abraham River) in Afqa, Lebanon, turns red each spring, which was said to be the blood of Adonis.

[4] See 1 Samuel 5.

A Leper once he lost[1] and gain'd a King,
Ahaz his sottish Conquerour, whom he drew
Gods Altar to disparage and displace
For one of *Syrian* mode, whereon to burn
His odious off'rings, and adore the Gods
Whom he had vanquisht. After these appear'd
A crew who under Names of old Renown,
Osiris, Isis, Orus and their Train[2]
With monstrous shapes and sorceries abus'd
Fanatic *Egypt* and her Priests, to seek
Thir wandring Gods disguis'd in brutish forms
Rather then human. Nor did *Israel* scape
Th' infection when thir borrow'd Gold compos'd
The Calf in *Oreb*: and the Rebel King[3]
Doubl'd that sin in *Bethel* and in *Dan*,
Lik'ning his Maker to the Grazed Ox,
Jehovah, who in one Night when he pass'd
From *Egypt* marching, equal'd with one stroke
Both her first born and all her bleating Gods.
Belial came last, then whom a Spirit more lewd
Fell not from Heaven, or more gross to love
Vice for it self: To him no Temple stood
Or Altar smoak'd; yet who more oft then hee
In Temples and at Altars, when the Priest
Turns Atheist, as did *Ely's* Sons, who fill'd
With lust and violence the house of God.[4]
In Courts and Palaces he also Reigns
And in luxurious Cities, where the noyse
Of riot ascends above thir loftiest Towrs,
And injury and outrage: And when Night
Darkens the Streets, then wander forth the Sons
Of *Belial,* flown with insolence and wine.
Witness the Streets of *Sodom,* and that night
In *Gibeah,* when the hospitable door

---

[1] Naaman
[2] Osiris was the Egyptian god of the dead; Isis, his sister and consort, was goddess of health and wisdom; and not only was their son Horus king of the gods, but the ruling pharaoh was worshipped as the living manifestation of Horus.
[3] Jeroboam
[4] The crimes of Eli's sons are detailed in 1 Samuel 2.

Expos'd a Matron to avoid worse rape.[1]
These were the prime in order and in might;
The rest were long to tell, though far renown'd,
Th' *Ionian* Gods, of *Javans* Issue[2] held
Gods, yet confest later then Heav'n and Earth
Thir boasted Parents; *Titan* Heav'ns first born
With his enormous brood, and birthright seis'd
By younger *Saturn,* he from mightier *Jove*
His own and *Rhea's* Son like measure found;
So Jove usurping reign'd: these first in *Creet*
And *Ida* known, thence on the Snowy top
Of cold *Olympus* rul'd the middle Air
Thir highest Heav'n; or on the *Delphian* Cliff,
Or in *Dodona,* and through all the bounds
Of *Doric* Land; or who with *Saturn* old
Fled over *Adria* to th' *Hesperian* Fields,
And ore the *Celtic* roam'd the utmost Isles.
All these and more came flocking; but with looks
Down cast and damp, yet such wherein appear'd
Obscure some glimps of joy, to have found thir chief
Not in despair, to have found themselves not lost
In loss it self; which on his count'nance cast
Like doubtful hue: but he his wonted pride
Soon recollecting, with high words, that bore
Semblance of worth, not substance, gently rais'd
Thir fainting courage, and dispel'd thir fears.
Then strait commands that at the warlike sound
Of Trumpets loud and Clarions be upreard
His mighty Standard; that proud honour claim'd
Azazel as his right, a Cherube tall:[3]
Who forthwith from the glittering Staff unfurld
Th' Imperial Ensign, which full high advanc't
Shon like a Meteor streaming to the Wind
With Gemms and Golden lustre rich imblaz'd,
Seraphic arms and Trophies: all the while

---

[1] See Judges 19.

[2] The offspring of Japheth, believed to be the ancestor of Europeans generally and of the Greeks particularly.

[3] Some translations render Leviticus 16:8, on the selection of the scapegoat, as "one for the LORD and one for Azazel," leading to the assumption that Azazel is the proper name of a demon. In Kabbalah, Azazel is one of Hell's standard-bearers.

Sonorous mettal blowing Martial sounds:
At which the universal Host upsent
A shout that tore Hells Concave, and beyond
Frighted the Reign of *Chaos* and old Night.
All in a moment through the gloom were seen
Ten thousand Banners rise into the Air
With Orient Colours waving: with them rose
A Forest huge of Spears: and thronging Helms
Appear'd, and serried shields in thick array
Of depth immeasurable: Anon they move
In perfect *Phalanx* to the *Dorian* mood
Of Flutes and soft Recorders; such as rais'd
To hight of noblest temper Hero's old
Arming to Battel, and in stead of rage
Deliberate valour breath'd, firm and unmov'd
With dread of death to flight or foul retreat,
Nor wanting power to mitigate and swage
With solemn touches, troubl'd thoughts, and chase
Anguish and doubt and fear and sorrow and pain
From mortal or immortal minds. Thus they
Breathing united force with fixed thought
Mov'd on in silence to soft Pipes that charm'd
Thir painful steps o're the burnt soyle; and now
Advanc't in view, they stand, a horrid Front
Of dreadful length and dazling Arms, in guise
Of Warriers old with order'd Spear and Shield,
Awaiting what command thir mighty Chief
Had to impose: He through the armed Files
Darts his experienc't eye, and soon traverse
The whole Battalion views, thir order due,
Thir visages and stature as of Gods,
Thir number last he summs. And now his heart
Distends with pride, and hardning in his strength
Glories: For never since created man,
Met such imbodied force, as nam'd with these
Could merit more then that small infantry
Warr'd on by Cranes: though all the Giant brood
Of *Phlegra*[1] with th' Heroic Race were joyn'd

---

[1] Site of the Gigantomachy (War against the Giants), according to Ovid.

That fought at *Theb's* and *Ilium,*[1] on each side
Mixt with auxiliar Gods; and what resounds
In Fable or *Romance* of *Uthers* Son[2]
Begirt with *British* and Armoric Knights;
And all who since, Baptiz'd or Infidel
Jousted in *Aspramont* or *Montalban,*
Damasco, or *Marocco,* or *Trebisond,*[3]
Or whom *Biserta* sent from *Afric* shore[4]
When *Charlemain* with all his Peerage fell
By *Fontarabbia.* Thus far these beyond
Compare of mortal prowess, yet observ'd
Thir dread commander: he above the rest
In shape and gesture proudly eminent
Stood like a Towr; his form had yet not lost
All her Original brightness, nor appear'd
Less then Arch Angel ruind, and th' excess
Of Glory obscur'd: As when the Sun new ris'n
Looks through the Horizontal misty Air
Shorn of his Beams, or from behind the Moon
In dim Eclips disastrous twilight sheds
On half the Nations, and with fear of change
Perplexes Monarchs. Dark'n'd so, yet shon
Above them all th' Arch Angel: but his face
Deep scars of Thunder had intrencht,[5] and care
Sat on his faded cheek, but under Browes
Of dauntless courage, and considerate Pride
Waiting revenge: cruel his eye, but cast
Signs of remorse and passion to behold
The fellows of his crime, the followers rather
(Far other once beheld in bliss) condemn'd
For ever now to have thir lot in pain,
Millions of Spirits for his fault amerc't[6]

---

[1] The seven heroes commemorated in Aeschylus' *Seven Against Thebes* and the Greek armies that besieged Troy (Ilium).

[2] Arthur

[3] Locations in chivalric romances like *Orlando Furioso,* especially connected with the Reconquista.

[4] Legendary embarkation point for the Muslim invasion of Spain, which actually happened long before Charlemagne was even born.

[5] entrenched (made trenches into)

[6] deprived

Of Heav'n, and from Eternal Splendors flung
For his revolt, yet faithfull how they stood,
Thir Glory witherd. As when Heavens Fire
Hath scath'd the Forrest Oaks, or Mountain Pines,
With singed top thir stately growth though bare
Stands on the blasted Heath. He now prepar'd
To speak; whereat thir doubl'd Ranks they bend
From wing to wing, and half enclose him round
With all his Peers: attention held them mute.
Thrice he assayd, and thrice in spight of scorn,
Tears such as Angels weep, burst forth: at last
Words interwove with sighs found out thir way.

"O Myriads of immortal Spirits, O Powers
Matchless, but with th' Almighty, and that strife
Was not inglorious, though th' event was dire,
As this place testifies, and this dire change
Hateful to utter: but what power of mind
Foreseeing or presaging, from the Depth
Of knowledge past or present, could have fear'd,
How such united force of Gods, how such
As stood like these, could ever know repulse?
For who can yet beleeve, though after loss,
That all these puissant Legions, whose exile
Hath emptied Heav'n, shall fail to re-ascend
Self-rais'd, and repossess thir native seat?
For mee be witness all the Host of Heav'n,
If counsels different, or danger shun'd
By me, have lost our hopes. But he who reigns
Monarch in Heav'n, till then as one secure
Sat on his Throne, upheld by old repute,
Consent or custome, and his Regal State
Put forth at full, but still his strength conceal'd,
Which tempted our attempt, and wrought our fall.
Henceforth his might we know, and know our own
So as not either to provoke, or dread
New warr, provok't; our better part remains
To work in close design, by fraud or guile
What force effected not: that he no less
At length from us may find, who overcomes

By force, hath overcome but half his foe.
Space may produce new Worlds; whereof so rife
There went a fame in Heav'n that he ere long
Intended to create, and therein plant
A generation, whom his choice regard
Should favour equal to the Sons of Heaven:
Thither, if but to pry, shall be perhaps
Our first eruption, thither or elsewhere:
For this Infernal Pit shall never hold
Cælestial Spirits in Bondage, nor th' Abyss
Long under darkness cover. But these thoughts
Full Counsel must mature: Peace is despaird,
For who can think Submission? Warr then, Warr
Open or understood must be resolv'd."

He spake: and to confirm his words, out-flew
Millions of flaming swords, drawn from the thighs[1]
Of mighty Cherubim; the sudden blaze
Far round illumin'd hell: highly they rag'd
Against the Highest, and fierce with grasped arms
Clash'd on thir sounding Shields the din of war,
Hurling defiance toward the vault of Heav'n.

There stood a Hill not far whose griesly top
Belch'd fire and rowling smoak; the rest entire
Shon with a glossie scurff, undoubted sign
That in his womb was hid metallic Ore,
The work of Sulphur. Thither wing'd with speed
A numerous Brigad hasten'd. As when Bands
Of Pioners with Spade and Pickax arm'd
Forerun the Royal Camp, to trench a Field,
Or cast a Rampart. *Mammon* led them on,
Mammon, the least erected Spirit that fell
From heav'n, for ev'n in heav'n his looks and thoughts
Were always downward bent, admiring more
The riches of Heav'ns pavement, trod'n Gold,
Then aught divine or holy else enjoy'd
In vision beatific: by him first

---

[1] i.e., the scabbards that rest against the thighs

Men also, and by his suggestion taught,
Ransack'd the Center, and with impious hands
Rifl'd the bowels of thir mother Earth
For Treasures better hid. Soon had his crew
Op'nd into the Hill a spacious wound
And dig'd out ribs of Gold. Let none admire
That riches grow in Hell; that soyle may best
Deserve the precious bane. And here let those
Who boast in mortal things, and wond'ring tell
Of *Babel,* and the works of *Memphian* Kings
Learn how thir greatest Monuments of Fame,
And Strength and Art are easily out-done
By Spirits reprobate, and in an hour
What in an age they with incessant toyle
And hands innumerable scarce perform.
Nigh on the Plain in many cells prepar'd,
That underneath had veins of liquid fire
Sluc'd from the Lake, a second multitude
With wondrous Art found out the massie Ore,
Severing each kind, and scum'd the Bullion dross:[1]
A third as soon had form'd within the ground
A various mould, and from the boyling cells
By strange conveyance fill'd each hollow nook,
As in an Organ from one blast of wind
To many a row of Pipes the sound-board breaths.
Anon out of the earth a Fabrick huge
Rose like an Exhalation, with the sound
Of Dulcet Symphonies and voices sweet,
Built like a Temple, where *Pilasters* round
Were set, and Doric pillars overlaid
With Golden Architrave; nor did there want
Cornice or Freeze, with bossy Sculptures grav'n,
The Roof was fretted Gold.[2] Not *Babilon,*
Nor great *Alcairo*[3] such magnificence
Equal'd in all thir glories, to inshrine

---

[1] Essentially, the demons are mining out the gold ore, smelting it, skimming off the impurities, and molding it into the shapes desired for building.

[2] The structure Milton describes here is a Greco-Roman temple like the Parthenon.

[3] Cairo

Belus[1] or *Serapis*[2] thir Gods, or seat
Thir Kings, when *Ægypt* with *Assyria* strove
In wealth and luxurie. Th' ascending pile
Stood fixt her stately highth, and strait the dores
Op'ning thir brazen foulds discover[3] wide
Within, her ample spaces, o're the smooth
And level pavement: from the arched roof
Pendant by suttle Magic many a row
Of Starry Lamps and blazing Cressets[4] fed
With *Naphtha* and *Asphaltus* yeilded light
As from a sky. The hasty multitude
Admiring enter'd, and the work some praise
And some the Architect: his hand was known
In Heav'n by many a Towred structure high,
Where Scepter'd Angels held thir residence,
And sat as Princes, whom the supreme King
Exalted to such power, and gave to rule,
Each in his Hierarchie, the Orders bright.
Nor was his name unheard or unador'd
In ancient *Greece*; and in *Ausonian* land
Men call'd him *Mulciber*;[5] and how he fell
From Heav'n, they fabl'd, thrown by angry *Jove*
Sheer o're the Chrystal Battlements: from Morn
To Noon he fell, from Noon to dewy Eve,
A Summers day; and with the setting Sun
Dropt from the Zenith like a falling Star,
On *Lemnos* th' *Ægean* Ile:[6] thus they relate,
Erring; for he with this rebellious rout
Fell long before; nor aught avail'd him now
To have built in Heav'n high Towrs; nor did he scape
By all his Engins, but was headlong sent

---

[1] Bel/Marduk/Baal. These were not necessarily all the same god in Babylonian and Canaanite mythology—*Bel* and *Baal* both mean merely "Lord," though *Bel* was usually connected exclusively with Marduk—but in Greek mythology they were all referred to as *Belus*.

[2] Hellenized version of Osiris, syncretized with Apis (the sacred bull) and other Greek and Roman gods.

[3] uncover

[4] Iron basket lamps. Naphtha, in the ancient world, was a volatile type of petroleum, and asphalt is a much stickier solid form of petroleum; both would make for effective, if stinky, lantern fuel.

[5] Another name for Hephaestus/Vulcan.

[6] One of the stories accounting for how Hephaestus became crippled.

With his industrious crew to build in hell.
Mean while the winged Haralds by command
Of Sovran power, with awful Ceremony
And Trumpets sound throughout the Host proclaim
A solemn Councel forthwith to be held
At *Pandæmonium*,[1] the high Capital
Of Satan and his Peers: thir summons call'd
From every Band and squared Regiment
By place or choice the worthiest; they anon
With hunderds and with thousands trooping came
Attended: all access was throng'd, the Gates
And Porches wide, but chief the spacious Hall
(Though like a cover'd field, where Champions bold
Wont[2] ride in arm'd, and at the Soldans[3] chair
Defi'd the best of *Paynim*[4] chivalry
To mortal combat or carreer with Lance)
Thick swarm'd, both on the ground and in the air,
Brusht with the hiss of russling wings. As Bees
In spring time, when the Sun with *Taurus* rides,[5]
Pour forth thir populous youth about the Hive
In clusters; they among fresh dews and flowers
Flie to and fro, or on the smoothed Plank,
The suburb of thir Straw-built Cittadel,
New rub'd with Baum, expatiate and confer
Thir State affairs. So thick the aerie crowd
Swarm'd and were straitn'd; till the Signal giv'n.
Behold a wonder! they but now who seemd
In bigness to surpass Earths Giant Sons
Now less then smallest Dwarfs, in narrow room
Throng numberless, like that Pigmean Race
Beyond the *Indian* Mount, or Faerie Elves,[6]
Whose midnight Revels, by a Forrest side

---

[1] Lit. "the place of all demons."
[2] Were accustomed to
[3] Sultan's
[4] pagan
[5] Late spring or early summer (Taurus is one of the signs of the zodiac, and in ancient times it was the constellation through which the sun rose on the vernal equinox)
[6] A significant change in the concept of the fae from the original Celtic legends! Milton is probably referring here to *A Midsummer Night's Dream*.

Or Fountain some belated Peasant sees,
Or dreams he sees, while over-head the Moon
Sits Arbitress, and neerer to the Earth
Wheels her pale course, they on thir mirth and dance
Intent, with jocond Music charm his ear;
At once with joy and fear his heart rebounds.
Thus incorporeal Spirits to smallest forms
Reduc'd thir shapes immense, and were at large,
Though without number still amidst the Hall
Of that infernal Court. But far within
And in thir own dimensions like themselves
The great Seraphic Lords and Cherubim
In close recess and secret conclave sat
A thousand Demy-Gods on golden seats,
Frequent and full. After short silence then
And summons read, the great consult began.

The End of the First Book.

Capt. John Smith
from The Generall Historie of Virginia

Smith perceiving (notwithstanding their late miserie) not any regarded but from hand to mouth (the company being well recovered) caused the Pinnace[1] to be provided with things fitting to get provision for the yeare following; but in the interim he made 3. or 4. journies and discovered the people of Chickahamania: yet what he carefully provided the rest carelessly spent. Wingfield and Kendall living in disgrace, seeing all things at randome in the absence of Smith, the companies dislike of their Presidents weaknes, and their small love to Martins never mending sicknes, strengthened themselves with the sailers, and other confederates to regaine their former credit and authority, or at least such meanes abord the Pinnace, (being fitted to saile as Smith had appointed for trade) to alter her course and to goe for England. Smith unexpectedly returning had the plot discovered to him, much trouble he had to prevent it, till with store of sakre[2] and musket shot he forced them stay or sinke in the river, which action cost the life of captaine Kendall. These brawles are so disgustfull, as some

---

[1] A type of ship
[2] An early type of cannon

will say they were better forgotten, yet all men of good judgement will conclude, at were better their basenes should be manifest to the world, then the busines beare the scorne and shame of their excused disorders. The President and captaine Archer not long after intended also to have abandoned the country, which project also was curbed, and suppressed by Smith. The Spaniard never more greedily desired gold then he victuall, nor his souldiers more to abandon the Country, then he to keepe it. But finding plentie of Corne[1] in the river of Chickahamania where hundreds of Salvages[2] in divers places stood with baskets expecting his comming. And now the winter approaching, the rivers became so covered with swans, geese, duckes, and cranes, that we daily feasted with good bread, Virginia pease, pumpions,[3] and putchamins,[4] fish, fowle, and diverse sorts of wild beasts as far as we could eate them: so that none of our Tuftaffaty[5] humorists desired to goe for England. But our Comædies never endured long without a Tragedie; some idle exceptions being muttered against Captaine Smith, for not discovering the head of Chickahamania river, and taxed by the Councell, to be too slow in so worthy an attempt. The next voyage hee proceeded so farre that with much labour by cutting of trees in sunder he made his passage, but when his Barge could passe no farther, he left her in a broad bay out of danger of shot, commanding none should goe a shore till his returne: himselfe with two English and two Salvages went up higher in a Canowe, but hee was not long absent, but his men went a shore, whose want of government, gave both occasion and opportunity to the Salvages to surprise one George Cassen, whom they slew, and much failed not to have cut of the boat and all the rest. Smith little dreaming of that accident, being got to the marshes at the rivers head, twentie myles in the desert, had his two men[6] slaine (as is supposed) sleeping by the Canowe, whilst himselfe by fowling sought them victuall, who finding he was beset with 200. Salvages, two of them hee slew, still defending himselfe with the ayd of a Salvage his guid, whom he bound to his arme with his garters, and used him as a buckler,[7] yet he was shot in his thigh a little, and had many arrowes that stucke in his cloathes but no great hurt, till at last they tooke him prisoner. When this newes came to James towne, much was their sorrow for his losse, fewe expecting what ensued. Sixe or seven weekes those Barbarians kept him prisoner, many strange triumphes and conjurations they made of him, yet hee so demeaned himselfe amongst them, as he not onely diverted them from surprising the Fort, but procured his owne libertie, and got himselfe and his company such estimation amongst them, that those

[1] Originally, "corn" was used for any grain and mainly meant wheat, but in this case, as later in *Of Plimouth Plantation*, it does indeed mean what we think of as corn (maize).
[2] Smith consistently spells "savages" this way.
[3] pumpkins
[4] This is the Algonquian word from which we get the name *persimmon* for the fruit Smith means here.
[5] tufted taffeta, used for luxurious clothing
[6] The marginal notes in the original version identify these men as Jehu Robinson and Thomas Emry.
[7] A type of shield

Salvages admired him more then their owne Quiyouckosucks. The manner how they used and delivered him, is as followeth.

The Salvages having drawne from George Cassen whether Captaine Smith was gone, prosecuting that opportunity they followed him with 300. bowmen, conducted by the King of Pamaunkee, who in divisions searching the turnings of the river, found Robinson and Emry by the fire side, those they shot full of arrowes and slew. Then finding the Captaine, as is said, that used the Salvage that was his guide as his shield (three of them being slaine and divers other so gauld[1]) all the rest would not come neere him. Thinking thus to have returned to his boat, regarding them, as he marched, more then his way, slipped up to the middle in an oasie creeke & his Salvage with him, yet durst they not come to him till being neere dead with cold, he threw away his armes. Then according to their composition they drew him forth and led him to the fire, where his men were slaine. Diligently they chafed his benummed limbs. He demanding for their Captaine, they shewed him Opechankanough, King[2] of Pamaunkee, to whom he gave a round Ivory double compass Dyall.[3] Much they marvailed at the playing of the Fly and Needle, which they could see so plainely, and yet not touch it, because of the glasse that covered them. But when he demonstrated by that Globe-like Jewell, the roundnesse of the earth, and skies, the spheare of the Sunne, Moone, and Starres, and how the Sunne did chase the night round about the world continually; the greatnesse of the Land and Sea, the diversitie of Nations, varietie of complexions, and how we were to them Antipodes,[4] and many other such like matters, they all stood as amazed with admiration. Notwithstanding, within an houre after they tyed him to a tree, and as many as could stand about him prepared to shoot him, but the King holding up the Compass in his hand, they all laid downe their Bowes and Arrowes, and in a triumphant manner led him to Orapaks, where he was after their manner kindly feasted, and well used.

Their order in conducting him was thus; Drawing themselves all in fyle, the King in the middest had all their Peeces[5] and Swords borne before him. Captaine Smith was led after him by three great Salvages, holding him fast by each arme: and on each side six went in fyle with their Arrowes nocked. But arriving at the Towne (which was but onely thirtie or fortie hunting houses made of Mats, which they remove as they please, as we our tents) all the

[1] galled (injured)

[2] Most European texts of this period misapply titles of European nobility, like king and emperor, for American Indian leaders. The Powhatans were a group of six allied tribes, each of which had a chief called a *weroance*; Powhatan himself was chief over the entire alliance and had the title *mamanatowick*. (Strikingly, Encyclopedia Britannica to this day refers to Powhatan's confederacy as "the Powhatan Empire.")

[3] dial

[4] The Greeks coined this term (lit. "feet in the opposite direction") to describe the Southern Hemisphere, though the idea that the inhabitants of the area walked upside down (relative to people in the Northern Hemisphere) gave rise to some very fanciful misunderstandings. When the South Pacific was being explored, the term was applied to the natives of the region, especially the Maori and Australian Aborigines. More generally, it refers to the point directly opposite any given point on a sphere.

[5] firearms

women and children staring to behold him, the souldiers first all in fyle performed the forme of a Bissom so well as could be, and on each flanke, officers as Serjeants to see them keepe their orders. A good time they continued this exercise, and then cast themselves in a ring, dauncing in such severall Postures, and singing and yelling out such hellish notes and screeches; being strangely painted, every one his quiver of Arrowes, and at his backe a club; on his arme a Fox or an Otters skinne, or some such matter for his vambrace; their heads and shoulders painted red, with Oyle and Pocones mingled together, which Scarlet-like colour made an exceeding handsome shew; his Bow in his hand, and the skinne of a Bird with her wings abroad dryed, tyed on his head, a peece of copper, a white shell, a long feather, with a small rattle growing at the tayles of their snaks tyed to it, or some such like toy. All this while Smith and the King stood in the middest guarded, as before is said, and after three dances they all departed. Smith they conducted to a long house, where thirtie or fortie tall fellowes did guard him, and ere long more bread and venison was brought him then would have served twentie men, I thinke his stomacke at that time was not very good; what he left they put in baskets and tyed over his head. About midnight they set the meate againe before him, all this time not one of them would eate a bit with him, till the next morning they brought him as much more, and then did they eate all the old, & reserved the new as they had done the other, which made him thinke they would fat him to eat him.[1] Yet in this desperate estate to defend him from the cold, one Maocassater brought him his gowne, in requitall of some beads and toyes Smith had given him at his first arrivall in Virginia.

Two dayes after a man would have slaine him (but that the guard prevented it) for the death of his sonne, to whom they conducted him to recover the poore man then breathing his last. Smith told them that at James towne he had a water would doe it, if they would let him fetch it, but they would not permit that; but made all the preparations they could to assault James towne, craving his advice, and for recompence he should have life, libertie, land, and women. In part of a Table booke he writ his minde to them at the Fort, what was intended, how they should follow that direction to affright the messengers, and without fayle send him such things as he writ for. And an Inventory with them. The difficultie and danger, he told the Salvages, of the Mines, great-gunnes, and other Engins exceedingly affrighted them, yet according to his request they went to James towne, in as bitter weather as could be of frost and snow, and within three dayes returned with an answer.

But when they came to Jame towne, seeing men sally out as he had told them they would, they fled; yet in the night they came againe to the same place where he had told them they should receive an answer, and such things as he had promised them, which they found accordingly, and with which they returned with no small expedition, to the wonder of them all that heard it, that he could either divine, or the paper could speake: then they led him to the Youthtanunds, the Mattapanients, the Payankatanks, the Nantaughtacunds, and Onawmanients upon the rivers of Raphanock, and Patawomek, over all those rivers, and

[1] More likely, this was a way of treating him as an honored guest.

backe againe by divers other severall Nations, to the Kings habitation at Pamaunkee, where they entertained him with most strange and fearefulle Conjurations;

> As if neare led to hell,
> Amongst the Devils to dwell.

Not long after, early in a morning a great fire was made in a long house, and a mat spread on the one side, as on the other; on the one they caused him to sit, and all the guard went out of the house, and presently came skipping in a great grim fellow, all painted over with coale, mingled with oyle; and many Snakes and Wesels skins stuffed with mosse, and all their tayles tyed together, so as they met on the crowne of his head in a tassell; and round about the tassell was as a Coronet of feathers, the skins hanging round about his head, backe, and shoulders, and in a manner covered his face; with a hellish voyce and a rattle in his hand. With most strange gestures and passions he began his invocation, and environed the fire with a circle of meale; which done, three more such like devils came rushing in with the like antique tricks, painted halfe blacke, halfe red: but all their eyes were painted white, and some red stroakes like 100 Mutchato's, along their cheekes: round about him those fiends daunced a pretty while, and then came in three more as ugly as the rest; with red eyes, and white stroakes over their blacke faces, at last they all sat downe right against him; three of them on the one hand of the chiefe Priest, and three on the other. Then all with their rattles began a song, which ended, the chiefe Priest layd downe five wheat cornes: then strayning his armes and hands with such violence that he sweat, and his veynes swelled, he began a short Oration: at the conclusion they all gave a short groane; and then layd down three graines more. After that, began their song againe, and then another Oration, ever laying downe so many cornes as before, till they had twice incircled the fire; that done, they tooke a bunch of little stickes prepared for that purpose, continuing still their devotion, and at the end of every song and Oration, they layd downe a sticke betwixt the divisions of Corne. Till night, neither he nor they did either eate or drinke, and then they feasted merrily, with the best provisions they could make. Three dayes they used this Ceremony; the meaning whereof they told him, was to know if he intended them well or no. The circle of meale signified their Country, the circles of corne the bounds of the Sea, and the stickes his Country. They imagined the world to be flat and round, like a trencher, and they in the middest. After this they brought him a bagge of gunpowder, which they carefully preserved till the next spring, to plant as they did their corne; because they would be acquainted with the nature of that seede.

Opitchapam the Kings brother invited him to his house, where, with as many platters of bread, foule, and wild beasts, as did environ him, he bid him wellcome; but not any of them would eate a bit with him, but put up all the remainder in Baskets. At his returne to Opechancanoughs, all the Kings women, and their children, flocked about him for their parts, as a due by Custome, to be merry with such fragments.

> But his waking mind in hydeous dreames did oft see wondrous shapes,
> Of bodies strange, and huge in growth, and of stupendious makes.

At last they brought him to Meronocomo, where was Powhatan their Emperor. Here more then two hundred of those grim Courtiers stood wondering at him, as he had beene a monster; till Powhatan and his trayne had put themselves in their greatest braveries. Before a fire upon a seat like a bedsted, he sat covered with a great robe, made of Rarowcun[1] skinnes, and all the tayles hanging by. On either hand did sit a young wench of 16 or 18 yeares, and along on each side the house, two rowes of men, and behind them as many women, with all their heads and shoulders painted red; many of their heads bedecked with the white downe of Birds; but every one with something: and a great chayne of white beads about their necks. At his entrance before the King, all the people gave a great shout. The Queene of Appamatuck was appointed to bring him water to wash his hands, and another brought him a bunch of feathers, in stead of a Towell to dry them: having feasted him after their best barbarous manner they could, a long consultation was held, but the conclusion was, two great stones were brought before Powhatan: then as many as could layd hands on him, dragged him to them, and thereon laid his head, and being ready with their clubs, to beate out his braines, Pocahontas the Kings dearest daughter, when no intreaty could prevaile, got his head in her armes, and laid her owne upon his to save him from death:[2] whereat the Emperour was contented he should live to make him hatchets, and her bells, beads, and copper; for they thought him aswell of all occupations as themselves. For the King himselfe will make his owne robes, shooes, bowes, arrowes, pots; plant, hunt, or doe any thing so well as the rest.[3]

> They say he bore a pleasant shew,
> But sure his heart was sad.
> For who can pleasant be, and rest,
> That lives in feare and dread:
> And having life suspected, doth
> It still suspected lead.

Two dayes after, Powhatan having disguised himselfe in the most fearefull manner he could, caused Capt. Smith to be brought forth to a great house in the woods, and there

---

[1] raccoon

[2] The consensus of modern scholarship is that this seeming attempt on Smith's life was actually an adoption ritual.

[3] Whether this statement is true or not—though it probably is true—Smith almost certainly means it as an implicit rebuke of the English gentry in Jamestown, who so disdained menial labor that they would have starved had Smith not made friends with the Powhatans.

upon a mat by the fire to be left alone. Not long after from behinde a mat that divided the house, was made the most dolefullest noyse he ever heard; then Powhatan more like a devill then a man with some two hundred more as blacke as himselfe, came unto him and told him now they were friends, and presently he should goe to James towne, to send him two great gunnes, and a gryndstone, for which he would give him the Country of Capahowosick, and for ever esteeme him as his sonne Nantaquoud. So to James towne with 12 guides Powhatan sent him. That night they quarterd in the woods, he still expecting (as he had done all this long time of his imprisonment) every houre to be put to one death or other: for all their feasting. But almightie God (by his divine providence) had mollified the hearts of those sterne Barbarians with compassion. The next morning betimes they came to the Fort, where Smith having used the Salvages with what kindnesse he could, he shewed Rawhunt, Powhatans trusty servant two demi-Culverings & a millstone to carry Powhatan: they found them somewhat too heavie; but when they did see him discharge them, being loaded with stones, among the boughs of a great tree loaded with Isickles, the yce and branches came so tumbling downe, that the poore Salvages ran away halfe dead with feare. But at last we regained some conference with them, and gave them such toyes; and sent to Powhatan, his women, and children such presents, as gave them in generall full content. Now in James Towne they were all in combustion, the strongest preparing once more to run away with the Pinnace; which with the hazzard of his life, with Sakre falcon and musket shot, Smith forced now the third time to stay or sinke. Some no better then they should be, had plotted with the President, the next day to have put him to death by the Leviticall law, for the lives of Robinson and Emry, pretending the fault was his that had led them to their ends: but he quickly tooke such order with such Lawyers, that he layd them by the heeles till he sent some of them prisoners for England. Now ever once in foure or five dayes, Pocahontas with her attendants, brought him so much provision, that saved many of their lives, that els[1] for all this had starved with hunger.

> Thus from numbe death our good God sent reliefe,
> The sweete asswager of all other griefe.

His relation of the plenty he had seene, especially at Werawocomoco, and of the state and bountie of Powhatan, (which till that time was unknowne) so revived their dead spirits (especially the love of Pocahontas) as all mens feare was abandoned. Thus you may see what difficulties still crossed any good indevour: and the good successe of the businesse being thus oft brought to the very period of destruction; yet you see by what strange means God hath still delivered it. As for the insufficiency of them admitted in Commission, that error could not be prevented by the Electors; there being no other choise, and all strangers to each others education, qualities, or disposition. And if any deeme it a shame to our Nation to have

---

[1] else (otherwise)

any mention made of those inormities, let them peruse the Histories of the Spanyards Discoveries and Plantations, where they may see how many mutinies, disorders, and dissentions have accompanied them, and crossed their attempts: which being knowne to be particular mens offences; doth take away the generall scorne and contempt, which malice, presumption, covetousnesse, or ignorance might produce; to the scandall and reproach of those, whose actions and valiant resolutions deserve a more worthy respect.

❧❧

William Bradford
from Of Plimoth Plantation[1]

The 1. Booke.
The 8. Chap.
Off the troubls that befell them on the coaste, and at sea being forced, after much trouble, to leave one of ther ships & some of their companie behind them.

Being thus put to sea they had not gone farr, but M^r. Reinolds y^{e2} master of ye leser ship complained that he found his ship so leak as he durst not put further to sea till she was mended.[3] So ye m^r.[4] of ye biger ship (caled M^r. Jonas) being consulted with, they both resolved to put into Dartmouth & have her ther searched & mended, which accordingly was done, to their great charg & losse of time and a faire winde. She was hear thorowly searcht from steme to sterne, some leaks were found & mended, and now it was conceived by the workmen & all, that she was sufficiente, & they might proceede without either fear or danger. So with good hopes from hence, they put to sea againe, conceiving they should goe comfortably on, not looking for any more lets of this kind; but it fell out otherwise, for after they were gone to sea againe above 100. leagues without[5] the Lands End, houlding company togeather all this while, the m^r. of ye small ship complained his ship was so leake as he must beare up or sinke at sea, for they could scarce free her with much pumping. So they came to consultation

---

[1] Notes on this text will incorporate footnotes from the 1898 edition published by Wright and Potter, which include notes added to the manuscript by Thomas Prince in 1728; these are denoted by "(P.)" at the end, and Bradford's original notes, of which there are a few, will be denoted with "(B.)". Notes from the unnamed editor of the Wright and Potter edition will be marked "(Ed.)". The original inconsistent spelling is retained.

[2] "Y^e" in this text is the conventional way of spelling "the." The *y* is used in place of the letter thorn (þ).

[3] The merchants with whom the Pilgrims had their contract had originally purchased two ships: a small one, the *Speedwell*, to take the Pilgrims from Leyden, Holland, to Southampton, England; and a large one, the *Mayflower*, to join the *Speedwell* at Southampton for the voyage to Virginia. They left Southampton on August 5, 1620.

[4] master (i.e., captain)

[5] past

againe, and resolved both ships to bear up backe againe & put into Plimoth,[1] which accordingly was done. But no spetiall leake could be founde, but it was judged to be yᵉ generall weaknes of yᵉ shipe, and that shee would not prove sufficiente for the voiage. Upon which it was resolved to dismise her & parte of yᵉ companie, and proceede with yᵉ other shipe. The which (though it was greevous, & caused great discouragmente) was put in execution. So after they had tooke out such provission as yᵉ other ship could well stow, and concluded both what number and what persons to send bak, they made another sad parting, yᵉ one ship going backe for London, and yᵉ other was to proceede on her viage. Those that went bak were for the most parte such as were willing so to doe, either out of some discontente, or feare they conceived of yᵉ ill success of yᵉ vioage, seeing so many croses[2] befale, & the year time so farr spente;[3] but others, in regarde of their owne weaknes, and charge of many yonge children, were thought least usefull, and most unfite to bear yᵉ brunte of this hard adventure; unto which worke of God, and judgmente of their brethern, they were contented to submite. And thus, like Gedions armie,[4] this small number was devided, as if yᵉ Lord by this worke of his providence thought these few to many for yᵉ great worke he had to doe. But here by the way let me show, how afterward it was found yᵗ[5] the leaknes of this ship was partly by being over masted, and too much pressed with sayles; for after she was sould & put into her old trime, she made many viages & performed her service very sufficiently, to yᵉ great profite of her owners. But more espetially, by the cuning & deceite of yᵉ mʳ. & his company, who were hired to stay a whole year in yᵉ cuntrie, and now fancying dislike & fearing wante of victeles, they ploted this strategem to free them selves; as afterwards was knowne, & by some of them confessed.[6] For they apprehended yᵗ the greater ship, being of force, & in whom most of yᵉ provissions were stowed, she would retayne enough for her selfe, what soever became of them or yᵉ passengers; & indeed shuch speeches had bene cast out by some of them; and yet, besids other incouragments, yᵉ cheefe of them that came from Leyden wente in this shipe to give yᵉ mʳ. contente. But so strong was self love & his fears, as he forgott all duty and former kindnesses, & delt thus falsly with them, though he pretended otherwise. Amongest those that returned was Mʳ. Cushman & his familie,

---

[1] A line over a consonant indicates that it should be doubled (i.e., "Plimmoth"). Such conventions were used in handwritten manuscripts to save space.

[2] crosses (misfortunes)

[3] Fall and winter are treacherous times to sail, especially on the North Atlantic, because of the bad weather.

[4] See Judges 7.

[5] that

[6] The area of sail available to catch the wind determines the amount of kinetic energy transferred from the wind to the hull; this force is normally greater than the ship's inertia and the resisting force of the water and pushes the ship forward. Increasing the ship's momentum also increases the force of the water against the hull, however, and a wooden hull can resist only so much water pressure before it begins to leak between the boards. According to Bradford, then, being afraid of the conditions in the New World, the captain and crew of the *Speedwell* sabotaged the ship by letting the sails out too far in order to get out of their contractual obligation not only to sail to Virginia but also to stay there for a year before returning to England.

whose hart & courage was gone from them before, as it seems, though his body was with them till now he departed; as may appear by a passionate letter he write[1] to a freind in London from Dartmouth, whilst yᵉ ship lay ther a mending; the which, besids yᵉ expressions of his owne fears, it shows much of yᵉ providence of God working for their good beyonde man's expectation, & other things concerning their condition in these streats. I will hear relate it. And though it discover some infirmities in him (as who under temtation is free), yet after this he continued to be a spetiall instrumente for their good, and to doe yᵉ offices of a loving freind & faithfull brother unto them, and pertaker of much comforte with them.

The letter is as followth.

To his loving friend Ed: S.[2] at Henige House in yᵉ Duks Place, these, &c. Dartmouth, Aug. 17.

Loving friend, my most kind remembrance to you & your wife, with loving E. M. &c. whom in this world I never looke to see againe. For besids yᵉ eminente dangers of this viage, which are no less then deadly, an infirmitie of body hath ceased[3] me, which will not in all lieᶜlyhoode leave me till death. What to call it I know not, but it is a bundle of lead, as it were, crushing my harte more & more these 14. days, as that allthough I doe yᵉ acctions of a liveing man, yet I am but as dead; but yᵉ will of God be done. Our pinass will not cease leaking, els I thinke we had been halfe way at Virginia, our viage hither hath been as full of crosses, as our selves have been of crokednes. We put in hear to trimē her, & I thinke, as others also, if we had stayed at sea but 3. or 4. howers more, shee would have sunke right downe. And though she was twise trimēd at Hamton, yet now shee is open and leakie as a seive; and ther was a borde, a man might have puld of with his fingers, 2 foote longe, wher yᵉ water came in as at a mole hole. We lay at Hamton 7. days, in fair weather, waiting for her, and now we lye hear waiting for her in as faire a wind as can blowe, and so have done these 4. days, and are like to lye 4. more, and by yᵗ time yᵉ wind will happily[4] turne as it did at Hampton. Our victualls will be halfe eaten up, I thinke, before we goe from the coaste of England, and if our viage last longe, we shall not have a months victialls when we come in yᵉ countrie. Neare 700ˡⁱ.[5] hath bene bestowed at Hampton, upon what I know not. Mr. Martin saith he neither can nor will give any accounte of it, and if he be called upon for accounts he crieth out of unthankfullnes for his paines & care, that we are susspitious of him, and flings away, & will end nothing. Also he so insultēh over our poore people, with shuch scorne & contempte, as if they were not

---

[1] writ (wrote)

[2] In Governor Bradford's *Collection of Letters*, this is Edward Southworth. (P.)

[3] seized

[4] haply (probably)

[5] pounds (£)

good enough to wipe his shoes. It would break your hart to see his dealing,[1] and yᵉ mourning of our people. They complaine to me, & alass! I can doe nothing for them; if I speake to him, he flies in my face, as mutinous, and saith no complaints shall be heard or received but by him selfe, and saith they are forwarde, & waspish, discontented people, & I doe ill to hear them. Ther are others yᵗ would lose all they have put in, or make satisfaction for what they have had, that they might departe: but he will not hear them, nor suffer them to goe ashore, least they should rune away. The sailors also are so offended at his ignorante bouldnes, in medling & controuling in things he knows not what belongs too, as yᵗ some threaten to misscheefe him, others say they will leave yᵉ shipe & goe their way. But at yᵉ best this cometh of it, yᵗ he maks him selfe a scorne & laughing stock unto them. As for Mʳ. Weston, excepte grace doe greatly swaye with him, he will hate us ten times more then ever he loved us, for not confirming yᵉ conditions. But now, since some pinches have taken them, they begine to reveile yᵉ trueth, & say Mʳ. Robinson was in yᵉ falte who charged them never to consente to those conditions, nor chuse me into office, but indeede apointed them to chose them they did chose.[2] But he & they will rue too late, they may now see, & all be ashamed when it is too late, that they were so ignorante, yea, & so inordinate in their courses. I am sure as they were resolved not to seale those conditions, I was not so resolute at Hampton to have left yᵉ whole bussines, excepte they would seale them, & better yᵉ vioage to have bene broken of then, then to have brought such miserie to our selves, dishonour to God, & detrimente to our loving freinds, as now it is like to doe. 4. or 5. of yᵉ cheefe of them which came from Leyden, came resolved never to goe on those conditions. And Mʳ. Martine, he said he never received no money on those conditions, he was not beholden to yᵉ marchants for a pine, they were bloudsuckers, & I know not what. Simple man, he indeed never made any conditions wᵗʰ the marchants, nor ever spake with them. But did all that money flie to Hampton, or was it his owne? Who will goe & lay out money so rashly & lavishly as he did, and never know how he comes by it, or on what conditions? 2ˡʸ. I tould him of yᵉ alteration longe agoe, & he was contente; but now he dominires, & said I had betrayed them into yᵉ hands of slaves; he is not beholden to them, he can set out 2. ships him selfe to a viage. When, good man? He hath but 50ˡⁱ. in, & if he should give up his accounts he would not have a penie left him, as I am persuaded,[3] &c. Freind, if ever we make a plantation, God works a mirakle; especially considering how scante we shall be of

---

[1] He was governour in yᵉ biger ship, & Mʳ. Cushman assistante. (B.)

[2] I thinke he was deceived in these things. (B.)

[3] This was found true afterward. (B.?)

victualls, and most of all ununited amongst our selves, & devoyd of good tutors & regimente. Violence will break all. Wher is yᵉ meek & humble spirite of Moyses? & of Nehemiah who reedified¹ yᵉ wals of Jerusalem, & yᵉ state of Israell? Is not yᵉ sound of Rehoboams braggs² daly hear amongst us? Have not yᵉ philosophers and all wise men observed yᵗ, even in setled comōne welths, violente governours bring either them selves, or people, or boath, to ruine; how much more in yᵉ raising of comōne wealths, when yᵉ morter is yet scarce tempered³ yᵗ should bind yᵉ wales.⁴ If I should write to you of all things which promiscuously forerune our ruine, I should over charge my weake head and greeve your tender hart; only this, I pray you prepare for evill tidings of us every day. But pray for us instantly, it may be yᵉ Lord will be yet entreated one way or other to make⁵ for us. I see not in reason how we shall escape even yᵉ gasping of hunger starved persons; but God can doe much, & his will be done. It is better for me to dye, then now for me to bear it, which I doe daly, & expecte it howerly;⁶ haveing received yᵉ sentance of death, both within me & without me. Poore William King & my selfe doe strive⁷ who shall be meate first for yᵉ fishes; but we looke for a glorious resurrection, knowing Christ Jesus after yᵉ flesh no more, but looking unto yᵉ joye yᵗ is before us, we will endure all these things and accounte them light in comparison of yᵗ joye we hope for. Remember me in all love to our freinds as if I named them, whose praiers I desire ernestly, & wish againe to see, but not till I can with more comforte looke them in yᵉ face. The Lord give us that true comforte which none can take from us. I had a desire to make a breefe relation of our estate to some freind. I doubte not but⁸ your wisdome will teach you seasonably to utter things as here after you shall be called to it. That which I have writen is treue, & many things more which I have forborne. I write it as upon my life, and last confession in England. What is of use to be spoken of presently, you may speake of it, and what is fitt

---

¹ re-edified (i.e., rebuilt)

² In 1 Kings 12, after Rehoboam succeeds Solomon as king of Israel, he receives an embassy from Jeroboam, who had been in charge of forced labor in northern Israel but had been exiled by Solomon for inciting rebellion. Jeroboam asks Rehoboam to reduce the burden on the people, and the elders advise Rehoboam to accede to the request; but the young men of the court urge Rehoboam to answer that he will be even harsher than Solomon had been. Rehoboam takes his buddies' advice, and as a result, Jeroboam successfully leads a civil war that ends with the division of the kingdom.

³ mixed

⁴ walls

⁵ provide

⁶ hourly

⁷ In the manuscript it is "strive dayly," but a pen has been drawn through the latter word. (Ed.)

⁸ I do not doubt that

to conceile, conceall. Pass by my weake maner, for my head is weake, & my body feeble, yᵉ Lord make me strong in him, & keepe both you & yours.

Your loving friend,

Robart Cushman.

Dartmouth, Aug. 17. 1620.

These being his conceptions & fears at Dartmouth, they must needs be much stronger now at Plimoth.

The 9. Chap.

Of their vioage, & how they passed yᵉ sea, and of their safe arrivall at Cape Codd.

Septʳ: 6. These troubls being blowne over, and now all being compacte togeather in one shipe, they put to sea againe with a prosperus winde, which continued diverce days togeather, which was some incouragmente unto them; yet according to yᵉ usuall maner many were afflicted with sea-sicknes. And I may not omite hear a spetiall worke of Gods providence. Ther was a proud & very profane yonge man, one of yᵉ sea-men, of a lustie,[1] able body, which made him the more hauty; he would allway be contemning yᵉ poore people in their sicknes, & cursing them dayly with greēous[2] execrations, and did not let to tell[3] them, that he hoped to help to cast halfe of them over board before they came to their jurneys end, and to make mery with what they had; and if he were by any gently reproved, he would curse and swear most bitterly. But it plased God before they came halfe seas over, to smite this yong man with a greeveous disease, of which he dyed in a desperate maner, and so was him selfe yᵉ first yᵗ was throwne overbord. Thus his curses light on his owne head; and it was an astonishmente to all his fellows, for they noted it to be yᵉ just hand of God upon him.

After they had injoyed faire winds and weather for a season, they were incountred many times with crosse winds, and mette with many feirce stormes, with which yᵉ shipe was shroudly[4] shaken, and her upper works made very leakie; and one of the maine beames in yᵉ midd ships was bowed & craked, which put them in some fear that yᵉ shipe could not be able to performe yᵉ vioage. So some of yᵉ cheefe of yᵉ company, perceiveing yᵉ mariners to feare yᵉ suffisiencie of yᵉ shipe, as appeared by their mutterings, they entred into serious consulltation with yᵉ mʳ. & other officers of yᵉ ship, to consider in time of yᵉ danger; and rather to returne then to cast them selves into a desperate & inevitable perill. And truly ther was great distraction & differance of opinion amongst yᵉ mariners them selves; faine would they doe what could be done for their wages sake, (being now halfe the seas over,) and on yᵉ

---

[1] In the sense of healthy and vigorous
[2] grievous
[3] never stopped telling
[4] severely

other hand they were loath to hazard their lives too desperatly. But in examening of all opinions, the m^r. & others affirmed they knew ye ship to be stronge & firme under water; and for the buckling of ye maine beame, ther was a great iron scrue ye passengers brought out of Holland, which would raise ye beame into his place;[1] ye which being done, the carpenter & m^r. affirmed that with a post put under it, set firme in ye lower deck, & otherways bounde, he would make it sufficiente. And as for ye decks & uper workes they would calke[2] them as well as they could, and though with ye workeing of ye ship they would not longe keepe stanch, yet ther would otherwise be no great danger, if they did not overpress her with sails. So they comīted them selves to ye will of God, & resolved to proseede. In sundrie of these stormes the winds were so feirce, & ye seas so high, as they could not beare a knote of saile, but were forced to hull, for diverce days togither.[3] And in one of them, as they thus lay at hull, in a mighty storme, a lustie yonge man (called John Howland) coming upon some occasion above ye grattings, was, with a seele[4] of the shipe throwne into [y^e] sea; but it pleased God y^t he caught hould of ye top-saile halliards, which hunge over board, & rane out at length; yet he held his hould (though he was sundrie fadomes under water) till he was hald up by ye same rope to ye brime of ye water, and then with a boat hooke & other means got into ye shipe againe, & his life saved; and though he was something ill with it, yet he lived many years after, and became a profitable member both in church & comōne wealthe. In all this viage ther died but one of ye passengers, which was William Butten, a youth, servant to Samuell Fuller, when they drew near ye coast. But to omite other things, (that I may be breefe,) after longe beating at sea they fell with that land which is called Cape Cod;[5] the which being made[6] & certainly knowne to be it, they were not a litle joyfull. After some deliberation had amongst them selves & with ye m^r. of ye ship, they tacked aboute and resolved to stande for ye southward (ye wind & weather being faire) to finde some place aboute Hudsons river for their habitation. But after they had sailed y^t course aboute halfe ye day, they fell amongst deangerous shoulds[7] and roring breakers, and they were so farr intangled ther with as they conceived them selves in great danger; & ye wind shrinking upon them withall, they resolved to bear up againe for the Cape, and thought them selves hapy to gett out of those dangers before night overtooke them, as by Gods providence they did. And ye next day they gott into ye Cape-harbor wher they ridd[8] in saftie. A word or too by ye way of this cape; it was thus

---

[1] It is unclear why the Pilgrims would have brought a massive iron jackscrew with them—but clearly they needed it now!

[2] caulk

[3] Hulling the ship meant raising the sails partially (short sail) or completely and might also include passing ropes under the ship's hull to add support.

[4] sail

[5] The storms had blown the *Mayflower* significantly off course, causing the Pilgrims to land much further north than the area of Virginia covered by their original charter.

[6] sighted

[7] dangerous shoals (shallows)

[8] rode (at anchor; i.e., the ship was anchored)

first named by Capten Gosnole & his company,[1] Anno: 1602, and after by Capten Smith was caled Cape James; but it retains yᵉ former name amongst seamen. Also yᵗ pointe which first shewed those dangerous shoulds unto them, they called Pointe Care, & Tuckers Terrour; but yᵉ French & Dutch to this day call it Malabarr, by reason of those perilous shoulds, and yᵉ losses they have suffered their.[2]

Being thus arived in a good harbor and brought safe to land, they fell upon their knees & blessed yᵉ God of heaven, who had brought them over yᵉ vast & furious ocean, and delivered them from all yᵉ periles & miseries therof, againe to set their feete on yᵉ firme and stable earth, their proper elemente. And no marvell if they were thus joyfull, seeing wise Seneca was so affected with sailing a few miles on yᵉ coast of his owne Italy; as he affirmed,[3] that he had rather remaine twentie years on his way by land, then pass by sea to any place in a short time; so tedious & dreadfull was yᵉ same unto him.

But hear I cannot but stay and make a pause, and stand half amased at this poore peoples presente condition; and so I thinke will the reader too, when he well considers yᵉ same. Being thus passed yᵉ vast ocean, and a sea of troubles before in their preparation (as may bc rcmembred by yᵗ which wente before), they had now no freinds to wellcome them, nor inns to entertaine or refresh their weatherbeaten bodys, no houses or much less townes to repaire too, to seeke for succoure. It is recorded in scripture[4] as a mercie to yᵉ apostle & his shipwraked company, yᵗ the barbarians shewed them no smale kindnes in refreshing them, but these savage barbarians, when they mette with them (as after will appeare) were readier to fill their sids full of arrows then otherwise. And for yᵉ season it was winter, and they that know yᵉ winters of yᵗ cuntrie[5] know them to be sharp & violent, & subjecte to cruell & feirce stormes, deangerous to travill to known places, much more to serch an unknown coast. Besids, what could they see but a hidious & desolate wildernes,[6] full of wild beasts & willd men? and what multituds ther might be of them they knew not. Nether could they, as it were, goe up to yᵉ tope of Pisgah,[7] to vew from this willdernes a more goodly cuntrie to feed their hops;[8] for which way soever they turnd their eys (save upward to yᵉ heavens) they could

---

[1] Because yᵉʸ tooke much of yᵗ fishe ther. (B.) (I.e., cod was the main fish Capt. Gosnole caught in these waters.)

[2] These shoals have apparently eroded to insignificance over the centuries; I can find no mention of them now.

[3] Epist: 53. (Ed.)

[4] Act. 28 (Ed.)

[5] Much worse in this period than now, in large part because the Little Ice Age was then in progress—not that present-day Massachusetts winters are pleasant.

[6] Great Britain had been settled for so long at this point that there were few true wilderness areas remaining. As will later become apparent, however, the absence of European-style settlements did not mean the land was unsettled or uncultivated.

[7] In Numbers 20, Moses lets his temper get the better of him and fails to follow God's instructions for creating the spring of Meriba properly. God thus forbids him from entering the Promised Land. However, in Deuteronomy 34, God does allow Moses to climb Mount Pisgah and look out over the Promised Land before his death.

[8] hopes

have litle solace or content in respecte of any outward objects.[1] For sumē being done, all things stand upon them with a wetherbeaten face; and yᵉ whole countrie, full of woods & thickets, represented a wild & savage heiw. If they looked behind them, ther was yᵉ mighty ocean which they had passed, and was now as a maine barr & goulfe to seperate them from all yᵉ civill parts of yᵉ world. If it be said they had a ship to sucour them, it is trew; but what heard they daly from yᵉ mʳ. & company? but yᵗ with speede they should looke out a place with their shallop,[2] wher they would be at some near distance; for yᵉ season was shuch as he would not stirr from thence till a safe harbor was discovered by them wher they would be, and he might goe without danger; and that victells consumed apace, but he must & would keepe sufficient for them selves & their returne. Yea, it was muttered by some, that if they gott not a place in time, they would turne them & their goods ashore & leave them. Let it also be considred what weake hopes of supply & succoure they left behinde them, yᵗ might bear up their minds in this sade condition and trialls they were under; and they could not but be very smale. It is true, indeed, yᵉ affections & love of their brethren at Leyden was cordiall & entire towards them, but they had litle power to help them, or them selves; and how yᵉ case stode betweene them & yᵉ marchants at their coming away, hath allready been declared. What could now sustaine them but the spirite of God & his grace? May not & ought not the children of these fathers rightly say: *Our faithers were Englishmen which came over this great ocean, and were ready to perish in this wilderness;[3] but they cried unto yᵉ Lord, and he heard their voyce, and looked on their adversitie, &c. Let them therfore praise yᵉ Lord, because he is good, & his mercies endure for ever.[4] Yea, let them which have been redeemed of yᵉ Lord, shew how he hath delivered them from yᵉ hand of yᵉ oppressour. When they wandered in yᵉ deserte willdernes out of yᵉ way, and found no citie to dwell in, both hungrie, & thirstie, their sowle was overwhelmed in them. Let them confess before yᵉ Lord his loving kindnes, and his wonderfull works before yᵉ sons of men.*

The 10. Chap.
Showing how they sought out a place of habitation, and what befell them theraboute.

Being thus arrived at Cap-Cod yᵉ 11. of November, and necessitie calling them to looke out a place for habitation, (as well as the maisters & mariners importunitie,) they having brought a large shalop with them out of England, stowed in quarters in yᵉ ship, they now gott her out & sett their carpenters to worke to trime her up; but being much brused & shatered in yᵉ shipe wᵗʰ foule weather, they saw she would be longe in mending. Wherupon a few of them tendered them selves to goe by land and discovere those nearest places, whilst yᵉ shallop

---

[1] Not only did most of the Pilgrims not have any experience as farmers, which would matter more in the spring when the weather was right for planting, but they also had no experience with foraging and probably only minimal experience with hunting.

[2] Small sailboat

[3] Deu: 26. 5, 7. (Ed.)

[4] 107 Psa: v. 1, 2, 4, 5, 8.

was in mending; and yᵉ rather because as they wente into yᵗ harbor ther seemed to be an opening some 2. or 3 leagues of, which yᵉ maister judged to be a river. It was conceived ther might be some danger in yᵉ attempte, yet seeing them resolute, they were permited to goe, being 16. of them well armed, under yᵉ conduct of Captain Standish, having shuch instructions given them as was thought meete. They sett forth yᵉ 15. of Noveᵇʳ: and when they had marched aboute the space of a mile by yᵉ sea side, they espied 5. or 6. persons with a dogg coming towards them, who were salvages; but they fled from them, & rane up into yᵉ woods, and yᵉ English followed them, partly to see if they could speake with them, and partly to discover if ther might not be more of them lying in ambush. But yᵉ Indeans seeing them selves thus followed, they againe forsooke the woods, & rane away on yᵉ sands as hard as they could, so as they could not come near them, but followed them by yᵉ tracte of their feet sundrie miles, and saw that they had come the same way. So, night coming on, they made their randevous[1] & set out their sentinels, and rested in quiete yᵗ *night*, and the next morning followed their tracte till they had headed a great creake, & so left the sands, & turned an other way into yᵉ woods. But they still followed them by geuss, hopeing to find their dwellings; but they soone lost both them & them selves, falling into shuch thickets as were ready to tear their cloaths & armore in peeces, but were most distresed for wante of drinke. But at length they found water & refreshed them selves, being yᵉ first New-England water they drunke of, and was now in thir great thirste as pleasante unto them as wine or bear[2] had been in for-times. Afterwards they directed their course to come to yᵉ other shore, for they knew it was a necke of land they were to crosse over, and so at length gott to yᵉ sea-side, and marched to this supposed river, & by yᵉ way found a pond of clear fresh water, and shortly after a good quantitie of clear ground wher yᵉ Indeans had formerly set corne, and some of their graves. And proceeding furder they saw new-stuble wher corne had been set yᵉ same year, also they found wher latly a house had been, wher some planks and a great ketle was remaining, and heaps of sand newly padled with their hands, which they, digging up, found in them diverce faire Indean baskets filled with corne, and some in eares, faire and good, of diverce collours, which seemed to them a very goodly sight, (haveing never seen any shuch before). This was near yᵉ place of that supposed river they came to seeck; unto which they wente and found it to open it selfe into 2. armes with a high cliffe of sand in yᵉ enterance, but more like to be crikes of salte water then any fresh, for ought they saw; and that ther was good harborige for their shalope; leaving it further to be discovered[3] by their shalop when she was ready. So their time limeted them being expired, they returned to yᵉ ship, least they should be in fear of their saftie; and tooke with them parte of yᵉ corne, and

---

[1] rendezvous

[2] Beer. Even had they not been so thirsty, the water probably would have tasted surprisingly sweet because clean water was hard to come by in England; most of the rivers were badly polluted because people had been using them as sewers for centuries.

[3] explored

buried up yᵉ rest, and so like yᵉ men from Eshcoll[1] carried with them of yᵉ fruits of yᵉ land, & showed their breethren; of which, & their returne, they were marvelusly glad, and their harts incouraged.

After this, yᵉ shalop being got ready, they set out againe for yᵉ better discovery of this place, & yᵉ mʳ. of yᵉ ship desired to goe him selfe, so ther went some 30. men, but found it to be no harbor for ships but only for boats; ther was allso found 2. of their houses covered with matts, & sundrie of their implements in them, but yᵉ people were rune away & could not be seen; also ther was found more of their corne, & of their beans of various collours. The corne & beans they brought away, purposing to give them full satisfaction when they should meete with any of them (as about some 6. months afterward they did, to their good contente). And here is to be noted a spetiall providence of God, and a great mercie to this poore people, that hear they gott seed to plant them corne yᵉ next year, or els they might have starved, for they had none, nor any liklyhood to get any till yᵉ season had beene past (as yᵉ sequell did manyfest). Neither is it lickly they had had this, if yᵉ first viage had not been made, for the ground was now all covered with snow, & hard frozen. But the Lord is never wanting unto his in their greatest needs; let his holy name have all yᵉ praise.

The month of November being spente in these affairs, & much foule weather falling in, the 6. *of Desemʳ*: they sente out their shallop againe with 10. of their principall men, & some sea men, upon further discovery, intending to circulate[2] that deepe bay of Cap-codd. The weather was very could, & it frose so hard as yᵉ sprea of yᵉ sea lighting on their coats, they were as if they had been glased; yet *that night* betimes they gott downe into yᵉ botome of yᵉ bay, and as they drue nere yᵉ shore they saw some 10. or 12. Indeans very busie aboute some thing. They landed aboute a league or 2. from them, and had much a doe to put a shore any wher, it lay so full of flats. Being landed, it grew late, and they made them selves a barricade with loggs & bowes as well as they could in yᵉ time, & set out their sentenill & betooke them to rest, and saw yᵉ smoake of yᵉ fire yᵉ savages made yᵗ night. When *morning* was come they devided their company, some to coaste along yᵉ shore in yᵉ boate, and the rest marched throw yᵉ woods to see yᵉ land, if any fit place might be for their dwelling. They came allso to yᵉ place wher they saw the Indans yᵉ night before, & found they had been cuting up a great fish like a grampus,[3] being some 2. inches thike of fate like a hogg, some peeces wher of they had left by yᵉ way; and yᵉ shallop found 2. more of these fishes dead on yᵉ sands, a thing usuall after storms in yᵗ place, by reason of yᵉ great flats of sand that lye of. So they ranged up and doune all yᵗ day, but found no people, nor any place they liked. When yᵉ sune grue low, they hasted out of yᵉ woods to meete with their shallop, to whom they made signes

---

[1] Valley where Hebrew spies cut down a giant cluster of grapes as a sample of Canaan's fruitfulness in their first attempt to cross the Jordan; the cluster was so large that it had to be carried on a pole between two men (see Numbers 13).

[2] circle around

[3] Small cetacean, possibly a dolphin that had been beached in a storm

to come to them into a *creeke* hardby, the which they did at highwater;[1] of which they were very glad, for they had not seen each other all y^t day, since ye morning. So they made them a barricado (as usually they did every night) with loggs, staks, & thike pine bowes, ye height of a man, leaving it open to leeward, partly to shelter them from ye could & wind (making their fire in ye midle, & lying round aboute it), and partly to defend them from any sudden assaults of ye savags, if they should surround them. So being very weary, they betooke them to rest. But aboute *midnight*, they heard a hideous & great crie, and their sentinell caled, "Arme, arme"; so they bestired them & stood to their armes, & shote of a cupple of moskets,[2] and then the noys seased. They concluded it was a companie of wolves, or such like willd beasts; for one of ye sea men tould them he had often heard shuch a noyse in New-found land. So they rested till about 5. of ye clock in the *morning*; for ye tide, & ther purpos to goe from thence, made them be stiring betimes. So after praier they prepared for breakfast, and it being day dawning, it was thought best to be carring things downe to ye boate. But some said it was not best to carrie ye armes downe, others said they would be the readier, for they had laped them up in their coats from ye dew. But some 3. or 4. would not cary theirs till they wente them selves, yet as it fell out, ye water being not high enough, they layed them downe on ye banke side, & came up to breakfast. But presently, all on ye sudain, they heard a great & strange crie, which they knew to be the same voyces they heard in ye night, though they varied their notes, & one of their company being abroad came runing in, & cried, "Men, Indeans, Indeans"; and w^thall, their arowes came flying amongst them. Their men rane with all speed to recover their armes, as by ye good providence of God they did. In ye mean time, of those that were ther ready, tow muskets were discharged at them, & 2. more stood ready in ye enterance of ther randevoue, but were comanded not to shoote till they could take full aime at them; & ye other 2. charged againe with all speed, for ther were only 4. had armes ther, & defended ye baricado which was first assalted. The crie of ye Indeans was dreadfull, espetially when they saw ther men rune out of ye randevoue towourds ye shallop, to recover their armes, the Indeans wheeling aboute upon them. But some runing out with coats of malle on, & cutlasses in their hands, they soone got their armes, & let flye amongs them, and quickly stopped their violence. Yet ther was a lustie man, and no less valiante, stood behind a tree within halfe a musket shot, and let his arrows flie at them. He was seen shoot 3. arrowes, which were all avoyded. He stood 3. shot of a musket, till one taking full aime at him, and made ye barke or splinters of ye tree fly about his ears, after which he gave an

---

[1] high tide

[2] Black-powder muskets had to be reloaded after every shot, which was much more time-consuming than it is with modern weapons. The attackers may have been trying to tempt the explorers to discharge all their weapons at once, with the intent of rushing them before they could reload; such tactics were practiced and perfected by the Comanches, and only the advent of the Colt revolver eliminated that weakness for settlers with firearms.

extraordinary shrike,[1] and away they wente all of them. They[2] left some to keep yᵉ shalop, and followed them aboute a quarter of a mille, and shouted once or twise, and shot of 2. or 3. peces, & so returned. This they did, that they might conceive that they were not affrade of them or any way discouraged. Thus it pleased God to vanquish their enimies, and give them deliverance; and by his spetiall providence so to dispose that not any one of them were either hurte, or hitt, though their arrows came close by them, & on every side them, and sundry of their coats, which hunge up in yᵉ barricado, were shot throw & throw.[3] Aterwards they gave God sollamne thanks & praise for their deliverance, & gathered up a bundle of their arrows, & sente them into England afterward by yᵉ mʳ. of yᵉ ship, and called that place yᵉ first encounter. From hence they departed, & costed all along, but discerned no place likly for harbor; & therfore hasted to a place that their pillote,[4] (one Mr. Coppin who had bine in yᵉ cuntrie before) did assure them was a good harbor, which he had been in, and they might fetch it before night; of which they were glad, for it begane to be foule weather. After some houres sailing, it begane to snow & raine, & about yᵉ midle of yᵉ afternoone, yᵉ wind increased, & yᵉ sea became very rough, and they broake their rudder, & it was as much as 2. men could doe to steere her with a cupple of oares. But their pillott bad them be of good cheere, for he saw yᵉ harbor; but yᵉ storme increasing, & night drawing on, they bore what saile they could to gett in, while they could see. But herwith they broake their mast in 3. peeces, & their saill fell over bord, in a very grown sea, so as they had like to have been cast away; yet by Gods mercie they recovered them selves, & having yᵉ floud with them, struck into yᵉ harbore. But when it came too, yᵉ pillott was deceived in yᵉ place, and said, yᵉ Lord be mercifull unto them, for his eys never saw yᵗ place before; & he & the mʳ. mate would have rune her ashore, in a cove full of breakers, before yᵉ winde. But a lusty seaman which steered, bad those which rowed, if they were men, about with her, or ells they were all cast away; the which they did with speed. So he bid them be of good cheere & row lustly, for ther was a faire sound before them, & he doubted not but they should find one place or other wher they might ride in saftie. And though it was *very darke*, and rained sore, yet in yᵉ end they gott under yᵉ lee[5] of a smalle iland, and remained ther all yᵗ night in saftie. But they knew not this to be an iland till morning, but were devided in their minds; some would keepe yᵉ boate for fear they might be amongst yᵉ Indians; others were so weake and could, they could not endure, but got a shore, & with much adoe got fire, (all things being so wett,) and yᵉ rest were glad to come to them; for after midnight yᵉ wind shifted to the north-west, & it frose hard. But though this had been a day & night of much trouble & danger unto them, yet God gave them a *morning* of comforte & refreshing (as usually he doth to his children), for yᵉ next day was a faire sunshinīg day, and they found them sellvs to be on an iland secure from yᵉ

---

[1] shriek

[2] i.e., the explorers

[3] through and through

[4] pilot

[5] The side sheltered from the wind

Indeans, wher they might drie their stufe, fixe their peeces, & rest them selves, and gave God thanks for his mercies, in their manifould deliverances. And this being the *last day of ye weeke*, they prepared ther to keepe y^e *Sabath*. On *Munday* they sounded ye harbor, and founde it fitt for shipping; and marched into ye land, & found diverse cornfeilds, & litle runing brooks, a place (as they supposed) fitt for situation; at least it was ye best they could find, and ye season, & their presente necessitie, made them glad to accepte of it. So they returned to their shipp againe with this news to ye rest of their people, which did much comforte their harts.

On ye 15. *of Desem^r*: they wayed[1] anchor to goe to ye place they had discovered, & came within 2. leagues of it, but were faine[2] to bear up againe; but ye 16. *day* ye winde came faire, and they arrived safe in this harbor. And after wards tooke better view of ye place, and resolved wher to pitch their dwelling; and ye 25. *day* begane to erecte ye first house for comõne use to receive them and their goods.

The 2. Booke.

The rest of this History (if God give me life, & opportunitie) I shall, for brevitis sake, handle by way of *annalls*, noteing only the heads of principall things, and passages as they fell in order of time, and may seeme to be profitable to know, or to make use of. And this may be as ye 2. Booke.

The remainder of An^o:[3] 1620.

I shall a litle returne backe and begine with a combination[4] made by them before they came ashore, being ye first foundation of their govermente in this place; occasioned partly by ye discontented & mutinous speeches that some of the strangers amongst them had let fall from them in ye ship—That when they came a shore they would use their owne libertie; for none had power to comãnd them, the patente they had being for Virginia, and not for New-england, which belonged to an other Goverment, with which ye Virginia Company had nothing to doe. And partly that shuch an acte by them done (this their condition considered) might be as firme as any patent, and in some respects more sure.

The forme was as followeth.

In ye name of God, Amen. We whose names are underwriten, the loyall subjects of our dread soveraigne Lord, King James, by ye grace of God, of Great Britaine, Franc, & Ireland king, defender of ye faith,& c., haveing undertaken, for ye glorie of God, and advancemente of ye Christian faith, and honour of our king

---

[1] weighed (to *weigh anchor* means to raise the anchor and set sail, hence "Anchors Aweigh")

[2] In this context: compelled

[3] Anno (year)

[4] This document is now known as the Mayflower Compact, one of the forerunners of the US Constitution.

& countrie, a voyage to plant yᵉ first colonie in yᵉ Northerne parts of Virginia, doe by these presents solemnly & mutualy in yᵉ presence of God, and one of another, covenant & combine our selves togeather into a civill body politick, for our better ordering & preservation & furtherance of yᵉ ends aforesaid; and by vertue hearof to enacte, constitute, and frame such just & equall lawes, ordinances, acts, constitutions, & offices, from time to time, as shall be thought most meete & convenient for yᵉ generall good of yᵉ Colonie, unto which we promise all due submission and obedience. In witnes wherof we have hereunder subscribed our names at Cap-Codd yᵉ 11. of November, in yᵉ year of yᵉ raigne of our soveraigne lord, King James, of England, France, & Ireland yᵉ eighteenth, and of Scotland yᵉ fiftie fourth. Anᵒ: Dom. 1620.

After this they chose, or rather confirmed, Mʳ. John Carver (a man godly & well approved amongst them) their Governour for that year. And after they had provided a place for their goods, or comone store, (which were long in unlading for want of boats, foulnes of winter weather, and sicknes of diverce,) and begune some small cottages for their habitation, as time would admitte, they mette and consulted of lawes & orders, both for their civill & military Govermente, as yᵉ necessitie of their condition did require, still adding therunto as urgent occasion in severall times, and as cases did require.

In these hard & difficulte beginings they found some discontents & murmurings arise amongst some, and mutinous speeches & carriags in other; but they were soone quelled & overcome by yᵉ wisdome, patience, and just & equall carrage of things by yᵉ Govʳ and better part, wᶜʰ clave faithfully togeather in yᵉ maine. But that which was most sadd & lamentable was, that in 2. or 3. moneths time halfe of their company dyed, espetialy in Jan: & February, being yᵉ depth of winter, and wanting houses & other comforts; being infected with yᵉ scurvie[1] & other diseases, which this long vioage & their inacomodate condition had brought upon them; so as ther dyed some times 2. or 3. of a day, in yᵉ foresaid time; that of 100. & odd persons, scarce 50. remained. And of these in yᵉ time of most distres, ther was but 6. or 7. sound persons, who, to their great comendations be it spoken, spared no pains, night nor day, but with abundance of toyle and hazard of their owne health, fetched them woode, made them fires, drest them meat, made their beads,[2] washed their lothsome cloaths, cloathed & uncloathed them; in a word, did all yᵉ homly & necessarie offices for them wᶜʰ dainty & quesie stomacks cannot endure to hear named; and all this willingly & cherfully, without any grudging in yᵉ least, shewing herein their true love unto their freinds & bretheren. A rare example & worthy to be remembred. Tow of these 7. were Mʳ. William Brewster, ther reverend Elder, & Myles Standish, ther Captein & military comander, unto

---

[1] Scurvy, or Vitamin C deficiency, was a particular problem on long sea voyages because of the lack of fresh fruit and green vegetables. Because its symptoms include soft gums and bleeding sores, it can be fatal if left untreated. The sickly appearance and fatigue of sailors afflicted with scurvy led to the name of the disease being used, especially by sea captains, as an adjective of contempt ("you scurvy dogs," etc.).

[2] beds

whom my selfe, & many others, were much beholden in our low & sicke condition. And yet the Lord so upheld these persons, as in this generall calamity they were not at all infected either with sicknes, or lamnes. And what I have said of these, I may say of many others who dyed in this generall vissitation, & others yet living, that whilst they had health, yea, or any strength continuing, they were not wanting to any that had need of them. And I doute not but their recompence is with ye Lord.

But I may not hear pass by an other remarkable passage not to be forgotten. As this calamitie fell among ye passengers that were to be left here to plant, and were hasted a shore and made to drinke water, that ye sea-men might have ye more bear, and one[1] in his sicknes desiring but a small cann of beere,[2] it was answered, that if he were their owne father he should have none; the disease begane to fall amongst them also, so as allmost halfe of their company dyed before they went away, and many of their officers and lustyest men, as ye boatson,[3] gunner, 3. quarter-maisters, the cooke, & others. At wch ye m^r. was something strucken[4] and sent to ye sick a shore and tould ye Govr he should send for beer for them that had need of it, though he drunke water homward bound. But now amongst his company ther was farr another kind of carriage in this miserie then amongst ye passengers; for they that before had been boone companions in drinking & joyllity in ye time of their health & wellfare, begane now to deserte one another in this calamitie, saing they would not hasard ther lives for them, they should be infected by coming to help them in their cabins, and so, after they came to dye by it, would doe litle or nothing for them, but if they dyed let them dye. But shuch of ye passengers as were yet abord shewed them what mercy they could, wch made some of their harts relente, as ye boatson (& some others), who was a prowd yonge man, and would often curse & scofe at ye passengers; but when he grew weak, they had compassion on him and helped him; then he confessed he did not deserve it at their hands, he had abused them in word & deed. O! saith he, you, I now see, shew your love like Christians indeed one to another, but we let one another lye & dye like doggs. Another lay cursing his wife, saing if it had not ben for her he had never come this unlucky viage, and anone cursing his felows, saing he had done this & that, for some of them, he had spente so much, & so much, amongst them, and they were now weary of him, and did not help him, having need. Another gave his companion all he had, if he died, to help him in his weaknes; he went and got a litle spise & made him a mess of meat once or twise, and because he dyed not so soone as he expected, he went amongst his fellows, & swore ye rogue would cousen[5] him, he would see him choaked before he made him any more meate; and yet ye pore fellow dyed before morning.

---

[1] Which was this author him selfe. (B.)

[2] Because alcohol kills bacteria, weak (or small) beer was often safer to drink in Europe than water was. Bradford gives no hint of what his ailment was, but he may have wanted the beer for the carbonation or for the comfort.

[3] bosun or boatswain

[4] stricken

[5] cozen (cheat)

All this while yᵉ Indians came skulking about them, and would sometimes show them selves aloofe of, but when any aproached near them, they would rune away. And once they stoale away their tools wher they had been at worke, & were gone to diner. But about yᵉ 16. *of March* a certaine Indian came bouldly amongst them, and spoke to them in broken English, which they could well understand, but marvelled at it. At length they understood by discourse with him, that he was not of these parts, but belonged to yᵉ eastrene parts, wher some English-ships came to fhish, with whom he was aquainted, & could name sundrie of them by their names, amongst whom he had gott his language. He became proftable to them in aquainting them with many things concerning yᵉ state of yᵉ cuntry in yᵉ east-parts wher he lived, which was afterwards profitable unto them; as also of yᵉ people hear, of their names, number, & strength; of their situation & distance from this place, and who was cheefe amongst them. His name was *Samaset*; he tould them also of another Indian whos name was *Squanto*, a native of this place, who had been in England & could speake better English then him selfe. Being, after some time of entertainmente & gifts, dismist, a while after he came againe, & 5. more with him, & they brought againe all yᵉ tooles that were stolen away before, and made way for yᵉ coming of their great Sachem,[1] called *Massasoyt*; who, about *4. or 5. days after*, came with the cheefe of his freinds & other attendance, with the aforesaid *Squanto*. With whom, after frendly entertainment, & some gifts given him, they made a peace with him[2] (which hath now continued this 24. years) in these terms.

1. That neither he nor any of his, should injurie or doe hurte to any of their peopl.
2. That if any of his did any hurte to any of theirs, he should send yᵉ offender, that they might punish him.
3. That if any thing were taken away from any of theirs, he should cause it to be restored; and they should doe yᵉ like to his.
4. If any did unjustly warr against him, they would aide him; if any did warr against them, he should aide them.
5. He should send to his neighbours confederats, to certifie them of this, that they might not wrong them, but might be likewise comprised in yᵉ conditions of peace.
6. That when ther men came to them, they should leave their bows & arrows behind them.

After these things he returned to his place caled *Sowams*, some 40. mile from this place, but *Squanto* continued with them, and was their interpreter, and was a spetiall instrument sent of God for their good beyond their expectation. He directed them how to set their corne, wher to take fish, and to procure other comodities, and was also their pilott to bring them to unknowne places for their profitt, and never left them till he dyed. He was a *native of this place*, & scarce any left alive besids him selfe. He was caried away with diverce others by one *Hunt*, a mʳ. of a ship, who thought to sell them for slaves in Spaine; but he got away for

[1] chief (usually chief of multiple bands or head of an alliance)
[2] i.e., with Massasoit

England, and was entertained by a marchante in London, & imployed to New-foundland & other parts, & lastly brought hither into these parts by one M^r. *Dermer*, a gentle-man imployed by Sr. Ferdinando Gorges & others, for discovery, & other designes in these parts. Of whom I shall say some thing, because it is mentioned in a booke set forth An^o: 1622. by the Presidente & Counsell for New-England, that he made ye peace betweene ye salvages of these parts & ye English; of which this plantation, as it is intimated, had ye benefite. But what a peace it was, may apeare by what befell him & his men.

This M^r. Dermer was hear the same year that these people came, as apears by a relation written by him, & given me by a friend, bearing date June 30. An^o: 1620. And they came in Novemb^r: following, so ther was but 4. months differance. In which relation to his honored freind, he hath these passages of this very place.

I will first begine (saith he) wth that place from whence *Squanto*, or *Tisquantem*, was taken away; wch in Cap: *Smiths mape* is called *Plimoth*: and I would that Plimoth had ye like comodities. I would that the first plantation might hear be seated, if ther come to the number of 50. persons, or upward. Otherwise at Charlton, because ther ye savages are lese to be feared. The *Pocanawkits*, which live to y^e *west* of *Plimoth*, bear an inveterate malice to ye English, and are of more streingth then all ye savags from thence to Penobscote. Their desire of revenge was occasioned by an English man, who having many of them on bord, made a great slaughter with their murderers & smale shot, when as (they say) they offered no injurie on their parts. Whether they were English or no, it may be douted; yet they beleeve they were, for ye Frenche have so possest them; for which cause *Squanto* canot deney but they would have kiled me when I was at *Namasket*, had he not entreated hard for me. The soyle of ye borders of this great bay, may be compared to most of ye plantations which I have seene in Virginia. The land is of diverce sorts; for *Patuxite* is a hardy but strong soyle, *Nawsel & Saughtughtett* are for ye most part a blakish & deep mould, much like that wher groweth ye best Tobaco in Virginia. In ye botume of y^t great bay is store of Codd & basse, or mulett, &c.

But above all he comends *Pacanawkite* for ye richest soyle, and much open ground fitt for English graine, &c.

Massachussets is about 9. leagues from *Plimoth*, & situate in ye mids betweene both, is full of ilands & peninsules very fertill for ye most parte.

With sundrie shuch relations which I forbear to transcribe, being now better knowne then they were to him.

He was taken prisoner by ye Indeans at *Manamoiak* (a place not farr from hence, now well knowne). He gave them what they demanded for his liberty, but when they had gott what they desired, they kept him still & indevored to kill his men; but he was freed by seasing on some of them, and kept them bound till they gave him a cannows load of corne. Of which, see Purch: lib. 9. fol. 1778. But this was An^o: 1619.

After yᵉ writing of yᵉ former relation he came to yᵉ Ile of *Capawack* (which lyes south of this place in yᵉ way to Virginia), and yᵉ foresaid *Squanto* wᵗʰ him, wher he going a shore amongst yᵉ Indans to trad, as he used to doe, was betrayed & assaulted by them, & *all his men slaine, but one that kept the boat*; but him selfe gott abord very sore wounded, & they had[1] cut of his head upon yᵉ cudy of his boat, had not yᵉ man reskued him with a sword. And so they got away, & made shift to gett into Virginia, wher he dyed; whether of his wounds or yᵉ diseases of yᵉ cuntrie, or both togeather, is uncertaine. By all which it may appeare how farr these people were from peace, and with what danger this plantation was begune, save as yᵉ powerfull hand of the Lord did protect them. These things were partly the reason why they kept aloofe & were so long before they came to the English. An other reason (as after them selvs made know͞) was how aboute 3. *years before*, a French-ship was cast away at *Cap-Codd*, but yᵉ men gott ashore, & saved their lives, and much of their victails, & other goods; but after yᵉ Indeans heard of it, they geathered togeather from these parts, and never left watching & dogging them till they got advantage, and *kild them all but 3. or 4.* which they kept, & sent from one Sachem to another, to make sporte with, and used them worse then slaves; (of which yᵉ foresaid Mʳ. Dermer redeemed 2. of them;) and they conceived this ship was now come to revenge it.

Also, (as after was made knowne,) before they came to yᵉ English to make freindship, they gott all the *Powachs* of yᵉ cuntrie, for 3. days togeather, in a horid and divellish maner to curse & execrate them with their cunjurations, which asembly & service they held in a darke & dismale swampe.

But to returne. The spring now approaching, it pleased God the mortalitie begane to cease amongst them, and yᵉ sick and lame recovered apace, which put as it were new life into them; though they had borne their sadd affliction with much patience & contentednes, as I thinke any people could doe. But it was yᵉ Lord which upheld them, and had beforehand prepared them; many having long borne yᵉ yoake, yea from their youth. Many other smaler maters I omite, sundrie of them having been allready published in a Jurnall made by one of the company; and some other passages of jurneys and relations allredy published, to which I referr those that are willing to know them more perticulerly. And being now come to yᵉ 25. of March I shall begine yᵉ year 1621.[2]

⋞⋟

---

[1] would have

[2] On the Julian calendar, the new year began on March 25, the Feast of the Annunciation, rather than on January 1.

Mary Rowlandson
from The Soveraignty and Goodness of God[1]

On the 10th of February, 1676, came the Indians with great numbers[2] upon Lancaster. Their first coming was about sun-rising. Hearing the noise of some guns, we looked out; several houses were burning, and the smoke ascending to heaven.

There were five persons taken in one house. The father and mother, and a sucking child, they knocked on the head; the other two they took and carried away alive. There were two others, who, being out of their garrison upon occasion, were set upon; one was knocked on the head, the other escaped. Another there was, who, running along, was shot and wounded, and fell down; he begged of them his life, promising them money, as they told me, but they would not hearken to him, but knocked him on the head, stripped him naked, and split open his bowels. Another, seeing many of the Indians about his barn, ventured and went out, but was quickly shot down. There were three others belonging to the same garrison who were killed. The Indians getting up on the roof of the barn, had advantage to shoot down upon them over their fortification. Thus these murderous wretches went on burning and destroying all before them.

At length they came and beset our house, and quickly it was the dolefulest day that ever mine eyes saw. The house stood upon the edge of a hill; some of the Indians got behind the hill, others into the barn, and others behind anything that would shelter them; from all which places they shot against the house, so that the bullets seemed to fly like hail, and quickly they wounded one man among us, then another, and then a third.

About two hours, according to my observation in that amazing time, they had been about the house before they prevailed to fire it, which they did with flax and hemp which they brought out of the barn, and there being no defence about the house, only two flankers at two opposite corners, and one of them not finished; they fired it once, and one ventured out and quenched it, but they quickly fired it again, and that took.

Now is the dreadful hour come that I have often heard of in time of the war, as it was the case of others, but now mine eyes see it. Some in our house were fighting for their lives, others wallowing in blood, the house on fire over our heads, and the bloody heathen ready to knock us on the head if we stirred out. Now might we hear mothers and children crying out for themselves and one another, "Lord, what shall we do?" Then I took my children, and one of my sisters (Mrs. Drew), hers to go forth and leave the house, but as soon as we came to the door and appeared, the Indians shot so thick that the bullets rattled against the house

---

[1] Unless otherwise noted, notes on this text come from *Captives among the Indians*, edited by Horace Kephart and published in 1915.

[2] Fifteen hundred Wamponoags, led by King Philip, and accompanied by the Narragansetts, his allies, and by the Nipmucks and Nashaways.

as if one had taken a handful of stones and threw them, so that we were forced to give back. We had six stout dogs belonging to our garrison, but none of them would stir, though at another time if an Indian had come to the door, they were ready to fly upon him and tear him down. The Lord hereby would make us the more to acknowledge his hand, and to see that our help is always in him. But out we must go, the fire increasing, and coming along behind us roaring, and the Indians gaping before us with their guns, spears and hatchets, to devour us.

No sooner were we out of the house, but my brother-in-law[1] (being before wounded in defending the house, in or near the throat) fell down dead, whereat the Indians scornfully shouted and hallooed, and were presently upon him, stripping off his clothes. The bullets flying thick, one went through my side, and the same, as would seem, through the bowels and hand of my poor child in my arms. One of my elder sister's children, named William, had then his leg broke, which the Indians perceiving, they knocked him on the head. Thus were we butchered by those merciless heathens, standing amazed, with the blood running down to our heels.

My eldest sister being yet in the house, and seeing those woful sights, the infidels hauling mothers one way and children another, and some wallowing in their blood; and her eldest son telling her that her son William was dead, and myself was wounded, she said, "Lord, let me die with them:" which was no sooner said but she was struck with a bullet, and fell down dead over the threshold. The Indians laid hold of us, pulling me one way and the children another, and said, "Come, go along with us." I told them they would kill me; they answered, if I were willing to go along with them they would not hurt me. [. . .]

There were twelve killed, some shot, some stabbed with their spears, some knocked down with their hatchets. When we are in prosperity, oh, the little that we think of such dreadful sights, to see our dear friends and relations lie bleeding out their heart's-blood upon the ground. There was one who was chopped in the head with a hatchet, and stripped naked, and yet was crawling up and down.

I had often before this said, that if the Indians should come, I should choose rather to be killed by them than taken alive, but when it came to the trial my mind changed; their glittering weapons so daunted my spirit that I chose rather to go along with those (as I may say) ravenous bears, than that moment to end my days. And that I may the better declare what happened to me during that grievous captivity, I shall particularly speak of the several removes we had up and down the wilderness.

The First Remove.—Now away we must go with those barbarous creatures, with our bodies wounded and bleeding, and our hearts no less than our bodies. About a mile we went that night, up on a hill within sight of the town where we intended to lodge. There was hard by a vacant house, deserted by the English before, for fear of the Indians. I asked them whether I might not lodge in the house that night; to which they answered, "What, will you

---

[1] Thomas Rowlandson, brother to the clergyman.

love Englishmen still?" This was the dolefulest night that ever my eyes saw. Oh, the roaring and singing and dancing and yelling of those black creatures in the night, which made the place a lively resemblance of hell! And miserable was the waste that was there made of horses, cattle, sheep, swine, calves, lambs, roasting pigs, and fowls (which they had plundered in the town), some roasting, some lying and burning, and some boiling, to feed our merciless enemies; who were joyful enough, though we were disconsolate.

To add to the dolefulness of the former day, and the dismalness of the present night, my thoughts ran upon my losses and sad, bereaved condition. All was gone, my husband gone (at least separated from me, he being in the Bay;[1] and, to add to my grief, the Indians told me they would kill him as he came homeward); my children gone, my relations and friends gone,[2] our house and home, and all our comforts within door and without—all was gone except my life, and I knew not but the next moment that might go too.[3]

There remained nothing to me but one poor, wounded babe; and it seemed at present worse than death, that it was in such a pitiful condition, bespeaking compassion, and I had no refreshing for it, nor suitable things to revive it. Little do many think what is the savageness and brutishness of this barbarous enemy, those even that seem to profess more than others among them, when the English have fallen into their hands.

The Second Remove.—But now (the next morning) I must turn my back upon the town, and travel with them into the vast and desolate wilderness, I know not whither. It is not my tongue or pen can express the sorrows of my heart, and bitterness of my spirit, that I had at this departure; but God was with me in a wonderful manner, carrying me along and bearing up my spirit, that it did not quite fail. One of the Indians carried my poor wounded babe upon a horse. It went moaning all along, "I shall die, I shall die!" I went on foot after it with sorrow that cannot be expressed. At length I took it off the horse, and carried it in my arms, till my strength failed and I fell down with it. Then they set me upon a horse with my wounded child in my lap, and there being no furniture on the horse's back, as we were going down a steep hill we both fell over the horse's head, at which they, like inhuman creatures, laughed, and rejoiced to see it, though I thought we should there have ended our days, overcome with so many difficulties. [. . .]

After this it quickly began to snow, and when night came on they stopped. And now down I must sit in the snow, by a little fire, and a few boughs behind me, with my sick child in my lap, and calling much for water, being now, through the wound, fallen into a violent fever; my own wound also growing so stiff that I could scarce sit down or rise up.

---

[1] Boston

[2] Seventeen of her family were put to death or captured.

[3] This sense of despair was often deliberately cultivated by Indian captors, especially when they intended to keep their captives as slaves or adopt them into the tribe; separating a captive from any relatives who might have been captured with them and lying about the status of anyone not in the immediate raiding party was a tactic the captors used to prevent escapes by convincing the captive that he or she had nothing to return to. (EGW)

The Third Remove.—The morning being come, they prepared to go on their way. One of the Indians got upon a horse, and they sat me up behind him, with my poor sick babe in my lap. A very wearisome and tedious day I had of it; what with my own wound, and my child being so exceeding sick, and in a lamentable condition with her wound, it may easily be judged what a poor, feeble condition we were in, there being not the least crumb of refreshing that came within either of our mouths from Wednesday night to Saturday night, except only a little cold water. This day in the afternoon, about an hour by sun, we came to the place where they intended, viz., an Indian town called Wenimesset (New Braintree), northward of Quabaug (Brookfield).

This day there came to me one Robert Pepper, a man belonging to Roxbury, who was taken at Captain Beers's fight, and had been now a considerable time with the Indians, and up with them almost as far as Albany, to see King Philip, as he told me, and was now very lately come into these parts. Hearing, I say, that I was in this Indian town, he obtained leave to come and see me. He told me he himself was wounded in the leg at Captain Beers's fight, and was not able some time to go, but as they carried him, and that he took oak leaves and laid to his wound, and by the blessing of God he was able to travel again. Then took I oak leaves and laid to my side, and with the blessing of God it cured me also.

I sat much alone with my poor wounded child in my lap, which moaned night and day, having nothing to revive the body or cheer the spirits of her; but instead of that, one Indian would come and tell me one hour, "Your master will knock your child on the head," and then a second, and then a third, "Your master will quickly knock your child on the head."

This was the comfort I had from them; miserable comforters were they all. Thus nine days I sat upon my knees, with my babe in my lap, till my flesh was raw again. My child being even ready to depart this sorrowful world, they bid me carry it out to another wigwam, I suppose because they would not be troubled with such spectacles; whither I went with a very heavy heart, and down I sat with the picture of death in my lap. About two hours in the night, my sweet babe, like a lamb, departed this life, on Feb. 18, 1676, it being about six years and five months old.

In the morning when they understood that my child was dead, they sent me home to my master's wigwam. By my master in this writing must be understood Quannopin, who was a sagamore,[1] and married King Philip's wife's sister; not that he first took me, but I was sold to him by a Narragansett Indian, who took me when I first came out of the garrison.

I went to take up my dead child in my arms to carry it with me, but they bid me let it alone. There was no resisting, but go I must, and leave it. When I had been a while at my master's wigwam, I took the first opportunity I could get to look after my dead child. When I came I asked them what they had done with it. They told me it was on the hill. Then they went and showed me where it was, where I saw the ground was newly digged, and where

---

[1] A chief subordinate to a sachem—in this case, to the Wampanoag sachem Metacom, known to the English as King Philip. (EGW)

they told me they had buried it. There I left that child in the wilderness, and must commit it and myself also in this wilderness condition to Him who is above all.

God having taken away this dear child, I went to see my daughter Mary, who was at the same Indian town, at a wigwam not very far off, though we had little liberty or opportunity to see one another. She was about ten years old, and taken from the door at first by a praying Indian,[1] and afterwards sold for a gun. When I came in sight she would fall a-weeping, at which they were provoked, and would not let me come near her, but bid me begone, which was a heart-cutting word to me. I could not sit still in this condition, but kept walking from one place to another; and as I was going along, my heart was even overwhelmed with the thoughts of my condition, and that I should have children, and a nation that I knew not ruled over them. Whereupon I earnestly entreated the Lord that he would consider my low estate, and show me a token for good, and if it were his blessed will, some sign and hope of some relief.

And, indeed, quickly the Lord answered in some measure my poor prayer; for as I was going up and down mourning and lamenting my condition, my son (Joseph) came to me and asked me how I did. I had not seen him before since the destruction of the town; and I knew not where he was, till I was informed by himself that he was among a smaller parcel of Indians, whose place was about six miles off. With tears in his eyes he asked me whether his sister Sarah was dead, and told me he had seen his sister Mary, and prayed me that I would not be troubled in reference to himself. The occasion of his coming to see me at this time was this: there was, as I said, about six miles from us, a small plantation of Indians, where it seems he had been during his captivity; and at this time there were some forces of the Indians gathered out of our company, and some also from them, among whom was my son's master, to go to assault and burn Medfield. In this time of his master's absence his dame brought him to see me.

Now the Indians began to talk of removing from this place, some one way and some another. There were now, besides myself, nine English captives in this place, all of them children except one woman. I got an opportunity to go and take my leave of them, they being to go one way and I another. I asked them whether they were earnest with God for deliverance. They told me they did as they were able, and it was some comfort to me that the Lord stirred up children to look to Him. The woman, viz., good-wife[2] Joslin, told me she should never see me again, and that she could not find it in her heart to run away by any means, for we were near thirty miles from any English town, and she with a child two years old; and bad rivers there were to go over, and we were feeble with our poor and coarse entertainment. [. . .]

The Fourth Remove.—And now must I part with the little company I had. Here I parted with my daughter Mary, whom I never saw again till I saw her in Dorchester,

---

[1] Convert to Christianity.

[2] Mrs. (EGW)

returned from captivity; and from four little cousins and neighbors, some of which I never saw afterwards; the Lord only knows the end of them. We travelled about a half a day or a little more, and came to a desolate place in the wilderness, where there were no wigwams or inhabitants before. We came about the middle of the afternoon to this place, cold, wet, and snowy, and hungry and weary, and no refreshing for man, but the cold ground to sit on, and our poor Indian cheer.

The Fifth Remove.—The occasion, as I thought, of their removing at this time was the English army's being near and following them; for they went as if they had gone for their lives for some considerable way. Then they made a stop, and chose out some of their stoutest men, and sent them back to hold the English army in play while the rest escaped; and then, like Jehu,[1] they marched on furiously with their old and young. Some carried their old, decrepit mothers; some carried one, and some another. Four of them carried a great Indian upon a bier; but, going through a thick wood with him, they were hindered, and could make no haste; whereupon they took him upon their backs, and carried him, one at a time, till we came to Baquaug River.

Upon Friday, a little after noon, we came to this river. When all the company was come up and were gathered together I thought to count the number of them, but they were so many, and being somewhat in motion, it was beyond my skill. In this travel, because of my wound, I was somewhat favored in my load. I carried only my knitting-work and two quarts of parched meal. Being very faint, I asked my mistress to give me one spoonful of the meal, but she would not give me a taste. They quickly fell to cutting dry trees to make rafts to carry them over the river, and soon my turn came to go over. By the advantage of some brush which they had laid upon the raft to sit on, I did not wet my foot, while many of themselves, at the other end, were mid-leg deep, which cannot but be acknowledged as a favor of God to my weakened body, it being a very cold time. I was not before acquainted with such kind of doings or dangers. A certain number of us got over the river that night, but it was the night after the Sabbath before all the company was got over. On the Saturday they boiled an old horse's leg which they had got, and so we drank of the broth as soon as they thought it was ready, and when it was almost all gone they filled it up again.

The first week of my being among them I hardly eat anything; the second week I found my stomach grow very faint for want of something, and yet it was very hard to get down their filthy trash; but the third week, though I could think how formerly my stomach would turn against this or that, and I could starve and die before I could eat such things, yet they were pleasant and savory to my taste.

I was at this time knitting a pair of cotton stockings for my mistress, and I had not yet wrought upon the Sabbath day. When the Sabbath came they bid me go to work. I told them it was Sabbath day, and desired them to let me rest, and told them I would do as much more work to-morrow; to which they answered me they would break my face.

---

[1] See 2 Kings 9. (EGW)

And here I cannot but take notice of the strange providence of God in preserving the heathen. They were many hundreds, old and young, some sick, and some lame; many had papooses at their backs; the greatest number at this time with us were squaws, and yet they travelled with all they had, bag and baggage, and they got over this river aforesaid; and on Monday they set their wigwams on fire, and away they went. On that very day came the English army after them to this river, and saw the smoke of their wigwams, and yet this river put a stop to them. God did not give them courage or activity to go over after us. We were not ready for so great a mercy as victory and deliverance; if we had been, God would have found out a way for the English to have passed this river as well as for the Indians, with their squaws and children and all their luggage.

The Sixth Remove.—On Monday, as I said, they set their wigwams on fire and went away. It was a cold morning, and before us there was a great brook with ice on it. Some waded through it up to the knees and higher, but others went till they came to a beaver-dam, and I among them, where, through the good providence of God, I did not wet my foot. I went along that day mourning and lamenting, leaving farther my own country, and travelling farther into the vast and howling wilderness, and I understood something of Lot's wife's temptation when she looked back. We came that day to a great swamp, by the side of which we took up our lodging that night. When we came to the brow of the hill that looked towards the swamp I thought we had been come to a great Indian town, though there were none but our own company; the Indians were as thick as the trees; it seemed as if there had been a thousand hatchets going at once.

The Seventh Remove.—After a restless and hungry night there we had a wearisome time of it the next day. The swamp by which we lay was, as it were, a deep dungeon, and an exceeding high and steep hill before it. Before I got to the top of the hill I thought my heart and legs and all would have broken and failed me. What with faintness and soreness of body, it was a grievous day of travel to me. As we went along, I saw a place where English cattle had been. That was a comfort to me, such as it was. Quickly after that we came to an English path, which so took me that I thought I could there have freely lain down and died.

That day, a little after noon, we came to Squaheag,[1] where the Indians quickly spread themselves over the deserted English fields, gleaning what they could find. Some picked up ears of wheat that were crickled down, some found ears of Indian corn, some found ground-nuts,[2] and others sheaves of wheat that were frozen together in the shock, and went to threshing of them out. Myself got two ears of Indian corn, and, whilst I did but turn my back, one of them was stole from me, which much troubled me.

There came an Indian to them at that time with a basket of horse-liver. I asked him to give me a piece. "What," says he, "can you eat horse-liver?" I told him I would try, if he

---

[1] Or Squakeag, now Northfield.
[2] *Apios tuberosa*. The Pilgrims, during their first winter, lived chiefly on these roots. The tubers vary from the size of a cherry to that of a hen's egg, and grow in strings of perhaps forty together.

would give me a piece, which he did; and I laid it on the coals to roast; but, before it was half ready, they got half of it away from me; so that I was forced to take the rest and eat it as it was, with the blood about my mouth, and yet a savory bit it was to me; for to the hungry soul every bitter thing was sweet.[1] A solemn sight methought it was to see whole fields of wheat and Indian corn forsaken and spoiled, and the remainder of them to be food for our merciless enemies. That night we had a mess of wheat for our supper.

The Eighth Remove.—On the morrow morning we must go over Connecticut River to meet with King Philip. Two canoes full they had carried over. The next turn myself was to go; but, as my foot was upon the canoe to step in, there was a sudden outcry among them, and I must step back; and instead of going over the river, I must go four or five miles up the river farther northward. Some of the Indians ran one way, and some another. The cause of this route was, as I thought, their espying some English scouts, who were thereabouts. In this travel up the river, about noon the company made a stop and sat down, some to eat and others to rest them. As I sat amongst them, musing on things past, my son Joseph unexpectedly came to me. [. . .]

We travelled on till night, and in the morning we must go over the river to Philip's crew. When I was in the canoe I could not but be amazed at the numerous crew of pagans that were on the bank on the other side. When I came ashore they gathered all about me, I sitting alone in the midst. I observed they asked one another questions, and laughed, and rejoiced over their gains and victories.

Then my heart began to fail, and I fell a-weeping; which was the first time, to my remembrance, that I wept before them. There one of them asked me why I wept. I could hardly tell what to say; yet I answered, they would kill me. "No," said he, "none will hurt you." Then came one of them and gave me two spoonfuls of meal to comfort me, and another gave me half a pint of peas, which was worth more than many bushels at another time.

Then I went to see King Philip. He bade me come in and sit down, and asked me whether I would smoke—a usual compliment nowadays among the saints and sinners; but this noway suited me; for though I had formerly used tobacco, yet I had left it ever since I was first taken. It seems to be a bait the devil lays to make men lose their precious time. I remember with shame how, formerly, when I had taken two or three pipes, I was presently ready for another, such a bewitching thing it is; but I thank God He has now given me power over it. Surely there are many who may be better employed than to sit sucking a stinking tobacco pipe.

---

[1] Starvation was another common tactic Indian captors used to break captives' spirits and force them to accept foods they would not otherwise have been willing to eat. In *Nine Years among the Indians*, Herman Lehmann recounts the ways in which his Apache captors conditioned him to eat raw meat; then, upon arrival at the Apache village several days later, they tested him by putting a piece of raw meat and a piece of cooked meat in front of him. Lehmann was so hungry that he scarfed down the raw meat as quickly as possible. Later, after his adoption by his captor, he found out that had he taken the cooked meat, he would have been killed on the spot. (EGW)

ॐ

The Indians, returning from Northampton,[1] brought with them some horses and sheep and other things which they had taken. I desired them that they would carry me to Albany upon one of those horses, and sell me for powder; for so they had sometimes discoursed. I was utterly helpless of getting home on foot, the way that I came. I could hardly bear to think of the many weary steps I had taken to this place.

The Ninth Remove.—But, instead of either going to Albany or homeward, we must go five miles up the river, and then go over it. Here we abode awhile. Here lived a sorry Indian, who spake to me to make him a shirt. When I had done it he would pay me nothing for it. But he, living by the river-side, where I often went to fetch water, I would often be putting him in mind, and calling for my pay; at last he told me if I would make another shirt for a papoose not yet born he would give me a knife, which he did when I had done it. I carried the knife in, and my master asked me to give it him, and I was not a little glad that I had anything that they would accept of and be pleased with.

My son being now about a mile from me, I asked liberty to go and see him. They bid me go, and away I went; but quickly lost myself, travelling over hills and through swamps, and could not find the way to him. And I cannot but admire at the wonderful power and goodness of God to me, in that though I was gone from home and met with all sorts of Indians, and those I had no knowledge of, and there being no Christian soul near me, yet not one of them offered the least imaginable miscarriage to me. I turned homeward again, and met with my master, and he showed me the way to my son. When I came to him I found him not well; and withal he had a boil on his side, which much troubled him. We bemoaned one another awhile, as the Lord helped us, and then I returned again. When I was returned I found myself as unsatisfied as I was before.

But I was fain to go look after something to satisfy my hunger; and, going among the wigwams, I went into one, and there found a squaw who showed herself very kind to me, and gave me a piece of bear. I put it into my pocket, and came home, but could not find an opportunity to broil it for fear they should get it from me. And there it lay all the day and night in my pocket. In the morning I went again to the same squaw, who had a kettle of ground-nuts boiling. I asked her to let me boil my piece of bear in the kettle, which she did, and gave me some ground-nuts to eat with it; and I cannot but think how pleasant it was to me. I have sometimes seen bear baked handsomely amongst the English, and some liked it, but the thoughts that it was bear made me tremble. But now that was savory to me that one would think was enough to turn the stomach of a brute creature.

One bitter cold day I could find no room to sit down before the fire. I went out, and could not tell what to do, but I went into another wigwam, where they were also sitting round the fire; but the squaw laid a skin for me, and bid me sit down, and gave me some

---

[1] Northampton was attacked March 14, 1676.

ground-nuts, and bid me come again, and told me they would buy me if they were able. And yet these were strangers to me that I never knew before.

The Tenth Remove.—That day a small part of the company removed about three quarters of a mile, intending farther the next day. When they came to the place they intended to lodge, and had pitched their wigwams, being hungry, I went again back to the place we were before at to get something to eat; being encouraged by the squaw's kindness, who bid me come again. When I was there, there came an Indian to look after me; who, when he had found me, kicked me all along. I went home and found venison roasting that night, but they would not give me one bit of it. Sometimes I met with favor, and sometimes with nothing but frowns.

The Eleventh Remove.—The next day, in the morning, they took their travel, intending a day's journey up the river; I took my load at my back, and quickly we came to wade over a river, and passed over tiresome and wearisome hills. One hill was so steep that I was fain to creep up upon my knees, and to hold by the twigs and bushes to keep myself from falling backwards. My head, also, was so light that I usually reeled as I went.

The Twelfth Remove.—It was upon a Sabbath-day morning that they prepared for their travel. This morning I asked my master whether he would sell me to my husband; he answered, nux; which did much rejoice my spirits. My mistress, before we went, was gone to the burial of a papoose, and returning she found me sitting and reading in my Bible. She snatched it hastily out of my hand and threw it out of doors. I ran out and caught it up, and put it in my pocket, and never let her see it afterwards. Then they packed up their things to be gone, and gave me my load; I complained it was too heavy, whereupon she gave me a slap on the face and bid me be gone. I lifted up my heart to God, hoping that redemption was not far off; and the rather because their insolence grew worse and worse.

೮つಅ

The Thirteenth Remove.—Instead of going towards the Bay, which was what I desired, I must go with them five or six miles down the river, into a mighty thicket of brush, where we abode almost a fortnight. Here one asked me to make a shirt for her papoose, for which she gave me a mess of broth which was thickened with meal made of the bark of a tree; and to make it better she had put into it about a handful of peas and a few roasted ground-nuts.

I had not seen my son a pretty while, and here was an Indian of whom I made inquiry after him, and asked him when he saw him. He answered me, that such a time his master roasted him, and that himself did eat a piece of him as big as his two fingers, and that he was very good meat. But the Lord upheld my spirit under this discouragement; and I considered their horrible addictedness to lying, and that there is not one of them that makes the least conscience of speaking the truth.

In this place, one cold night, as I lay by the fire, I removed a stick which kept the heat from me; a squaw moved it down again, at which I looked up, and she threw a handful of ashes in my eyes. I thought I should have been quite blinded and never have seen more; but, lying down, the water ran out of my eyes, and carried the dirt with it, that by the morning I recovered my sight again.

About this time they came yelping from Hadley, having there killed three Englishmen, and brought one captive with them, viz., Thomas Reed. They all gathered about the poor man, asking him many questions. I desired also to go and see him; and when I came, he was crying bitterly, supposing they would quickly kill him. Whereupon I asked one of them whether they intended to kill him; he answered me they would not. He being a little cheered with that, I asked him about the welfare of my husband; he told me he saw him such a time in the Bay, and he was well, but very melancholy. By which I certainly understood, though I suspected it before, that whatsoever the Indians told me respecting him was vanity and lies. Some of them told me he was dead, and they had killed him; some said he was married again, and that the governor wished him to marry, and told him that he should have his choice; and that all persuaded him that I was dead. So like were these barbarous creatures to him who was a liar from the beginning.

As I was sitting once in the wigwam here, Philip's maid came with the child in her arms, and asked me to give her a piece of my apron to make a flap for it. I told her I would not; then my mistress bid me give it, but I still said no. The maid told me if I would not give her a piece, she would tear a piece off it. I told her I would tear her coat then. With that my mistress rises up, and takes up a stick big enough to have killed me, and struck at me with it, but I stepped out, and she struck the stick into the mat of the wigwam. But while she was pulling it out, I ran to the maid, and gave her all my apron, and so that storm went over.

Hearing that my son was come to this place, I went to see him, and told him his father was well, but very melancholy. He told me he was as much grieved for his father as for himself. I wondered at his speech, for I thought I had enough upon my spirit, in reference to myself, to make me mindless of my husband and every one else, they being safe among their friends. He told me also, that a while before, his master, together with other Indians, were going to the French for powder; but by the way the Mohawks met with them, and killed four of their company, which made the rest turn back again. For which I desire that myself and he may ever bless the Lord; for it might have been worse with him had he been sold to the French, than it proved to be in his remaining with the Indians.

I asked his master to let him stay awhile with me, that I might comb his head and look over him, for he was almost overcome with lice. He told me when I had done that he was very hungry, but I had nothing to relieve him, but bid him go into the wigwams as he went along, and see if he could get anything among them; which he did, and, it seems, tarried a little too long, for his master was angry with him, and beat him, and then sold him. Then he came running to tell me he had a new master, and that he had given him some ground-nuts already. Then I went along with him to his new master, who told me he loved him, and he should not want. So his master carried him away, and I never saw him afterwards till I saw him at Piscataqua, in Portsmouth.

That night they bid me go out of the wigwam again; my mistress's papoose was sick, and it died that night; and there was one benefit in it, that there was more room. I went to a wigwam and they bid me come in, and gave me a skin to lie upon, and a mess of venison and ground-nuts, which was a choice dish among them. On the morrow they buried the papoose; and afterwards, both morning and evening, there came a company to mourn and howl with her; though I confess I could not much condole with them.

ଅଚ

The Sixteenth Remove.—We began this remove with wading over Baquaug River. The water was up to our knees, and the stream very swift, and so cold that I thought it would have cut me in sunder. I was so weak and feeble that I reeled as I went along, and thought there I must end my days at last, after my bearing and getting through so many difficulties. The Indians stood laughing to see me staggering along, but in my distress the Lord gave me experience of the truth and goodness of that promise, Isa. xliii., 2—"When thou passeth through the waters I will be with thee, and through the rivers, they shall not overflow thee." Then I sat down to put on my stockings and shoes, with the tears running down my eyes, and many sorrowful thoughts in my heart. But I got up to go along with them.

Quickly there came up to us an Indian who informed them that I must go to Wachusett[1] to my master, for there was a letter come from the council to the sagamores about redeeming the captives, and that there would be another in fourteen days, and that I must be there ready. My heart was so heavy before that I could scarce speak or go in the path, and yet now so light that I could run. My strength seemed to come again, and to recruit my feeble knees and aching heart; yet it pleased them to go but one mile that night, and there we staid two days.

In that time came a company of Indians to us, near thirty, all on horseback. My heart skipped within me, thinking they had been Englishmen, at the first sight of them; for they were dressed in English apparel, with hats, white neckcloths, and sashes about their waists, and ribbons upon their shoulders. But when they came near there was a vast difference between the lovely faces of Christians and the foul looks of those heathen, which much damped my spirits again.

The Seventeenth Remove.—A comfortable remove it was to me, because of my hopes. They gave me my pack and along we went cheerfully. But quickly my will proved more than my strength; having little or no refreshment my strength failed, and my spirits were almost quite gone. At night we came to an Indian town, and the Indians sat down by a wigwam discoursing, but I was almost spent and could scarce speak. I laid down my load and went

---

[1] Princeton. The mountain in this town still retains the name of Wachusett.

into the wigwam, and there sat an Indian boiling of horse-feet, they being wont to eat the flesh first, and when the feet were old and dried, and they had nothing else, they would cut off the feet and use them. I asked him to give me a little of his broth, or water they were boiling it in. He took a dish and gave me one spoonful of samp, and bid me take as much of the broth as I would. Then I put some of the hot water to the samp, and drank it up, and my spirits came again.

The Eighteenth Remove.—We took up our packs, and along we went; but a wearisome day I had of it. As we went along I saw an Englishman stripped naked and lying dead upon the ground, but knew not who he was. Then we came to another Indian town where we staid all night. In this town there were four English children captives, and one of them my own sister's. I went to see how she did, and she was well, considering her captive condition. I would have tarried that night with her, but they that owned her would not suffer it. Then I went to another wigwam, where they were boiling corn and beans, which was a lovely sight to see, but I could not get a taste thereof. Then I went home to my mistress's wigwam, and they told me I disgraced my master with begging, and if I did so any more they would knock me on the head. I told them they had as good do that as starve me to death.

The Nineteenth Remove.—They said when we went out that we must travel to Wachusett this day. But a bitter weary day I had of it, travelling now three days together, without resting any day between. Going along, having indeed my life, but little spirit, Philip, who was in the company, came up, and took me by the hand, and said, "Two weeks more and you shall be mistress again." I asked him if he spoke true. He said, "Yes, and quickly you shall come to your master again;" who had been gone from us three weeks.

My master had three squaws, living sometimes with one and sometimes with another: Onux, this old squaw at whose wigwam I was, and with whom my master had been these three weeks. Another was Wettimore, with whom I had lived and served all this while. A severe and proud dame she was, bestowing every day in dressing herself near as much time as any of the gentry of the land; powdering her hair and painting her face, going with her necklaces, with jewels in her ears, and bracelets upon her hands. When she had dressed herself, her work was to make girdles of wampum and beads. The third squaw was a younger one, by whom he had two papooses.

By that time I was refreshed by the old squaw, Wettimore's maid came to call me home, at which I fell a-weeping. Then the old squaw told me, to encourage me, that when I wanted victuals I should come to her, and that I should lie in her wigwam. Then I went with the maid, and quickly I came back and lodged there. The squaw laid a mat under me, and a good rug over me; the first time that I had any such kindness showed me. I understood that Wettimore thought that if she should let me go and serve with the old squaw she should be in danger to lose not only my service, but the redemption-pay also. And I was not a little glad to hear this; being by it raised in my hopes that in God's due time there would be an end of this sorrowful hour. Then came an Indian and asked me to knit him three pair of stockings, for which I had a hat and a silk handkerchief. Then another asked me to make her a shift, for which she gave me an apron.

Then came Tom and Peter with the second letter from the council, about the captives. Though they were Indians, I gat them by the hand, and burst out into tears; my heart was so full that I could not speak to them; but recovering myself, I asked them how my husband did, and all my friends and acquaintance. They said they were well, but very melancholy. They brought me two biscuits and a pound of tobacco. The tobacco I soon gave away. When it was all gone one asked me to give him a pipe of tobacco. I told him it was all gone. Then he began to rant and threaten. I told him when my husband came I would give him some. "Hang him, rogue," says he; "I will knock out his brains if he comes here." And then again at the same breath they would say that if there should come an hundred without guns they would do them no hurt; so unstable and like madmen they were. So that, fearing the worst, I durst not send to my husband, though there were some thoughts of his coming to redeem and fetch me, not knowing what might follow; for there was little more trust to them than to the master they served.

When the letter was come, the sagamores met to consult about the captives, and called me to them to inquire how much my husband would give to redeem me. When I came I sat down among them, as I was wont to do, as their manner is. Then they bid me stand up, and said they were the general court. They bid me speak what I thought he would give. Now knowing that all we had was destroyed by the Indians, I was in a great strait. I thought if I should speak of but a little, it would be slighted and hinder the matter; if of a great sum, I knew not where it would be procured. Yet at a venture I said twenty pounds, yet desired them to take less; but they would not hear of that, but sent the message to Boston, that for twenty pounds I should be redeemed. It was a praying Indian that wrote their letters for them.

About that time there came an Indian to me, and bid me come to his wigwam at night, and he would give me some pork and groundnuts, which I did; and as I was eating, another Indian said to me, "He seems to be your good friend, but he killed two Englishmen at Sudbury,[1] and there lie the clothes behind you." I looked behind me, and there I saw bloody clothes, with bullet-holes in them. Yet the Lord suffered not this wretch to do me any hurt; yea, instead of that, he many times refreshed me: five or six times did he and his squaw refresh my feeble carcass. If I went to their wigwam at any time they would always give me something, and yet they were strangers that I never saw before. Another squaw gave me a piece of fresh pork, and a little salt with it, and lent me her frying-pan to fry it; and I cannot but remember what a sweet, pleasant, and delightful relish that bit had to me, to this day. So little do we prize common mercies when we have them to the full.

The Twentieth Remove.—It was their usual manner to remove when they had done any mischief, lest they should be found out; and so they did at this time. We went about three

---

[1] Sudbury was attacked 21st April.

or four miles, and there they built a great wigwam, big enough to hold an hundred Indians, which they did in preparation to a great day of dancing. They would now say among themselves that the governor would be so angry for his loss at Sudbury that he would send no more about the captives, which made me grieve and tremble.

My sister being not far from this place, and hearing that I was here, desired her master to let her come and see me, and he was willing to it, and would come with her, but she, being ready first, told him she would go before, and was come within a mile or two of the place. Then he overtook her, and began to rant as if he had been mad, and made her go back again in the rain; so that I never saw her till I saw her in Charlestown. But the Lord requited many of their ill doings, for this Indian, her master, was hanged afterwards at Boston.

They began now to come from all quarters, against their merry dancing day. Among some of them came one good-wife Kettle. I told her my heart was so heavy that it was ready to break. "So is mine too," said she, "but yet I hope we shall hear some good news shortly." I could hear how earnestly my sister desired to see me, and I earnestly desired to see her; yet neither of us could get an opportunity. My daughter was now but a mile off, and I had not seen her for nine or ten weeks, as I had not seen my sister since our first taking. I desired them to let me go and see them; yea, I entreated, begged, and persuaded them to let me see my daughter, and yet so hard-hearted were they that they would not suffer it. They made use of their tyrannical power while they had it, but through the Lord's wonderful mercy their time was now but short.

On a Sabbath day, the sun being about an hour high in the afternoon, came Mr. John Hoar (the council permitting him, and his own forward spirit inclining him), together with the two forementioned Indians, Tom and Peter, with the third letter from the council. When they came near I was abroad. They presently called me in, and bid me sit down and not stir. Then they catched up their guns and away they ran as if an enemy had been at hand, and the guns went off apace. I manifested some great trouble, and asked them what was the matter. I told them I thought they had killed the Englishman (for they had in the meantime told me that an Englishman was come). They said no; they shot over his horse, and under, and before his horse, and they pushed him this way and that way, at their pleasure, showing him what they could do. Then they let him come to their wigwams.

I begged of them to let me see the Englishman, but they would not; but there was I fain to sit their pleasure. When they had talked their fill with him, they suffered me to go to him. We asked each other of our welfare, and how my husband did, and all my friends. He told me they were all well, and would be glad to see me. Among other things which my husband sent me, there came a pound of tobacco, which I sold for nine shillings in money; for many of them for want of tobacco smoked hemlock and ground-ivy. It was a great mistake in any who thought I sent for tobacco, for through the favor of God that desire was overcome.

I now asked them whether I should go home with Mr. Hoar. They answered no, one and another of them, and it being late, we lay down with that answer. In the morning Mr.

Hoar invited the sagamores to dinner; but when we went to get it ready, we found they had stolen the greatest part of the provisions Mr. Hoar had brought. And we may see the wonderful power of God in that one passage, in that when there was such a number of them together, and so greedy of a little good food, and no English there but Mr. Hoar and myself, that there they did not knock us on the head and take what we had; there being not only some provision, but also trading cloth, a part of the twenty pounds agreed upon. But instead of doing us any mischief, they seemed to be ashamed of the fact, and said it was the matchit[1] Indians that did it. Oh, that we could believe that there was nothing too hard for God. God showed His power over the heathen in this, as He did over the hungry lions when Daniel was cast into the den.

Mr. Hoar called them betime to dinner, but they ate but little, they being so busy in dressing themselves and getting ready for their dance, which was carried on by eight of them, four men and four squaws, my master and mistress being two. He was dressed in his Holland shirt, with great stockings, his garters hung round with shillings, and had girdles of wampom upon his head and shoulders. She had a kersey coat, covered with girdles of wampom from the loins upward. Her arms from her elbows to her hands were covered with bracelets; there were handfuls of necklaces about her neck, and several sorts of jewels in her ears. She had fine red stockings, and white shoes, her hair powdered, and her face painted red, that was always before black. And all the dancers were after the same manner.

There were two others singing and knocking on a kettle for their music. They kept hopping up and down one after another, with a kettle of water in the midst, standing warm upon some embers, to drink of when they were dry. They held on till almost night, throwing out their wampom to the standers-by. At night I asked them again if I should go home. They all as one said no, except my husband would come for me. When we were lain down, my master went out of the wigwam, and by and by sent in an Indian called James the printer, who told Mr. Hoar that my master would let me go home to-morrow if he would let him have one pint of liquor. Then Mr. Hoar called his own Indians, Tom and Peter, and bid them all go and see if he would promise it before them three, and if he would he should have it; which he did and had it.

Philip, smelling the business, called me to him, and asked me what I would give him to tell me some good news, and to speak a good word for me, that I might go home to-morrow. I told him I could not tell what to give him, I would anything I had, and asked him what he would have. He said two coats, and twenty shillings in money, half a bushel of seed corn, and some tobacco. I thanked him for his love, but I knew that good news as well as that crafty fox.

On Tuesday morning they called their General Court, as they styled it, to consult and determine whether I should go home or no. And they all seemingly consented that I should go, except Philip, who would not come among them.

---

[1] Wicked

At first they were all against it, except my husband would come for me; but afterwards they assented to it, and seeming to rejoice in it; some asking me to send them some bread, others some tobacco, others shaking me by the hand, offering me a hood and scarf to ride in; not one moving hand or tongue against it. Thus hath the Lord answered my poor desires, and the many earnest requests of others put up unto God for me.

In my travels an Indian came to me and told me, if I were willing, he and his squaw would run away, and go home along with me. I told them no, I was not willing to run away, but desired to wait God's time, that I might go home quietly and without fear. And now God hath granted me my desire. Oh, the wonderful power of God that I have seen, and the experiences that I have had! I have been in the midst of those roaring lions and savage bears that feared neither God nor man nor the devil, by night and day, alone and in company, sleeping all sorts together, and yet not one of them ever offered the least abuse of unchastity to me in word or action; though some are ready to say I speak it for my own credit; but I speak it in the presence of God, and to His glory. God's power is as great now as it was to save Daniel in the lions' den or the three children in the fiery furnace. Especially that I should come away in the midst of so many hundreds of enemies, and not a dog move his tongue.

So I took my leave of them, and in coming along my heart melted into tears more than all the while I was with them, and I was almost swallowed up with the thoughts that ever I should go home again. About the sun's going down Mr. Hoar, myself, and the two Indians came to Lancaster; and a solemn sight it was to me. There had I lived many comfortable years among my relations and neighbors, and now not one Christian to be seen, or one house left standing. We went on to a farmhouse that was yet standing, where we lay all night; and a comfortable lodging we had, though nothing but straw to lie on. The Lord preserved us in safety that night, raised us up again in the morning, and carried us along, that before noon we came to Concord. Now was I full of joy, and yet not without sorrow; joy to see such a lovely sight, so many Christians together, and some of them my neighbors.

Being recruited with food and raiment, we went to Boston that day, where I met with my dear husband; but the thoughts of our dear children—one being dead and the other we could not tell where—abated our comfort in each other. I was not before so much hemmed in by the merciless and cruel heathen, but now as much with pitiful, tender-hearted, and compassionate Christians. In that poor and beggarly condition I was received in I was kindly entertained in several houses. [. . .] The twenty pounds, the price of my redemption, was raised by some Boston gentlewomen, and Mr. Usher, whose bounty and charity I would not forget to make mention of. Then Mr. Thomas Shepard, of Charlestown, received us into his house, where we continued eleven weeks; and a father and mother they were unto us. And many more tender-hearted friends we met with in that place. We were now in the midst of love, yet not without much and frequent heaviness of heart for our poor children and other relations who were still in affliction.

The week following, after my coming in, the governor and council sent to the Indians again, and that not without success; for they brought in my sister and good-wife Kettle.

About this time the council had ordered a day of public thanksgiving, though I had still cause of mourning; and being unsettled in our minds, we thought we would ride eastward, to see if we could hear anything concerning our children. As we were riding along between Ipswich and Rowley we met with William Hubbard, who told us our son Joseph and my sister's son were come into Major Waldren's. I asked him how he knew it. He said the major himself told him so. So along we went till we came to Newbury; and their minister being absent, they desired my husband to preach the thanksgiving for them; but he was not willing to stay there that night, but he would go over to Salisbury to hear farther, and come again in the morning, which he did, and preached there that day.

At night, when he had done, one came and told him that his daughter was come into Providence. Here was mercy on both hands. Now we were between them, the one on the east, and the other on the west. Our son being nearest, we went to him first, to Portsmouth, where we met with him, and with the major also, who told us he had done what he could, but could not redeem him under seven pounds, which the good people thereabouts were pleased to pay. On Monday we came to Charlestown, where we heard that the Governor of Rhode Island had sent over for our daughter, to take care of her, being now within his jurisdiction; which should not pass without our acknowledgments. But she being nearer Rehoboth than Rhode Island, Mr. Newman went over and took care of her, and brought her to his own house. And the goodness of God was admirable to us in our low estate, in that he raised up compassionate friends on every side, when we had nothing to recompense any for their love.

Our family being now gathered together, the South Church in Boston hired a house for us. Then we removed from Mr. Shepard's (those cordial friends) and went to Boston, where we continued about three quarters of a year.[1] Still the Lord went along with us, and provided graciously for us. I thought it somewhat strange to set up house-keeping with bare walls; but as Solomon says, "Money answers all things" and that we had through the benevolence of Christian friends, some in this town, and some in that, and others; and some from England; that in a little time we might look, and see the house furnished with love. The Lord hath been exceeding good to us in our low estate, in that when we had neither house nor home, nor other necessaries, the Lord so moved the hearts of these and those towards us, that we wanted neither food, nor raiment for ourselves or ours: "There is a Friend which sticketh closer than a Brother" (Proverbs 18.24). And how many such friends have we found, and now living amongst? And truly such a friend have we found him to be unto us, in whose house we lived, viz. Mr. James Whitcomb, a friend unto us near hand, and afar off.

I can remember the time when I used to sleep quietly without workings in my thoughts, whole nights together, but now it is other ways with me. When all are fast about me, and no eye open, but His who ever waketh, my thoughts are upon things past, upon the

---

[1] The remainder of this text is supplied from the 1720 edition; Kephart leaves out most of Rowlandson's spiritual reflections, but this concluding segment strikes me as particularly important. (EGW)

awful dispensation of the Lord towards us, upon His wonderful power and might, in carrying of us through so many difficulties, in returning us in safety, and suffering none to hurt us. I remember in the night season, how the other day I was in the midst of thousands of enemies, and nothing but death before me. It is then hard work to persuade myself, that ever I should be satisfied with bread again. But now we are fed with the finest of the wheat, and, as I may say, with honey out of the rock. Instead of the husk, we have the fatted calf. The thoughts of these things in the particulars of them, and of the love and goodness of God towards us, make it true of me, what David said of himself, "I watered my Couch with my tears" (Psalm 6.6). Oh! the wonderful power of God that mine eyes have seen, affording matter enough for my thoughts to run in, that when others are sleeping mine eyes are weeping.

I have seen the extreme vanity of this world: One hour I have been in health, and wealthy, wanting nothing. But the next hour in sickness and wounds, and death, having nothing but sorrow and affliction.

Before I knew what affliction meant, I was ready sometimes to wish for it. When I lived in prosperity, having the comforts of the world about me, my relations by me, my heart cheerful, and taking little care for anything, and yet seeing many, whom I preferred before myself, under many trials and afflictions, in sickness, weakness, poverty, losses, crosses, and cares of the world, I should be sometimes jealous least I should have my portion in this life, and that Scripture would come to my mind, "For whom the Lord loveth he chasteneth, and scourgeth every Son whom he receiveth" (Hebrews 12.6). But now I see the Lord had His time to scourge and chasten me. The portion of some is to have their afflictions by drops, now one drop and then another; but the dregs of the cup, the wine of astonishment, like a sweeping rain that leaveth no food, did the Lord prepare to be my portion. Affliction I wanted, and affliction I had, full measure (I thought), pressed down and running over. Yet I see, when God calls a person to anything, and through never so many difficulties, yet He is fully able to carry them through and make them see, and say they have been gainers thereby. And I hope I can say in some measure, as David did, "It is good for me that I have been afflicted." The Lord hath showed me the vanity of these outward things. That they are the vanity of vanities, and vexation of spirit, that they are but a shadow, a blast, a bubble, and things of no continuance. That we must rely on God Himself, and our whole dependance must be upon Him. If trouble from smaller matters begin to arise in me, I have something at hand to check myself with, and say, why am I troubled? It was but the other day that if I had had the world, I would have given it for my freedom, or to have been a servant to a Christian. I have learned to look beyond present and smaller troubles, and to be quieted under them. As Moses said, "Stand still and see the salvation of the Lord" (Exodus 14.13).

ๅๅ

Isaac Watts

When I Survey the Wond'rous Cross

When I survey the wond'rous Cross
On which the Prince of Glory dy'd,
My richest Gain I count but Loss,
And pour Contempt on all my Pride.

Forbid it, Lord, that I should boast,
Save in the Death of Christ my God:
All the vain Things that charm me most,
I sacrifice them to his Blood.

See from his Head, his Hands, his feet,
Sorrow and Love flow mingled down!
Did e'er such Love and Sorrow meet?
Or Thorns compose so rich a Crown?

His dying Crimson, like a Robe,
Spreads o'er his Body on the Tree;
Then am I dead to all the Globe,
And all the Globe is dead to me.

Were the whole Realm of Nature mine,
That were a Present far too small;
Love so amazing, so divine,
Demands my Soul, my Life, my All.

The Messiah's Coming and Kingdom

Joy to the World; the Lord is come;
Let Earth receive her King;
Let ev'ry Heart prepare him Room,
And Heav'n and Nature sing.

Joy to the Earth, the Saviour reigns,
Let Men their Songs employ;

While Fields and Floods, Rocks, Hills and Plains,
Repeat the sounding Joy.

No more let Sins and Sorrows grow,
Nor Thorns infest the Ground;
He comes to make his Blessings flow
Far as the Curse is found.

He rules the World with Truth and Grace,
And makes the Nations prove
The Glories of his Righteousness,
And Wonders of his Love.

Charles Wesley

Love Divine, All Loves Excelling

Love divine, all love excelling,
Joy of heaven to earth come down!
Fix in us thine humble dwelling,
All thy faithful mercies crown;
Jesus! thou art all compassion,
Pure unbounded love thou art,
Visit us with thy salvation,
Enter ev'ry trembling heart!

Breathe! O breathe thy lovely spirit
Into ev'ry troubled breast!
Let us all in thee inherit,
Let us find the promis'd rest;
Take away the power of sinning,
Alpha and Omega be,
End of faith, as its beginning,
Set our hearts at liberty.

Come! Almighty to deliver,
Let us all thy life receive!

Suddenly return, and never,
Never more thy temples leave!
Thee we would be always blessing,
Serve thee as thy hosts above,
Pray, and praise thee without ceasing,
Glory in thy precious love.

Finish then thy new creation,
Pure, unspotted may we be,
Let us see thy great salvation,
Perfectly restor'd by thee!
Chang'd from glory into glory,
Till in heaven we take our place,
Till we cast our crowns before thee,
Lost in wonder, love and praise!

Christ the Lord Is Risen Today[1]

Christ the Lord is ris'n to day,
Sons of Men and Angels say!
Raise your Joys and Triumphs high,
Sing, ye Heav'ns, and Earth, reply.

Love's redeeming Work is done,
Fought the Fight, the Battle won:
Lo! our Sun's Eclipse is o'er,
Lo! he sets in Blood no more.

Vain the Stone, the Watch, the Seal,
Christ hath burst the Gates of Hell:
Death in vain forbids his Rise,
Christ hath open'd Paradise.

Lives again our glorious King,
Where, O Death, is now thy Sting?
Once he dy'd our Souls to save;
Where's thy Victory, O Grave?

---

[1] There is considerable variation in the texts of this hymn in early hymnals, but they all omit the "Alleluia" at the end of each line found in modern hymnals.

Soar we now where Christ hath led,
Foll'wing our exalted Head;
Made like him, like him we rise,
Ours the Cross, the Grave, the Skies.

What tho' once we perish'd all,
Partners of our Parents Fall;
Second Life we all receive,
In our heav'nly Adam live.

Hail, the Lord of Earth and Heav'n!
Praise to thee by both be giv'n!
Thee we greet Triumphant now
Hail the Resurrection—thou!

King of Glory! Soul of bliss!
Everlasting Life is this—
Thee to know—thy Pow'r to prove,
Thus to sing, and thus to love.

William Cowper

Praise for the Fountain Opened

There is a fountain filled with blood
Drawn from EMMANUEL'S veins;
And sinners, plunged beneath that flood,
Loose all their guilty stains.

The dying thief rejoiced to see
That fountain in his day;
And there have I, as vile as he,
Washed all my sins away.

Dear dying Lamb, thy precious blood
Shall never lose its pow'r;

Till all the ransomed church of God
Be saved, to sin no more.

E'er since, by faith, I saw the stream
Thy flowing wounds supply:
Redeeming love has been my theme,
And shall be till I die.

Then in a nobler sweeter song
I'll sing thy pow'r to save
When this poor lisping stamm'ring tongue
Lies silent in the grave.

Lord, I believe thou hast prepared
(Unworthy though I be)
For me a blood-bought free reward,
A golden harp for me!

'Tis strung, and tuned, for endless years,
And formed by pow'r divine;
To sound, in God the Father's ears,
No other name but thine.

Light Shining out of Darkness

God moves in a mysterious way
his wonders to perform.
He plants his footsteps in the sea
and rides upon the storm.

Deep in unfathomable mines
of never-failing skill,
he treasures up his bright designs
and works his sovereign will.

You fearful saints, fresh courage take;
the clouds you so much dread
are big with mercy and shall break
in blessings on your head.

Judge not the LORD by feeble sense,
But trust him for his grace;
Behind a frowning providence,
He hides a smiling face.

His purposes will ripen fast,
unfolding every hour.
The bud may have a bitter taste,
but sweet will be the flower.

Blind unbelief is sure to err
and scan his work in vain.
GOD is his own interpreter,
and he will make it plain.

༺༻

John Newton

Zion, or The City of God

Glorious things of thee are spoken,
Zion, city of our God!
He, whose word cannot be broken,
Formed thee for his own abode:
On the rock of ages founded,
What can shake thy sure repose?
With salvation's walls surrounded
Thou may'st smile at all thy foes.

See! the streams of living waters
Springing from eternal love;
Well supply thy sons and daughters,
And all fear of want remove:
Who can faint while such a river
Ever flows their thirst t' assuage?
Grace, which like the LORD, the giver,
Never fails from age to age.

Round each habitation hov'ring
See the cloud and fire appear!
For a glory and a cov'ring,
Showing that the LORD is near:
Thus deriving from their banner
Light by night and shade by day;
Safe they feed upon the Manna
Which he gives them when they pray.

Blest inhabitants of Zion,
Washed in the Redeemer's blood!
Jesus, whom their souls rely on,
Makes them kings and priests to GOD:
'Tis his love his people raises
Over self to reign as kings
And as priests, his solemn praises
Each for a thank-offering brings.

Savior, if of Zion's city
I through grace a member am;
Let the world deride or pity,
I will glory in thy name.
Fading is the worldling's pleasure,
All his boasted pomp and show;
Solid joys and lasting treasure,
None but Zion's children know.

❧❧

John Wesley
from Sermons on Several Occasions

Preface to the First Series (1747)

1. The following Sermons contain the substance of what I have been preaching for between eight and nine years last past. During that time I have frequently spoken in public, on every subject in the ensuing collection; and I am not conscious, that there is any one point of doctrine, on which I am accustomed to speak in public, which is not here, incidentally, if not professedly, laid before every Christian reader. Every serious man who peruses these, will

therefore see, in the clearest manner, what these doctrines are which I embrace and teach as the essentials of true religion.

2. But I am throughly sensible, these are not proposed in such a manner as some may expect. Nothing here appears in an elaborate, elegant, or oratorical dress. If it had been my desire or design to write thus, my leisure would not permit. But, in truth, I, at present, designed nothing less; for I now write, as I generally speak, ad populum, — to the bulk of mankind, to those who neither relish nor understand the art of speaking; but who, notwithstanding, are competent judges of those truths which are necessary to present and future happiness. I mention this, that curious readers may spare themselves the labour of seeking for what they will not find.

3. I design plain truth for plain people: Therefore, of set purpose, I abstain from all nice and philosophical speculations; from all perplexed and intricate reasonings; and, as far as possible, from even the show of learning, unless in sometimes citing the original Scripture. I labour to avoid all words which are not easy to be understood, all which are not used in common life; and, in particular, those kinds of technical terms that so frequently occur in Bodies of Divinity; those modes of speaking which men of reading are intimately acquainted with, but which to common people are an unknown tongue. Yet I am not assured, that I do not sometimes slide into them unawares: It is so extremely natural to imagine, that a word which is familiar to ourselves is so to all the world.

4. Nay, my design is, in some sense, to forget all that ever I have read in my life. I mean to speak, in the general, as if I had never read one author, ancient or modern (always excepting the inspired). I am persuaded, that, on the one hand, this may be a means of enabling me more clearly to express the sentiments of my heart, while I simply follow the chain of my own thoughts, without entangling myself with those of other men; and that, on the other, I shall come with fewer weights upon my mind, with less of prejudice and prepossession, either to search for myself, or to deliver to others, the naked truths of the gospel.

5. To candid, reasonable men, I am not afraid to lay open what have been the inmost thoughts of my heart. I have thought, I am a creature of a day, passing through life as an arrow through the air. I am a spirit come from God, and returning to God: Just hovering over the great gulf; till, a few moments hence, I am no more seen; I drop into an unchangeable eternity! I want to know one thing, — the way to heaven; how to land safe on that happy shore. God himself has condescended to teach the way: For this very end he came from heaven. He hath written it down in a book. O give me that book! At any price, give me the book of God! I have it: Here is knowledge enough for me. Let me be homo unius libri. [A man of one book.] Here then I am, far from the busy ways of men. I sit down alone: Only God is here. In his presence I open, I read his book; for this end, to find the way to heaven. Is there a doubt concerning the meaning of what I read? Does anything appear dark or intricate? I lift up my heart to the Father of Lights: — "Lord, is it not thy word, 'If any man lack wisdom, let him ask of God?' Thou 'givest liberally, and upbraidest not.' Thou hast said,

'If any be willing to do thy will, he shall know.' I am willing to do, let me know, thy will." I then search after and consider parallel passages of Scripture, "comparing spiritual things with spiritual." I meditate thereon with all the attention and earnestness of which my mind is capable. If any doubt still remains, I consult those who are experienced in the things of God; and then the writings whereby, being dead, they yet speak. And what I thus learn, that I teach.

6. I have accordingly set down in the following sermons what I find in the Bible concerning the way to heaven; with a view to distinguish this way of God from all those which are the inventions of men. I have endeavoured to describe the true, the scriptural, experimental religion, so as to omit nothing which is a real part thereof, and to add nothing thereto which is not. And herein it is more especially my desire, First, to guard those who are just setting their faces toward heaven, (and who, having little acquaintance with the things of God, are the more liable to be turned out of the way,) from formality, from mere outside religion, which has almost driven heart-religion out of the world; and, Secondly, to warn those who know the religion of the heart, the faith which worketh by love, lest at any time they make void the law through faith, and so fall back into the snare of the devil.

7. By the advice and at the request of some of my friends, I have prefixed to the other sermons contained in this volume, three sermons of my own, and one of my Brother's, preached before the University of Oxford. My design required some discourses on those heads; and I preferred these before any others, as being a stronger answer than any which can be drawn up now, to those who have frequently asserted that we have changed our doctrine of late, and do not preach now what we did some years ago. Any man of understanding may now judge for himself, when he has compared the latter with the former sermons.

8. But some may say, I have mistaken the way myself, although I take upon me to teach it to others. It is probable many will think this, and it is very possible that I have. But I trust, whereinsoever I have mistaken, my mind is open to conviction. I sincerely desire to be better informed. I say to God and man, "What I know not, teach thou me!"

9. Are you persuaded you see more clearly than me? It is not unlikely that you may. Then treat me as you would desire to be treated yourself upon a change of circumstances. Point me out a better way than I have yet known. Show me it is so, by plain proof of Scripture. And if I linger in the path I have been accustomed to tread, and am therefore unwilling to leave it, labour with me a little; take me by the hand, and lead me as I am able to bear. But be not displeased if I entreat you not to beat me down in order to quicken my pace: I can go but feebly and slowly at best; then, I should not be able to go at all. May I not request of you, further, not to give me hard names in order to bring me into the right way. Suppose I were ever so much in the wrong, I doubt this would not set me right. Rather, it would make me run so much the farther from you, and so get more and more out of the way.

10. Nay, perhaps, if you are angry, so shall I be too; and then there will be small hopes of finding the truth. If once anger arise, *Eute kapnos*, (as Homer somewhere expresses it,) this

smoke will so dim the eyes of my soul, that I shall be able to see nothing clearly. For God's sake, if it be possible to avoid it, let us not provoke one another to wrath. Let us not kindle in each other this fire of hell; much less blow it up into a flame. If we could discern truth by that dreadful light, would it not be loss, rather than gain? For, how far is love, even with many wrong opinions, to be preferred before truth itself without love! We may die without the knowledge of many truths, and yet be carried into Abraham's bosom. But, if we die without love, what will knowledge avail? Just as much as it avails the devil and his angels! The God of love forbid we should ever make the trial! May he prepare us for the knowledge of all truth, by filling our hearts with his love, and with all joy and peace in believing!

Preface to the Second Series (1788)

1. A gentleman in the west of England informed me a few days ago, that a Clergyman in his neighbourhood designed to print, in two or three volumes, the Sermons which had been published in the ten volumes of the Arminian Magazine. I had been frequently solicited to do this myself, and had as often answered, "I leave this for my executors." But if it must be done before I go hence, methinks I am the properest person to do it.

2. I intend, therefore, to set about it without delay: And if it pleases God to continue to me a little longer the use of my understanding and memory, I know not that I can employ them better. And perhaps I may be better able than another to revise my own writings; in order either to retrench what is redundant, to supply what is wanting, or to make any farther alterations which shall appear needful.

3. To make these plain Discourses more useful, I purpose now to range them in proper order; placing those first which are intended to throw light on some important Christian doctrines; and afterwards those which more directly relate to some branch of Christian practice: And I shall endeavour to place them all in such an order that one may illustrate and confirm the other. There may be the greater need of this, because they were occasionally written, during a course of years, without any order or connexion at all; just as this or the other subject either occurred to my own mind, or was suggested to me at various times by one or another friend.

4. To complete the number of twelve Sermons in every volume, I have added six Sermons to those printed in the Magazines; and I did this the rather, because the subjects were important, and cannot be too much insisted on.

5. Is there need to apologize to sensible persons for the plainness of my style? A gentleman, whom I much love and respect, lately informed me, with much tenderness and courtesy, that men of candour made great allowance for the decay of my faculties; and did not expect me to write now, either with regard to sentiment or language, as I did thirty or forty years ago. Perhaps they are decayed; though I am not conscious of it. But is not this a fit occasion to explain myself concerning the style I use from choice, not necessity? I could even now write as floridly and rhetorically as ever the admired Dr. B—; but I dare not;

because I seek the honour that cometh of God only. What is the praise of man to *me*, that have one foot in the grave, and am stepping into the land whence I shall not return? Therefore, I dare no more write in a *fine style* than wear a fine coat. But were it otherwise, had I time to spare, I should still write just as I do. I should purposely decline, what many admire, an highly ornamental style. I cannot admire French oratory: I despise it from my heart. Let those that please be in raptures at the pretty, elegant sentences of Massillon or Bourdabue;[1] but give me the plain, nervous style of Dr. South, Dr. Bates, or Mr. John Howe: And for elegance, show me any French writer who exceeds Dean Young, or Mr. Seed. Let who will admire the French frippery, I am still for plain, sound English.

6. I think a preacher or a writer of Sermons has lost his way when he imitates any of the French orators; even the most famous of them; even Massillon, or Bourdabue. Only let his language be plain, proper, and clear, and it is enough. God himself has told us how to speak, both as to the matter and the manner: "If any man speak," in the name of God, "let him speak as the oracles of God;" and if he would imitate any part of these above the rest, let it be the First Epistle of St. John. This is the style, the most excellent style, for every gospel preacher. And let him aim at no more ornament than he finds in that sentence, which is the sum of the whole gospel, "We love Him, because He first loved us."

London,
January 1, 1788.

Sermon 2[2]
The Almost Christian[3]

"Almost thou persuadest me to be a Christian."
Acts 26:28.

AND many there are who go thus far: ever since the Christian religion was in the world, there have been many in every age and nation who were almost persuaded to be Christians. But seeing it avails nothing before God to go *only thus* far, it highly imports us to consider,

First. What is implied in being *almost*,
Secondly. What in being *altogether, a Christian*.

---

[1] Famous French orators of the day.
[2] This text follows the 1872 edition.
[3] Preached at St. Mary's, Oxford, before the University, on July 25, 1741. (Ed.) (The full name of St. Mary's is The University Church of St. Mary the Virgin; it is the official church of Oxford University, and many major figures have preached from its pulpit. C. S. Lewis preached "The Weight of Glory" there. – EGW)

I. (I.) 1. Now, in the being *almost a Christian* is implied, First, heathen honesty. No one, I suppose, will make any question of this; especially, since by heathen honesty here, I mean, not that which is recommended in the writings of their philosophers only, but such as the common heathens expected one of another, and many of them actually practised.[1] By the rules of this they were taught that they ought not to be unjust; not to take away their neighbour's goods, either by robbery or theft; not to oppress the poor, neither to use extortion toward any; not to cheat or overreach either the poor or rich, in whatsoever commerce they had with them; to defraud no man of his right; and, if it were possible, to owe no man anything.

2. Again: the common heathens allowed, that some regard was to be paid to truth, as well as to justice. And, accordingly, they not only held him in abomination who was forsworn, who called God to witness to a lie; but him also who was known to be a slanderer of his neighbour, who falsely accused any man. And indeed, little better did they esteem wilful liars of any sort, accounting them the disgrace of human kind, and the pests of society.

3. Yet again: there was a sort of love and assistance which they expected one from another. They expected whatever assistance any one could give another, without prejudice to himself. And this they extended not only to those little offices of humanity which are performed without any expense or labour, but likewise to the feeding the hungry, if they had food to spare; the clothing the naked with their own superfluous raiment; and, in general. the giving, to any that needed, such things as they needed not themselves. Thus far, in the lowest account of it, heathen honesty went; the first thing implied in the being *almost a Christian*.

(II.) 4. A second thing implied in the being *almost a Christian*, is, the having a form of godliness; of that godliness which is prescribed in the gospel of Christ; the having the *outside of a real Christian*. Accordingly, the almost Christian does nothing which the gospel forbids. He taketh not the name of God in vain; he blesseth, and curseth not; he sweareth not at all, but his communication is, yea, yea; nay, nay. He profanes not the day of the Lord, nor suffers it to be profaned, even by the stranger that is within his gates. He not only avoids all actual adultery, fornication, and uncleanness, but every word or look that either directly or indirectly tends thereto; nay, and all idle words, abstaining both from detraction, backbiting, talebearing, evil speaking, and from "all foolish talking and jesting"—*eutrapelia*, a kind of virtue in the heathen moralist's account;—briefly, from all conversation that is not "good to the use of edifying," and that, consequently, "grieves the Holy Spirit of God, whereby we are sealed to the day of redemption."

5. He abstains from "wine wherein is excess"; from revellings and gluttony. He avoids, as much as in him lies, all strife and contention, continually endeavouring to live peaceably with all men. And, if he suffer wrong, he avengeth not himself, neither returns

---

[1] This is what Lewis calls "the Tao" in *The Abolition of Man*.

evil for evil. he is no railer, no brawler, no scoffer, either at the faults or infirmities of his neighbour. he does not willingly wrong, hurt, or grieve any man; but in all things act and speaks by that plain rule, "Whatsoever thou wouldest not he should do unto thee, that do not thou to another."[1]

6. And in doing good, he does not confine himself to cheap and easy offices of kindness, but labours and suffers for the profit of many, that by all means he may help some. In spite of toil or pain, "whatsoever his hand findeth to do, he doeth it with his might;" whether it be for his friends, or for his enemies; for the evil, or for the good. For being "not slothful" in this, or in any "business," as he "hath opportunity" he doeth "good," all manner of good, "to all men;" and to their souls as well as their bodies. he reproves the wicked, instructs the ignorant, confirms the wavering, quickens the good, and comforts the afflicted. he labours to awaken those that sleep; to lead those whom God hath already awakened to the "Fountain opened for sin and for uncleanness," that they may wash therein and be clean; and to stir up those who are saved through faith, to adorn the gospel of Christ in all things.

7. He that hath the form of godliness uses also the means of grace; yea, all of them, and at all opportunities. He constantly frequents the house of God; and that, not as the manner of some is, who come into the presence of the Most High, either loaded with gold and costly apparel, or in all the gaudy vanity of dress, and either by their unseasonable civilities to each other, or the impertinent gaiety of their behaviour, disclaim all pretensions to the form as well as to the power of godliness. Would to God there were none even among ourselves who fall under the same condemnation! who come into this house, it may be, gazing about, or with all the signs of the most listless, careless indifference, though sometimes they may *seem* to use a prayer to God for his blessing on what they are entering upon; who, during that awful service, are either asleep, or reclined in the most convenient posture for it; or, as though they supposed God was asleep, talking with one another, or looking round, as utterly void of employment. Neither let these be accused of the form of godliness. No; he who has even this, behaves with seriousness and attention, in every part of that solemn service. More especially, when he approaches the table of the Lord, it is not with a light or careless behaviour, but with an air, gesture, and deportment which speaks nothing else but "God be merciful to me a sinner!"

8. To this, if we add the constant use of family prayer, by those who are masters of families, and the setting times apart for private addresses to God, with a daily seriousness of behaviour; he who uniformly practises this outward religion, has the form of godliness. There needs but one thing more in order to his being *almost a Christian*, and that is, sincerity.

(III.) 9. By sincerity I mean, a real, inward principle of religion, from whence these outward actions flow. And, indeed if we have not this, we have not heathen honesty; no, not so much

---

[1] In *The Abolition of Man*, Lewis notes that this *negative* form of the Golden Rule is common among non-Christian cultures; it took Jesus to put it in the stronger positive form we know from the Gospels.

of it as will answer the demand of a heathen Epicurean poet. Even this poor wretch, in his sober intervals, is able to testify,

> *Oderunt peccare boni, virtutis amore;*
> *Oderunt peccare mali, formidine poenae.*
> [Good men avoid sin from the love of virtue;
> Wicked men avoid sin from a fear of punishment.]

So that, if a man only abstains from doing evil in order to avoid punishment, *Non pasces in cruce corvos*, [Thou shalt not be hanged.], saith the Pagan; there, "thou hast thy reward." But even he will not allow such a harmless man as this to be so much as a *good heathen*. If, then, any man, from the same motive, viz., to avoid punishment, to avoid the loss of his friends, or his gain, or his reputation, should not only abstain from doing evil, but also do ever so much good; yea, and use all the means of grace; yet we could not with any propriety say, this man is even *almost a Christian*. If he has no better principle in his heart, he is only a hypocrite altogether.

10. Sincerity, therefore, is necessarily implied in the being *almost a Christian*; a real design to serve God, a hearty desire to do his will. It is necessarily implied, that a man have a sincere view of pleasing God in all things; in all his conversation; in all his actions; in all he does or leaves undone. This design, if any man be *almost a Christian*, runs through the whole tenor of his life. This is the moving principle, both in his doing good, his abstaining from evil, and his using the ordinances of God.

11. But here it will probably be inquired, "Is it possible that any man living should go so far as this, and, nevertheless, be *only almost a Christian*"? What more than this, can be implied in the being *a Christian altogether*? I answer, First, that it is possible to go thus far, and yet be but *almost a Christian*, I learn, not only from the oracles of God, but also from the sure testimony of experience.

12. Brethren, great is "my boldness towards you in this behalf." And "forgive me this wrong," if I declare my own folly upon the house-top, for yours and the gospel's sake. — Suffer me, then, to speak freely of myself, even as of another man. I am content to be abased, so ye may be exalted, and to be yet more vile for the glory of my Lord.

13. I did go thus far for many years, as many of this place can testify; using diligence to eschew all evil, and to have a conscience void of offence; redeeming the time; buying up every opportunity of doing all good to all men; constantly and carefully using all the public and all the private means of grace; endeavouring after a steady seriousness of behaviour, at all times, and in all places; and, God is my record, before whom I stand, doing all this in sincerity; having a real design to serve God; a hearty desire to do his will in all things; to please him who had called me to "fight the good fight," and to "lay hold of eternal life." Yet my own conscience beareth me witness in the Holy Ghost, that all this time I was but *almost a Christian*.

II. If it be inquired, "What more than this is implied in the being *altogether a Christian*?" I answer,

(I.) 1. First. The love of God. For thus saith his word, "Thou shalt love the Lord thy God with all thy heart, and with all thy soul, and with all thy mind, and with all thy strength." Such a love is this, as engrosses the whole heart, as rakes up all the affections, as fills the entire capacity of the soul and employs the utmost extent of all its faculties. he that thus loves the Lord his God, his spirit continually "rejoiceth in God his Saviour." his delight is in the Lord, his Lord and his All, to whom "in everything he giveth thanks. All his desire is unto God, and to the remembrance of his name." his heart is ever crying out, "Whom have I in heaven but Thee? and there is none upon earth that I desire beside Thee." Indeed, what can he desire beside God? Not the world, or the things of the world: for he is "crucified to the world, and the world crucified to him." he is crucified to "the desire of the flesh, the desire of the eye, and the pride of life." Yea, he is dead to pride of every kind: for "love is not puffed up" but "he that dwelling in love, dwelleth in God, and God in him," is less than nothing in his own eyes.

(II.) 2. The Second thing implied in the being *altogether a Christian* is, the love of our neighbour. For thus said our Lord in the following words, "Thou shalt love thy neighbour as thyself" If any man ask, "Who is my neighbour?" we reply, Every man in the world; every child of his who is the Father of the spirits of all flesh. Nor may we in any wise except our enemies or the enemies of God and their own souls. But every Christian loveth these also as himself, yea, "as Christ loved us." he that would more fully understand what manner of love this is, may consider St. Paul's description of it. It is "long-suffering and kind." It "envieth not." It is not rash or hasty in judging. It "is not puffed up;" but maketh him that loves, the least, the servant of all. Love "doth not behave itself unseemly," but becometh "all things to all men." She "seeketh not her own;" but only the good of others, that they may be saved. "Love is not provoked." It casteth out wrath, which he who hath is wanting in love. "It thinketh no evil. It rejoiceth not in iniquity, but rejoiceth in the truth. It covereth all things, believeth all things, hopeth all things, endureth all things."

(III.) 3. There is yet one thing more that may be separately considered, though it cannot actually be separate from the preceding, which is implied in the being *altogether a Christian*; and that is the ground of all, even faith. Very excellent things are spoken of this throughout the oracles of God. "Every one," saith the beloved disciple, "that believeth is born of God." "To as many as received him, gave he power to become the sons of God. even to them that believe on his name." And "this is the victory that overcometh the world, even our faith." Yea, our Lord himself declares, "He that believeth in the Son hath everlasting life; and cometh not into condemnation, but is passed from death unto life."

4. But here let no man deceive his own soul. "It is diligently to be noted, the faith which bringeth not forth repentance, and love, and all good works, is not that right living faith, but a dead and devilish one. For, even the devils believe that Christ was born of a virgin: that he wrought all kinds of miracles, declaring himself very God: that, for our sakes, he suffered a most painful death, to redeem us from death everlasting; that he rose again the third day: that he ascended into heaven, and sitteth at the right hand of the Father and at the end of the world shall come again to judge both the quick and dead. These articles of our faith the devils believe, and so they believe all that is written in the Old and New Testament. And yet for all this faith, they be but devils. They remain still in their damnable estate lacking the very true Christian faith." [Homily on the Salvation of Man.]

5. "The right and true Christian faith is" (to go on the words of our own Church), "not only to believe that Holy Scripture and the Articles of our Faith are true, but also to have a sure trust and confidence to be saved from everlasting damnation by Christ. It is a sure trust and confidence which a man hath in God, that, by the merits of Christ, his sins are forgiven, and he reconciled to the favour of God; whereof doth follow a loving heart, to obey his commandments."

6. Now, whosoever has this faith, which "purifies the heart" (by the power of God, who dwelleth therein) from "pride, anger, desire, from all unrighteousness" from "all filthiness of flesh and spirit;" which fills it with love stronger than death, both to God and to all mankind; love that doeth the works of God, glorying to spend and to be spent for all men, and that endureth with joy, not only the reproach of Christ, the being mocked, despised, and hated of all men, but whatsoever the wisdom of God permits the malice of men or devils to inflict,—whosoever has this faith thus working by love is not almost only, but altogether, a Christian.

7. But who are the living witnesses of these things? I beseech you, brethren, as in the presence of that God before whom "hell and destruction are without a covering—how much more the hearts of the children of men?"—that each of you would ask his own heart, "Am I of that number? Do I so far practise justice, mercy, and truth, as even the rules of heathen honesty require? If so, have I the very *outside* of a Christian? the form of godliness? Do I abstain from evil,—from whatsoever is forbidden in the written Word of God? Do I, whatever good my hand findeth to do, do it with my might? Do I seriously use all the ordinances of God at all opportunities? And is all this done with a sincere design and desire to please God in all things?"

8. Are not many of you conscious, that you never came thus far; that you have not been even *almost a Christian*; that you have not come up to the standard of heathen honesty; at least, not to the form of Christian godliness?—much less hath God seen sincerity in you, a real design of pleasing him in all things. You never so much as intended to devote all your words and works. your business, studies, diversions, to his glory. You never even designed or desired, that whatsoever you did should be done "in the name of the Lord Jesus," and as such should be "a spiritual sacrifice, acceptable to God through Christ."

9. But, supposing you had, do good designs and good desires make a Christian? By no means, unless they are brought to good effect. "Hell is paved," saith one, "with good intentions." The great question of all, then, still remains. Is the love of God shed abroad in your heart? Can you cry out, "My God, and my All"? Do you desire nothing but him? Are you happy in God? Is he your glory, your delight, your crown of rejoicing? And is this commandment written in your heart, "That he who loveth God love his brother also"? Do you then love your neighbour as yourself? Do you love every man, even your enemies, even the enemies of God, as your own soul? as Christ loved you? Yea, dost thou believe that Christ loved thee, and gave himself for thee? Hast thou faith in his blood? Believest thou the Lamb of God hath taken away thy sins, and cast them as a stone into the depth of the sea? that he hath blotted out the handwriting that was against thee, taking it out of the way, nailing it to his cross? Hast thou indeed redemption through his blood, even the remission of thy sins? And doth his Spirit bear witness with thy spirit, that thou art a child of God?

10. The God and Father of our Lord Jesus Christ, who now standeth in the midst of us, knoweth, that if any man die without this faith and this love, good it were for him that he had never been born. Awake, then, thou that sleepest, and call upon thy God: call in the day when he may be found. Let him not rest, till he make his "goodness to pass before thee;" till he proclaim unto thee the name of the Lord, "The Lord, the Lord God, merciful and gracious, long-suffering, and abundant in goodness and truth, keeping mercy for thousands, forgiving iniquity, and transgression, and sin." Let no man persuade thee, by vain words, to rest short of this prize of thy high calling. But cry unto him day and night, who, "while we were without strength, died for the ungodly," until thou knowest in whom thou hast believed, and canst say, "My Lord, and my God!" Remember, "always to pray, and not to faint," till thou also canst lift up thy hand unto heaven, and declare to him that liveth for ever and ever, "Lord, Thou knowest all things, Thou knowest that I love Thee."

11. May we all thus experience what it is to be, not almost only; but altogether Christians; being justified freely by his grace, through the redemption that is in Jesus; knowing we have peace with God through Jesus Christ; rejoicing in hope of the glory of God; and having the love of God shed abroad in our hearts, by the Holy Ghost given unto us!

&

Thomas Paine
from The Crisis[1]

THESE are the times that try men's souls. The summer soldier and the sunshine patriot will, in this crisis, shrink from the service of their country; but he that stands by it now, deserves the love and thanks of man and woman. Tyranny, like hell, is not easily conquered; yet we have this consolation with us, that the harder the conflict, the more glorious the triumph. What we obtain too cheap, we esteem too lightly: it is dearness only that gives every thing its value. Heaven knows how to put a proper price upon its goods; and it would be strange indeed if so celestial an article as FREEDOM should not be highly rated. Britain, with an army to enforce her tyranny, has declared that she has a right (not only to TAX) but "to BIND us in ALL CASES WHATSOEVER" and if being bound in that manner, is not slavery, then is there not such a thing as slavery upon earth. Even the expression is impious; for so unlimited a power can belong only to God.

Whether the independence of the continent was declared too soon, or delayed too long, I will not now enter into as an argument; my own simple opinion is, that had it been eight months earlier, it would have been much better. We did not make a proper use of last winter, neither could we, while we were in a dependent state. However, the fault, if it were one, was all our own;[2] we have none to blame but ourselves. But no great deal is lost yet. All that Howe has been doing for this month past, is rather a ravage than a conquest, which the spirit of the Jerseys, a year ago, would have quickly repulsed, and which time and a little resolution will soon recover.

I have as little superstition in me as any man living, but my secret opinion has ever been, and still is, that God Almighty will not give up a people to military destruction, or leave them unsupportedly to perish, who have so earnestly and so repeatedly sought to avoid the calamities of war, by every decent method which wisdom could invent. Neither have I so much of the infidel in me, as to suppose that He has relinquished the government of the world, and given us up to the care of devils; and as I do not, I cannot see on what grounds the king of Britain can look up to heaven for help against us: a common murderer, a highwayman, or a house-breaker, has as good a pretence as he.

'Tis surprising to see how rapidly a panic will sometimes run through a country. All nations and ages have been subject to them. Britain has trembled like an ague at the report of a French fleet of flat-bottomed boats; and in the fourteenth[3] century the whole English

---

[1] Notes on this text will include Paine's original footnote, denoted with "(P.)" at the end.

[2] The present winter is worth an age, if rightly employed; but, if lost or neglected, the whole continent will partake of the evil; and there is no punishment that man does not deserve, be he who, or what, or where he will, that may be the means of sacrificing a season so precious and useful. (P.)

[3] The Battle of Agincourt, to which Paine is referring here, actually took place in 1415, and Joan's great victory at Orléans was in 1429; so this ought to read "fifteenth" instead of "fourteenth."

army, after ravaging the kingdom of France, was driven back like men petrified with fear; and this brave exploit was performed by a few broken forces collected and headed by a woman, Joan of Arc. Would that heaven might inspire some Jersey maid to spirit up her countrymen, and save her fair fellow sufferers from ravage and ravishment! Yet panics, in some cases, have their uses; they produce as much good as hurt. Their duration is always short; the mind soon grows through them, and acquires a firmer habit than before. But their peculiar advantage is, that they are the touchstones of sincerity and hypocrisy, and bring things and men to light, which might otherwise have lain forever undiscovered. In fact, they have the same effect on secret traitors, which an imaginary apparition would have upon a private murderer. They sift out the hidden thoughts of man, and hold them up in public to the world. Many a disguised Tory has lately shown his head, that shall penitentially solemnize with curses the day on which Howe arrived upon the Delaware.

As I was with the troops at Fort Lee, and marched with them to the edge of Pennsylvania, I am well acquainted with many circumstances, which those who live at a distance know but little or nothing of. Our situation there was exceedingly cramped, the place being a narrow neck of land between the North River and the Hackensack. Our force was inconsiderable, being not one-fourth so great as Howe could bring against us. We had no army at hand to have relieved the garrison, had we shut ourselves up and stood on our defence. Our ammunition, light artillery, and the best part of our stores, had been removed, on the apprehension that Howe would endeavor to penetrate the Jerseys, in which case Fort Lee could be of no use to us; for it must occur to every thinking man, whether in the army or not, that these kind of field forts are only for temporary purposes, and last in use no longer than the enemy directs his force against the particular object which such forts are raised to defend. Such was our situation and condition at Fort Lee on the morning of the 20th of November, when an officer arrived with information that the enemy with 200 boats had landed about seven miles above; Major General Green,[1] who commanded the garrison, immediately ordered them under arms, and sent express to General Washington at the town of Hackensack, distant by the way of the ferry = six miles. Our first object was to secure the bridge over the Hackensack, which laid up the river between the enemy and us, about six miles from us, and three from them. General Washington arrived in about three-quarters of an hour, and marched at the head of the troops towards the bridge, which place I expected we should have a brush for; however, they did not choose to dispute it with us, and the greatest part of our troops went over the bridge, the rest over the ferry, except some which passed at a mill on a small creek, between the bridge and the ferry, and made their way through some marshy grounds up to the town of Hackensack, and there passed the river. We brought off as much baggage as the wagons could contain, the rest was lost. The simple object was to bring off the garrison, and march them on till they could be strengthened by the Jersey or Pennsylvania militia, so as to be enabled to make a stand. We staid four days at

---

[1] Nathanael Greene, who gained a reputation as Washington's most able sub-commander.

Newark, collected our out-posts with some of the Jersey militia, and marched out twice to meet the enemy, on being informed that they were advancing, though our numbers were greatly inferior to theirs. Howe, in my little opinion, committed a great error in generalship in not throwing a body of forces off from Staten Island through Amboy, by which means he might have seized all our stores at Brunswick, and intercepted our march into Pennsylvania; but if we believe the power of hell to be limited, we must likewise believe that their agents are under some providential control.

I shall not now attempt to give all the particulars of our retreat to the Delaware; suffice it for the present to say, that both officers and men, though greatly harassed and fatigued, frequently without rest, covering, or provision, the inevitable consequences of a long retreat, bore it with a manly and martial spirit. All their wishes centred in one, which was, that the country would turn out and help them to drive the enemy back. Voltaire has remarked that King William never appeared to full advantage but in difficulties and in action; the same remark may be made on General Washington, for the character fits him. There is a natural firmness in some minds which cannot be unlocked by trifles, but which, when unlocked, discovers[1] a cabinet of fortitude; and I reckon it among those kind of public blessings, which we do not immediately see, that God hath blessed him with uninterrupted health, and given him a mind that can even flourish upon care.

I shall conclude this paper with some miscellaneous remarks on the state of our affairs; and shall begin with asking the following question, Why is it that the enemy have left the New England provinces, and made these middle ones the seat of war? The answer is easy: New England is not infested with Tories, and we are. I have been tender in raising the cry against these men, and used numberless arguments to show them their danger, but it will not do to sacrifice a world either to their folly or their baseness. The period is now arrived, in which either they or we must change our sentiments, or one or both must fall. And what is a Tory? Good God! What is he? I should not be afraid to go with a hundred Whigs against a thousand Tories, were they to attempt to get into arms. Every Tory is a coward; for servile, slavish, self-interested fear is the foundation of Toryism; and a man under such influence, though he may be cruel, never can be brave.

But, before the line of irrecoverable separation be drawn between us, let us reason the matter together: Your conduct is an invitation to the enemy, yet not one in a thousand of you has heart enough to join him. Howe is as much deceived by you as the American cause is injured by you. He expects you will all take up arms, and flock to his standard, with muskets on your shoulders. Your opinions are of no use to him, unless you support him personally, for 'tis soldiers, and not Tories, that he wants.

I once felt all that kind of anger, which a man ought to feel, against the mean principles that are held by the Tories: a noted one, who kept a tavern at Amboy, was standing at his door, with as pretty a child in his hand, about eight or nine years old, as I ever saw, and after

---

[1] reveals

speaking his mind as freely as he thought was prudent, finished with this unfatherly expression, "Well! give me peace in my day." Not a man lives on the continent but fully believes that a separation must some time or other finally take place, and a generous parent should have said, "If there must be trouble, let it be in my day, that my child may have peace;" and this single reflection, well applied, is sufficient to awaken every man to duty. Not a place upon earth might be so happy as America. Her situation is remote from all the wrangling world, and she has nothing to do but to trade with them. A man can distinguish himself between temper and principle, and I am as confident, as I am that God governs the world, that America will never be happy till she gets clear of foreign dominion. Wars, without ceasing, will break out till that period arrives, and the continent must in the end be conqueror; for though the flame of liberty may sometimes cease to shine, the coal can never expire.

America did not, nor does not want[1] force; but she wanted a proper application of that force. Wisdom is not the purchase of a day, and it is no wonder that we should err at the first setting off. From an excess of tenderness, we were unwilling to raise an army, and trusted our cause to the temporary defence of a well-meaning militia. A summer's experience has now taught us better; yet with those troops, while they were collected, we were able to set bounds to the progress of the enemy, and, thank God! they are again assembling. I always considered militia as the best troops in the world for a sudden exertion, but they will not do for a long campaign. Howe, it is probable, will make an attempt on this city;[2] should he fail on this side the Delaware, he is ruined. If he succeeds, our cause is not ruined. He stakes all on his side against a part on ours; admitting he succeeds, the consequence will be, that armies from both ends of the continent will march to assist their suffering friends in the middle states; for he cannot go everywhere, it is impossible. I consider Howe as the greatest enemy the Tories have; he is bringing a war into their country, which, had it not been for him and partly for themselves, they had been clear of. Should he now be expelled, I wish with all the devotion of a Christian, that the names of Whig and Tory may never more be mentioned; but should the Tories give him encouragement to come, or assistance if he come, I as sincerely wish that our next year's arms may expel them from the continent, and the Congress appropriate their possessions to the relief of those who have suffered in well-doing. A single successful battle next year will settle the whole. America could carry on a two years' war by the confiscation of the property of disaffected persons, and be made happy by their expulsion. Say not that this is revenge, call it rather the soft resentment of a suffering people, who, having no object in view but the good of all, have staked their own all upon a seemingly doubtful event. Yet it is folly to argue against determined hardness; eloquence may strike the ear, and the language of sorrow draw forth the tear of compassion, but nothing can reach the heart that is steeled with prejudice.

---

[1] lack

[2] Philadelphia

Quitting this class of men, I turn with the warm ardor of a friend to those who have nobly stood, and are yet determined to stand the matter out: I call not upon a few, but upon all: not on this state or that state, but on every state: up and help us; lay your shoulders to the wheel; better have too much force than too little, when so great an object is at stake. Let it be told to the future world, that in the depth of winter, when nothing but hope and virtue could survive, that the city and the country, alarmed at one common danger, came forth to meet and to repulse it. Say not that thousands are gone, turn out your tens of thousands; throw not the burden of the day upon Providence, but "show your faith by your works," that God may bless you. It matters not where you live, or what rank of life you hold, the evil or the blessing will reach you all. The far and the near, the home counties and the back, the rich and the poor, will suffer or rejoice alike. The heart that feels not now is dead; the blood of his children will curse his cowardice, who shrinks back at a time when a little might have saved the whole, and made them happy. I love the man that can smile in trouble, that can gather strength from distress, and grow brave by reflection. 'Tis the business of little minds to shrink; but he whose heart is firm, and whose conscience approves his conduct, will pursue his principles unto death. My own line of reasoning is to myself as straight and clear as a ray of light. Not all the treasures of the world, so far as I believe, could have induced me to support an offensive war, for I think it murder; but if a thief breaks into my house, burns and destroys my property, and kills or threatens to kill me, or those that are in it, and to "bind me in all cases whatsoever" to his absolute will, am I to suffer it? What signifies it to me, whether he who does it is a king or a common man; my countryman or not my countryman; whether it be done by an individual villain, or an army of them? If we reason to the root of things we shall find no difference; neither can any just cause be assigned why we should punish in the one case and pardon in the other. Let them call me rebel and welcome, I feel no concern from it; but I should suffer the misery of devils, were I to make a whore of my soul by swearing allegiance to one whose character is that of a sottish, stupid, stubborn, worthless, brutish man. I conceive likewise a horrid idea in receiving mercy from a being, who at the last day shall be shrieking to the rocks and mountains to cover him, and fleeing with terror from the orphan, the widow, and the slain of America.

There are cases which cannot be overdone by language, and this is one. There are persons, too, who see not the full extent of the evil which threatens them; they solace themselves with hopes that the enemy, if he succeed, will be merciful. It is the madness of folly, to expect mercy from those who have refused to do justice; and even mercy, where conquest is the object, is only a trick of war; the cunning of the fox is as murderous as the violence of the wolf, and we ought to guard equally against both. Howe's first object is, partly by threats and partly by promises, to terrify or seduce the people to deliver up their arms and receive mercy. The ministry recommended the same plan to Gage, and this is what the Tories call making their peace, "a peace which passeth all understanding" indeed! A peace which would be the immediate forerunner of a worse ruin than any we have yet thought of. Ye men of Pennsylvania, do reason upon these things! Were the back counties to give up their arms, they would fall an easy prey to the Indians, who are all armed: this perhaps is what some Tories would not be sorry for. Were the home counties to deliver up their arms, they would be exposed to the resentment of the back counties who would then have it in their power to chastise their defection at pleasure. And were any one state to give up its arms, that state must be garrisoned by all Howe's army of Britons and Hessians to preserve it from the anger of the rest. Mutual fear is the principal link in the chain of mutual love, and woe be to that state that breaks the compact. Howe is mercifully inviting you to barbarous destruction, and men must be either rogues or fools that will not see it. I dwell not upon the vapors of imagination; I bring reason to your ears, and, in language as plain as A, B, C, hold up truth to your eyes.

I thank God, that I fear not. I see no real cause for fear. I know our situation well, and can see the way out of it. While our army was collected, Howe dared not risk a battle; and it is no credit to him that he decamped from the White Plains, and waited a mean opportunity to ravage the defenceless Jerseys; but it is great credit to us, that, with a handful of men, we sustained an orderly retreat for near an hundred miles, brought off our ammunition, all our field pieces, the greatest part of our stores, and had four rivers to pass. None can say that our retreat was precipitate, for we were near three weeks in performing it, that the country might have time to come in. Twice we marched back to meet the enemy, and remained out till dark. The sign of fear was not seen in our camp, and had not some of the cowardly and disaffected inhabitants spread false alarms through the country, the Jerseys had never been ravaged. Once more we are again collected and collecting; our new army at both ends of the continent is recruiting fast, and we shall be able to open the next campaign with sixty thousand men, well armed and clothed. This is our situation, and who will may know it. By perseverance and fortitude we have the prospect of a glorious issue; by cowardice and submission, the sad choice of a variety of evils – a ravaged country – a depopulated city – habitations without safety, and slavery without hope – our homes turned into barracks and bawdy-houses for Hessians, and a future race to provide for, whose fathers we shall doubt of. Look on this picture and weep over it! and if there yet remains one thoughtless wretch who believes it not, let him suffer it unlamented.

❧❧

from The Federalist Papers

Federalist No. 51[1]

To the People of the State of New York:

TO WHAT expedient, then, shall we finally resort, for maintaining in practice the necessary partition of power among the several departments, as laid down in the Constitution? The only answer that can be given is, that as all these exterior provisions are found to be inadequate, the defect must be supplied, by so contriving the interior structure of the government as that its several constituent parts may, by their mutual relations, be the means of keeping each other in their proper places. Without presuming to undertake a full development of this important idea, I will hazard a few general observations, which may perhaps place it in a clearer light, and enable us to form a more correct judgment of the principles and structure of the government planned by the convention.

In order to lay a due foundation for that separate and distinct exercise of the different powers of government, which to a certain extent is admitted on all hands to be essential to the preservation of liberty, it is evident that each department should have a will of its own; and consequently should be so constituted that the members of each should have as little agency as possible in the appointment of the members of the others. Were this principle rigorously adhered to, it would require that all the appointments for the supreme executive, legislative, and judiciary magistracies should be drawn from the same fountain of authority, the people, through channels having no communication whatever with one another. Perhaps such a plan of constructing the several departments would be less difficult in practice than it may in contemplation appear. Some difficulties, however, and some additional expense would attend the execution of it. Some deviations, therefore, from the principle must be admitted. In the constitution of the judiciary department in particular, it might be inexpedient to insist rigorously on the principle: first, because peculiar qualifications being essential in the members, the primary consideration ought to be to select that mode of choice which best secures these qualifications; secondly, because the permanent tenure by which the appointments are held in that department, must soon destroy all sense of dependence on the authority conferring them.

It is equally evident, that the members of each department should be as little dependent as possible on those of the others, for the emoluments annexed to their offices. Were the executive magistrate, or the judges, not independent of the legislature in this particular, their independence in every other would be merely nominal.

---

[1] Originally published February 8, 1788, and written probably by either Alexander Hamilton or James Madison. (Hamilton, Madison, and John Jay collaborated and all shared the pen name "Publius" in writing these essays.)

But the great security against a gradual concentration of the several powers in the same department, consists in giving to those who administer each department the necessary constitutional means and personal motives to resist encroachments of the others. The provision for defense must in this, as in all other cases, be made commensurate to the danger of attack. Ambition must be made to counteract ambition. The interest of the man must be connected with the constitutional rights of the place. It may be a reflection on human nature, that such devices should be necessary to control the abuses of government. But what is government itself, but the greatest of all reflections on human nature? If men were angels, no government would be necessary. If angels were to govern men, neither external nor internal controls on government would be necessary. In framing a government which is to be administered by men over men, the great difficulty lies in this: you must first enable the government to control the governed; and in the next place oblige it to control itself. A dependence on the people is, no doubt, the primary control on the government; but experience has taught mankind the necessity of auxiliary precautions.

This policy of supplying, by opposite and rival interests, the defect of better motives, might be traced through the whole system of human affairs, private as well as public. We see it particularly displayed in all the subordinate distributions of power, where the constant aim is to divide and arrange the several offices in such a manner as that each may be a check on the other that the private interest of every individual may be a sentinel over the public rights. These inventions of prudence cannot be less requisite in the distribution of the supreme powers of the State.

But it is not possible to give to each department an equal power of self-defense. In republican government, the legislative authority necessarily predominates. The remedy for this inconveniency is to divide the legislature into different branches; and to render them, by different modes of election and different principles of action, as little connected with each other as the nature of their common functions and their common dependence on the society will admit. It may even be necessary to guard against dangerous encroachments by still further precautions. As the weight of the legislative authority requires that it should be thus divided, the weakness of the executive may require, on the other hand, that it should be fortified. An absolute negative on the legislature appears, at first view, to be the natural defense with which the executive magistrate should be armed. But perhaps it would be neither altogether safe nor alone sufficient. On ordinary occasions it might not be exerted with the requisite firmness, and on extraordinary occasions it might be perfidiously abused. May not this defect of an absolute negative be supplied by some qualified connection between this weaker department and the weaker branch of the stronger department, by which the latter may be led to support the constitutional rights of the former, without being too much detached from the rights of its own department?

If the principles on which these observations are founded be just, as I persuade myself they are, and they be applied as a criterion to the several State constitutions, and to the federal Constitution it will be found that if the latter does not perfectly correspond with them, the former are infinitely less able to bear such a test.

There are, moreover, two considerations particularly applicable to the federal system of America, which place that system in a very interesting point of view.

First. In a single republic, all the power surrendered by the people is submitted to the administration of a single government; and the usurpations are guarded against by a division of the government into distinct and separate departments. In the compound republic of America, the power surrendered by the people is first divided between two distinct governments, and then the portion allotted to each subdivided among distinct and separate departments. Hence a double security arises to the rights of the people. The different governments will control each other, at the same time that each will be controlled by itself.

Second. It is of great importance in a republic not only to guard the society against the oppression of its rulers, but to guard one part of the society against the injustice of the other part. Different interests necessarily exist in different classes of citizens. If a majority be united by a common interest, the rights of the minority will be insecure. There are but two methods of providing against this evil: the one by creating a will in the community independent of the majority that is, of the society itself; the other, by comprehending in the society so many separate descriptions of citizens as will render an unjust combination of a majority of the whole very improbable, if not impracticable. The first method prevails in all governments possessing an hereditary or self-appointed authority. This, at best, is but a precarious security; because a power independent of the society may as well espouse the unjust views of the major, as the rightful interests of the minor party, and may possibly be turned against both parties. The second method will be exemplified in the federal republic of the United States. Whilst all authority in it will be derived from and dependent on the society, the society itself will be broken into so many parts, interests, and classes of citizens, that the rights of individuals, or of the minority, will be in little danger from interested combinations of the majority. In a free government the security for civil rights must be the same as that for religious rights. It consists in the one case in the multiplicity of interests, and in the other in the multiplicity of sects. The degree of security in both cases will depend on the number of interests and sects; and this may be presumed to depend on the extent of country and number of people comprehended under the same government. This view of the subject must particularly recommend a proper federal system to all the sincere and considerate friends of republican government, since it shows that in exact proportion as the territory of the Union may be formed into more circumscribed Confederacies, or States oppressive combinations of a majority will be facilitated: the best security, under the republican forms, for the rights of every class of citizens, will be diminished: and consequently the stability and independence of some member of the government, the only other security, must be proportionately increased. Justice is the end of government. It is the end of civil society. It ever has been and ever will be pursued until it be obtained, or until liberty be lost in the pursuit. In a society under the forms of which the stronger faction can readily unite and oppress the weaker, anarchy may as truly be said to reign as in a state of nature, where the weaker individual is not secured against the violence of the stronger; and as, in the latter state, even the stronger individuals are prompted, by the uncertainty of their condition, to submit to a government which may protect the weak as well as themselves; so, in the former state, will the more powerful factions or parties be gradnally induced, by a like motive, to wish for a government which will protect all parties, the weaker as well as the more powerful. It can be little doubted that if the State of Rhode Island was separated from the Confederacy and left to itself, the insecurity of rights under the popular form of government within such narrow limits would be displayed by such reiterated oppressions of factious majorities that some power altogether independent of the people would soon be called for by the voice of the very factions whose misrule had proved the necessity of it. In the extended republic of the United States, and among the great variety of interests, parties, and sects which it embraces, a coalition of a majority of the whole society could seldom take place on any other principles than those of justice and the general good; whilst there being thus less danger to a minor from the will of a major party, there must be less pretext, also, to provide for the security of the former, by introducing into the government a will not dependent on the latter, or, in other words, a will independent of the society itself. It is no less certain than it is important, notwithstanding the contrary opinions which have been entertained, that the larger the society, provided it lie within a practical sphere, the more duly capable it will be of self-government. And happily for the REPUBLICAN CAUSE, the practicable sphere may be carried to a very great extent, by a judicious modification and mixture of the FEDERAL PRINCIPLE.

PUBLIUS.

⚚

Phillis Wheatley
Liberty and Peace

LO! Freedom comes. Th' prescient Muse foretold,
 All Eyes th' accomplish'd Prophecy behold:
Her Port describ'd, "*She moves divinely fair,*
"*Olive and Laurel bind her golden Hair.*"
She, the bright Progeny of Heaven, descends,
And every Grace her sovereign Step attends;
For now kind Heaven, indulgent to our Prayer,
In smiling *Peace* resolves the Din of *War*.

Fix'd in *Columbia*[1] her illustrious Line,
And bids in thee her future Councils shine.
To every Realm her Portals open'd wide,
Receives from each the full commercial Tide.
Each Art and Science now with rising Charms
Th' expanding Heart with Emulation warms.
E'en great *Britannia* sees with dread Surprize,
And from the dazzling Splendor turns her Eyes!
Britain, whose Navies swept th' *Atlantic* o'er,
And Thunder sent to every distant Shore;
E'en thou, in Manners cruel as thou art,
The Sword resign'd, resume the friendly Part!
For *Galia's*[2] Power espous'd *Columbia's* Cause,
And new-born *Rome* shall give *Britannia* Law,
Nor unremember'd in the grateful Strain,
Shall princely *Louis'* friendly Deeds remain;
The generous Prince th' impending Vengeance eye's,
Sees the fierce Wrong, and to the rescue flies.
Perish that Thirst of boundless Power, that drew
On *Albion's* Head the Curse to Tyrants due.
But thou appeas'd submit to Heaven's decree,
That bids this Realm of Freedom rival thee!
Now sheathe the Sword that bade the Brave attone
With guiltless Blood for Madness not their own.
Sent from th' Enjoyment of their native Shore
Ill-fated – never to behold her more!
From every Kingdom on *Europa's* Coast
Throng'd various Troops, their Glory, Strength and Boast.
With heart-felt pity fair *Hibernia*[3] saw
Columbia menac'd by the Tyrant's Law:
On hostile Fields fraternal Arms engage,
And mutual Deaths, all dealt with mutual Rage:
The Muse's Ear hears mother Earth deplore
Her ample Surface smoak with kindred Gore:
The hostile Field destroys the social Ties,
And every-lasting Slumber seals their Eyes.

---

[1] A common personification of America.
[2] France
[3] Ireland

Columbia mourns, the haughty Foes deride,
Her Treasures plunder'd, and her Towns destroy'd:
Witness how *Charlestown's* curling Smoaks arise,
In sable Columns to the clouded Skies!
The ample Dome, high-wrought with curious Toil,
In one sad Hour the savage Troops despoil.
Descending *Peace* and Power of War confounds;
From every Tongue celestial *Peace* resounds:
As for the East th' illustrious King of Day,
With rising Radiance drives the Shades away,
So Freedom comes array'd with Charms divine,
And in her Train Commerce and Plenty shine.
Britannia owns her Independent Reign,
Hibernia, Scotia, and the Realms of *Spain;*
And great *Germania's* ample Coast admires
The generous Spirit that *Columbia* fires.
Auspicious Heaven shall fill with fav'ring Gales,
Where e'er *Columbia* spreads her swelling Sails:
To every Realm shall *Peace* her Charms display,
And Heavenly *Freedom* spread her golden Ray.

Alexis de Tocqueville
from Democracy in America
Translated by Henry Reeve[1]

Volume II

Section 1
Chapter V
Of The Manner In Which Religion In The United States Avails Itself Of Democratic Tendencies

I have laid it down in a preceding chapter that men cannot do without dogmatical belief; and even that it is very much to be desired that such belief should exist amongst them. I now add, that of all the kinds of dogmatical belief the most desirable appears to me to be dogmatical belief in matters of religion; and this is a very clear inference, even from no higher

---

[1] Notes on this text are taken from Reeve's translation.

consideration than the interests of this world. There is hardly any human action, however particular a character be assigned to it, which does not originate in some very general idea men have conceived of the Deity, of his relation to mankind, of the nature of their own souls, and of their duties to their fellow-creatures. Nor can anything prevent these ideas from being the common spring from which everything else emanates. Men are therefore immeasurably interested in acquiring fixed ideas of God, of the soul, and of their common duties to their Creator and to their fellow-men; for doubt on these first principles would abandon all their actions to the impulse of chance, and would condemn them to live, to a certain extent, powerless and undisciplined.

This is then the subject on which it is most important for each of us to entertain fixed ideas; and unhappily it is also the subject on which it is most difficult for each of us, left to himself, to settle his opinions by the sole force of his reason. None but minds singularly free from the ordinary anxieties of life—minds at once penetrating, subtle, and trained by thinking—can even with the assistance of much time and care, sound the depth of these most necessary truths. And, indeed, we see that these philosophers are themselves almost always enshrouded in uncertainties; that at every step the natural light which illuminates their path grows dimmer and less secure; and that, in spite of all their efforts, they have as yet only discovered a small number of conflicting notions, on which the mind of man has been tossed about for thousands of years, without either laying a firmer grasp on truth, or finding novelty even in its errors. Studies of this nature are far above the average capacity of men; and even if the majority of mankind were capable of such pursuits, it is evident that leisure to cultivate them would still be wanting. Fixed ideas of God and human nature are indispensable to the daily practice of men's lives; but the practice of their lives prevents them from acquiring such ideas.

The difficulty appears to me to be without a parallel. Amongst the sciences there are some which are useful to the mass of mankind, and which are within its reach; others can only be approached by the few, and are not cultivated by the many, who require nothing beyond their more remote applications: but the daily practice of the science I speak of is indispensable to all, although the study of it is inaccessible to the far greater number.

General ideas respecting God and human nature are therefore the ideas above all others which it is most suitable to withdraw from the habitual action of private judgment, and in which there is most to gain and least to lose by recognizing a principle of authority. The first object and one of the principal advantages of religions, is to furnish to each of these fundamental questions a solution which is at once clear, precise, intelligible to the mass of mankind, and lasting. There are religions which are very false and very absurd; but it may be affirmed, that any religion which remains within the circle I have just traced, without aspiring to go beyond it (as many religions have attempted to do, for the purpose of enclosing on every side the free progress of the human mind), imposes a salutary restraint on the intellect; and it must be admitted that, if it do not save men in another world, such religion is at least very conducive to their happiness and their greatness in this. This is more especially true of men living in free countries. When the religion of a people is destroyed, doubt gets hold of the highest portions of the intellect, and half paralyzes all the rest of its powers. Every man accustoms himself to entertain none but confused and changing notions on the subjects most interesting to his fellow-creatures and himself. His opinions are ill-defended and easily abandoned: and, despairing of ever resolving by himself the hardest problems of the destiny of man, he ignobly submits to think no more about them. Such a condition cannot but enervate the soul, relax the springs of the will, and prepare a people for servitude. Nor does it only happen, in such a case, that they allow their freedom to be wrested from them; they frequently themselves surrender it. When there is no longer any principle of authority in religion any more than in politics, men are speedily frightened at the aspect of this unbounded independence. The constant agitation of all surrounding things alarms and exhausts them. As everything is at sea in the sphere of the intellect, they determine at least that the mechanism of society should be firm and fixed; and as they cannot resume their ancient belief, they assume a master.

For my own part, I doubt whether man can ever support at the same time complete religious independence and entire public freedom. And I am inclined to think, that if faith be wanting in him, he must serve; and if he be free, he must believe.

Perhaps, however, this great utility of religions is still more obvious amongst nations where equality of conditions prevails than amongst others. It must be acknowledged that equality, which brings great benefits into the world, nevertheless suggests to men (as will be shown hereafter) some very dangerous propensities. It tends to isolate them from each other, to concentrate every man's attention upon himself; and it lays open the soul to an inordinate love of material gratification. The greatest advantage of religion is to inspire diametrically contrary principles. There is no religion which does not place the object of man's desires above and beyond the treasures of earth, and which does not naturally raise his soul to regions far above those of the senses. Nor is there any which does not impose on man some sort of duties to his kind, and thus draws him at times from the contemplation of himself. This occurs in religions the most false and dangerous. Religious nations are therefore naturally strong on the very point on which democratic nations are weak; which shows of what importance it is for men to preserve their religion as their conditions become more equal.

I have neither the right nor the intention of examining the supernatural means which God employs to infuse religious belief into the heart of man. I am at this moment considering religions in a purely human point of view: my object is to inquire by what means they may most easily retain their sway in the democratic ages upon which we are entering. It has been shown that, at times of general cultivation and equality, the human mind does not consent to adopt dogmatical opinions without reluctance, and feels their necessity acutely in spiritual matters only. This proves, in the first place, that at such times religions ought, more cautiously than at any other, to confine themselves within their own precincts; for in seeking to extend their power beyond religious matters, they incur a risk of not being believed at all.

The circle within which they seek to bound the human intellect ought therefore to be carefully traced, and beyond its verge the mind should be left in entire freedom to its own guidance. Mahommed professed to derive from Heaven, and he has inserted in the Koran, not only a body of religious doctrines, but political maxims, civil and criminal laws, and theories of science. The gospel, on the contrary, only speaks of the general relations of men to God and to each other—beyond which it inculcates and imposes no point of faith. This alone, besides a thousand other reasons, would suffice to prove that the former of these religions will never long predominate in a cultivated and democratic age, whilst the latter is destined to retain its sway at these as at all other periods.

But in continuation of this branch of the subject, I find that in order for religions to maintain their authority, humanly speaking, in democratic ages, they must not only confine themselves strictly within the circle of spiritual matters: their power also depends very much on the nature of the belief they inculcate, on the external forms they assume, and on the obligations they impose. The preceding observation, that equality leads men to very general and very extensive notions, is principally to be understood as applied to the question of religion. Men living in a similar and equal condition in the world readily conceive the idea of the one God, governing every man by the same laws, and granting to every man future happiness on the same conditions. The idea of the unity of mankind constantly leads them back to the idea of the unity of the Creator; whilst, on the contrary, in a state of society where men are broken up into very unequal ranks, they are apt to devise as many deities as there are nations, castes, classes, or families, and to trace a thousand private roads to heaven.

It cannot be denied that Christianity itself has felt, to a certain extent, the influence which social and political conditions exercise on religious opinions. At the epoch at which the Christian religion appeared upon earth, Providence, by whom the world was doubtless prepared for its coming, had gathered a large portion of the human race, like an immense flock, under the sceptre of the Caesars. The men of whom this multitude was composed were distinguished by numerous differences; but they had thus much in common, that they all obeyed the same laws, and that every subject was so weak and insignificant in relation to the imperial potentate, that all appeared equal when their condition was contrasted with his. This novel and peculiar state of mankind necessarily predisposed men to listen to the general truths which Christianity teaches, and may serve to explain the facility and rapidity with which they then penetrated into the human mind. The counterpart of this state of things was exhibited after the destruction of the empire. The Roman world being then as it were shattered into a thousand fragments, each nation resumed its pristine individuality. An infinite scale of ranks very soon grew up in the bosom of these nations; the different races were more sharply defined, and each nation was divided by castes into several peoples. In the midst of this common effort, which seemed to be urging human society to the greatest conceivable amount of voluntary subdivision, Christianity did not lose sight of the leading general ideas which it had brought into the world. But it appeared, nevertheless, to lend itself, as much as was possible, to those new tendencies to which the fractional distribution of mankind had given birth. Men continued to worship an only God, the Creator and Preserver of all things; but every people, every city, and, so to speak, every man, thought to obtain some distinct privilege, and win the favor of an especial patron at the foot of the Throne of Grace. Unable to subdivide the Deity, they multiplied and improperly enhanced the importance of the divine agents. The homage due to saints and angels became an almost idolatrous worship amongst the majority of the Christian world; and apprehensions might be entertained for a moment lest the religion of Christ should retrograde towards the superstitions which it had subdued. It seems evident, that the more the barriers are removed which separate nation from nation amongst mankind, and citizen from citizen amongst a people, the stronger is the bent of the human mind, as if by its own impulse, towards the idea of an only and all-powerful Being, dispensing equal laws in the same manner to every man. In democratic ages, then, it is more particularly important not to allow the homage paid to secondary agents to be confounded with the worship due to the Creator alone.

Another truth is no less clear—that religions ought to assume fewer external observances in democratic periods than at any others. In speaking of philosophical method among the Americans, I have shown that nothing is more repugnant to the human mind in an age of equality than the idea of subjection to forms. Men living at such times are impatient of figures; to their eyes symbols appear to be the puerile artifice which is used to conceal or to set off truths, which should more naturally be bared to the light of open day: they are unmoved by ceremonial observances, and they are predisposed to attach a secondary importance to the details of public worship. Those whose care it is to regulate the external forms of religion in a democratic age should pay a close attention to these natural propensities of the human mind, in order not unnecessarily to run counter to them. I firmly believe in the necessity of forms, which fix the human mind in the contemplation of abstract truths, and stimulate its ardor in the pursuit of them, whilst they invigorate its powers of retaining them steadfastly. Nor do I suppose that it is possible to maintain a religion without external observances; but, on the other hand, I am persuaded that, in the ages upon which we are entering, it would be peculiarly dangerous to multiply them beyond measure; and that they ought rather to be limited to as much as is absolutely necessary to perpetuate the doctrine itself, which is the substance of religions of which the ritual is only the form.[1] A religion which should become more minute, more peremptory, and more surcharged with small observances at a time in which men are becoming more equal, would soon find itself reduced to a band of fanatical zealots in the midst of an infidel people.

I anticipate the objection, that as all religions have general and eternal truths for their object, they cannot thus shape themselves to the shifting spirit of every age without forfeiting their claim to certainty in the eyes of mankind. To this I reply again, that the principal

---

[1] In all religions there are some ceremonies which are inherent in the substance of the faith itself, and in these nothing should, on any account, be changed. This is especially the case with Roman Catholicism, in which the doctrine and the form are frequently so closely united as to form one point of belief.

opinions which constitute belief, and which theologians call articles of faith, must be very carefully distinguished from the accessories connected with them. Religions are obliged to hold fast to the former, whatever be the peculiar spirit of the age; but they should take good care not to bind themselves in the same manner to the latter at a time when everything is in transition, and when the mind, accustomed to the moving pageant of human affairs, reluctantly endures the attempt to fix it to any given point. The fixity of external and secondary things can only afford a chance of duration when civil society is itself fixed; under any other circumstances I hold it to be perilous.

We shall have occasion to see that, of all the passions which originate in, or are fostered by, equality, there is one which it renders peculiarly intense, and which it infuses at the same time into the heart of every man: I mean the love of well-being. The taste for well-being is the prominent and indelible feature of democratic ages. It may be believed that a religion which should undertake to destroy so deep seated a passion, would meet its own destruction thence in the end; and if it attempted to wean men entirely from the contemplation of the good things of this world, in order to devote their faculties exclusively to the thought of another, it may be foreseen that the soul would at length escape from its grasp, to plunge into the exclusive enjoyment of present and material pleasures. The chief concern of religions is to purify, to regulate, and to restrain the excessive and exclusive taste for well-being which men feel at periods of equality; but they would err in attempting to control it completely or to eradicate it. They will not succeed in curing men of the love of riches: but they may still persuade men to enrich themselves by none but honest means.

This brings me to a final consideration, which comprises, as it were, all the others. The more the conditions of men are equalized and assimilated to each other, the more important is it for religions, whilst they carefully abstain from the daily turmoil of secular affairs, not needlessly to run counter to the ideas which generally prevail, and the permanent interests which exist in the mass of the people. For as public opinion grows to be more and more evidently the first and most irresistible of existing powers, the religious principle has no external support strong enough to enable it long to resist its attacks. This is not less true of a democratic people, ruled by a despot, than in a republic. In ages of equality, kings may often command obedience, but the majority always commands belief: to the majority, therefore, deference is to be paid in whatsoever is not contrary to the faith.

I showed in my former volumes how the American clergy stand aloof from secular affairs. This is the most obvious, but it is not the only, example of their self-restraint. In America religion is a distinct sphere, in which the priest is sovereign, but out of which he takes care never to go. Within its limits he is the master of the mind; beyond them, he leaves men to themselves, and surrenders them to the independence and instability which belong to their nature and their age. I have seen no country in which Christianity is clothed with fewer forms, figures, and observances than in the United States; or where it presents more distinct, more simple, or more general notions to the mind. Although the Christians of America are divided into a multitude of sects, they all look upon their religion in the same light. This applies to Roman Catholicism as well as to the other forms of belief. There are no Romish priests who show less taste for the minute individual observances for extraordinary or peculiar means of salvation, or who cling more to the spirit, and less to the letter of the law, than the Roman Catholic priests of the United States. Nowhere is that doctrine of the Church, which prohibits the worship reserved to God alone from being offered to the saints, more clearly inculcated or more generally followed. Yet the Roman Catholics of America are very submissive and very sincere.

Another remark is applicable to the clergy of every communion. The American ministers of the gospel do not attempt to draw or to fix all the thoughts of man upon the life to come; they are willing to surrender a portion of his heart to the cares of the present; seeming to consider the goods of this world as important, although as secondary, objects. If they take no part themselves in productive labor, they are at least interested in its progression, and ready to applaud its results; and whilst they never cease to point to the other world as the great object of the hopes and fears of the believer, they do not forbid him honestly to court prosperity in this. Far from attempting to show that these things are distinct and contrary to one another, they study rather to find out on what point they are most nearly and closely connected.

All the American clergy know and respect the intellectual supremacy exercised by the majority; they never sustain any but necessary conflicts with it. They take no share in the altercations of parties, but they readily adopt the general opinions of their country and their age; and they allow themselves to be borne away without opposition in the current of feeling and opinion by which everything around them is carried along. They endeavor to amend their contemporaries, but they do not quit fellowship with them. Public opinion is therefore never hostile to them; it rather supports and protects them; and their belief owes its authority at the same time to the strength which is its own, and to that which they borrow from the opinions of the majority. Thus it is that, by respecting all democratic tendencies not absolutely contrary to herself, and by making use of several of them for her own purposes, religion sustains an advantageous struggle with that spirit of individual independence which is her most dangerous antagonist.

Chapter VI
Of The Progress Of Roman Catholicism In The United States

America is the most democratic country in the world, and it is at the same time (according to reports worthy of belief) the country in which the Roman Catholic religion makes most progress. At first sight this is surprising. Two things must here be accurately distinguished: equality inclines men to wish to form their own opinions; but, on the other hand, it imbues them with the taste and the idea of unity, simplicity, and impartiality in the power which governs society. Men living in democratic ages are therefore very prone to shake off all religious authority; but if they consent to subject themselves to any authority of this kind, they choose at least that it should be single and uniform. Religious powers not radiating from a common centre are naturally repugnant to their minds; and they almost as readily conceive that there should be no religion, as that there should be several. At the present time, more than in any preceding one, Roman Catholics are seen to lapse into infidelity, and Protestants to be converted to Roman Catholicism. If the Roman Catholic faith be considered within the pale of the church, it would seem to be losing ground; without that pale, to be gaining it. Nor is this circumstance difficult of explanation. The men of our days are naturally disposed to believe; but, as soon as they have any religion, they immediately find in themselves a latent propensity which urges them unconsciously towards Catholicism. Many of the doctrines and the practices of the Romish Church astonish them; but they feel a secret admiration for its discipline, and its great unity attracts them. If Catholicism could at length withdraw itself from the political animosities to which it has given rise, I have hardly any doubt but that the same spirit of the age, which appears to be so opposed to it, would become so favorable as to admit of its great and sudden advancement. One of the most ordinary weaknesses of the human intellect is to seek to reconcile contrary principles, and to purchase peace at the expense of logic. Thus there have ever been, and will ever be, men who, after having submitted some portion of their religious belief to the principle of authority, will seek to exempt several other parts of their faith from its influence, and to keep their minds floating at random between liberty and obedience. But I am inclined to believe that the number of these thinkers will be less in democratic than in other ages; and that our posterity will tend more and more to a single division into two parts—some relinquishing Christianity entirely, and others returning to the bosom of the Church of Rome.

Chapter VII
Of The Cause Of A Leaning To Pantheism Amongst Democratic Nations

I shall take occasion hereafter to show under what form the preponderating taste of a democratic people for very general ideas manifests itself in politics; but I would point out, at the present stage of my work, its principal effect on philosophy. It cannot be denied that pantheism has made great progress in our age. The writings of a part of Europe bear visible marks of it: the Germans introduce it into philosophy, and the French into literature. Most of the works of imagination published in France contain some opinions or some tinge caught from pantheistical doctrines, or they disclose some tendency to such doctrines in their authors. This appears to me not only to proceed from an accidental, but from a permanent cause. When the conditions of society are becoming more equal, and each individual man becomes more like all the rest, more weak and more insignificant, a habit grows up of ceasing to notice the citizens to consider only the people, and of overlooking individuals to think only of their kind. At such times the human mind seeks to embrace a multitude of different objects at once; and it constantly strives to succeed in connecting a variety of consequences with a single cause. The idea of unity so possesses itself of man, and is sought for by him so universally, that if he thinks he has found it, he readily yields himself up to repose in that belief. Nor does he content himself with the discovery that nothing is in the world but a creation and a Creator; still embarrassed by this primary division of things, he seeks to expand and to simplify his conception by including God and the universe in one great whole. If there be a philosophical system which teaches that all things material and immaterial, visible and invisible, which the world contains, are only to be considered as the several parts of an immense Being, which alone remains unchanged amidst the continual change and ceaseless transformation of all that constitutes it, we may readily infer that such a system, although it destroy the individuality of man—nay, rather because it destroys that individuality—will have secret charms for men living in democracies. All their habits of thought prepare them to conceive it, and predispose them to adopt it. It naturally attracts and fixes their imagination; it fosters the pride, whilst it soothes the indolence, of their minds. Amongst the different systems by whose aid philosophy endeavors to explain the universe, I believe pantheism to be one of those most fitted to seduce the human mind in democratic ages. Against it all who abide in their attachment to the true greatness of man should struggle and combine.

Section 2
Chapter XV
That Religious Belief Sometimes Turns The Thoughts Of The Americans To Immaterial Pleasures

In the United States, on the seventh day of every week, the trading and working life of the nation seems suspended; all noises cease; a deep tranquillity, say rather the solemn calm of meditation, succeeds the turmoil of the week, and the soul resumes possession and contemplation of itself. Upon this day the marts of traffic are deserted; every member of the community, accompanied by his children, goes to church, where he listens to strange language which would seem unsuited to his ear. He is told of the countless evils caused by pride and covetousness: he is reminded of the necessity of checking his desires, of the finer pleasures which belong to virtue alone, and of the true happiness which attends it. On his return home, he does not turn to the ledgers of his calling, but he opens the book of Holy Scripture; there he meets with sublime or affecting descriptions of the greatness and goodness of the Creator, of the infinite magnificence of the handiwork of God, of the lofty destinies of man, of his duties, and of his immortal privileges. Thus it is that the American at times steals an hour from himself; and laying aside for a while the petty passions which agitate his life, and the ephemeral interests which engross it, he strays at once into an ideal world, where all is great, eternal, and pure.

I have endeavored to point out in another part of this work the causes to which the maintenance of the political institutions of the Americans is attributable; and religion appeared to be one of the most prominent amongst them. I am now treating of the Americans in an individual capacity, and I again observe that religion is not less useful to each citizen than to the whole State. The Americans show, by their practice, that they feel the high necessity of imparting morality to democratic communities by means of religion. What they think of themselves in this respect is a truth of which every democratic nation ought to be thoroughly persuaded.

I do not doubt that the social and political constitution of a people predisposes them to adopt a certain belief and certain tastes, which afterwards flourish without difficulty amongst them; whilst the same causes may divert a people from certain opinions and propensities, without any voluntary effort, and, as it were, without any distinct consciousness, on their part. The whole art of the legislator is correctly to discern beforehand these natural inclinations of communities of men, in order to know whether they should be assisted, or whether it may not be necessary to check them. For the duties incumbent on the legislator differ at different times; the goal towards which the human race ought ever to be tending is alone stationary; the means of reaching it are perpetually to be varied.

If I had been born in an aristocratic age, in the midst of a nation where the hereditary wealth of some, and the irremediable penury of others, should equally divert men from the idea of bettering their condition, and hold the soul as it were in a state of torpor fixed on the contemplation of another world, I should then wish that it were possible for me to rouse that people to a sense of their wants; I should seek to discover more rapid and more easy means for satisfying the fresh desires which I might have awakened; and, directing the most strenuous efforts of the human mind to physical pursuits, I should endeavor to stimulate it to promote the well-being of man. If it happened that some men were immoderately incited to the pursuit of riches, and displayed an excessive liking for physical gratifications, I should not be alarmed; these peculiar symptoms would soon be absorbed in the general aspect of the people.

The attention of the legislators of democracies is called to other cares. Give democratic nations education and freedom, and leave them alone. They will soon learn to draw from this world all the benefits which it can afford; they will improve each of the useful arts, and will day by day render life more comfortable, more convenient, and more easy. Their social condition naturally urges them in this direction; I do not fear that they will slacken their course.

But whilst man takes delight in this honest and lawful pursuit of his wellbeing, it is to be apprehended that he may in the end lose the use of his sublimest faculties; and that whilst he is busied in improving all around him, he may at length degrade himself. Here, and here only, does the peril lie. It should therefore be the unceasing object of the legislators of democracies, and of all the virtuous and enlightened men who live there, to raise the souls of their fellow-citizens, and keep them lifted up towards heaven. It is necessary that all who feel an interest in the future destinies of democratic society should unite, and that all should make joint and continual efforts to diffuse the love of the infinite, a sense of greatness, and a love of pleasures not of earth. If amongst the opinions of a democratic people any of those pernicious theories exist which tend to inculcate that all perishes with the body, let men by whom such theories are professed be marked as the natural foes of such a people.

The materialists are offensive to me in many respects; their doctrines I hold to be pernicious, and I am disgusted at their arrogance. If their system could be of any utility to man, it would seem to be by giving him a modest opinion of himself. But these reasoners show that it is not so; and when they think they have said enough to establish that they are brutes, they show themselves as proud as if they had demonstrated that they are gods. Materialism is, amongst all nations, a dangerous disease of the human mind; but it is more especially to be dreaded amongst a democratic people, because it readily amalgamates with that vice which is most familiar to the heart under such circumstances. Democracy encourages a taste for physical gratification: this taste, if it become excessive, soon disposes men to believe that all is matter only; and materialism, in turn, hurries them back with mad impatience to these same delights: such is the fatal circle within which democratic nations are driven round. It were well that they should see the danger and hold back.

Most religions are only general, simple, and practical means of teaching men the doctrine of the immortality of the soul. That is the greatest benefit which a democratic people derives, from its belief, and hence belief is more necessary to such a people than to all others. When therefore any religion has struck its roots deep into a democracy, beware lest you disturb them; but rather watch it carefully, as the most precious bequest of aristocratic ages. Seek not to supersede the old religious opinions of men by new ones; lest in the passage from one faith to another, the soul being left for a while stripped of all belief, the love of physical gratifications should grow upon it and fill it wholly.

The doctrine of metempsychosis is assuredly not more rational than that of materialism; nevertheless if it were absolutely necessary that a democracy should choose one of the two, I should not hesitate to decide that the community would run less risk of being brutalized by believing that the soul of man will pass into the carcass of a hog, than by believing that the soul of man is nothing at all. The belief in a supersensual and immortal principle, united for a time to matter, is so indispensable to man's greatness, that its effects are striking even when it is not united to the doctrine of future reward and punishment; and when it holds no more than that after death the divine principle contained in man is absorbed in the Deity, or transferred to animate the frame of some other creature. Men holding so imperfect a belief will still consider the body as the secondary and inferior portion of their nature, and they will despise it even whilst they yield to its influence; whereas they have a natural esteem and secret admiration for the immaterial part of man, even though they sometimes refuse to submit to its dominion. That is enough to give a lofty cast to their opinions and their tastes, and to bid them tend with no interested motive, and as it were by impulse, to pure feelings and elevated thoughts.

It is not certain that Socrates and his followers had very fixed opinions as to what would befall man hereafter; but the sole point of belief on which they were determined—that the soul has nothing in common with the body, and survives it—was enough to give the

Platonic philosophy that sublime aspiration by which it is distinguished. It is clear from the works of Plato, that many philosophical writers, his predecessors or contemporaries, professed materialism. These writers have not reached us, or have reached us in mere fragments. The same thing has happened in almost all ages; the greater part of the most famous minds in literature adhere to the doctrines of a supersensual philosophy. The instinct and the taste of the human race maintain those doctrines; they save them oftentimes in spite of men themselves, and raise the names of their defenders above the tide of time. It must not then be supposed that at any period or under any political condition, the passion for physical gratifications, and the opinions which are superinduced by that passion, can ever content a whole people. The heart of man is of a larger mould: it can at once comprise a taste for the possessions of earth and the love of those of heaven: at times it may seem to cling devotedly to the one, but it will never be long without thinking of the other.

If it be easy to see that it is more particularly important in democratic ages that spiritual opinions should prevail, it is not easy to say by what means those who govern democratic nations may make them predominate. I am no believer in the prosperity, any more than in the durability, of official philosophies; and as to state religions, I have always held, that if they be sometimes of momentary service to the interests of political power, they always, sooner or later, become fatal to the Church. Nor do I think with those who assert, that to raise religion in the eyes of the people, and to make them do honor to her spiritual doctrines, it is desirable indirectly to give her ministers a political influence which the laws deny them. I am so much alive to the almost inevitable dangers which beset religious belief whenever the clergy take part in public affairs, and I am so convinced that Christianity must be maintained at any cost in the bosom of modern democracies, that I had rather shut up the priesthood within the sanctuary than allow them to step beyond it.

What means then remain in the hands of constituted authorities to bring men back to spiritual opinions, or to hold them fast to the religion by which those opinions are suggested? My answer will do me harm in the eyes of politicians. I believe that the sole effectual means which governments can employ in order to have the doctrine of the immortality of the soul duly respected, is ever to act as if they believed in it themselves; and I think that it is only by scrupulous conformity to religious morality in great affairs that they can hope to teach the community at large to know, to love, and to observe it in the lesser concerns of life.

❧❧

G. K. Chesterton
from What I Saw in America

Chapter 1
What is America?

I have never managed to lose my old conviction that travel narrows the mind. At least a man must make a double effort of moral humility and imaginative energy to prevent it from narrowing his mind. Indeed there is something touching and even tragic about the thought of the thoughtless tourist, who might have stayed at home loving Laplanders, embracing Chinamen, and clasping Patagonians to his heart in Hampstead or Surbiton, but for his blind and suicidal impulse to go and see what they looked like. This is not meant for nonsense; still less is it meant for the silliest sort of nonsense, which is cynicism. The human bond that he feels at home is not an illusion. On the contrary, it is rather an inner reality. Man is inside all men. In a real sense any man may be inside any men. But to travel is to leave the inside and draw dangerously near the outside. So long as he thought of men in the abstract, like naked toiling figures in some classic frieze, merely as those who labour and love their children and die, he was thinking the fundamental truth about them. By going to look at their unfamiliar manners and customs he is inviting them to disguise themselves in fantastic masks and costumes. Many modern internationalists talk as if men of different nationalities had only to meet and mix and understand each other. In reality that is the moment of supreme danger—the moment when they meet. We might shiver, as at the old euphemism by which a meeting meant a duel.

Travel ought to combine amusement with instruction; but most travellers are so much amused that they refuse to be instructed. I do not blame them for being amused; it is perfectly natural to be amused at a Dutchman for being Dutch or a Chinaman for being Chinese. Where they are wrong is that they take their own amusement seriously. They base on it their serious ideas of international instruction. It was said that the Englishman takes his pleasures sadly; and the pleasure of despising foreigners is one which he takes most sadly of all. He comes to scoff and does not remain to pray, but rather to excommunicate. Hence in international relations there is far too little laughing, and far too much sneering. But I believe that there is a better way which largely consists of laughter; a form of friendship between nations which is actually founded on differences. To hint at some such better way is the only excuse of this book.

Let me begin my American impressions with two impressions I had before I went to America. One was an incident and the other an idea; and when taken together they illustrate the attitude I mean. The first principle is that nobody should be ashamed of thinking a thing funny because it is foreign; the second is that he should be ashamed of thinking it wrong because it is funny. The reaction of his senses and superficial habits of mind against something new, and to him abnormal, is a perfectly healthy reaction. But the mind which imagines that mere unfamiliarity can possibly prove anything about inferiority is a very inadequate mind. It is inadequate even in criticising things that may really be inferior to the things involved here. It is far better to laugh at a negro for having a black face than to sneer at him for having a sloping skull. It is proportionally even more preferable to laugh rather than judge in dealing with highly civilised peoples. Therefore I put at the beginning two working examples of what I felt about America before I saw it; the sort of thing that a man has a right to enjoy as a joke, and the sort of thing he has a duty to understand and respect, because it is the explanation of the joke.

When I went to the American consulate to regularise my passports, I was capable of expecting the American consulate to be American. Embassies and consulates are by tradition like islands of the soil for which they stand; and I have often found the tradition corresponding to a truth. I have seen the unmistakable French official living on omelettes and a little wine and serving his sacred abstractions under the last palm-trees fringing a desert. In the heat and noise of quarrelling Turks and Egyptians, I have come suddenly, as with the cool shock of his own shower-bath, on the listless amiability of the English gentleman. The officials I interviewed were very American, especially in being very polite; for whatever may have been the mood or meaning of Martin Chuzzlewit,[1] I have always found Americans by far the politest people in the world. They put in my hands a form to be filled up, to all appearance like other forms I had filled up in other passport offices. But in reality it was very different from any form I had ever filled up in my life. At least it was a little like a freer form of the game called 'Confessions' which my friends and I invented in our youth; an examination paper containing questions like, 'If you saw a rhinoceros in the front garden, what would you do?' One of my friends, I remember, wrote, 'Take the pledge.' But that is another story, and might bring Mr. Pussyfoot Johnson on the scene before his time.

One of the questions on the paper was, 'Are you an anarchist?' To which a detached philosopher would naturally feel inclined to answer, 'What the devil has that to do with you? Are you an atheist?' along with some playful efforts to cross-examine the official about what constitutes an ἀρχη.[2] Then there was the question, 'Are you in favour of subverting the government of the United States by force?' Against this I should write, 'I prefer to answer that question at the end of my tour and not the beginning.' The inquisitor, in his more than morbid curiosity, had then written down, 'Are you a polygamist?' The answer to this is, 'No such luck' or 'Not such a fool,' according to our experience of the other sex. But perhaps a better answer would be that given to W. T. Stead when he circulated the rhetorical question,

---

[1] Main character of a novel by Charles Dickens, which was hugely controversial due to its disparaging portrayal of Americans.

[2] *archê*: rule or government

'Shall I slay my brother Boer?'—the answer that ran, 'Never interfere in family matters.' But among many things that amused me almost to the point of treating the form thus disrespectfully, the most amusing was the thought of the ruthless outlaw who should feel compelled to treat it respectfully. I like to think of the foreign desperado, seeking to slip into America with official papers under official protection, and sitting down to write with a beautiful gravity, 'I am an anarchist. I hate you all and wish to destroy you.' Or, 'I intend to subvert by force the government of the United States as soon as possible, sticking the long sheath-knife in my left trouser-pocket into Mr. Harding at the earliest opportunity.' Or again, 'Yes, I am a polygamist all right, and my forty-seven wives are accompanying me on the voyage disguised as secretaries.' There seems to be a certain simplicity of mind about these answers; and it is reassuring to know that anarchists and polygamists are so pure and good that the police have only to ask them questions and they are certain to tell no lies.

Now that is a model of the sort of foreign practice, founded on foreign problems, at which a man's first impulse is naturally to laugh. Nor have I any intention of apologising for my laughter. A man is perfectly entitled to laugh at a thing because he happens to find it incomprehensible. What he has no right to do is to laugh at it as incomprehensible, and then criticise it as if he comprehended it. The very fact of its unfamiliarity and mystery ought to set him thinking about the deeper causes that make people so different from himself, and that without merely assuming that they must be inferior to himself.

Superficially this is rather a queer[1] business. It would be easy enough to suggest that in this America has introduced a quite abnormal spirit of inquisition; an interference with liberty unknown among all the ancient despotisms and aristocracies. About that there will be something to be said later; but superficially it is true that this degree of officialism is comparatively unique. In a journey which I took only the year before I had occasion to have my papers passed by governments which many worthy people in the West would vaguely identify with corsairs and assassins; I have stood on the other side of Jordan, in the land ruled by a rude Arab chief, where the police looked so like brigands that one wondered what the brigands looked like. But they did not ask me whether I had come to subvert the power of the Shereef; and they did not exhibit the faintest curiosity about my personal views on the ethical basis of civil authority. These ministers of ancient Moslem despotism did not care about whether I was an anarchist; and naturally would not have minded if I had been a polygamist. The Arab chief was probably a polygamist himself. These slaves of Asiatic autocracy were content, in the old liberal fashion, to judge me by my actions; they did not inquire into my thoughts. They held their power as limited to the limitation of practice; they did not forbid me to hold a theory. It would be easy to argue here that Western democracy persecutes where even Eastern despotism tolerates or emancipates. It would be easy to develop the fancy that, as compared with the sultans of Turkey or Egypt, the American Constitution is a thing like the Spanish Inquisition.

---

[1] strange

Only the traveller who stops at that point is totally wrong; and the traveller only too often does stop at that point. He has found something to make him laugh, and he will not suffer it to make him think. And the remedy is not to unsay what he has said, not even, so to speak, to unlaugh what he has laughed, not to deny that there is something unique and curious about this American inquisition into our abstract opinions, but rather to continue the train of thought, and follow the admirable advice of Mr. H. G. Wells, who said, 'It is not much good thinking of a thing unless you think it out.' It is not to deny that American officialism is rather peculiar on this point, but to inquire what it really is which makes America peculiar, or which is peculiar to America. In short, it is to get some ultimate idea of what America is; and the answer to that question will reveal something much deeper and grander and more worthy of our intelligent interest.

It may have seemed something less than a compliment to compare the American Constitution to the Spanish Inquisition. But oddly enough, it does involve a truth; and still more oddly perhaps, it does involve a compliment. The American Constitution does resemble the Spanish Inquisition in this: that it is founded on a creed. America is the only nation in the world that is founded on a creed. That creed is set forth with dogmatic and even theological lucidity in the Declaration of Independence; perhaps the only piece of practical politics that is also theoretical politics and also great literature. It enunciates that all men are equal in their claim to justice, that governments exist to give them that justice, and that their authority is for that reason just. It certainly does condemn anarchism, and it does also by inference condemn atheism, since it clearly names the Creator as the ultimate authority from whom these equal rights are derived. Nobody expects a modern political system to proceed logically in the application of such dogmas, and in the matter of God and Government it is naturally God whose claim is taken more lightly. The point is that there is a creed, if not about divine, at least about human things.

Now a creed is at once the broadest and the narrowest thing in the world. In its nature it is as broad as its scheme for a brotherhood of all men. In its nature it is limited by its definition of the nature of all men. This was true of the Christian Church, which was truly said to exclude neither Jew nor Greek, but which did definitely substitute something else for Jewish religion or Greek philosophy. It was truly said to be a net drawing in of all kinds; but a net of a certain pattern, the pattern of Peter the Fisherman. And this is true even of the most disastrous distortions or degradations of that creed; and true among others of the Spanish Inquisition. It may have been narrow touching theology, it could not confess to being narrow about nationality or ethnology. The Spanish Inquisition might be admittedly Inquisitorial; but the Spanish Inquisition could not be merely Spanish. Such a Spaniard, even when he was narrower than his own creed, had to be broader than his own empire. He might burn a philosopher because he was heterodox; but he must accept a barbarian because he was orthodox. And we see, even in modern times, that the same Church which is blamed for making sages heretics is also blamed for making savages priests. Now in a much vaguer and more evolutionary fashion, there is something of the same idea at the back of the great

American experiment; the experiment of a democracy of diverse races which has been compared to a melting-pot. But even that metaphor implies that the pot itself is of a certain shape and a certain substance; a pretty solid substance. The melting-pot must not melt. The original shape was traced on the lines of Jeffersonian democracy; and it will remain in that shape until it becomes shapeless. America invites all men to become citizens; but it implies the dogma that there is such a thing as citizenship. Only, so far as its primary ideal is concerned, its exclusiveness is religious because it is not racial. The missionary can condemn a cannibal, precisely because he cannot condemn a Sandwich Islander.[1] And in something of the same spirit the American may exclude a polygamist, precisely because he cannot exclude a Turk.

Now for America this is no idle theory. It may have been theoretical, though it was thoroughly sincere, when that great Virginian gentleman declared it in surroundings that still had something of the character of an English countryside. It is not merely theoretical now. There is nothing to prevent America being literally invaded by Turks, as she is invaded by Jews or Bulgars. In the most exquisitely inconsequent of the Bab Ballads,[2] we are told concerning Pasha Bailey Ben:—

> One morning knocked at half-past eight
> A tall Red Indian at his gate.
> In Turkey, as you 'r' p'raps aware,
> Red Indians are extremely rare.

But the converse need by no means be true. There is nothing in the nature of things to prevent an emigration of Turks increasing and multiplying on the plains where the Red Indians wandered; there is nothing to necessitate the Turks being extremely rare. The Red Indians, alas, are likely to be rarer. And as I much prefer Red Indians to Turks, not to mention Jews, I speak without prejudice; but the point here is that America, partly by original theory and partly by historical accident, does lie open to racial admixtures which most countries would think incongruous or comic. That is why it is only fair to read any American definitions or rules in a certain light, and relatively to a rather unique position. It is not fair to compare the position of those who may meet Turks in the back street with that of those who have never met Turks except in the Bab Ballads. It is not fair simply to compare America with England in its regulations about the Turk. In short, it is not fair to do what almost every Englishman probably does; to look at the American international examination paper, and laugh and be satisfied with saying, 'We don't have any of that nonsense in England.'

---

[1] The Sandwich Islands are now known by their original name: Hawai'i.

[2] Silly lyric poems by W. S. Gilbert (of the writing team Gilbert and Sullivan), written under the pen name "Bab" for the magazine *Fun* in the late nineteenth century. "Pasha Bailey Ben" was published on June 6, 1865.

We do not have any of that nonsense in England because we have never attempted to have any of that philosophy in England. And, above all, because we have the enormous advantage of feeling it natural to be national, because there is nothing else to be. England in these days is not well governed; England is not well educated; England suffers from wealth and poverty that are not well distributed. But England is English; *esto perpetua.*[1] England is English as France is French or Ireland Irish; the great mass of men taking certain national traditions for granted. Now this gives us a totally different and a very much easier task. We have not got an inquisition, because we have not got a creed; but it is arguable that we do not need a creed, because we have got a character. In any of the old nations the national unity is preserved by the national type. Because we have a type we do not need to have a test.

Take that innocent question, 'Are you an anarchist?' which is intrinsically quite as impudent as 'Are you an optimist?' or 'Are you a philanthropist?' I am not discussing here whether these things are right, but whether most of us are in a position to know them rightly. Now it is quite true that most Englishmen do not find it necessary to go about all day asking each other whether they are anarchists. It is quite true that the phrase occurs on no British forms that I have seen. But this is not only because most of the Englishmen are not anarchists. It is even more because even the anarchists are Englishmen. For instance, it would be easy to make fun of the American formula by noting that the cap would fit all sorts of bald academic heads. It might well be maintained that Herbert Spencer[2] was an anarchist. It is practically certain that Auberon Herbert[3] was an anarchist. But Herbert Spencer was an extraordinarily typical Englishman of the Nonconformist middle class. And Auberon Herbert was an extraordinarily typical English aristocrat of the old and genuine aristocracy. Every one knew in his heart that the squire would not throw a bomb at the Queen, and the Nonconformist would not throw a bomb at anybody. Every one knew that there was something subconscious in a man like Auberon Herbert, which would have come out only in throwing bombs at the enemies of England; as it did come out in his son and namesake, the generous and unforgotten, who fell flinging bombs from the sky far beyond the German line.[4] Every one knows that normally, in the last resort, the English gentleman is patriotic. Every one knows that the English Nonconformist is national even when he denies that he is patriotic. Nothing is more notable indeed than the fact that nobody is more stamped with the mark of his own nation than the man who says that there ought to be no nations. Somebody called

[1] May it be so perpetually (which is, ironically enough and whether Chesterton knew it or not, the motto of the State of Idaho)

[2] English philosopher who developed social Darwinism

[3] English philosopher and politician who built on Spencer's work to develop the idea of voluntaryism: that governments should never employ force except for defense and that taxation, in particular, ought to be voluntary. His father was the 3rd Earl of Carnarvon.

[4] Herbert's second son, Auberon Thomas, succeeded his maternal uncle as Lord Lucas and Dingwall in 1907, then had a very colorful career in politics before joining the Royal Flying Corps in 1916. In November of that year, he was shot down in France and died of his wounds.

Cobden the International Man;[1] but no man could be more English than Cobden. Everybody recognises Tolstoy[2] as the iconoclast of all patriotism; but nobody could be more Russian than Tolstoy. In the old countries where there are these national types, the types may be allowed to hold any theories. Even if they hold certain theories, they are unlikely to do certain things. So the conscientious objector, in the English sense, may be and is one of the peculiar by-products of England. But the conscientious objector will probably have a conscientious objection to throwing bombs.

Now I am very far from intending to imply that these American tests are good tests, or that there is no danger of tyranny becoming the temptation of America. I shall have something to say later on about that temptation or tendency. Nor do I say that they apply consistently this conception of a nation with the soul of a church, protected by religious and not racial selection. If they did apply that principle consistently, they would have to exclude pessimists and rich cynics who deny the democratic ideal; an excellent thing but a rather improbable one. What I say is that when we realise that this principle exists at all, we see the whole position in a totally different perspective. We say that the Americans are doing something heroic, or doing something insane, or doing it in an unworkable or unworthy fashion, instead of simply wondering what the devil they are doing.

When we realise the democratic design of such a cosmopolitan commonwealth, and compare it with our insular reliance or instincts, we see at once why such a thing has to be not only democratic but dogmatic. We see why in some points it tends to be inquisitive or intolerant. Any one can see the practical point by merely transferring into private life a problem like that of the two academic anarchists, who might by a coincidence be called the two Herberts. Suppose a man said, 'Buffle, my old Oxford tutor, wants to meet you; I wish you'd ask him down for a day or two. He has the oddest opinions, but he's very stimulating.' It would not occur to us that the oddity of the Oxford don's opinions would lead him to blow up the house; because the Oxford don is an English type. Suppose somebody said, 'Do let me bring old Colonel Robinson down for the week-end; he's a bit of a crank but quite interesting.' We should not anticipate the colonel running amuck with a carving-knife and offering up human sacrifice in the garden; for these are not among the daily habits of an old English colonel; and because we know his habits, we do not care about his opinions. But suppose somebody offered to bring a person from the interior of Kamskatka[3] to stay with us for a week or two, and added that his religion was a very extraordinary religion, we should feel a little more inquisitive about what kind of religion it was. If somebody wished to add a Hairy Ainu to the family party at Christmas, explaining that his point of view was so

---

[1] Richard Cobden, a mid-nineteenth-century politician who was (for the time) very radical and advocated free trade. The "someone" Chesterton is thinking of here is Drouyn de Lhuys, French minister of foreign affairs, who called Cobden "an international man" in a special dispatch to France's ambassador to the UK expressing condolences to the British government on Cobden's death in 1865.

[2] Leo Tolstoy, one of the great nineteenth-century Russian novelists.

[3] A large peninsula on the Pacific coast of Russia, more usually spelled *Kamchatka* in English.

individual and interesting, we should want to know a little more about it and him. We should be tempted to draw up as fantastic an examination paper as that presented to the emigrant going to America. We should ask what a Hairy Ainu was, and how hairy he was, and above all what sort of Ainu he was. Would etiquette require us to ask him to bring his wife? And if we did ask him to bring his wife, how many wives would he bring? In short, as in the American formula, is he a polygamist? Merely as a point of housekeeping and accommodation the question is not irrelevant. Is the Hairy Ainu content with hair, or does he wear any clothes? If the police insist on his wearing clothes, will he recognise the authority of the police? In short, as in the American formula, is he an anarchist?

Of course this generalisation about America, like other historical things, is subject to all sorts of cross divisions and exceptions, to be considered in their place. The negroes are a special problem, because of what white men in the past did to them. The Japanese are a special problem, because of what men fear that they in the future may do to white men. The Jews are a special problem, because of what they and the Gentiles, in the past, present, and future, seem to have the habit of doing to each other. But the point is not that nothing exists in America except this idea; it is that nothing like this idea exists anywhere except in America. This idea is not internationalism; on the contrary it is decidedly nationalism. The Americans are very patriotic, and wish to make their new citizens patriotic Americans. But it is the idea of making a new nation literally out of any old nation that comes along. In a word, what is unique is not America but what is called Americanisation. We understand nothing till we understand the amazing ambition to Americanise the Kamskatkan and the Hairy Ainu. We are not trying to Anglicise thousands of French cooks or Italian organ-grinders. France is not trying to Gallicise thousands of English trippers or German prisoners of war. America is the one place in the world where this process, healthy or unhealthy, possible or impossible, is going on. And the process, as I have pointed out, is not internationalisation. It would be truer to say it is the nationalisation of the internationalised. It is making a home out of vagabonds and a nation out of exiles. This is what at once illuminates and softens the moral regulations which we may really think faddist or fanatical. They are abnormal; but in one sense this experiment of a home for the homeless is abnormal. In short, it has long been recognised that America was an asylum. It is only since Prohibition that it has looked a little like a lunatic asylum.

It was before sailing for America, as I have said, that I stood with the official paper in my hand and these thoughts in my head. It was while I stood on English soil that I passed through the two stages of smiling and then sympathising; of realising that my momentary amusement, at being asked if I were not an Anarchist, was partly due to the fact that I was not an American. And in truth I think there are some things a man ought to know about America before he sees it. What we know of a country beforehand may not affect what we see that it is; but it will vitally affect what we appreciate it for being, because it will vitally affect what we expect it to be. I can honestly say that I had never expected America to be what nine-tenths of the newspaper critics invariably assume it to be. I never thought it was a sort of Anglo-Saxon colony, knowing that it was more and more thronged with crowds of very different colonists. During the war I felt that the very worst propaganda for the Allies was the propaganda for the Anglo-Saxons. I tried to point out that in one way America is nearer to Europe than England is. If she is not nearer to Bulgaria, she is nearer to Bulgars; if she is not nearer to Bohemia,[1] she is nearer to Bohemians. In my New York hotel the head waiter in the dining-room was a Bohemian; the head waiter in the grill-room was a Bulgar. Americans have nationalities at the end of the street which for us are at the ends of the earth. I did my best to persuade my countrymen not to appeal to the American as if he were a rather dowdy Englishman, who had been rusticating in the provinces and had not heard the latest news about the town. I shall record later some of those arresting realities which the traveller does not expect; and which, in some cases I fear, he actually does not see because he does not expect. I shall try to do justice to the psychology of what Mr. Belloc[2] has called 'Eye-Openers in Travel.' But there are some things about America that a man ought to see even with his eyes shut. One is that a state that came into existence solely through its repudiation and abhorrence of the British Crown is not likely to be a respectful copy of the British Constitution. Another is that the chief mark of the Declaration of Independence is something that is not only absent from the British Constitution, but something which all our constitutionalists have invariably thanked God, with the jolliest boasting and bragging, that they had kept out of the British Constitution. It is the thing called abstraction or academic logic. It is the thing which such jolly people call theory; and which those who can practise it call thought. And the theory or thought is the very last to which English people are accustomed, either by their social structure or their traditional teaching. It is the theory of equality. It is the pure classic conception that no man must aspire to be anything more than a citizen, and that no man should endure to be anything less. It is by no means especially intelligible to an Englishman, who tends at his best to the virtues of the gentleman and at his worst to the vices of the snob. The idealism of England, or if you will the romance of England, has not been primarily the romance of the citizen. But the idealism of America, we may safely say, still revolves entirely round the citizen and his romance. The realities are quite another matter, and we shall consider in its place the question of whether the ideal will be able to shape the realities or will merely be beaten shapeless by them. The ideal is besieged by inequalities of the most towering and insane description in the industrial and economic field. It may be devoured by modern capitalism, perhaps the worst inequality that ever existed among men. Of all that we shall speak later. But citizenship is still the American ideal; there is an army of actualities opposed to that ideal; but there is no ideal opposed to that ideal. American plutocracy has never got itself respected like English aristocracy. Citizenship is the American ideal; and it has never been the English ideal. But it is surely an ideal that may stir

---

[1] Western part of the present-day Czech Republic, and sometimes (especially in the historical sense) applied to the Czech Republic as a whole.
[2] Hillaire Belloc, one of Chesterton's best friends.

some imaginative generosity and respect in an Englishman, if he will condescend to be also a man. In this vision of moulding many peoples into the visible image of the citizen, he may see a spiritual adventure which he can admire from the outside, at least as much as he admires the valour of the Moslems and much more than he admires the virtues of the Middle Ages. He need not set himself to develop equality, but he need not set himself to misunderstand it. He may at least understand what Jefferson and Lincoln meant, and he may possibly find some assistance in this task by reading what they said. He may realise that equality is not some crude fairy tale about all men being equally tall or equally tricky; which we not only cannot believe but cannot believe in anybody believing. It is an absolute of morals by which all men have a value invariable and indestructible and a dignity as intangible as death. He may at least be a philosopher and see that equality is an idea; and not merely one of these soft-headed sceptics who, having risen by low tricks to high places, drink bad champagne in tawdry hotel lounges, and tell each other twenty times over, with unwearied iteration, that equality is an illusion.

In truth it is inequality that is the illusion. The extreme disproportion between men, that we seem to see in life, is a thing of changing lights and lengthening shadows, a twilight full of fancies and distortions. We find a man famous and cannot live long enough to find him forgotten; we see a race dominant and cannot linger to see it decay. It is the experience of men that always returns to the equality of men; it is the average that ultimately justifies the average man. It is when men have seen and suffered much and come at the end of more elaborate experiments, that they see men as men under an equal light of death and daily laughter; and none the less mysterious for being many. Nor is it in vain that these Western democrats have sought the blazonry of their flag in that great multitude of immortal lights that endure behind the fires we see, and gathered them into the corner of Old Glory whose ground is like the glittering night. For veritably, in the spirit as well as in the symbol, suns and moons and meteors pass and fill our skies with a fleeting and almost theatrical conflagration; and wherever the old shadow stoops upon the earth, the stars return.

The Victorian and Modern Eras

Mark Twain
from A Connecticut Yankee in King Arthur's Court

Chapter V
An Inspiration

I was so tired that even my fears were not able to keep me awake long.

When I next came to myself, I seemed to have been asleep a very long time. My first thought was, "Well, what an astonishing dream I've had! I reckon I've waked only just in time to keep from being hanged or drowned or burned or something.... I'll nap again till the whistle blows, and then I'll go down to the arms factory and have it out with Hercules."

But just then I heard the harsh music of rusty chains and bolts, a light flashed in my eyes, and that butterfly, Clarence, stood before me! I gasped with surprise; my breath almost got away from me.

"What!" I said, "you here yet? Go along with the rest of the dream! scatter!"

But he only laughed, in his light-hearted way, and fell to making fun of my sorry plight.

"All right," I said resignedly, "let the dream go on; I'm in no hurry."

"Prithee[1] what dream?"

"What dream? Why, the dream that I am in Arthur's court—a person who never existed; and that I am talking to you, who are nothing but a work of the imagination."

"Oh, la, indeed! and is it a dream that you're to be burned to-morrow? Ho-ho—answer me that!"

The shock that went through me was distressing. I now began to reason that my situation was in the last degree serious, dream or no dream; for I knew by past experience of the lifelike intensity of dreams, that to be burned to death, even in a dream, would be very far from being a jest, and was a thing to be avoided, by any means, fair or foul, that I could contrive. So I said beseechingly:

"Ah, Clarence, good boy, only friend I've got,—for you *are* my friend, aren't you?—don't fail me; help me to devise some way of escaping from this place!"

"Now do but hear thyself! Escape? Why, man, the corridors are in guard and keep of men-at-arms."

"No doubt, no doubt. But how many, Clarence? Not many, I hope?"

"Full a score. One may not hope to escape." After a pause—hesitatingly: "and there be other reasons—and weightier."

"Other ones? What are they?"

"Well, they say—oh, but I daren't, indeed daren't!"

---

[1] Short for "I pray thee"

"Why, poor lad, what is the matter? Why do you blench? Why do you tremble so?"

"Oh, in sooth, there is need! I do want to tell you, but—"

"Come, come, be brave, be a man—speak out, there's a good lad!"

He hesitated, pulled one way by desire, the other way by fear; then he stole to the door and peeped out, listening; and finally crept close to me and put his mouth to my ear and told me his fearful news in a whisper, and with all the cowering apprehension of one who was venturing upon awful ground and speaking of things whose very mention might be freighted with death.

"Merlin, in his malice, has woven a spell about this dungeon, and there bides not the man in these kingdoms that would be desperate enough to essay to cross its lines with you! Now God pity me, I have told it! Ah, be kind to me, be merciful to a poor boy who means thee well; for an thou betray me I am lost!"

I laughed the only really refreshing laugh I had had for some time; and shouted:

"Merlin has wrought a spell! *Merlin*, forsooth! That cheap old humbug, that maundering old ass? Bosh, pure bosh, the silliest bosh in the world! Why, it does seem to me that of all the childish, idiotic, chuckle-headed, chicken-livered superstitions that ev—oh, damn Merlin!"

But Clarence had slumped to his knees before I had half finished, and he was like to go out of his mind with fright.

"Oh, beware! These are awful words! Any moment these walls may crumble upon us if you say such things. Oh, call them back before it is too late!"

Now this strange exhibition gave me a good idea and set me to thinking. If everybody about here was so honestly and sincerely afraid of Merlin's pretended magic as Clarence was, certainly a superior man like me ought to be shrewd enough to contrive some way to take advantage of such a state of things. I went on thinking, and worked out a plan. Then I said:

"Get up. Pull yourself together; look me in the eye. Do you know why I laughed?"

"No—but for our blessed Lady's sake, do it no more."

"Well, I'll tell you why I laughed. Because I'm a magician myself."

"Thou!" The boy recoiled a step, and caught his breath, for the thing hit him rather sudden; but the aspect which he took on was very, very respectful. I took quick note of that; it indicated that a humbug didn't need to have a reputation in this asylum; people stood ready to take him at his word, without that. I resumed.

"I've known Merlin seven hundred years, and he—"

"Seven hun—"

"Don't interrupt me. He has died and come alive again thirteen times, and traveled under a new name every time: Smith, Jones, Robinson, Jackson, Peters, Haskins, Merlin—a new alias every time he turns up. I knew him in Egypt three hundred years ago; I knew him in India five hundred years ago—he is always blethering around in my way, everywhere I go; he makes me tired. He don't amount to shucks, as a magician; knows some of the old common tricks, but has never got beyond the rudiments, and never will. He is well enough for the provinces—one-night stands and that sort of thing, you know—but dear me, *he* oughtn't to set up for an expert—anyway not where there's a real artist. Now look here, Clarence, I am going to stand your friend, right along, and in return you must be mine. I want you to do me a favor. I want you to get word to the king that I am a magician myself— and the Supreme Grand High-yu-Muck-amuck and head of the tribe, at that; and I want him to be made to understand that I am just quietly arranging a little calamity here that will make the fur fly in these realms if Sir Kay's project is carried out and any harm comes to me. Will you get that to the king for me?"

The poor boy was in such a state that he could hardly answer me. It was pitiful to see a creature so terrified, so unnerved, so demoralized. But he promised everything; and on my side he made me promise over and over again that I would remain his friend, and never turn against him or cast any enchantments upon him. Then he worked his way out, staying himself with his hand along the wall, like a sick person.

Presently this thought occurred to me: how heedless I have been! When the boy gets calm, he will wonder why a great magician like me should have begged a boy like him to help me get out of this place; he will put this and that together, and will see that I am a humbug.

I worried over that heedless blunder for an hour, and called myself a great many hard names, meantime. But finally it occurred to me all of a sudden that these animals didn't reason; that *they* never put this and that together; that all their talk showed that they didn't know a discrepancy when they saw it. I was at rest, then.

But as soon as one is at rest, in this world, off he goes on something else to worry about. It occurred to me that I had made another blunder: I had sent the boy off to alarm his betters with a threat—I intending to invent a calamity at my leisure; now the people who are the readiest and eagerest and willingest to swallow miracles are the very ones who are hungriest to see you perform them; suppose I should be called on for a sample? Suppose I should be asked to name my calamity? Yes, I had made a blunder; I ought to have invented my calamity first. "What shall I do? what can I say, to gain a little time?" I was in trouble again; in the deepest kind of trouble...

"There's a footstep!—they're coming. If I had only just a moment to think.... Good, I've got it. I'm all right."

You see, it was the eclipse. It came into my mind in the nick of time, how Columbus, or Cortez, or one of those people, played an eclipse as a saving trump once, on some savages, and I saw my chance. I could play it myself, now, and it wouldn't be any plagiarism, either, because I should get it in nearly a thousand years ahead of those parties.

Clarence came in, subdued, distressed, and said: "I hasted the message to our liege the king, and straightway he had me to his presence. He was frighted even to the marrow, and was minded to give order for your instant enlargement, and that you be clothed in fine raiment and lodged as befitted one so great; but then came Merlin and spoiled all; for he persuaded the king that you are mad, and know not whereof you speak; and said your threat is but foolishness and idle vaporing. They disputed long, but in the end, Merlin, scoffing, said, 'Wherefore hath he not *named* his brave calamity? Verily it is because he cannot.' This thrust did in a most sudden sort close the king's mouth, and he could offer naught to turn the argument; and so, reluctant, and full loth to do you the discourtesy, he yet prayeth you to consider his perplexed case, as noting how the matter stands, and name the calamity—if so be you have determined the nature of it and the time of its coming. Oh, prithee delay not; to delay at such a time were to double and treble the perils that already compass thee about. Oh, be thou wise—name the calamity!"

I allowed silence to accumulate while I got my impressiveness together, and then said: "How long have I been shut up in this hole?"

"Ye were shut up when yesterday was well spent. It is 9 of the morning now."

"No! Then I have slept well, sure enough. Nine in the morning now! And yet it is the very complexion of midnight, to a shade. This is the 20th, then?"

"The 20th—yes."

"And I am to be burned alive to-morrow." The boy shuddered.

"At what hour?"

"At high noon."

"Now then, I will tell you what to say." I paused, and stood over that cowering lad a whole minute in awful silence; then, in a voice deep, measured, charged with doom, I began, and rose by dramatically graded stages to my colossal climax, which I delivered in as sublime and noble a way as ever I did such a thing in my life: "Go back and tell the king that at that hour I will smother the whole world in the dead blackness of midnight; I will blot out the sun, and he shall never shine again; the fruits of the earth shall rot for lack of light and warmth, and the peoples of the earth shall famish and die, to the last man!"

I had to carry the boy out myself, he sunk into such a collapse. I handed him over to the soldiers, and went back.

Chapter VI
The Eclipse

In the stillness and the darkness, realization soon began to supplement knowledge. The mere knowledge of a fact is pale; but when you come to *realize* your fact, it takes on color. It is all the difference between hearing of a man being stabbed to the heart, and seeing it done. In the stillness and the darkness, the knowledge that I was in deadly danger took to itself deeper and deeper meaning all the time; a something which was realization crept inch by inch through my veins and turned me cold.

But it is a blessed provision of nature that at times like these, as soon as a man's mercury has got down to a certain point there comes a revulsion, and he rallies. Hope springs up, and cheerfulness along with it, and then he is in good shape to do something for himself, if anything can be done. When my rally came, it came with a bound. I said to myself that my eclipse would be sure to save me, and make me the greatest man in the kingdom besides; and straightway my mercury went up to the top of the tube, and my solicitudes all vanished. I was as happy a man as there was in the world. I was even impatient for to-morrow to come, I so wanted to gather in that great triumph and be the center of all the nation's wonder and reverence. Besides, in a business way it would be the making of me; I knew that.

Meantime there was one thing which had got pushed into the background of my mind. That was the half-conviction that when the nature of my proposed calamity should be reported to those superstitious people, it would have such an effect that they would want to compromise. So, by and by when I heard footsteps coming, that thought was recalled to me, and I said to myself, "As sure as anything, it's the compromise. Well, if it is good, all right, I will accept; but if it isn't, I mean to stand my ground and play my hand for all it is worth."

The door opened, and some men-at-arms appeared. The leader said: "The stake is ready. Come!"

The stake! The strength went out of me, and I almost fell down. It is hard to get one's breath at such a time, such lumps come into one's throat, and such gaspings; but as soon as I could speak, I said:

"But this is a mistake—the execution is to-morrow."

"Order changed; been set forward a day. Haste thee!"

I was lost. There was no help for me. I was dazed, stupefied; I had no command over myself, I only wandered purposely about, like one out of his mind; so the soldiers took hold of me, and pulled me along with them, out of the cell and along the maze of underground corridors, and finally into the fierce glare of daylight and the upper world. As we stepped into the vast enclosed court of the castle I got a shock; for the first thing I saw was the stake, standing in the center, and near it the piled fagots and a monk. On all four sides of the court the seated multitudes rose rank above rank, forming sloping terraces that were rich with color. The king and the queen sat in their thrones, the most conspicuous figures there, of course.

To note all this, occupied but a second. The next second Clarence had slipped from some place of concealment and was pouring news into my ear, his eyes beaming with triumph and gladness. He said: "Tis through *me* the change was wrought! And main hard have I worked to do it, too. But when I revealed to them the calamity in store, and saw how mighty was the terror it did engender, then saw I also that this was the time to strike! Wherefore I diligently pretended, unto this and that and the other one, that your power against the sun could not reach its full until the morrow; and so if any would save the sun and the world, you must be slain to-day, while your enchantments are but in the weaving and lack potency. Odsbodikins, it was but a dull lie, a most indifferent invention, but you should have seen them seize it and swallow it, in the frenzy of their fright, as it were salvation sent from heaven; and all the while was I laughing in my sleeve the one moment, to see them so cheaply deceived, and glorifying God the next, that He was content to let the meanest of

His creatures be His instrument to the saving of thy life. Ah how happy has the matter sped! You will not need to do the sun a *real* hurt—ah, forget not that, on your soul forget it not! Only make a little darkness—only the littlest little darkness, mind, and cease with that. It will be sufficient. They will see that I spoke falsely,—being ignorant, as they will fancy—and with the falling of the first shadow of that darkness you shall see them go mad with fear; and they will set you free and make you great! Go to thy triumph, now! But remember—ah, good friend, I implore thee remember my supplication, and do the blessed sun no hurt. For *my* sake, thy true friend."

I choked out some words through my grief and misery; as much as to say I would spare the sun; for which the lad's eyes paid me back with such deep and loving gratitude that I had not the heart to tell him his good-hearted foolishness had ruined me and sent me to my death.

As the soldiers assisted me across the court the stillness was so profound that if I had been blindfold I should have supposed I was in a solitude instead of walled in by four thousand people. There was not a movement perceptible in those masses of humanity; they were as rigid as stone images, and as pale; and dread sat upon every countenance. This hush continued while I was being chained to the stake; it still continued while the fagots were carefully and tediously piled about my ankles, my knees, my thighs, my body. Then there was a pause, and a deeper hush, if possible, and a man knelt down at my feet with a blazing torch; the multitude strained forward, gazing, and parting slightly from their seats without knowing it; the monk raised his hands above my head, and his eyes toward the blue sky, and began some words in Latin; in this attitude he droned on and on, a little while, and then stopped. I waited two or three moments; then looked up; he was standing there petrified. With a common impulse the multitude rose slowly up and stared into the sky. I followed their eyes, as sure as guns, there was my eclipse beginning! The life went boiling through my veins; I was a new man! The rim of black spread slowly into the sun's disk, my heart beat higher and higher, and still the assemblage and the priest stared into the sky, motionless. I knew that this gaze would be turned upon me, next. When it was, I was ready. I was in one of the most grand attitudes I ever struck, with my arm stretched up pointing to the sun. It was a noble effect. You could *see* the shudder sweep the mass like a wave. Two shouts rang out, one close upon the heels of the other:

"Apply the torch!"

"I forbid it!"

The one was from Merlin, the other from the king. Merlin started from his place—to apply the torch himself, I judged. I said: "Stay where you are. If any man moves—even the king—before I give him leave, I will blast him with thunder, I will consume him with lightnings!"

The multitude sank meekly into their seats, and I was just expecting they would. Merlin hesitated a moment or two, and I was on pins and needles during that little while. Then he sat down, and I took a good breath; for I knew I was master of the situation now.

The king said: "Be merciful, fair sir, and essay no further in this perilous matter, lest disaster follow. It was reported to us that your powers could not attain unto their full strength until the morrow; but—"

"Your Majesty thinks the report may have been a lie? It *was* a lie."

That made an immense effect; up went appealing hands everywhere, and the king was assailed with a storm of supplications that I might be bought off at any price, and the calamity stayed.

The king was eager to comply. He said: "Name any terms, reverend sir, even to the halving of my kingdom; but banish this calamity, spare the sun!"

My fortune was made. I would have taken him up in a minute, but I couldn't stop an eclipse; the thing was out of the question. So I asked time to consider. The king said: "How long—ah, how long, good sir? Be merciful; look, it growth darker, moment by moment. Prithee how long?"

"Not long. Half an hour—maybe an hour."

There were a thousand pathetic protests, but I couldn't shorten up any, for I couldn't remember how long a total eclipse lasts. I was in a puzzled condition, anyway, and wanted to think. Something was wrong about that eclipse, and the fact was very unsettling. If this wasn't the one I was after, how was I to tell whether this was the sixth century, or nothing but a dream? Dear me, if I could only prove it was the latter! Here was a glad new hope. If the boy was right about the date, and this was surely the 20th, it *wasn't* the sixth century. I reached for the monk's sleeve, in considerable excitement, and asked him what day of the month it was.

Hang him, he said it was the *twenty-first*! It made me turn cold to hear him. I begged him not to make any mistake about it; but he was sure; he knew it was the 21st. So, that feather-headed boy had botched things again! The time of the day was right for the eclipse; I had seen that for myself, in the beginning, by the dial that was near by. Yes, I was in King Arthur's court, and I might as well make the most out of it I could.

The darkness was steadily growing, the people becoming more and more distressed. I now said:

"I have reflected, Sir King. For a lesson, I will let this darkness proceed, and spread night in the world; but whether I blot out the sun for good, or restore it, shall rest with you. These are the terms, to wit: You shall remain king over all your dominions, and receive all the glories and honors that belong to the kingship; but you shall appoint me your perpetual minister and executive, and give me for my services one per cent of such actual increase of revenue over and above its present amount as I may succeed in creating for the state. If I can't live on that, I sha'n't ask anybody to give me a lift. Is it satisfactory?"

There was a prodigious roar of applause, and out of the midst of it the king's voice rose, saying: "Away with his bonds, and set him free! and do him homage, high and low, rich and poor, for he is become the king's right hand, is clothed with power and authority, and his seat is upon the highest step of the throne! Now sweep away this creeping night, and bring the light and cheer again, that all the world may bless thee."

But I said: "That a common man should be shamed before the world, is nothing; but it were dishonor to the *king* if any that saw his minister naked should not also see him delivered from his shame. If I might ask that my clothes be brought again—"

"They are not meet," the king broke in. "Fetch raiment of another sort; clothe him like a prince!"

My idea worked. I wanted to keep things as they were till the eclipse was total, otherwise they would be trying again to get me to dismiss the darkness, and of course I couldn't do it. Sending for the clothes gained some delay, but not enough. So I had to make another excuse. I said it would be but natural if the king should change his mind and repent to some extent of what he had done under excitement; therefore I would let the darkness grow a while, and if at the end of a reasonable time the king had kept his mind the same, the darkness should be dismissed. Neither the king nor anybody else was satisfied with that arrangement, but I had to stick to my point.

It grew darker and darker and blacker and blacker, while I struggled with those awkward sixth-century clothes. It got to be pitch dark, at last, and the multitude groaned with horror to feel the cold uncanny night breezes fan through the place and see the stars come out and twinkle in the sky. At last the eclipse was total, and I was very glad of it, but everybody else was in misery; which was quite natural. I said: "The king, by his silence, still stands to the terms." Then I lifted up my hands—stood just so a moment—then I said, with the most awful solemnity: "Let the enchantment dissolve and pass harmless away!"

There was no response, for a moment, in that deep darkness and that graveyard hush. But when the silver rim of the sun pushed itself out, a moment or two later, the assemblage broke loose with a vast shout and came pouring down like a deluge to smother me with blessings and gratitude; and Clarence was not the last of the wash, to be sure.

Chapter VII
Merlin's Tower

Inasmuch as I was now the second personage in the Kingdom, as far as political power and authority were concerned, much was made of me. My raiment was of silks and velvets and cloth of gold, and by consequence was very showy, also uncomfortable. But habit would soon reconcile me to my clothes; I was aware of that. I was given the choicest suite of apartments in the castle, after the king's. They were aglow with loud-colored silken hangings, but the stone floors had nothing but rushes on them for a carpet, and they were misfit rushes at that, being not all of one breed. As for conveniences, properly speaking, there weren't any. I mean *little* conveniences; it is the little conveniences that make the real comfort of life. The big oaken chairs, graced with rude carvings, were well enough, but that was the stopping place. There was no soap, no matches, no looking-glass—except a metal one, about as powerful as a pail of water. And not a chromo.[1] I had been used to chromos for years, and I saw now that without my suspecting it a passion for art had got worked into the fabric of my being, and was become a part of me. It made me homesick to look around over this proud and gaudy but heartless barrenness and remember that in our house in East Hartford, all unpretending as it was, you couldn't go into a room but you would find an insurance-chromo, or at least a three-color God-Bless-Our-Home over the door; and in the parlor we had nine. But here, even in my grand room of state, there wasn't anything in the nature of a picture except a thing the size of a bedquilt, which was either woven or knitted (it had darned places in it), and nothing in it was the right color or the right shape;[2] and as for proportions, even Raphael himself couldn't have botched them more formidably, after all his practice on those nightmares they call his "celebrated Hampton Court cartoons." Raphael was a bird. We had several of his chromos; one was his "Miraculous Draught of Fishes," where he puts in a miracle of his own—puts three men into a canoe which wouldn't have held a dog without upsetting. I always admired to study R.'s art, it was so fresh and unconventional.

There wasn't even a bell or a speaking-tube in the castle. I had a great many servants, and those that were on duty lolled in the anteroom; and when I wanted one of them I had to go and call for him. There was no gas, there were no candles; a bronze dish half full of boarding-house butter with a blazing rag floating in it was the thing that produced what was regarded as light. A lot of these hung along the walls and modified the dark, just toned it down enough to make it dismal. If you went out at night, your servants carried torches. There were no books, pens, paper or ink, and no glass in the openings they believed to be windows.[3] It is a little thing—glass is—until it is absent, then it becomes a big thing. But perhaps the worst of all was, that there wasn't any sugar, coffee, tea, or tobacco.[4] I saw that I was just another Robinson Crusoe cast away on an uninhabited island, with no society but some more or less tame animals, and if I wanted to make life bearable I must do as he did—invent, contrive, create, reorganize things; set brain and hand to work, and keep them busy. Well, that was in my line.

One thing troubled me along at first—the immense interest which people took in me. Apparently the whole nation wanted a look at me. It soon transpired that the eclipse had scared the British world almost to death; that while it lasted the whole country, from one end to the other, was in a pitiable state of panic, and the churches, hermitages, and monkeries overflowed with praying and weeping poor creatures who thought the end of the world was

---

[1] Chromolithograph, a colored art print mass-produced using a series of lithographic plates.

[2] The technique of making and painting with oil paints was lost when Rome fell, was not rediscovered until the High Middle Ages, and did not become standard until the Renaissance, so living quarters in Camelot genuinely would not have had any form of art on the walls beyond tapestries.

[3] Also accurate: books, parchment, and glass were all extremely expensive and would not be found in most living quarters.

[4] Sugar existed but was terribly expensive and mostly used for medicine; coffee and tea didn't reach England until the seventeenth century; and tobacco is a New World plant.

come. Then had followed the news that the producer of this awful event was a stranger, a mighty magician at Arthur's court; that he could have blown out the sun like a candle, and was just going to do it when his mercy was purchased, and he then dissolved his enchantments, and was now recognized and honored as the man who had by his unaided might saved the globe from destruction and its peoples from extinction. Now if you consider that everybody believed that, and not only believed it, but never even dreamed of doubting it, you will easily understand that there was not a person in all Britain that would not have walked fifty miles to get a sight of me. Of course I was all the talk—all other subjects were dropped; even the king became suddenly a person of minor interest and notoriety. Within twenty-four hours the delegations began to arrive, and from that time onward for a fortnight they kept coming. The village was crowded, and all the countryside. I had to go out a dozen times a day and show myself to these reverent and awe-stricken multitudes. It came to be a great burden, as to time and trouble, but of course it was at the same time compensatingly agreeable to be so celebrated and such a center of homage. It turned Brer Merlin green with envy and spite, which was a great satisfaction to me. But there was one thing I couldn't understand—nobody had asked for an autograph. I spoke to Clarence about it. By George! I had to explain to him what it was. Then he said nobody in the country could read or write but a few dozen priests. Land! think of that.

There was another thing that troubled me a little. Those multitudes presently began to agitate for another miracle. That was natural. To be able to carry back to their far homes the boast that they had seen the man who could command the sun, riding in the heavens, and be obeyed, would make them great in the eyes of their neighbors, and envied by them all; but to be able to also say they had seen him work a miracle themselves—why, people would come a distance to see *them*. The pressure got to be pretty strong. There was going to be an eclipse of the moon, and I knew the date and hour, but it was too far away. Two years. I would have given a good deal for license to hurry it up and use it now when there was a big market for it. It seemed a great pity to have it wasted so, and come lagging along at a time when a body wouldn't have any use for it, as like as not. If it had been booked for only a month away, I could have sold it short; but, as matters stood, I couldn't seem to cipher out any way to make it do me any good, so I gave up trying. Next, Clarence found that old Merlin was making himself busy on the sly among those people. He was spreading a report that I was a humbug, and that the reason I didn't accommodate the people with a miracle was because I couldn't. I saw that I must do something. I presently thought out a plan.

By my authority as executive I threw Merlin into prison—the same cell I had occupied myself. Then I gave public notice by herald and trumpet that I should be busy with affairs of state for a fortnight, but about the end of that time I would take a moment's leisure and blow up Merlin's stone tower by fires from heaven; in the meantime, whoso listened to evil reports about me, let him beware. Furthermore, I would perform but this one miracle at this time, and no more; if it failed to satisfy and any murmured, I would turn the murmurers into horses, and make them useful. Quiet ensued.

I took Clarence into my confidence, to a certain degree, and we went to work privately. I told him that this was a sort of miracle that required a trifle of preparation, and that it would be sudden death to ever talk about these preparations to anybody. That made his mouth safe enough. Clandestinely we made a few bushels of first-rate blasting powder, and I superintended my armorers while they constructed a lightning-rod and some wires. This old stone tower was very massive—and rather ruinous, too, for it was Roman, and four hundred years old. Yes, and handsome, after a rude fashion, and clothed with ivy from base to summit, as with a shirt of scale mail. It stood on a lonely eminence, in good view from the castle, and about half a mile away.

Working by night, we stowed the powder in the tower—dug stones out, on the inside, and buried the powder in the walls themselves, which were fifteen feet thick at the base. We put in a peck at a time, in a dozen places. We could have blown up the Tower of London with these charges. When the thirteenth night was come we put up our lightning-rod, bedded it in one of the batches of powder, and ran wires from it to the other batches. Everybody had shunned that locality from the day of my proclamation, but on the morning of the fourteenth I thought best to warn the people, through the heralds, to keep clear away— a quarter of a mile away. Then added, by command, that at some time during the twenty-four hours I would consummate the miracle, but would first give a brief notice; by flags on the castle towers if in the daytime, by torch-baskets in the same places if at night.

Thunder-showers had been tolerably frequent of late, and I was not much afraid of a failure; still, I shouldn't have cared for a delay of a day or two; I should have explained that I was busy with affairs of state yet, and the people must wait.

Of course, we had a blazing sunny day—almost the first one without a cloud for three weeks; things always happen so. I kept secluded, and watched the weather. Clarence dropped in from time to time and said the public excitement was growing and growing all the time, and the whole country filling up with human masses as far as one could see from the battlements. At last the wind sprang up and a cloud appeared—in the right quarter, too, and just at nightfall. For a little while I watched that distant cloud spread and blacken, then I judged it was time for me to appear. I ordered the torch-baskets to be lit, and Merlin liberated and sent to me. A quarter of an hour later I ascended the parapet and there found the king and the court assembled and gazing off in the darkness toward Merlin's Tower. Already the darkness was so heavy that one could not see far; these people and the old turrets, being partly in deep shadow and partly in the red glow from the great torch-baskets overhead, made a good deal of a picture.

Merlin arrived in a gloomy mood. I said: "You wanted to burn me alive when I had not done you any harm, and latterly you have been trying to injure my professional reputation. Therefore I am going to call down fire and blow up your tower, but it is only fair to give you a chance; now if you think you can break my enchantments and ward off the fires, step to the bat, it's your innings." "I can, fair sir, and I will. Doubt it not."

He drew an imaginary circle on the stones of the roof, and burnt a pinch of powder in it, which sent up a small cloud of aromatic smoke, whereat everybody fell back and began to cross themselves and get uncomfortable. Then he began to mutter and make passes in the air with his hands. He worked himself up slowly and gradually into a sort of frenzy, and got to thrashing around with his arms like the sails of a windmill. By this time the storm had about reached us; the gusts of wind were flaring the torches and making the shadows swash about, the first heavy drops of rain were falling, the world abroad was black as pitch, the lightning began to wink fitfully. Of course, my rod would be loading itself now. In fact, things were imminent. So I said: "You have had time enough. I have given you every advantage, and not interfered. It is plain your magic is weak. It is only fair that I begin now."

I made about three passes in the air, and then there was an awful crash and that old tower leaped into the sky in chunks, along with a vast volcanic fountain of fire that turned night to noonday, and showed a thousand acres of human beings groveling on the ground in a general collapse of consternation. Well, it rained mortar and masonry the rest of the week. This was the report; but probably the facts would have modified it.

It was an effective miracle. The great bothersome temporary population vanished. There were a good many thousand tracks in the mud the next morning, but they were all outward bound. If I had advertised another miracle I couldn't have raised an audience with a sheriff.

Merlin's stock was flat. The king wanted to stop his wages; he even wanted to banish him, but I interfered. I said he would be useful to work the weather, and attend to small matters like that, and I would give him a lift now and then when his poor little parlor-magic soured on him. There wasn't a rag of his tower left, but I had the government rebuild it for him, and advised him to take boarders; but he was too high-toned for that. And as for being grateful, he never even said thank you. He was a rather hard lot, take him how you might; but then you couldn't fairly expect a man to be sweet that had been set back so.

❧❧

Alfred, Lord Tennyson
The Lady of Shalott

Part I

On either side the river lie
Long fields of barley and of rye,
That clothe the wold and meet the sky;
And thro' the field the road runs by
To many-tower'd Camelot;

And up and down the people go,
Gazing where the lilies blow
Round an island there below,
    The island of Shalott.[1]

Willows whiten, aspens quiver,
Little breezes dusk and shiver
Thro' the wave that runs for ever
By the island in the river
    Flowing down to Camelot.
Four gray walls, and four gray towers,
Overlook a space of flowers,
And the silent isle imbowers
    The Lady of Shalott.

By the margin, willow-veil'd
Slide the heavy barges trail'd
By slow horses; and unhail'd
The shallop flitteth silken-sail'd
    Skimming down to Camelot:
But who hath seen her wave her hand?
Or at the casement seen her stand?
Or is she known in all the land,
    The Lady of Shalott?

Only reapers, reaping early
In among the bearded barley,
Hear a song that echoes cheerly
From the river winding clearly,
    Down to tower'd Camelot:
And by the moon the reaper weary,
Piling sheaves in uplands airy,
Listening, whispers "'Tis the fairy
    Lady of Shalott".

---

[1] This place name comes from an Italian version of the legend of Elaine of Astolat, but Tennyson's version is only very loosely based on it.

Part II

There she weaves by night and day
A magic web with colours gay.
She has heard a whisper say,
A curse is on her if she stay
      To look down to Camelot.
She knows not what the curse may be,
And so she weaveth steadily,
And little other care hath she,
      The Lady of Shalott.

And moving thro' a mirror clear
That hangs before her all the year,
Shadows of the world appear.
There she sees the highway near
      Winding down to Camelot:
There the river eddy whirls,
And there the surly village-churls,
And the red cloaks of market girls,
      Pass onward from Shalott.

Sometimes a troop of damsels glad,
An abbot on an ambling pad,
Sometimes a curly shepherd-lad,
Or long-hair'd page in crimson clad,
      Goes by to tower'd Camelot;
And sometimes thro' the mirror blue
The knights come riding two and two:
She hath no loyal knight and true,
      The Lady of Shalott.

But in her web she still delights
To weave the mirror's magic sights,
For often thro' the silent nights
A funeral, with plumes and lights,
      And music, went to Camelot:
Or when the moon was overhead,
Came two young lovers lately wed;

"I am half-sick of shadows," said
    The Lady of Shalott.

Part III

A bow-shot from her bower-eaves,
He rode between the barley sheaves,
The sun came dazzling thro' the leaves,
And flamed upon the brazen greaves
    Of bold Sir Lancelot.
A redcross knight for ever kneel'd
To a lady in his shield,
That sparkled on the yellow field,
    Beside remote Shalott.

The gemmy bridle glitter'd free,
Like to some branch of stars we see
Hung in the golden Galaxy.
The bridle bells rang merrily
    As he rode down to Camelot:
And from his blazon'd baldric slung
A mighty silver bugle hung,
And as he rode his armour rung,
    Beside remote Shalott.

All in the blue unclouded weather
Thick-jewell'd shone the saddle-leather,
The helmet and the helmet-feather
Burn'd like one burning flame together,
    As he rode down to Camelot.
As often thro' the purple night,
Below the starry clusters bright,
Some bearded meteor, trailing light,
    Moves over still Shalott.

His broad clear brow in sunlight glow'd;
On burnish'd hooves his war-horse trode;
From underneath his helmet flow'd
His coal-black curls as on he rode,
    As he rode down to Camelot.

From the bank and from the river
He flashed into the crystal mirror,
"Tirra lirra," by the river
    Sang Sir Lancelot.

She left the web, she left the loom;
She made three paces thro' the room,
She saw the water-lily bloom,
She saw the helmet and the plume,
    She look'd down to Camelot.
Out flew the web and floated wide;
The mirror crack'd from side to side;
"The curse is come upon me," cried
    The Lady of Shalott.

Part IV

In the stormy east-wind straining,
The pale yellow woods were waning,
The broad stream in his banks complaining,
Heavily the low sky raining
    Over tower'd Camelot;
Down she came and found a boat
Beneath a willow left afloat,
And round about the prow she wrote
    The Lady of Shalott.

And down the river's dim expanse
Like some bold seër in a trance,
Seeing all his own mischance
With a glassy countenance
    Did she look to Camelot.
And at the closing of the day
She loosed the chain, and down she lay;
The broad stream bore her far away,
    The Lady of Shalott.

Lying, robed in snowy white
That loosely flew to left and right
The leaves upon her falling light

Thro' the noises of the night
  She floated down to Camelot;
And as the boat-head wound along
The willowy hills and fields among,
They heard her singing her last song,
  The Lady of Shalott.

Heard a carol, mournful, holy,
Chanted loudly, chanted lowly,
Till her blood was frozen slowly,
And her eyes were darken'd wholly,
  Turn'd to tower'd Camelot;
For ere she reach'd upon the tide
The first house by the water-side,
Singing in her song she died,
  The Lady of Shalott.

Under tower and balcony,
By garden-wall and gallery,
A gleaming shape she floated by,
Dead-pale between the houses high,
  Silent into Camelot.
Out upon the wharfs they came,
Knight and burgher, lord and dame,
And round the prow they read her name,
  The Lady of Shalott.

Who is this? and what is here?
And in the lighted palace near
Died the sound of royal cheer;
And they cross'd themselves for fear,
  All the knights at Camelot:
But Lancelot mused a little space;
He said, "She has a lovely face;
God in his mercy lend her grace,
  The Lady of Shalott".

Rudyard Kipling
from Just So Stories[1]

The Elephant's Child

In the High and Far-Off Times the Elephant, O Best Beloved, had no trunk. He had only a blackish, bulgy nose, as big as a boot, that he could wriggle about from side to side; but he couldn't pick up things with it. But there was one Elephant—a new Elephant—an Elephant's Child—who was full of 'satiable curtiosity, and that means he asked ever so many questions. *And* he lived in Africa, and he filled all Africa with his 'satiable curtiosities. He asked his tall aunt, the Ostrich, why her tail-feathers grew just so, and his tall aunt the Ostrich spanked him with her hard, hard claw. He asked his tall uncle, the Giraffe, what made his skin spotty, and his tall uncle, the Giraffe, spanked him with his hard, hard hoof. And still he was full of 'satiable curtiosity! He asked his broad aunt, the Hippopotamus, why her eyes were red, and his broad aunt, the Hippopotamus, spanked him with her broad, broad hoof; and he asked his hairy uncle, the Baboon, why melons tasted just so, and his hairy uncle, the Baboon, spanked him with his hairy, hairy paw. And *still* he was full of 'satiable curtiosity! He asked questions about everything that he saw, or heard, or felt, or smelt, or touched, and all his uncles and his aunts spanked him. And still he was full of 'satiable curtiosity!

One fine morning in the middle of the Precession of the Equinoxes this 'satiable Elephant's Child asked a new fine question that he had never asked before. He asked, 'What does the Crocodile have for dinner?' Then everybody said, 'Hush!' in a loud and dretful tone, and they spanked him immediately and directly, without stopping, for a long time.

By and by, when that was finished, he came upon Kolokolo Bird sitting in the middle of a wait-a-bit thorn-bush, and he said, 'My father has spanked me, and my mother has spanked me; all my aunts and uncles have spanked me for my 'satiable curtiosity; and *still* I want to know what the Crocodile has for dinner!'

Then Kolokolo Bird said, with a mournful cry, 'Go to the banks of the great grey-green, greasy Limpopo River, all set about with fever-trees, and find out.'

That very next morning, when there was nothing left of the Equinoxes, because the Precession had preceded according to precedent, this 'satiable Elephant's Child took a hundred pounds of bananas (the little short red kind), and a hundred pounds of sugar-cane (the long purple kind), and seventeen melons (the greeny-crackly kind), and said to all his dear families, 'Goodbye. I am going to the great grey-green, greasy Limpopo River, all set about with fever-trees, to find out what the Crocodile has for dinner.' And they all spanked him once more for luck, though he asked them most politely to stop.

---

[1] Much as I love Kipling's illustrations for *Just So Stories*, I have elected not to include them because of the difficulty of getting high-resolution scans.

Then he went away, a little warm, but not at all astonished, eating melons, and throwing the rind about, because he could not pick it up.

He went from Graham's Town to Kimberley, and from Kimberley to Khama's Country, and from Khama's Country he went east by north, eating melons all the time, till at last he came to the banks of the great grey-green, greasy Limpopo River, all set about with fever-trees, precisely as Kolokolo Bird had said.

Now you must know and understand, O Best Beloved, that till that very week, and day, and hour, and minute, this 'satiable Elephant's Child had never seen a Crocodile, and did not know what one was like. It was all his 'satiable curtiosity.

The first thing that he found was a Bi-Coloured-Python-Rock-Snake curled round a rock.

''Scuse me,' said the Elephant's Child most politely, 'but have you seen such a thing as a Crocodile in these promiscuous parts?'

'*Have* I seen a Crocodile?' said the Bi-Coloured-Python-Rock-Snake, in a voice of dretful scorn. 'What will you ask me next?'

''Scuse me,' said the Elephant's Child, 'but could you kindly tell me what he has for dinner?'

Then the Bi-Coloured-Python-Rock-Snake uncoiled himself very quickly from the rock, and spanked the Elephant's Child with his scalesome, flailsome tail.

'That is odd,' said the Elephant's Child, 'because my father and my mother, and my uncle and my aunt, not to mention my other aunt, the Hippopotamus, and my other uncle, the Baboon, have all spanked me for my 'satiable curtiosity—and I suppose this is the same thing.'

So he said good-bye very politely to the Bi-Coloured-Python-Rock-Snake, and helped to coil him up on the rock again, and went on, a little warm, but not at all astonished, eating melons, and throwing the rind about, because he could not pick it up, till he trod on what he thought was a log of wood at the very edge of the great grey-green, greasy Limpopo River, all set about with fever-trees.

But it was really the Crocodile, O Best Beloved, and the Crocodile winked one eye—like this!

''Scuse me,' said the Elephant's Child most politely, 'but do you happen to have seen a Crocodile in these promiscuous parts?'

Then the Crocodile winked the other eye, and lifted half his tail out of the mud; and the Elephant's Child stepped back most politely, because he did not wish to be spanked again.

'Come hither, Little One,' said the Crocodile. 'Why do you ask such things?'

''Scuse me,' said the Elephant's Child most politely, 'but my father has spanked me, my mother has spanked me, not to mention my tall aunt, the Ostrich, and my tall uncle, the Giraffe, who can kick ever so hard, as well as my broad aunt, the Hippopotamus, and my hairy uncle, the Baboon, *and* including the Bi-Coloured-Python-Rock-Snake, with the scalesome, flailsome tail, just up the bank, who spanks harder than any of them; and *so*, if it's quite all the same to you, I don't want to be spanked any more.'

'Come hither, Little One,' said the Crocodile, 'for I am the Crocodile,' and he wept crocodile-tears to show it was quite true.

Then the Elephant's Child grew all breathless, and panted, and kneeled down on the bank and said, 'You are the very person I have been looking for all these long days. Will you please tell me what you have for dinner?'

'Come hither, Little One,' said the Crocodile, 'and I'll whisper.'

Then the Elephant's Child put his head down close to the Crocodile's musky, tusky mouth, and the Crocodile caught him by his little nose, which up to that very week, day, hour, and minute, had been no bigger than a boot, though much more useful.

'I think, said the Crocodile—and he said it between his teeth, like this—'I think to-day I will begin with Elephant's Child!'

At this, O Best Beloved, the Elephant's Child was much annoyed, and he said, speaking through his nose, like this, 'Led go! You are hurtig be!'

Then the Bi-Coloured-Python-Rock-Snake scuffled down from the bank and said, 'My young friend, if you do not now, immediately and instantly, pull as hard as ever you can, it is my opinion that your acquaintance in the large-pattern leather ulster[1]' (and by this he meant the Crocodile) 'will jerk you into yonder limpid stream before you can say Jack Robinson.'

This is the way Bi-Coloured-Python-Rock-Snakes always talk.

Then the Elephant's Child sat back on his little haunches, and pulled, and pulled, and pulled, and his nose began to stretch. And the Crocodile floundered into the water, making it all creamy with great sweeps of his tail, and *he* pulled, and pulled, and pulled.

And the Elephant's Child's nose kept on stretching; and the Elephant's Child spread all his little four legs and pulled, and pulled, and pulled, and his nose kept on stretching; and the Crocodile threshed his tail like an oar, and *he* pulled, and pulled, and pulled, and at each pull the Elephant's Child's nose grew longer and longer—and it hurt him hijjus!

Then the Elephant's Child felt his legs slipping, and he said through his nose, which was now nearly five feet long, 'This is too butch for be!'

Then the Bi-Coloured-Python-Rock-Snake came down from the bank, and knotted himself in a double-clove-hitch round the Elephant's Child's hind legs, and said, 'Rash and inexperienced traveller, we will now seriously devote ourselves to a little high tension, because if we do not, it is my impression that yonder self-propelling man-of-war[2] with the armour-plated upper deck' (and by this, O Best Beloved, he meant the Crocodile), 'will permanently vitiate your future career.'

That is the way all Bi-Coloured-Python-Rock-Snakes always talk.

---

[1] A long, heavy overcoat made in Northern Ireland.
[2] A type of battleship.

So he pulled, and the Elephant's Child pulled, and the Crocodile pulled; but the Elephant's Child and the Bi-Coloured-Python-Rock-Snake pulled hardest; and at last the Crocodile let go of the Elephant's Child's nose with a plop that you could hear all up and down the Limpopo.

Then the Elephant's Child sat down most hard and sudden; but first he was careful to say 'Thank you' to the Bi-Coloured-Python-Rock-Snake; and next he was kind to his poor pulled nose, and wrapped it all up in cool banana leaves, and hung it in the great grey-green, greasy Limpopo to cool.

'What are you doing that for?' said the Bi-Coloured-Python-Rock-Snake.

''Scuse me,' said the Elephant's Child, 'but my nose is badly out of shape, and I am waiting for it to shrink.'

'Then you will have to wait a long time,' said the Bi-Coloured-Python-Rock-Snake. 'Some people do not know what is good for them.'

The Elephant's Child sat there for three days waiting for his nose to shrink. But it never grew any shorter, and, besides, it made him squint. For, O Best Beloved, you will see and understand that the Crocodile had pulled it out into a really truly trunk same as all Elephants have to-day.

At the end of the third day a fly came and stung him on the shoulder, and before he knew what he was doing he lifted up his trunk and hit that fly dead with the end of it.

''Vantage number one!' said the Bi-Coloured-Python-Rock-Snake. 'You couldn't have done that with a mere-smear nose. Try and eat a little now.'

Before he thought what he was doing the Elephant's Child put out his trunk and plucked a large bundle of grass, dusted it clean against his fore-legs, and stuffed it into his own mouth.

''Vantage number two!' said the Bi-Coloured-Python-Rock-Snake. 'You couldn't have done that with a mear-smear nose. Don't you think the sun is very hot here?'

'It is,' said the Elephant's Child, and before he thought what he was doing he schlooped up a schloop of mud from the banks of the great grey-green, greasy Limpopo, and slapped it on his head, where it made a cool schloopy-sloshy mud-cap all trickly behind his ears.

''Vantage number three!' said the Bi-Coloured-Python-Rock-Snake. 'You couldn't have done that with a mere-smear nose. Now how do you feel about being spanked again?'

''Scuse me,' said the Elephant's Child, 'but I should not like it at all.'

'How would you like to spank somebody?' said the Bi-Coloured-Python-Rock-Snake.

'I should like it very much indeed,' said the Elephant's Child.

'Well,' said the Bi-Coloured-Python-Rock-Snake, 'you will find that new nose of yours very useful to spank people with.'

'Thank you,' said the Elephant's Child, 'I'll remember that; and now I think I'll go home to all my dear families and try.'

So the Elephant's Child went home across Africa frisking and whisking his trunk. When he wanted fruit to eat he pulled fruit down from a tree, instead of waiting for it to fall as he used to do. When he wanted grass he plucked grass up from the ground, instead of going on his knees as he used to do. When the flies bit him he broke off the branch of a tree and used it as fly-whisk; and he made himself a new, cool, slushy-squshy mud-cap whenever the sun was hot. When he felt lonely walking through Africa he sang to himself down his trunk, and the noise was louder than several brass bands.

He went especially out of his way to find a broad Hippopotamus (she was no relation of his), and he spanked her very hard, to make sure that the Bi-Coloured-Python-Rock-Snake had spoken the truth about his new trunk. The rest of the time he picked up the melon rinds that he had dropped on his way to the Limpopo—for he was a Tidy Pachyderm.

One dark evening he came back to all his dear families, and he coiled up his trunk and said, 'How do you do?' They were very glad to see him, and immediately said, 'Come here and be spanked for your 'satiable curtiosity.'

'Pooh,' said the Elephant's Child. 'I don't think you peoples know anything about spanking; but I do, and I'll show you.' Then he uncurled his trunk and knocked two of his dear brothers head over heels.

'O Bananas!' said they, 'where did you learn that trick, and what have you done to your nose?'

'I got a new one from the Crocodile on the banks of the great grey-green, greasy Limpopo River,' said the Elephant's Child. 'I asked him what he had for dinner, and he gave me this to keep.'

'It looks very ugly,' said his hairy uncle, the Baboon.

'It does,' said the Elephant's Child. 'But it's very useful,' and he picked up his hairy uncle, the Baboon, by one hairy leg, and hove[1] him into a hornet's nest.

Then that bad Elephant's Child spanked all his dear families for a long time, till they were very warm and greatly astonished. He pulled out his tall Ostrich aunt's tail-feathers; and he caught his tall uncle, the Giraffe, by the hind-leg, and dragged him through a thorn-bush; and he shouted at his broad aunt, the Hippopotamus, and blew bubbles into her ear when she was sleeping in the water after meals; but he never let any one touch Kolokolo Bird.

At last things grew so exciting that his dear families went off one by one in a hurry to the banks of the great grey-green, greasy Limpopo River, all set about with fever-trees, to borrow new noses from the Crocodile. When they came back nobody spanked anybody any more; and ever since that day, O Best Beloved, all the Elephants you will ever see, besides all those that you won't, have trunks precisely like the trunk of the 'satiable Elephant's Child.

---

[1] Past tense of heave.

I keep six honest serving-men:
    (They taught me all I knew)
Their names are What and Where and When
    And How and Why and Who.
I send them over land and sea,
I send them east and west;
    But after they have worked for me,
I give them all a rest.

I let them rest from nine till five.
    For I am busy then,
As well as breakfast, lunch, and tea,
    For they are hungry men:
But different folk have different views:
    I know a person small—
She keeps ten million serving-men,
    Who get no rest at all!
She sends 'em abroad on her own affairs,
    From the second she opens her eyes—
One million Hows, two million Wheres,
    And seven million Whys!

The Sing-Song of Old Man Kangaroo

Not always was the Kangaroo as now we do behold him, but a Different Animal with four short legs. He was grey and he was woolly, and his pride was inordinate: he danced on an outcrop in the middle of Australia, and he went to the Little God Nqa.

He went to Nqa at six before breakfast, saying, 'Make me different from all other animals by five this afternoon.'

Up jumped Nqa from his seat on the sandflat and shouted, 'Go away!'

He was grey and he was woolly, and his pride was inordinate: he danced on a rock-ledge in the middle of Australia, and he went to the Middle God Nquing.

He went to Nquing at eight after breakfast, saying, 'Make me different from all other animals; make me, also, wonderfully popular by five this afternoon.'

Up jumped Nquing from his burrow in the spinifex[1] and shouted, 'Go away!'

He was grey and he was woolly, and his pride was inordinate: he danced on a sandbank in the middle of Australia, and he went to the Big God Nqong.

He went to Nqong at ten before dinner-time, saying, 'Make me different from all other animals; make me popular and wonderfully run after by five this afternoon.'

Up jumped Nqong from his bath in the salt-pan and shouted, 'Yes, I will!'

---

[1] Type of sharp-bladed Australian grass

Nqong called Dingo—Yellow-Dog Dingo—always hungry, dusty in the sunshine, and showed him Kangaroo. Nqong said, 'Dingo! Wake up, Dingo! Do you see that gentleman dancing on an ashpit? He wants to be popular and very truly run after. Dingo, make him SO!'

Up jumped Dingo—Yellow-Dog Dingo—and said, 'What, that cat-rabbit?'

Off ran Dingo—Yellow-Dog Dingo—always hungry, grinning like a coal-scuttle,[1]—ran after Kangaroo.

Off went the proud Kangaroo on his four little legs like a bunny.

This, O Beloved of mine, ends the first part of the tale!

He ran through the desert; he ran through the mountains; he ran through the salt-pans; he ran through the reed-beds; he ran through the blue gums; he ran through the spinifex; he ran till his front legs ached.

He had to!

Still ran Dingo—Yellow-Dog Dingo—always hungry, grinning like a rat-trap, never getting nearer, never getting farther,—ran after Kangaroo.

He had to!

Still ran Kangaroo—Old Man Kangaroo. He ran through the ti-trees; he ran through the mulga; he ran through the long grass; he ran through the short grass; he ran through the Tropics of Capricorn and Cancer; he ran till his hind legs ached.

He had to!

Still ran Dingo—Yellow-Dog Dingo—hungrier and hungrier, grinning like a horse-collar, never getting nearer, never getting farther; and they came to the Wollgong River.

Now, there wasn't any bridge, and there wasn't any ferry-boat, and Kangaroo didn't know how to get over; so he stood on his legs and hopped.

He had to!

He hopped through the Flinders; he hopped through the Cinders; he hopped through the deserts in the middle of Australia. He hopped like a Kangaroo.

First he hopped one yard; then he hopped three yards; then he hopped five yards; his legs growing stronger; his legs growing longer. He hadn't any time for rest or refreshment, and he wanted them very much.

Still ran Dingo—Yellow-Dog Dingo—very much bewildered, very much hungry, and wondering what in the world or out of it made Old Man Kangaroo hop.

For he hopped like a cricket; like a pea in a saucepan; or a new rubber ball on a nursery floor.

He had to!

He tucked up his front legs; he hopped on his hind legs; he stuck out his tail for a balance-weight behind him; and he hopped through the Darling Downs.

He had to!

---

[1] Bucket for holding coal

Still ran Dingo—Tired-Dog Dingo—hungrier and hungrier, very much bewildered, and wondering when in the world or out of it would Old Man Kangaroo stop.

Then came Nqong from his bath in the salt-pans, and said, 'It's five o'clock.'

Down sat Dingo—Poor Dog Dingo—always hungry, dusky in the sunshine; hung out his tongue and howled.

Down sat Kangaroo—Old Man Kangaroo—stuck out his tail like a milking-stool behind him, and said, 'Thank goodness *that's* finished!'

Then said Nqong, who is always a gentleman, 'Why aren't you grateful to Yellow-Dog Dingo? Why don't you thank him for all he has done for you?'

Then said Kangaroo—Tired Old Kangaroo—'He's chased me out of the homes of my childhood; he's chased me out of my regular meal-times; he's altered my shape so I'll never get it back; and he's played Old Scratch[1] with my legs.'

Then said Nqong, 'Perhaps I'm mistaken, but didn't you ask me to make you different from all other animals, as well as to make you very truly sought after? And now it is five o'clock.'

'Yes,' said Kangaroo. 'I wish that I hadn't. I thought you would do it by charms and incantations, but this is a practical joke.'

'Joke!' said Nqong from his bath in the blue gums. 'Say that again and I'll whistle up Dingo and run your hind legs off.'

'No,' said the Kangaroo. 'I must apologise. Legs are legs, and you needn't alter 'em so far as I am concerned. I only meant to explain to Your Lordliness that I've had nothing to eat since morning, and I'm very empty indeed.'

'Yes,' said Dingo—Yellow-Dog Dingo,—'I am just in the same situation. I've made him different from all other animals; but what may I have for my tea?'

Then said Nqong from his bath in the salt-pan, 'Come and ask me about it tomorrow, because I'm going to wash.'

So they were left in the middle of Australia, Old Man Kangaroo and Yellow-Dog Dingo, and each said, 'That's *your* fault.'

> This is the mouth-filling song
> Of the race that was run by a Boomer,
> Run in a single burst—only event of its kind—
> Started by big God Nqong from Warrigaborrigarooma,
> Old Man Kangaroo first: Yellow-Dog Dingo behind.
>
> Kangaroo bounded away,
> His back-legs working like pistons—
> Bounded from morning till dark,
> Twenty-five feet to a bound.

---

[1] A nickname for the Devil

Yellow-Dog Dingo lay
Like a yellow cloud in the distance—
Much too busy to bark.
My! but they covered the ground!

Nobody knows where they went,
Or followed the track that they flew in,
For that Continent
Hadn't been given a name.
They ran thirty degrees,
From Torres Straits to the Leeuwin
(Look at the Atlas, please),
And they ran back as they came.

S'posing you could trot
From Adelaide to the Pacific,
For an afternoon's run—
Half what these gentlemen did—
You would feel rather hot,
But your legs would develop terrific—
Yes, my importunate son,
You'd be a Marvellous Kid!

Sources

Hesiod. *Theogony.* Tr. and ed. Hugh Evelyn-White. *Hesiod, the Homeric Hymns, and Homerica.* London: W. Heinemann, 1914.

P. Vergilius Maro. *Aeneid.* Tr. John Dryden. 1697.

Mackenzie, Donald A. "Balder the Beautiful." *Teutonic Myth and Legend.* London: Gresham, 1912.

Gregory, Lady Augusta, tr. "The Coming of the Tuatha de Danaan." *Gods and Fighting Men.* London: John Murray, 1904.

Mooney, James. *Myths of the Cherokee: Extract from the Nineteenth Annual Report of the Bureau of American Ethnology.* Washington: GPO, 1902.

Garnett, James M., tr. *The Dream of the Rood. Elene; Judith; Athelstan, or the Fight at Brunanburh; Byrhtnoth, or the Fight at Maldon; and the Dream of the Rood: Anglo-Saxon Poems.* 3rd ed. Boston: Ginn-Athenaeum, 1911.

Geoffrey of Monmouth. *The History of the Kings of Britain.* Tr. J. A. Giles. *Six Old English Chronicles.* London: G. Henry Bohn, 1848.

Layamon. *Brut.* Tr. Eugene Mason. *Arthurian Chronicles.* London: Dent, 1912.

Marie de France. *Sir Launfal.* Tr. Jessie L. Weston. *Guingamor, Lanval, Tyolet, Bisclaveret.* London: David Nutt, 1900.

Chrétien de Troyes. *Lancelot: or, The Knight of the Cart.* Tr. William Wistar Comfort. New York: E. P. Dutton, 1913.

Malory, Thomas. *Le Morte D'Arthur.* Ed. William Caxton. 1485. Ed. Alfred W. Pollard. New York: Macmillan, 1900.

Donne, John. *Poems of John Donne.* Vol. 1. Ed. E. K. Chambers. London: Lawrence & Bullen, 1896.

Herbert, George. *The Poetical Works of George Herbert.* New York: D. Appleton and Co., 1857.

Bunyan, John. *The Pilgrim's Progress.* Vol. XV, Part 1. The Harvard Classics. New York: P.F. Collier & Son, 1909–14.

Milton, John. *Paradise Lost.* Rev. ed. 1674.

Smith, John. *The Generall Historie of Virginia, New England & the Summer Isles.* 1624. *The Travels of Captaine John Smith, in Two Volumes.* Vol. 1. Glasgow: James MacLehose and Sons, 1907.

Bradford, William. *Of Plimoth Plantation.* 1647. Boston: Wright and Potter, 1898.

Rowlandson, Mary. *The Soveraignty and Goodness of God, Together with the Faithfulness of His Promises Displayed: Being a Narrative of the Captivity and Restauration of Mrs. Mary Rowlandson.* 2nd ed. Boston: Thomas Fleet, 1720.

Kephart, Horace, ed. *Captives among the Indians.* Outing Adventure Library. New York: Outing, 1915.

Watts, Isaac. "When I Survey the Wond'rous Cross." *Appendix, Containing a Number of Hymns, Taken Chiefly from Dr. Watts' Scripture Collection.* Boston: T. Leverett, 1760.

---. "The Messiah's Coming and Kingdom." *The Psalms of David: Imitated in the Language of the New Testament.* Philadelphia, 1740.

Wesley, Charles. "Breathing after Holiness" [Love Divine, All Loves Excelling]. *A Collection of Hymn Tunes from the Most Modern and Approved Authors.* Ed. Andrew Law. Cheshire, CT: Wm. Law, 1783.

---. "Christ the Lord Is Risen Today." *The Christians Duty, Exhibited, in a Series of Hymns.* Germantown, PA: Peter Leibert, 1791.

Newton, John, ed. *Olney Hymns*. London, 1779.

Wesley, John. *Sermons on Several Occasions*. 1771.

Paine, Thomas. *The Crisis*. Philadelphia, 1776.

Publius [Alexander Hamilton, James Madison, and John Jay]. *The Federalist*. 2 vols. 1788.

Peters [Wheatley], Phillis. *Liberty and Peace*. Boston: Warden and Russell, 1784.

De Tocqueville, Alexis. *Democracy in America*. Vol. 2. Tr. Henry Reeve. 1835.

Chesterton, G. K. *What I Saw in America*. London: Hodder and Stoughton, 1922.

Twain, Mark. *A Connecticut Yankee in King Arthur's Court*. New York: Charles L. Webster, 1889.

Tennyson, Alfred. "The Lady of Shalott." *The Early Poems of Alfred, Lord Tennyson*. Ed. John Churton Collins. London: Meuthen, 1899.

Kipling, Rudyard. *Just So Stories*. London: Macmillan, 1902.

Websites Used

Project Gutenberg: http://www.gutenberg.org

Internet Sacred Text Archive: http://www.sacred-texts.com

The Camelot Project: http://d.lib.rochester.edu/camelot-project

Bartleby: http://www.bartleby.com

The John Milton Reading Room:
    http://www.dartmouth.edu/~milton/reading_room/contents/text.shtml

Hymnary: http://www.hymnary.org

Christian Classics Ethereal Library: http://www.ccel.org

USHistory.org

Founding Fathers: http://www.foundingfathers.info

A Celebration of Women Writers, ed. Mary Mark Ockerbloom:
    http://digital.library.upenn.edu/women/writers.html

Made in United States
North Haven, CT
06 November 2023